EARLY NORTHAMPTON WILLS

Frontispiece: Brass of Henry and Anne Jarman (or German) in Geddington church. They are dressed in growns worn by the well-to-do in the 15th century (*Source*: F. Hudson *Memorial Brasses of Northamptonshire*)

EARLY NORTHAMPTON WILLS

Preserved in Northamptonshire Record Office

TRANSCRIBED, TRANSLATED AND EDITED BY
DOROTHY EDWARDS, MARGARET FORREST, JACQUELINE MINCHINTON, MICHAEL SHAW, BERYL TYNDALL AND PATIENCE WALLIS

Published by Northamptonshire Record Society
2005

A Publication

of the

Northamptonshire Record Society

Founded in 1920

Volume XLII

General Editor: R.L. Greenall

ISBN No

0 901275 646

Contents

Part 1

Part 2

Acknowledgements

We would like to thank the staff of Northamptonshire Record Office for allowing us to work in their seminar room on numerous Saturday mornings and for their general encouragement over the course of this project.

Our thanks also go to Steve Parry and Myk Flitcroft of Northamptonshire County Council for providing digital copies of some historic maps.

Last, but not least, we would like to thank Ron Greenall, Hon. General Editor of the Record Society, not only for his very helpful editorial advice, but also for undertaking the tracking down and acquisition of good copies of maps and illustrations to enhance the text.

Maps and Illustrations

1

Project and Contributors

In 1994 a group of family and local historians began to meet once a month at Northamptonshire Record Office under the guidance of Jacqui Minchinton in order to improve their palaeographic skills and knowledge of medieval Latin. After one term some felt that they had, at least temporarily, reached their limits, but a group of enthusiasts wanted to continue. Rather than work on a random selection of documents they decided to tackle some of Northamptonshire's early wills in order to make them more easily available to the general public. As the project continued they became increasingly aware of the insight that these wills afforded into the life and times of Medieval Northampton and, with the encouragement of Northamptonshire Record Society, this volume came into existence.

Dorothy Edwards became interested in local history in 1975 when she moved to an old house in the village of Wootton. She began to research the house and the village and this led on to a Local History Certificate course at Northampton's University Centre, followed by an MA and PhD in History at Leicester University.

Margaret Forrest followed a similar route to an MA at Leicester University but her focus of interest was the village of Harlestone. Margaret taught French and German for many years and her general linguistic expertise has been very helpful to the project.

Jacqueline Minchinton has been the leading expert in the group. Without her knowledge of palaeography and medieval Latin the project would not have been possible. For many years Jacqueline was an archivist at Northamptonshire Record Office and is a long standing Council member of the Record Society. After a career break to have a family, she now works at Northampton Central Museum. In addition to her invaluable expertise throughout the project she has contributed the chapter on religion.

Michael Shaw is a professional archaeologist with an interest in local history. His links with Northampton began as a member of the archaeological team that carried out major excavations in the town under the auspices of Northampton Development Corporation. He was also a major contributor to the Royal Commission on Historical Monuments volume on archaeological sites and churches in Northampton. Michael is currently the Archaeologist for the Black Country but has maintained an interest in Northampton and used his specialist knowledge and expertise to produce the chapter on topography.

Beryl Tyndall came to the project as a family historian wanting to improve her skill in palaeography, but she soon proved her worth with her background in Latin. Beryl read Latin and French at Liverpool University. Having taught French throughout her career she has welcomed this opportunity to utilise her Latin.

Patience Wallis is also an experienced family historian with a desire to improve her skills in palaeography and Latin. She initiated the group after a gruelling but inspiring summer school on Latin for Family and Local Historians at Keele University, where she and Dorothy met.

2

Introduction

Northamptonshire Record Office has in its collections a bound volume of early wills for part of the county - approximately 650 wills in all, dating from 1462 to 1509. Before the Probate Act of 1857 (which came into force on the 12th January 1858) wills were proved by an ecclesiastical court rather than at a probate registry. The ecclesiastical courts were organised into three tiers. At the top were the courts of the Archbishops of Canterbury and York. Beneath these two were the diocesan courts of the bishops and at the bottom of the hierarchy were the archdeaconry courts which were where the wills of most 'middling' people were presented. When a will was proved before a court the clerk of that court would copy the will into a register. Northamptonshire wills were presented to the Archdeaconry Court of Northampton which was in the diocese of Lincoln. We learn from the few cases where probate or administration has also been recorded that this court had at least two meeting places - All Saints Church and the Hospital of St John the Baptist situated at the lower end of Bridge Street.

The survival of this volume of Northamptonshire wills is extraordinary. Its existence had been known for some time but not its whereabouts. Serjeantson and Longden[1] note that Bishop Kennett had made copious extracts from the volume and that these[2] had been used in their research. Then in 1935 the District Probate Registrar of the Peterborough Registry sent the volume to Birmingham to be placed with the records relating to Northamptonshire which had been transferred there from Northampton. In a subsequent letter he explained that it had been brought in be a local solicitor who discovered it among the papers of an ancestor who was thought to have been the Registrar at one time, and had been kept at Peterborough for about two years 'for the benefit of local people.'

The word volume is slightly misleading. The current binding of covered board with marbled paper and 'Northants Copies of Wills Early Act Book Entries 1467–1506' written in capitals on the spine

1 R.M. Serjeantson & H. Isham Longden, The Parish Churches and Religious Houses of Northamptonshire, *Archaeological Journal* 70 and 2nd series volume 20 No. 4, pp. 217–452, published by the Royal Archaeological Institute, London, 1913.

2 Lansdowne MS, No. 1028.

would seem to date from the nineteenth century as the end paper to which the first page of the index is attached has an 1871 watermark. The first three folios record 36 inductions to livings from 4 January 1469/70 to 15 September 1470. The first will entered is that of John Bykyrston which appears on the verso of Folium septimum. A further foliation in Arabic numerals was introduced so that the will of William Sawter of Evenley (will 2) is on Folium octavum or 2. This latter is the foliation used for reference purposes. Interspersed between will 2 and will 7 (William Russhden) are groups of registered entries of grants of probate or administration, some 65 in all. In view of the other material included the book does not seem to have been originally intended as a register of wills alone.

The volume consists of seven gatherings with some of the first and central folios being parchment rather than paper. There also appear to have been some pages cut out as well as pages which have been inserted individually. Some wills have been written on a single side of paper. The final pages (f190r & v) have been used for notes and doodles. However the collections of papers originated, the index currently at the front of the book was apparently written in 1579.

Between 1467 and 1496 the wills are almost exclusively in Latin but from 1496 to 1504 the reverse is the case. During the fifteenth century Latin was still the language of the church and the law, but its use was steadily being eroded as English became the dominant language. Already in 1362 a law had been passed that courts should conduct their affairs in English, although they were to be recorded in Latin, and this remained the custom until the eighteenth century. These wills illustrate this ongoing process.

A number of assertions generally made about wills are not entirely consistent with the wills of Northampton. It is generally accepted that if a person held property or goods to the value of £5 or over in more than one archdeaconry then his will would have to be proved in the superior court of a bishop or even archbishop. While this probably holds true for most cases in Northampton, as the majority of the wills are of the middling classes and trades people with property in Northampton itself or surrounding villages, there are a number of examples where men hold substantial property across county boundaries. For example John Leycestr' (74) leaves land in Northamptonshire and Leicestershire, William Prentece (363) leaves land and property in Oxfordshire and William Hobbis (488) leaves land in Buckinghamshire and Bedfordshire.

It is also accepted that before the Married Women's Property Act of 1882, wills for married women were extremely rare because women and their property were treated as possessions of the husband. The Northampton collection does not contain many wills for married women but there are three clear cases - Joan Ball (11), Ricardina Mose

(12) and Alice Wyng (368). Joan and Alice had definitely been married before because their previous husbands are named, and it would seem that property from these marriages was treated as their own to dispose of, perhaps with the permission of their present husbands. Ricardina too had possibly had an earlier marriage as she had a daughter with a different surname described as her 'natural daughter'.[3]

Today we use the phrase 'last will and testament' fairly loosely but at one time there was a clear distinction between the two. A will was the devising of a man's 'real' property *ie.* his land and buildings, and for many years there were restrictions on how this could be done. For most of England the rule of primogeniture applied where most of the 'real estate' had to go to the eldest son. This can be assumed in most of the Northampton wills because quite often the only mention that the eldest son gets is being appointed as an executor. Some property owners tried to avoid this restriction by transferring land to trustees who held it for the use of a named individual or individuals. They might do this by deed during their lifetime or at their death by will. The Statute of Uses of 1535 prohibited this kind of transfer, but all of the Northampton wills are from before this date.[4] The notion of a 'legal heir' comes through quite strongly in a number of wills, especially when men were making provision in case all of the named beneficiaries died. A man was more free to bequeath at least some of his personal belongings to whomsoever he chose and this was done by testament, but even then there were restrictions. Ecclesiastical law held that a third of a man's possessions should go to his wife and a further third to his children.

In England a will and a testament could be covered by the same document and gradually the two terms came to mean the same thing; influenced no doubt by the latin word 'testamentum' which seems to cover both, but ironically we now more commonly use the word will. Many of the Northampton examples should more correctly be called testaments because they deal exclusively with personal possessions, and in a few instances it is clear that another will exists. Some of the wills, however, do deal with both real estate and personal possessions.

By the fifteenth century a set pattern had already been established for wills. They began with the invocation to Almighty God followed by the date and the name of the testator. Usually his place of abode and occupation was then given but sometimes one or both of these details was omitted. A statement was then made about the testator's

3 A phrase which originally meant legitimate but from the late sixteenth century it changed to mean illegitimate. In this case it probably means her own daughter rather than one of her stepdaughters.

4 This Act did not survive for very long as the Statute of Wills Act of 1540 made it legal for a man to devise real property to anyone of their own choosing rather than to the legal heir, and from 1661 this applied to all land.

state of mind and occasionally about his health, especially if he was already sick. The first disposition was always the very important one concerning the soul which was left to Almighty God, followed by instructions as to the place of burial. This was sometimes specified very precisely and included details of a monument, if one was to be erected. The legacy section following was much more varied both in length and content but very often began with bequests to the parish church and sometimes the priest for 'tithes forgotten'. The final legacy was for the residue[5] of the estate which was left in the hands of executors and supervisors to be disposed as they thought best for the health of the testator's soul. The will finished with a list of names and often occupations of witnesses.

The Northampton wills all follow this general pattern with variations in detail. For example, some of the them give a great deal of information concerning the disposition of the soul, while others just say "Almighty God etceteras". As this volume is a copy of the original there is no way of knowing whether the testator or witnesses could actually sign their own names. A will should be followed by a probate clause showing when it was presented and proved before the court but only in a few instances has this been recorded. Sometimes a will was proved and then cancelled because a later version came to light. In the Northampton examples there is usually very little difference between the two versions. In the case of Thomas Harrowden (93) the only significant difference was that the cancelled version was in Latin while the valid will was in English. There are at least two instances of two versions being inscribed into the register without any indication of one of them being cancelled. Richard Bruester's two wills (312 and 314) were written on the same day and Richard Sherd's (575 and 597) were just three days apart. In both cases the differences in wording were very minor and the lack of cancellation was perhaps an oversight on the part of a busy clerk.

The wills in this study are mainly made by the tradespeople of Northampton, with a sprinkling of priests and minor gentry. The forty year period covered takes us from the Yorkist dynasty to the early Tudors. Apart from their obvious value for family historians these wills afford an insight into the life and times of medieval Northampton. There is information to be gleaned about the local churches and their associated fraternities, almshouses, and monastic institutions. Much useful detail about local properties and land is given, with street names and specific town sites being mentioned. Most of the wills state the occupation of the deceased, which tells us about the trades and businesses in the town in the late fifteenth and early sixteenth centuries. From the items bequeathed we learn of a family's

---

5 This catch-all phrase makes it impossible to assess the full value of an estate.

possessions and property such as animals, jewellery, furniture, clothing, bedding, kitchen utensils, etc. Women figure prominently both as executrices trusted to administer the estate, and as testatrices who often were clearly playing a full role in the business community.

Testators would have expressed their wishes in English, which would then have been put into legal language by a clerk, no longer necessarily a good scholar, so that the Latin used is becoming anglicised. For example 'scryvenor' (10) is used instead of the latin 'scriptor'. 'Goala', a word of unknown origin which in Middle English means a boundary, has been Latinised in its modern sense to mean gaol (357). Words like 'unam shopam' (91) - a shop - have crept in. Then as the clerks found it difficult to find an appropriate word in Latin, they used the familiar English names. Colours are regularly in English - 'coloris russett', 'coloris violett'. Then we find "Item lego to the paving of Northyate in Northampton iijs iiijd" (111) and "unam potte et unam panne et unam red corse gyrdell harnesyt with silver" (86). In will 84 the scribe even uses the Latin word and the English equivalent in the same line "Item lego Agneti Pope lx oves ... Johanni Coleor lxxxvj shepe".[6] The word 'vocatum' - called - is often used to herald an English word of phrase - 'vocatam a standing maser' (90), 'vocata London sheets' (336). Will 86 goes further: it begins in Latin and then switches to English, presumably as the scribe found it impossible to find a Latin equivalent for a long list of household and farming items. Just occasionally the opposite happens and a Latin word creeps into an English text such as 'dimidium' being used for 'half' (298).

Anglo-Saxon, much influenced by Norman French, had by this time become Middle English, with a few traces of French. Some words which later disappear are clearly French in derivation; compare the various words for warming objects such as 'chaffer' (86), 'chawferen' (575) with 'chauffer' - to heat; 'cawsee'/'causeway' (83) with 'chausse' (road); 'cowcher' (370) with 'coucher' (to sleep). The spelling of 'freres' (brothers) is closer to the French than the later 'friars'. The introduction of 'le' also seems to indicate the use of an English word or phrase in a Latin text. For example 'le Oxford Waye' (83) and 'le wering clothes'(336).

The English of the wills is understandable to modern readers with the exception of words no longer in use and listed in the glossary, and, of course idiosyncratic spelling which had not yet been fixed by printing. 'Qwysshons' for cushions is a delightful and quite typical example of words which are clear on reflection, though 'aye-ways' for highways (568) takes some thought. There are certain standard variations such as 'y' for 'i' and 'tion' endings spelt 'con' as in

6 I bequeath to Agnes Pope 60 sheep ... to John Coleor 86 sheep.

'reparacon' and 'discrecon'. Some spellings are still related to former Old English letter, as in the use of the thorn represented as 'y' for 'th', still frequently used as a false archaism in expressions such as 'ye olde teashop'. 'Y' also figures as a substitute for another obsolete letter, near to the modern 'g' as in 'yate' (539) for 'gate' (a variation which is still used in Yorkshire dialect) and 'yoven' (342) for 'given'.

Perhaps more of a problem to comprehension are the many words which are regularly run into one another such as shalbe, wilbe, aswel, wilnott or thapurtenances (356). The 'n' or 'an' is often attached to the next word as in 'a nother' and 'a naumbry'. There are clues about the pronunciation of English at that time: 'thygh' for 'the high' showing that the initial 'h' was not pronounced; 'warke' for 'work' (428) and 'auter' regularly for 'altar'. Occasionally the spelling is misleading, for example 'beds' (410) should be read as 'beads' and 'wode' (347) should be 'woad'. Grammar is almost all as today. The occasional 'e' on the end of a word is a relic of Old English when the grammatical function of a word was indicated by the word ending. The plural of 'child' as 'childer' is the most obvious reminder of this inflected language, comparable with the modern German 'kind' with its plural 'kinder' (child and children).

While on the subject of language and change it is worth noting that even by this time surnames were not always fixed. When surnames were first developed they were sometimes associated with the place that a person had come from or derived from their occupation. Both examples can be readily found in the wills as can several examples of major revisions indicated by 'alias' (otherwise known as). In the case of Richard Barker (567) alias Dyer in 1502 it is easy to see why the change was made as he is by then a dyer, but other changes are not so simple. In his will of 1490 John Leycestre (74) describes himself as alias Atylburgh (the old name for Irthlingborough) and in 1477 he was referred to as Atylburgh by Robert Gybson (39). The fact that both of these surnames are place names is unusual. Similarly in 1474 William Haryson (26) and Ralph West (27) both refer to John Bukby senior, but in his own will of 1490 John calls himself James alias Bukby (332). He was presumably originally from Long Buckby but as he was a tanner his occupation does not explain his alternate surname. William Clerk, vintner, probably became William Jakelyn (109) but it is not clear whether John Adams (389), draper, has become John Umfrey, or vice versa.

There are approximately six hundred and fifty wills in this Northamptonshire volume[7] but this book deals only with the one hundred and forty five wills made by residents of the town of

7 To give the reader an appreciation of the full scope of the volume, we have included a complete index as Appendix 1.

Northampton itself. Chapter 2 consists of an analysis of these wills in terms of what they tell us about the people of Northampton, their occupations, attitudes and general lifestyle. Chapter 3 is a detailed examination by Michael Shaw of topographical information and Chapter 4 is a similar consideration by Jacqueline Minchinton of the fraternities and religious institutions. We then move on to the transcriptions and, where necessary, translations of the wills themselves, which make up the bulk of this book.

3

Society and Customs

There are very few surviving sources of information on how ordinary people lived and worked in the later fifteenth century. An analysis of these wills can provide some interesting detail on the people of Northampton, their occupations, attitudes and customs and a little of their lifestyle in the way of clothing, possessions and house furnishings.

Occupations

Many of the 145 wills specify the occupation of the testator; in only 25 cases can an occupation not be assigned. The available sample can be increased to 692 by taking account of people mentioned in the wills as recipients, supervisors or witnesses. This is quite a significant sample of an estimated population of between 2,500 and 2,800 at the turn of the fifteenth/sixteenth centuries. Both occupation figures, however, need to be subject to some reduction.

Of the testators themselves the usable figure needs to be reduced to 91 to take account of the many wives and widows, because to classify 'widow' as an occupation would unbalance all calculations. Of the larger figure, 350 people do not have an occupation listed, or are wives and widows, and a further 45 belong to other towns or villages. This brings the total down to 297. A further reduction is necessary because of the particular nature of wills and the circumstances in which they were made. In many cases the small gap between the date a will was made and the date when probate was granted suggests that many people were already close to death and had a priest present. Almost a quarter of the 297 Northampton residents are described as priests, chaplains or monks. This exaggerates the true percentage of clergy in the population and it seems more realistic to remove this category from calculations. This leaves a grand total 239 people to analyse for occupation patterns.

A further note of caution must be sounded in that wills represent only those people in the population who were wealthy enough to make a will, plus a lower order of people who worked for those testators. This tends to limit the sample to the gentlemen and tradespeople of the town plus a significant group which comes under the general heading of servants. We should remember, however, that until the detailed census returns of the nineteenth century all data that has been used to analyse and discuss occupations has suffered from similar limitations.

Results

Most of the analysis has been made in respect of the larger sample but it is worth comparing the two, especially with regard to the most common occupations, as a simple but important check on the validity of the data. We find very little difference in the composition of lists of the most common occupations and in many cases percentages are also very similar. The only significant difference is the large group of servants who appear in the whole group sample as recipients but, not surprisingly, do not appear at all as testators. There is also quite a large difference between the two samples in the number of occupations identified - 33 in the case of testators but rising to 51 in the whole group. The similarity between the two samples suggest that even with the limitations mentioned above the data extracted from these wills does give a good indication of occupations in Northampton.

Most Common Occupations

Testators (91 in sample) (33 occupations)		Whole sample (239 in sample) (51 occupations)	
mercers/drapers	15.4%	mercers/drapers	12.1%
		servants	11.3%
gentry	7.7%	gentry	10.9%
weavers	7.7%	weavers	7.5%
fullers	7.7%	fullers	5.7%
bakers	6.6%	bakers	5.4%
dyers	5.6%	dyers	5.4%
shoemakers	4.4%	shoemakers	5.9%
innholders	4.4%	innholders	2.5%
butchers	4.4%	butchers	3.3%
tanners	4.4%	tanners	2.9%
priests	4.4%		

In the main sample 51 different occuptions are mentioned but almost half have only one representative and only eight reach double figures. Two of the largest groups are the servants at twenty-seven (11.3%) and the gentry with twenty six (10.9%). This is not unexpected given the special nature of wills and, perhaps, social expectations on the part of testators to provide for servants, but the largest group of all, with twenty-nine mercers and drapers (12.1%), is very clear evidence of their status and wealth. Even though they were probably not all in business at the same time, given the nearly fifty-year span of the wills, it does suggest that Northampton was an important centre for selling cloth. The percentage is even higher among the testators themselves, with 15.4% being described as mercers or drapers (the latter term being more common in later wills). We might wonder whether the term 'mercer' was being used to describe a wider range of merchants, but all evidence relating to the nature of goods being bequeathed supports the accepted view of mercers as men dealing in cloth.

In all a massive 34.7% of the sample was involved in one way or another with cloth: 21.3% with preparing wool and weaving woollen cloth and 12.1%, as already mentioned, in selling cloth and clothing. The importance of the cloth industry is reinforced by Helen Cam's analysis of the different trades of men who held the position of town bailiff between 1386 and 1461. She finds that 19 mercers and 11 drapers head the lists which include 8 dyers and 6 fullers,[8] and even by the assessment for taxation towards the great subsidy of 1524/5 the cloth trades were still the third largest group of craftsmen.[9] There is very little indication, however, of the processing of wool before weavers or dyers took over, with no mention of woolcombers or sorters, apart from one cardmaker.[10] Perhaps these were lower status occupations and not so involved in making wills.[11] Similar low numbers in these occupations are found in the subsidy surveys of 1524/5.[12]

It is perhaps not so surprising that the production and sale of cloth had become so important, as Donald King points out, "After food and drink, man's most compelling need is that of clothing."[13] Most of the textile occupations that have been mentioned are related to the woollen industry. Once woolcombers, carders and spinners had produced woollen thread it needed weavers to turn it into cloth, which fullers felted in troughs and stretched on tenterhooks to dry and then shearmen trimmed it. The dyers either dyed the thread or the finished cloth. Their part of the operation required particular skill, and knowledge of chemical interactions in order to fix the colours. Perhaps the level of skill required led to dyers being acknowledged as some of the town's leading citizens. Three of the four dyers who

8 H. Cam in *The Victoria History of the County of Northampton*, vol 3, 1930, p. 28.

9 Alan Dyer, 'Northampton in 1524', *Northamptonshire Past and Present*, vol 6, No. 2, 1979, p. 76.

10 Cards were used for combing wool.

11 A view reinforced by the fact that both woolcombers and sorters appear in the 1777 Militia Lists in all but the East Ward which was the wealthier side of town. V. Hatley (ed), *Northants Militia List 1777*, Northamptonshire Record Society, 1973, pp. 185–191.

12 Alan Dyer, *ibid*. p. 79.

13 D. King in *The Flowering of the Middle Ages*, ed. Joan Evans, 1985, p. 218.

made wills in this period had held the position of mayor. Since at least the thirteenth century Northampton had a national reputation for dyed cloth and it is probable that London cloth was sent to Northampton to be dyed.[14]

A considerably smaller, but still significant, group was involved with leather; either in tanning hides or using the leather to make shoes, gloves and saddles. Although this was well before the major expansion of the shoe industry in Northampton in the seventeenth century[15] which led to 21% of the population of Northampton making shoes in 1777, the fairly significant 5.9% who were working in the trade (twelve shoemakers, one pattenmaker and one cobbler) does suggest that the town was already making more shoes than were needed for its own inhabitants, as does the fact that leather workers had become the largest trade group of all by 1525.[16]

The basics of life by way of food and drink are also well represented. Over 10% of the sample were involved with selling bread, meat and fish, with the thirteen bakers suggesting that private houses did not have ovens or baking facilities. Another 3.9% were involved in handling or selling drink. The six innholders and three vintners would have provided for both local residents and passing travellers.

None of the other occupations occurs in any significant numbers, but the three bowyers and one fletcher are a reminder that archers still provided the main line of defence. There is very little evidence of agriculture being important to the town with only one yeoman and one grazier, but several other testators do mention land and animals.

Occupational distribution within the town

Almost all of the 145 testators specify at which church or other religious establishment they wish to be buried. We might expect that this would provide evidence of occupation patterns within the town but no really significant areas emerge. As Michael Shaw discusses later, street names seem to be a better indicator of occupational areas.[17] Nine Northampton churches are mentioned in the wills plus the religious establishments of St James' Abbey, St Andrew's Priory, Delapre Abbey and St John's Hospital. It is reasonable to assume that the choice of church for burial in most cases indicates the parish of residence and probable place of work of the testator in question. The

---

14 J. Laughton in *Northampton in the Late Middle Ages*, E.T. Jones, J. Laughton and P. Clark, Centre for Urban History, University of Leicester, Working Paper 10, 2000, pp. 77 – 78.

15 Hatley, *ibid*. p. xvii.

16 Dyer, *ibid*. pp. 76–79.

17 See Chapter 4 on topography.

case of the abbeys and St John's Hospital is more open to interpretation. Some tradespeople may well have been permanent lay residents of religious establishments but, on the other hand, they may have been there as retirees or invalids. This is particularly likely in the case of St John's Hospital.

Ninety-three of the testators choose All Saints which certainly endorses its position as the major church of Northampton but most of the named occupations are represented in this number. The main exceptions are the tanners and esquires, plus five occupations which have only one person listed (carpenter, clothier, grazier, haberdasher, wiredrawer).

Of the four tanners, two are from St Peter's parish, one from St Gregory's and the final one is from the district of St James. The parishes of St Peter and St Gregory both have good river frontage as has St James. St Gregory's parish also has two of the seven fullers, plus a fulling house (67), and one of the five dyers - trades which also require water. The other four dyers, however, are all from All Saints, as are three of the fullers which suggests that the old parish boundaries stretched down to the river. There is also a fuller at St Edmund's End.

Of the four esquires only two give a parish and that is St Giles where they are joined by two of the gentlemen, three widows and the 'clean' occupations of wiredrawing and carpentry. This corresponds to its reputation as the most 'respectable' end of the town. St Giles also has the one grazier and one shearman, which might indicate that it was still a relatively rural parish on the edge of the town.

All of the mercers, innkeepers, corvisors, barbers and butchers are from All Saints, the commercial heart of the town, but the bakers and weavers are from a range of parishes. This ties in well with fresh bread being a very local concern and weaving being a home industry.

Tesatators Occupations and Parishes

mercers/drapers	100% All Saints
barbers	100% All Saints
innkeepers	100% All Saints
gents/esquires	All Saints and St Giles
butchers	100% All Saints
dyers	4 All Saints, 1 St Gregory
fullers	3 All Saints, 2 St Gregory, 1 each St Peter & St Edmund
tanners	2 St Peter, 1 St Gregory, 1 St James Abbey
weavers	2 All Saints, 1 each St Mary, St Peter & St Michael, 2 St John's Hospital

Farming

Northampton was clearly a place of trade and urban occupations but there is evidence that some inhabitants also maintained more rural activities. A number of them kept animals on the edge of town and elsewhere. In the case of Edward Atwell (86), butcher, this is not surprising as even into the early twentieth century butchers were often also graziers - buying in and fattening up their own beasts. Edward kept a wide range of animals and there is evidence of other aspects of farming with ploughs, carts and oxen. It is not known exactly where he carried on this activity but Northampton did have its own extensive fields. Most of them were owned by the Abbey of St Andrew, but would have been let out to people from the town or elsewhere.

William Atwell (87), on the other hand, also a butcher, mentions two hundred sheep at Grafton Woodville and another two hundred at Eastcote. Thomas Pounce (99), fisher, leaves three hundred sheep but does not say where they are located though he does mention a piece of arable land outside the east wall next to the cemetery of St Giles. As already mentioned, Thomas Pepe (84), grazier, also lived in the parish of St Giles as did Richard Hobbis (488) whose occupation is not given, but who mentions growing crops of corn, beans and peas. He also mentions land in Bedfordshire and Buckinghamshire which could be where his farming interests lay. On the other side of town, Nicholas Smallay (488) of St Peter's leaves twenty sheep and five lambs, and John Bukby (94), barber, leaves sheep "wherever they may be in this realm of England".

Attitudes and customs

The role of women in local society

Women clearly played an important part in the society of trades people and above. Twenty seven of the testators were women, of whom three were wives. These three were obviously ladies of some wealth. Joan Ball (11) wished to be buried next to her first husband, William Wellys, a mercer, but she included the former wife of her present husband, Simon Ball, in her dedications. She clearly had money and possessions of her own to leave to beneficiaries. Alice Wynge (368), who had had three husbands, made many monetary bequests to churches and fraternities in the town. She was the possessor of several fine gowns and silver spoons and a maser or drinking cup called 'ower lady' which had once belonged to Richard

Daffron, her second husband.[18] Ricardina Mose (12) had land of her own in the towns of Cranfield and Wroxhill and made personal bequests to her 'natural daughter' Joan Dyve, possibly the daughter of a first husband. Of the remaining twenty-four women, twenty-two were stated to be widows and the remaining two, Isobel Geffron (257) and Margaret Hanred (390) were almost certainly so.

We are accustomed to think that, until the twentieth century, women were confined to domestic affairs, but this may be the result of social change in the Victorian era. Fifteenth century women were sometimes trusted to take over the family business[19] and almost always expected to manage family affairs. In all but two cases, when a testator had a surviving wife she was made an executor of his will. Sometimes this was a task to be shared with an eldest son or trusted friend but quite often she was made sole executrix, maybe with the support of an experienced supervisor, who was sometimes of a higher social status than the testator and his family. As executrix she was entrusted with the residue of all goods not formerly bequeathed and with arrangements for the health of her husband's soul and that of others as requested. Richard Hobbis (488) is one of the two exceptions, he made his son his sole executor, but he did leave his purchased lands to his wife. William Marchall (609) is the other, and he made two of his friends his executors in spite of the fact that his wife seemed to be still alive. She was only mentioned in passing and everything was left to his four sons and one daughter. Perhaps his wife had been previously provided for as the law would certainly accord her a share of the estate.

The remarriage of a widow was understandably of concern to some testators. William Perwyn (297) trusted his wife enough to make her his sole executrix, with his eldest son as supervisor, but if she remarried the legacies to his other sons were to be placed out of her hands for security. John Leycestre (74) had a rather more benevolent attitude; if his widow married a man of good character who treated her well then they were to be allowed to purchase, at a reduced price, those lands and tenements that he had left to his wife for her lifetime. Roger Butler (387) is possibly even more generous as, if his widow remarried, she was to be allowed to keep forever one half of everything left to her for life. The other half was to go immediately to the son. This concern over remarriage was obviously not without foundation, as widows, especially the rich ones, do seem to have been sought after. Agnes Chambre (56) had been married three times and left property in Derngate and Abingdon Street. The widow of a

18 See will 83.
19 Medieval law actually gave them the legal right to do so.

freeman was a particularly attractive proposition because, in Northampton, a new husband could acquire the same status.

Rather than remarrying, however, some widows may have continued with the family business. Agnes Clerke (58) widow of Thomas Clerke, mercer, leaves linen cloth in her will, which could suggest the business survived, but in some cases the evidence is even stronger. William Goldwyre (68), fisher, leaves his stall in the fishmarket to his wife Joan, even though he had an adult son, and Simon Brafeld (347), dyster, leaves wool, madder, wood (woad) and alum for the use of his wife. Margaret Hancock (54) also seems to have carried on her late husband's trade as a dyster because she refers to her apprentice and leaves an old leaden vessel and a wooden vat, items connected with dyeing.

Daughters of the family were often treated equally. For example, Thomas Wylliamson (91) leaves to each of his two daughters five marks of 'good English money', a maser, six silver spoons and a girdle. John Leynowe (338) leaves £10 to both of his daughters and an equal share of a silver salt with cover. There were more likely to be conditions attached to a daughter's inheritance. Richard Daffron's daughter, Alice, was to receive five marks of good money only if "she governs herself well and honestly and lives a praiseworthy life". His daughter Joan would inherit a garden and tenement "if she behaves well and takes honest governance". Margaret Harowdon (10) only mentions daughters and seems particularly anxious that Margery should not be deprived of the main inheritance, perhaps fearing that her influential relatives, the Vauxes and the Knightleys, would try to take advantage of her.

Lifestyle

Clothing

We get an impression of a society which enjoyed dressing-up in colourful clothes and rich fabrics. Maybe their everyday work clothes were more drab and serviceable and did not warrant a mention in a will, but many of the testators owned a number of fancy garments which were clearly regarded as valuable items to be passed on to appropriate recipients. Indeed, in some cases, clothes represent the only items of value to be mentioned in a will eg. John Bykyrston (1) leaves two gowns - one green and one rone russet alongside only a primer (a religious book). The colour of a gown is significant because some colours were restricted by law to certain levels of society, but there is little difference between the sexes. The one mulberry gown (87) belonged to a man, but all other colours were worn by both men and women.

For the men, violet and russet seem to have been particularly favoured colours, with John Hancok (36) leaving a violet gown with a hood, Thomas More (70), William Wellynburgh (351) and John Kyng (357) leaving long violet gowns, and Richard Pakeman (349) and William Prentece (363) short violet gowns. William Multon (90) also left a violet gown but his was trimmed with polecat while William Wellynburgh left another violet gown trimmed with white lamb. Blue, black, scarlet, crimson, sanguine,[20] tawny, and green gowns are all mentioned, many trimmed with fur. Several of the russet gowns were trimmed with lambskin; black in the case of William Wynge (382) and white for John Fawcett (625), but John Page's gown (463) was trimmed with fox fur. Hugh Wodsall (336) left a sanguine gown trimmed with beaver, while Roger Butler (387) left a blue gown furred with frychens,[21] and a sanguine gown furred with lamb. Otter and squirrel fur was also used as trimming (83, 324). These gowns were sometimes accessorized with belts or girdles ornamented with silver (36, 83).[22]

Most of the men left only one or two gowns although William Wellynburgh left a colourful wardrobe of five - two of violet and one each of blue, tawny and russet. William Rutter (341) left an even more extensive wardrobe of seven gowns - two of sanguine trimmed with fur, two of russet trimmed with black fur, two green and one blue. At the other end of the scale Thomas Fyssh (224) left only the outer layer of his russet gown. William Wellynburgh is the only one to give clues, perhaps, of more everyday wear by also leaving two doublets of blue worsted and a smock.

Women's clothing was equally rich and colourful. Alice Wynge (368) left only one gown of violet trimmed with fur and Margaret Hancok (54) a single blue gown ornamented with silver, gold and gilt, but Isabel Peche (45) left a crimson gown trimmed with marten, a back gown with bands of black velvet, a tawny gown trimmed with shankys[23] and a green gown lined with buckram[24] with black velvet around the collar. These latter two women also left silk girdles ornamented with silver, as did Agnes Roberdes (389). Isabelle Peche also left white and mulberry silk headresses.

Only sixteen testators mention jewellery and most of that is in the form of religious rosaries. Coral, jet and amber are the only stones mentioned. Perhaps more elaborate pieces were still confined to the upper classes. Margaret Harowdon (101), a member of a gentry family, left a gold cross, a gold ring and her best jewel for her mortuary. Most

20 Blood red colour.

21 Polecat.

22 The frontispiece shows typical clothing, with fur trimming and lining clearly visible on the man's gown.

23 Fur from the lower legs of an animal.

24 At this date buckram was not the stiff fabric that we know today.

notable among the rosary bequests are those of Margaret Hancok (54), who left coral rosary beads with gold and silver, and jet rosary beads with silver, and Agnes Roberdes (389), who left coral beads with silver gilt 'gaudis'.[25] Three men mention jewellery - William Rutter (341), a draper, who left a jet rosary with silver gilt beads and a gold cross called an Anthony Cross; John Kyng (357) who left an amber rosary; and John Page (463) who left a gold ring. Nicholas Bowker (410) also left beads, brooches and rings, but these were already in the possession of his wife and are described as hanging from her girdles, and Richard Barker (567) left his daughter "a silver device known as a brooch" which had belonged to his wife.

Furnishings and possessions

As for their houses, many of the testators lived in some comfort. Feather beds and considerable quantities of sheets, blankets and pillows are frequently mentioned. John Kyng (357) left a bed with curtains hanging around it. Some of the bed covers were very decorative. For example Agnes Roberdes (389) left a bed cover with bands of blue; John Palmer (426) left a coverlet decorated with white lilies, and Joan Getyn (649) left a green coverlet with red lions.

Furniture appears less often, chests are the most frequently mentioned item, often of spruce, or painted, as in the case of Alice Peny (112). Chairs are left by eight testators and benches or stools by another two, sometimes with 'whysshons' or 'kuschyns' (575, 649) in the later wills. Other items left are cupboards, which could merely be flat surfaces or shelves rather than our view of a cupboard, and tables which are described as folding, counter or trestle.

Towels and tablecloths are in use and a number of testators mention wall hangings. John Kyng (357) just describes his hanging as 'painted' but Margaret Hancok (54) describes one painted with pictures of saints and another with angels. This latter was large enough to leave in three parts - one part each to the Hospital of St John, the church of St Michael and the almshouse of St Thomas the Martyr.

Household ware of platters, basins, ewers and candlesticks was mainly made of pewter, latten and brass. Some of the bowls were very large, with Margaret Hancok (54) leaving a brass bowl holding eighteen gallons. Silver spoons were frequently mentioned in wills and were often shared between the various sons, daughters and maybe grandchildren of the family. Knives are not mentioned even

25 The eleventh bead in a rosary.

Mazer.—A rather shallow and capacious drinking-bowl, usually made of maple-wood, and mounted in silver or silver-gilt. Drinking-cups, or bowls, of this form, are depicted on the Bayeux tapestry. In the centre, within the bowl, is generally an ornamental metal boss, called the "print"; the metallic rim is sometimes inscribed.

Mazer.

Fig. 1. A mediavel maser (or mazer) (Source: *Handbook of English Antiquities*)

though daggers, at least, would have been used at table for cutting meat.[26] Perhaps this is an early indication of the superstition that it is unlucky to give anyone a knife, or maybe they were just too common to single out. A number of people left silver items. For example John Hancok (36) left a silver salt with a cover, a silver bowl and a maser with a band of silver, and Hugh Hopwod (44) left a silver gilt bowl worth £6. The will of William Harysson (26) is a good example of the range of goods in a better-off household.

Among the more unusual items are a maser left by Richard Daffron (83), which is described as having the names of the three kings of Cologne around the band. William Rutter (341) left several items of silver one of which is called a "nutte of silver gilt with a cover" which is indicative of a new fashion at the time for a cup to be fashioned from a coconut shell. Simon Rowland (356) similarly left a "copp callyt a nutt" and Richard Hobbis (488) left a maser 'nutt' with a cover decorated with silver and gilt.

Other items worth mentioning are the drinking horn chased with silver left by John Longe (139) and the red goblet left by Alice Peny (112). This could have been glass and if so would be the only mention of this material. Richard Sherd (578) left two puzzling items - a "St John's head" and a pair of tables "with men" (a form of board game such as backgammon). Another unusual item is the horn left by Thomas Symson (440) to the chapel of Corpus Christi "... to the use of Robyn Hode to have on Wytson Monday and all othyr tymes when hee need" - probably a reference to the mummers' play performed on Whit Monday.[27]

Very few testators left books, Edward Atwell (86) mentions books in the plural, but all the others are single bequests and always a religious book. John Bykyrston (1) and William Rutter (341) left primers and Thomas Arderon (4) left a book called *Speculum Christianorum* to a chaplain. Isabel Peche (45) and John Wellys (107) left missals and

26 Forks had not come into use at this period.

27 See Chapter 5 on Religion.

John Kyng (357), a priest, left his book of the Offices of the dead to his grandson. An indication of how expensive books could be comes from the will of John Whyte (372). He directed that an Antiphoner[28] was to be purchased for the church of St Mary. For this he left 40 shillings, to be paid over six years at 6s 8d a year.

There are only a few indications of the trade of a testator in items bequeathed. John Bukby (94), a tanner, left leather and bark; Thomas Fyssh (224), a barber, left knives in a pouch; Simon Brafeld (347), a dyster, left woad, madder and alum, important constituents of the dying process; and William Halowton (408), a fuller, left Walker's earth used in fulling cloth.

Outside influences

One of the more striking features of the wills is, perhaps not surprisingly, a complete lack of information on anything of wider significance. There are, however, two small clues that might just suggest some individual participation in the Wars of the Roses. Three of the testators ask to be buried where God wills[29] which could show an expectation of not necessarily being at Northampton at the time of death. All of these wills are written in 1485 and two of the testators, John Barnard (88) and Thomas Harowdon (93), identify themselves as esquires, a class which could well have been involved in actual fighting. The twenty second of August 1485 saw the last major battle of the Wars of the Roses - the Battle of Bosworth where the Lancastrian army defeated Richard III and the Yorkists and the will of Thomas Harowdon is dated the twenty first of August, the day before the battle. The other small clue to involvement with weapns is that William Marchall (609) left his son William a pair of briganders and a salet. Briganders were light pieces of armour formed by sewing metal plates onto leather and a salet was a globular headpiece of armour. As William was a mercer this is a reminder that fighting was not confined to knights and esquires, common soldiers were always needed.

Another major cause of death during the middle ages was from the various outbreaks of plague. The wills of St Albans for a similar period mention an outbreak in August 1479[30] but there are no references in the Northampton wills and no significant clustering of deaths in the town itself. On the other hand if one looks at the register for the county

---

28 A religious book of musical or verbal responses.

29 A similar phrase was used by Henry Kilbyffe of St Albans in 1492 but he goes on to say that he is 'preparing to travel overseas with the most illustrious Lord King about his intended wars'. Susan Flood (ed), *St Albans Wills*, Hertfordshire Record Publications 1993, pp. 106–7.

30 Flood, *ibid.*, p. 49.

as a whole there are a lot of deaths in 1498. There are seventy county wills recorded between John Nutman (154) and Thomas Fyssh (224) and a smaller, but still significant, county cluster in 1501 with forty wills recorded between Robert Testwod (499) and Richard Chead (539). The plague was almost certainly a factor in these cases.

A reminder, however, that Northampton did have links with national affairs comes with references to the Catesby family and to Richard Empson. The Catesbys of Ashby St Leger had property in Northampton and William Catesby was an executor for Richard Haroweden (49). The family were not only prominent in local affairs, but were also royal servants throughout the Wars of the Roses. Initially they were trusted Lancastrians but changed sides when Edward IV was securely on the throne. William Catesby Esq. was particularly close to Richard of Gloucester and remained loyal when Richard usurped the throne. This attachment led to his execution after the Battle of Bosworth. The appointment of Richard Empson[31] as supervisor for two of the testators (334, 347) was in some ways not a surprising occurence as Empson was a local lawyer from a minor land-owning family of Towcester, but even as a young man he began to move in royal circles and is better known for his links to Henry VII. He and Edmund Dudley became trusted advisers of the king and were instumental in helping Henry to recover money from his noblemen for long forgotten obligations, a deeply resented activity which led to the pair being accused of treason on trumped-up charges after Henry's death. In spite of their undoubted innocence they were executed in 1510 in a move by Henry VIII to court popularity amongst his nobility.

31 His name is always written as Emson but invariably becomes Empson in print.

4

Topography

Michael Shaw

The wills do, of course, contain a wealth of topographical information. This is not, however, the place to attempt a detailed examination of the topography of late medieval Northampton. Rather I have tried to help the reader and researcher using this volume by providing a brief introduction to the history of the town and a short commentary on the topographical information in the wills.[32] In order to clarify text I have provided plans reconstructing the topography of the late medieval town, showing the street pattern with the insertion of sites, monuments, street names and suburbs mentioned in the wills.[33]

In order to understand the topography of the town in the fifteenth century we need a short summary of its earlier growth. The Northampton area has been an important centre from prehistoric times, but the area of the later town can first be identified as a major

---

32 The best starting point for anyone wishing to study the topography of the town is the Northampton volume of the Royal Commission on Historical Monuments study of Northamptonshire - *An Inventory of the Historical Monuments of the County of Northampton, Volume 5: Archaeological Sites and Churches in Northampton*, HMSO, 1985. Unfortunately the actual inventory of sites in the town was consigned to microfiche but a bound printout of the fiche is available at Northamptonshire Record Office and Northampton Central Library. This volume also gives a full listing of sources available prior to its publication. Later publications can be found in the volumes of *Northamptonshire Past and Present* and *Northamptonshire Archaeology*, and by consulting the Northamptonshire Sites and Monuments Record, held by Northamptonshire County Council.

33 The maps have been compiled digitally. I have used the 1st edition Ordnance Survey mapping of the 1880s as a base map and added topographical detail from the earlier town maps, chiefly Speed's map of 1610, but also the Noble and Butlin map of 1746, the Roper and Cole map of 1807 and the Wood and Law map of 1847. Speed's map is in fact a remarkably accurate survey of the town. Although distorted, the street pattern when compared with that shown on later maps can be seen to be almost totally accurate, while his location of the major ecclesiastical sites is generally accurate, although he wrongly labels the site of the Whitefriars as the Greyfriars. For the location of the monuments mentioned in the documents, I have largely used those given in Fig. 7 of the RCHME volume, which locates the sites and monuments on a modern map base. As to have attempted to show everything on a single map would have been confusing, I have provided two versions of the map, Fig. 2 with sites and monuments labelled and Fig. 5 with the streets and suburbs labelled.

centre in the middle Saxon period, around the eighth to ninth centuries AD, when there was a major royal/ecclesiastical complex in the south west corner of the later town around St Peter's church. By the end of the ninth century the settlement was in the hands of the Danes and archaeological evidence suggests that by this time Northampton was already a commercial and industrial centre. The English drove out the Danes in 917 and soon after the settlement's importance is demonstrated by its status as the head of the shire of Northamptonshire. By the time of the Domesday survey (1086) Northampton was a middling shire town, paying an annual tax to the crown of £30.10s, a similar sum to that paid by other county towns such as Nottingham and Derby.[34] In the twelfth century, however, the town underwent an unparalleled transformation in status, becoming one of the chief towns in the kingdom. Its farm was increased to £100 in 1130 and £120 in 1184, a sum exceeded only by those of London, Lincoln, Winchester and Dunwich.[35] This status was not to last, however. Northampton was already complaining of decline in the late thirteenth century and by the fourteenth century it was once again a middle ranking county town.[36]

This economic growth is mirrored by an exponential increase in size. Topographical analysis and archaeological evidence demonstrate that the late Saxon town was largely confined to an area of around 20 ha (50 acres) in the south west corner of the later town. In the medieval period, probably by the mid-twelfth century, the town walls enclosed around 65 ha (220 acres), one of the largest enclosed areas in the country, and in addition there were extensive suburbs outside the town's main gates. The town's population has been estimated as around 3,000 towards the end of the fourteenth century.[37] Unfortunately we do not have any data on which to estimate its twelfth to thirteenth century population but it is likely to have been substantially higher. By the early sixteenth century, however, there is evidence of a further slight decrease to around 2,500.[38]

Churches, chapels and colleges

The wills emphasise the central role of the church in the life of the town. Like many towns which were already important by the eleventh to twelfth centuries Northampton possessed a multiplicity of churches.

---

34 James Tait, *The Medieval English Borough*, 1936, p. 184.
35 Martin Biddle (ed), *Winchester in the Early Middle Ages*, 1976, p. 500.
36 W.G. Hoskins, *Local History in England*, 3rd edn 1984, p. 278.
37 Christopher Dyer and T.R. Slater, 'The Midlands', p. 627, in D.M. Palliser (ed), *The Cambridge Urban History of Britain*, vol.1, (600–1540), 2000.
38 Dyer, *ibid.*, pp. 73–80.

Seven within the town walls are mentioned in the wills: All Saints, St Giles', St Peter's, Holy Sepulchre, St Gregory's, St Mary's and St Michael's. All were in existence by the early twelfth century. The first four were the most important and survive to the present day. Of these the most important of all was All Saints. It is the most common recipient of bequests and was clearly regarded as the town church. Of the remaining three, St Gregory's receives a number of mentions because of its possession of a holy relic - The Rood in the Wall, a stone crucifix. Nevertheless St Gregory, along with St Mary and St Michael fell into disuse and all three were annexed to other churches in the later sixteenth century (after the Reformation) - St Gregory and St Mary to All Saints and St Michael to Holy Sepulchre. Associated with All Saints church were the College of All Saints and the chapel and churchyard of St Katherine. The college was founded in the fifteenth century to enable the guild chaplains of All Saints church to live together under a common rule. The cemetery at St Katherine's, also known as the 'new cemetery' and 'the Pardon churchyard', was used for the burial of plague victims. It is thought to have been founded in the fifteenth century although there are thirteenth century references to a 'new cemetery'.

The wills mention three churches in the suburbs outside the town, these are our best evidence that, despite the size of its walled area, the town possessed suburbs from an early date. The eastern suburb of St Edmund's was served by St Edmund's church which was in existence by the early twelfth century. The western suburb of St James' End lay within Duston parish but was served by the chapel of St Margaret, which is recorded from the thirteenth century. The southern suburb, Cotton End or East Cotton, lay within the parish of Hardingstone but was served by St Leonard's chapel. The chapel lay within the hospital of St Leonard, which is known from the mid-twelfth century, but acquired semi-parochial rights for the inhabitants of the southern suburb.[39]

Religious Houses

There were three monastic houses at Northampton. The Cluniac priory of St Andrew occupied a large site within the town walls at the northern end of the town. It had possessed the advowson of all the town's churches since the early twelfth century. The Augustinian abbey of St James lay around 1 km west of the town in the parish of

39 There was a fourth suburb beyond the north gate of the town with its own church to serve it - St Bartholomew (later St Lawrence), which is recorded from the twelfth century (see J.H. Williams, 'Northampton's Medieval Parishes', *Northamptonshire Archaeology,* 17,1982, pp. 74–84). There is no mention of this church or suburb in the wills, however; indicating that this was an early suburb which had lost its importance by this time.

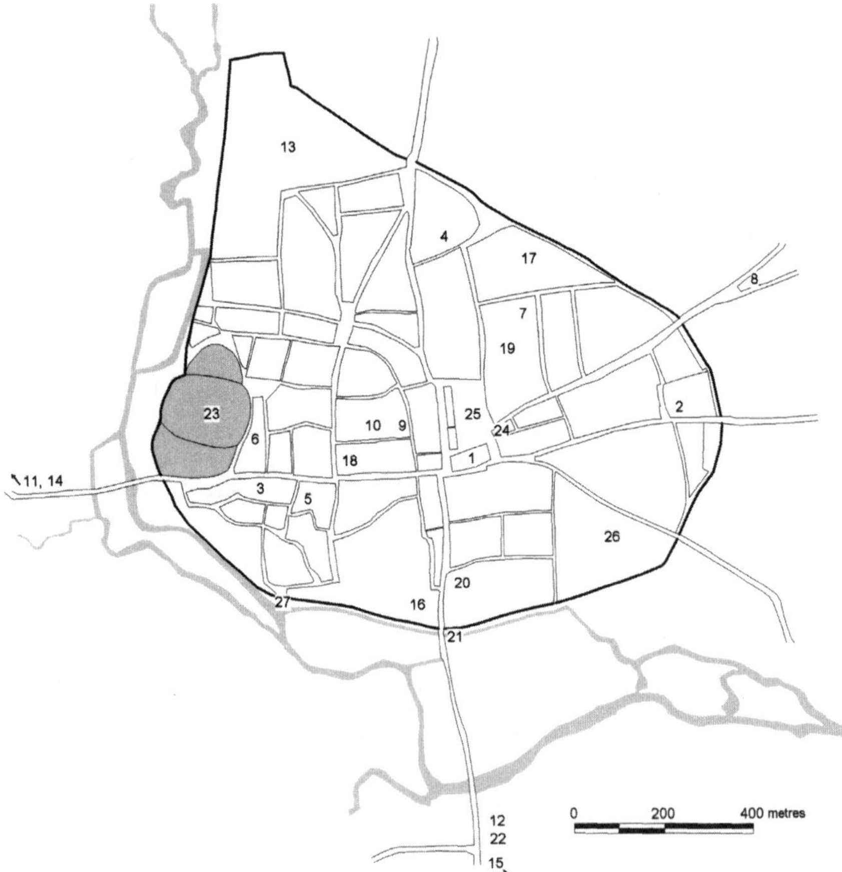

Churches: 1 – All Saints; 2 – St Giles; 3 – St Peter; 4 – Holy Sepulchre; 5 – St Gregory; 6 – St Mary; 7 – St Michael; 8 – St Edmund; **College:** 9 – All Saints; **Chapel:** 10 – St Katherine; 11 – St Margaret; 12 – St Leonard; **Priory:** 13 – St Andraw; **Abbey:** 14 – St James; **Nunnery:** 15 – Delapré; **Friaries:** 16 – Augustinian; 17 – Carmelite (Whitefriars); 18 – Dominican (Blackfriars); Franciscan (Greyfriars); **Hospitals:** 20 – St John; 21 – St Thomas; 22 – St Leonard; **Lay Sites:** 23 – Castle; 24 – Town Hall; 25 – Market Square; 26 – The Tower (Latimer's Tower)

Fig. 2 Sites and Monuments in 15th century Northampton mentioned in the wills

Duston, while the Cluniac nunnery of Delapre lay a similar distance to the south in the parish of Hardingstone. All three owned extensive property in the town, especially St Andrew's. None, however, figured prominently in the minds of the testators when bequests were made.

Far more common are bequests to the friaries. Northampton's importance in the thirteenth century is shown by the foundation of houses of all four major orders - the Augustinian, Carmelite (White-friars), Dominican (Blackfriars), and Franciscan (Greyfriars). It is notable that, unlike the situation at many towns, there was sufficient space for all four to be fitted within the town walls (an indication both of the unusually large area enclosed by the town walls and also perhaps that this included a speculative element of empty space not taken up until the foundation of the friaries).

Bequests to hospitals are also common, especially the hospital of St John, which lay within the walls at the south end of the town, and the hospital of St Thomas which lay immediately outside the south gate of the town. The hospital of St Leonard is also mentioned, both as a recipient of bequests and also as owning property within the town. The hospital, whose chapel has already been mentioned as possessing quasi-parochial rights, lay 500m south of the town.

Lay Institutions

Although it was a major topographical feature within the town, covering a large area by the west gate, Northampton castle was used only for county administration and justice by this time and the only references to it in the wills are incidental ones - 'church of the Blessed Mary by the king's castle' (86) and 'Castle green' (547).

There are two references to the town hall (341) or common hall (349) also known as the guild hall. It lay in the centre of the town on the corner of Abington Street and Wood Hill, adjacent to All Saints church and the market place. It appears to have been an early fourteenth century structure[40] but was demolished in 1864 when the present Guildhall was constructed to the east on St Giles' Street.

The gates within the defences receive quite frequent mentions. We hear of the North Gate at the top of Sheep Street; the West Gate at the bottom of Gold Street;[41] the South Gate at the bottom of Bridge Street; the East Gate at the top of Abington Street; the Derngate which lay at the bottom of Swinewell Street[42] and also of a postern gate which lay to the south of St Giles' church at the bottom of St Giles' Street.

Three of the wills refer to the Conduit (58, 75, 82). They probably refer to the Great Conduit which had recently been built at the southern end of the Market Place. It was supplied with water by pipes from a spring to the east of the town. There was also an older conduit, the Little Conduit, which stood at the south-west corner of All Saints churchyard.[43]

Of the secular private properties mentioned the most interesting is 'the Tower'. This building is shown on Speed's map of 1610[44] but its

---

40 See Fig. 3, taken from the Noble and Butlin map of 1746.

41 The bottom end of Gold Street was later renamed Marefair; Rev J.C. Cox (ed), *The Records of the Borough of Northampton*, vol. 2, 1898, p. 252.

42 The street itself was later renamed Derngate, Cox *op. cit.*, p. 519.

43 Cam, *ibid.*, p. 25, 51; Cox *op. cit.* pp. 252–60.

44 See Fig. 4.

Fig. 3 The 15th century Guild Hall, from Noble and Butlin's map of 1746.

function has been widely misunderstood. Cox suggested that it had formed part of a putative Anglo-Norman defensive line.[45] No evidence for such a defence has ever been found, however. Will 334 clears up much of the confusion. John Chauncey bequeaths, to his son Anthony, Latimer's Tower for his mansion, two closes, three gardens and a tenement yard set beside the tower. Hence there would appear to have been a major town house here which acquired the name of its chief feature, the Tower, and, on occasions, of its builder or at least its best known occupier, Lord Latimer. The Northampton Town Survey of 1504 gives an alternative name, the Grange, for this complex.[46]

Latimer's Tower is referred to as early as 1377 when it was granted by John Neville, Lord Latimer, to John de Etton.[47] It is likely that the tower was a solar tower to which a hall and perhaps other buildings were attached. Margaret Wood describes these in a rural context.[48] Perhaps the best example is Longthorpe Tower, near Peterborough,

45 Cox, *op. cit.* pp. 239, 527. The line of the supposed defence was included on a map accompanying Cox's volume and seems to have been traced on to a copy of the Roper and Cole 1807 map of Northampton. (Fig. 6) This copy has been reproduced in Cam (*op. cit.*) opposite page 310 and described as plan of Northampton in 1810 and in the RCHME volume (*op. cit.*) plate 10 and on versions of the map sold by Northampton libraries. It should be emphasised therefore that this line is not on the original map. Early copies in the Northamptonshire Record Office have been checked to confirm this and in any case close examination, even with the naked eye, shows that the line has been crudely drawn in a different style to the original.

46 NRO, Northampton Borough Records, Royal Charters 29.

47 Cox, *ibid.*, p. 239.

48 Margaret Wood, *The English Medieval House*, 1965, p. 166.

which is early fourteenth century.[49] In an urban context, Schofield[50] has pointed to a fashion for building solar towers within London houses in the thirteenth to fourteenth centuries. We can see therefore that the Tower was a major element within an important aristocratic town house, perhaps dating back to the fourteenth century. Indeed perhaps we are seeing a distant reflection of the fashion for towers around this time in Renaissance Italian cities such as Sienna and San Gimignano.

Of the other properties mentioned in the town, the most common is the tenement (*tenementum*). In only one case is there reference to size. In will 107, the mercer John Wellys refers to his large tenement (magnum tenementum) in Abington Street. The use of the term messuages is less common. One in Newlands belonging to John Asplond (59) is, however, described as a capital messuage. The numerous mentions of houses presumably refer generally to smaller structures, as do those to cottages.[51] In addition to dwellings, we hear of other structures within the town such as stables and dovecotes. In one case (1) we hear of five cottages or stables with some rooms above, perhaps suggesting conversion from cottage to stables, but also demonstrating two-storey structures.

We also have mention of commercial and industrial activities, inns, shops, a fish stall, a woolhouse, a 'yelyng' house,[52] and there are of course many more examples of trade and industry both in descriptions of the person's trade, in their title and in their possessions.

There is a single mention of a mill (106) when the tanner Richard Horpoll leaves his house with a mill and garden to his wife Alice, allowing his brother, William Horpoll, also a tanner, free access to the pond. Subsequently Alice leaves the pond yard to William (441). As the testators live in St Peter's parish the mill referred to is probably Marvell's mill which lay at the bottom of Tanner Street. It would seem that at this time the mill, or at least its surrounding area, was being used as a tannery.

Noticeable is the space within the town that allows for gardens, closes, crofts, dovecotes, stables, orchards, etc. This is of course commonplace within medieval towns but would have been all the more noticeable in Northampton because of its huge size due to its early growth and importance.

49 E. Clive Rouse, *Longthorpe Tower*, 1987, English Heritage Handbook.

50 John Schofield, *Medieval London Houses*, 1994, pp. 36, 38, 69.

51 The usage of the terms tenement (tenementum) and messuage (messuagium) in the wills is imprecise and interchangeable. Both are used to refer to properties with houses within them. Smaller properties and houses are described as simply house (domus) or cottage (cotagium). A useful discussion of terms used in contemporary documents at Winchester can be found in Derek Keene, *Survey of Medieval Winchester*, vol 2, part 1, pp. 137–9, 1985.

52 We have been unable to determine the function of this structure.

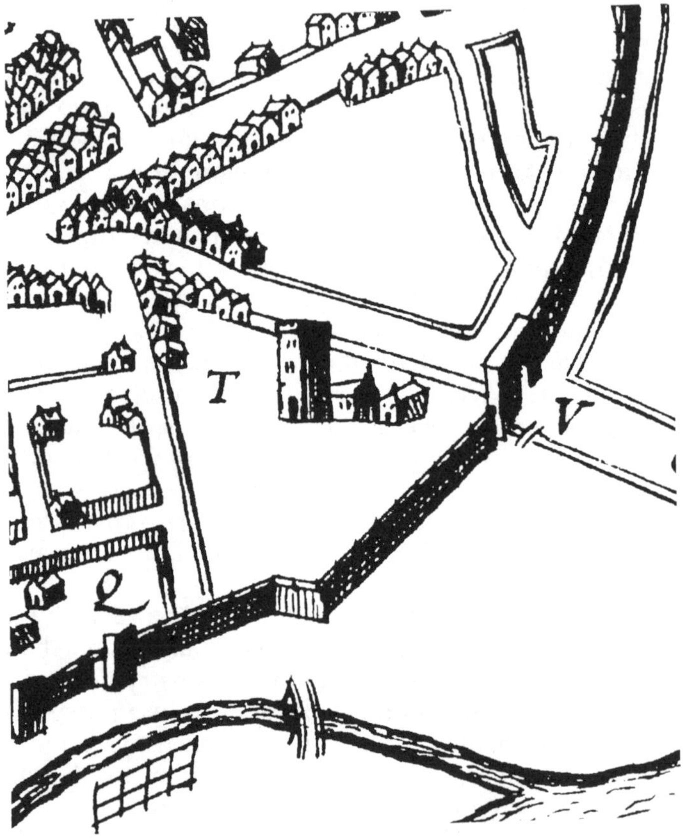

Fig. 4 The Tower, from Speed's map of 1610.

Streets

All of the streets mentioned in the wills whose locations can be traced are marked on Fig 5. The majority of street names still exist or are shown on earlier maps. A small number which can be deduced from documentary references are discussed below.

Berker Street, alias Barker Street (17b), I have discussed the evidence for Barker Street elsewhere.[53] It lay in the south-west quarter of the town and ran from the castle south-east, following the line of the inside of the town's defences roughly along the line of the present St Peter's Way. On the Noble and Butlin map of 1746 its north western end is described as Bakewell Street, while its south eastern arm is marked as The Green/

53 Michael Shaw, 'The excavation of a late 15th to 17th century tanning complex at The Green, Northampton', *Post-Medieval Archaeology*, 30, 1996, p. 108.

Palmer's Street.[54] The south-west quarter of the town was largely given over to tanning at this time (barker is synonymous with tanner, the name arising from the tanner's use of oak bark in the tanning process); hence the name Barker's End (31) which also refers to this area.

Butchers' Row (335) lay within the Market Square.[55]

Carfax corner (363). Alderman Frank Lee locates Carfax as the junction of Horseshoe Street/Horseshoe Lane and Gold Street/ Marefair, although he gives no reason for this.[56]

Cow Lane, later became Swan Street.

Crope Lane, alias Grope Lane (374, 553), was later Dychurch Street.[57]

Les Delvys (115) Delves are quarry pits. The description in the will suggests that the quarry stood within the town wall walls between St Giles' church and the East Gate. Although this may seem surprising, quarry pits have been commonly found during archaeological excavations within the medieval town, a number to the north of St Giles' church.[58]

Fishmarket (68, 391) lay within the Market Square. Fish Street still survives in this area.[59]

Fleshmonger Street (17b, 335) Cox suggests that Fleshmonger Street lay within the Market Square close to Butchers' Row, while Gover *et al* suggest that it is an alternative name for Butchers' Row.[60] However, will 17b refers to a garden and will 335 to principal tenements in the street. These would seem unlikely to have been located in a crowded market area and hence this street must be regarded as unlocated.

Knight Street (610), was later Angel Lane.[61]

Master's Street (102, 335) possibly an earlier or alternative name for College Street where All Saints College was located.

North Street (609) is an earlier name for the northern end of Sheep Street leading to the North Gate.[62]

---

54 In my original article I had assumed that Bakewell Street only was the earlier Barker Street. Since, however, will 363 describes the street as lying in St Gregory's parish, while Bakewell Street lies in St Peter's, I now think it likely that it included also the continuation of the line of Bakewell Street to the east, described on Noble and Butlin as The Green and Palmer's Street as they lie within St Gregory's parish. The parish boundaries are marked on the Noble and Butlin map and are discussed in J H Williams 1982 *ibid.*

55 Cox, *op. cit.*, p. 517; J.E.B. Gover, A. Mawer and F.M. Stenton, *The Place Names of Northamptonshire* (1933), p. 7.

56 Alderman Frank Lee, 'A New Theory of the Origins and Growth of Northampton', *Archaeological Journal* 110, 1954, p. 169.

57 Cox, *op. cit.*, p. 519.

58 Michael Shaw, 'Excavations on a medieval site at Derngate, Northampton, 1984', *Northamptonshire Archaeology* 19xx, p. 74.

59 Cox, *op. cit.*, p. 520.

60 Cox, *op. cit.*, p. 520; Gover et al, p. 8.

61 Cox, *op. cit.*, p. 524.

62 Cox, *op. cit.*, p. 525.

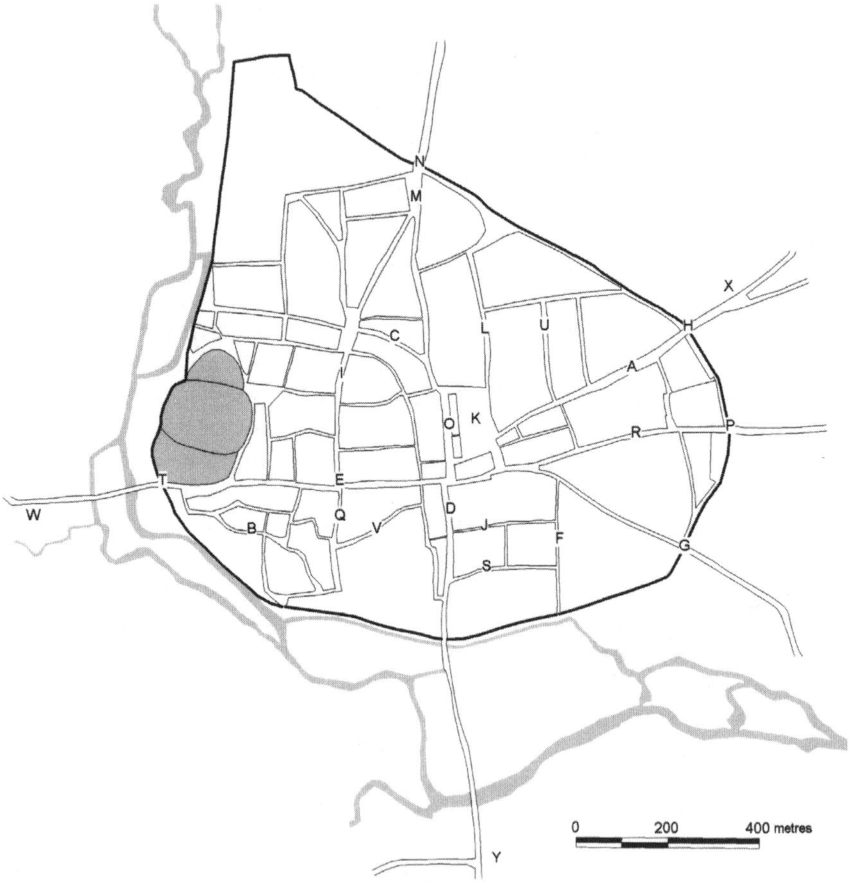

A – Abington Street; B – Barker Street; C – Bearward Street; D – Bridge Street; E – Carfax Corner;
F– Cow Lane; G – Derngate; H – East Gate; I – Horsemarket; J – Knight Street; L – Newland;
M – North Street; N – North Gate; O – (Old) Drapery; P – Postern Gate (by St Giles' Church);
Q – Le Rye Lane; R – St Giles' Street; S – St John's Lane; T – West Bridge; U – Whitefriars Lane;
V – Woolmonger Street; W – St James' End; X – St Edmund's End; Y – Cotton End;

Fig. 5 Northampton streets and suburbs mentioned in the text

Le Rye (308) The will locates le Rye as being in St Gregory's parish. It may be the same place as Roya which occurs as a place name in the 1504 town rental, again in St Gregory's parish. Five properties 'in Roya' are recorded.[63] Welsh has used deeds in Northamptonshire Record Office to demonstrate that The Rye is the lane leading from Horsemarket down to Marvell's Mill, which was later known as Horseshoe Lane.[64]

63 NRO, Royal Charters 29.

64 Tom Welsh, 'Northampton Alternatives: conjecture and counter-conjecture', *Northamptonshire Archaeology* 27, 1996–7, p. 173, and pers comm.

5

Religion and the People

Jacqueline Minchinton

In addition to general social and topographical information, these wills cast valuable light on life when it was not divided into the neat compartments of home, work and religion. In Northampton, as elsewhere, before the factory forced conformity on employees, work was not necessarily tied to fixed hours. Masters of a trade, assisted by members of the family, would normally work in the same premises as they lived. Other employees might live in the same house; they would certainly live nearby. Similarly, religion was not confined to observance of services on Sunday, nor was it regarded as a matter of concern for individuals and their consciences alone. Religion was corporate and social and a part of everyday life.

These wills are a valuable record of the outward forms and trappings of conventional religion. The convictions of those who made them are harder to uncover. At this date the home of the prosperous citizen of Northampton might well be decorated with objects with a religious theme. Margaret Hancok (54) had a painted cloth with the images of St John the Baptist, St John the Evangelist and St Christopher. She left part of a cloth painted with angels and other garlands to the infirmary of the Hospital of St John. It would seem likely that the other part of the cloth, which was left to the church of St Michael, might well have depicted St Michael the Archangel. A halling[65] with the Image of St Dorothy is mentioned in the will of Agnes Rynglond (43).

As Michael Shaw indicates above, Northampton in the fifteenth century was provided with ten parish and other churches, a college of priests, three monastic houses and friaries of each of the main mendicant orders. Priests, friars and monks, as well as those in minor orders, would have been a familiar sight to everyone in the town. Indeed as the wills show many people had relatives among them e.g. '... to Sir William Daffron priest son of Richard Daffron late my husband 6 silver spoons' (Alice Wyng 368).

Not only were those leading the religious life visible in the town, but church services were part of daily life whether or not one attended

65 A wall hanging - probably tapestry.

them. In the church of All Saints, for example, the Morrow mass was said at 4 am-5 am, there was a further mass at Prime (6 a.m.). and another mass with music between 9 am-11 am. In addition there were the daily offices prime, sext, nones and lauds, mattins and vespers, before the day ended with compline. Passers-by would have been alerted to the most solemn moment of Mass by the ringing of the sanctus bell. Indeed the sound of bells both from the churches within the town and from the outlying religious houses was an everyday fact of life.

The private conviction and devotion of those who made the wills can only be surmised. As has been mentioned[66] the wills conventionally begin 'In the name of God Amen' and continue with the bequest of the soul to Almighty God and his saints, who may be specified by name. There are obvious difficulties in using this convention as a guide to the religious views of the testator. These are after all only copies of wills, in many cases turned into Latin by someone who was in all probability in Holy Orders and who, directly or indirectly, may have influenced the testator.

The common form in the earlier Latin wills is 'Deo Omnipotenti Beate Marie eius genitrici et omnibus sanctis curie celestis', (18a, 20, 26 etc.) (To Almighty God, the Blessed Mary his mother and all the saints of heaven), a form of words which changes to 'sue genitrici', (54, 56, 57 etc.). Linking the name of the Blessed Virgin with Almighty God is a reminder of Mary's importance as an intercessor. When the later wills were registered it became the practice to use et cetera after Deo Omnipotenti. This may be of no great significance. It is probable that the clerk who copied the will saw no point in recording the same lengthy phrase over and over again. It is possible that he may also have been similarly deterred by lengthy commendations to a variety of saints. The Lollard views for which Northampton had been known in the early part of the fifteenth century are not shown in these wills. There are, however, a few which do appear to convey the convictions of the testator. In 1469 Thomas Arderon (4) bequeaths and commends his soul '... to God the Father Almighty, Jesus Christ his only son my creator and redeemer, the Blessed Mary my only advocate and to all the orders of the courts of heaven interceding and supplicating on my behalf at the day of judgement'. It could be argued that Thomas, who was a resident at Delapre Abbey, is a special case. There are others however who express what appear to be personal devotions and convictions. Thomas Merton (62) leaves his soul to Almighty God '... by the intercession of the Blessed Virgin Mary, of the Blessed Bishop Nicholas and of all the Saints of God'; Roger Butler (387) '... First I betake my soul to Almighty God and to His mercy'; Margaret

66 See Introduction, p. 5.

Harowdon (101) in '... faithful belief of Holy Church disposed to make me ready to the mercy of the most gracious Lord Our Saviour Jesus Christ when it shall please him to call me out of this mortal life... I commend my soul to the mercy of Almighty God'.

When contemplating the disposal of their mortal remains the testators viewed the funeral rites in the same social and communal light with spiritual services, charitable donations and the involvement of others. Many testators had a specific place marked out for their burial within the church itself if they had sufficient status or wealth. Joan, wife of Simon Ball wished to be buried in the Chapel of the Fraternity of Corpus Christi next to the tomb of her first husband William Wellys (11). Isabel Peche's first husband William Tresham had been buried in St James Abbey where she too wished to be buried (45). There are frequent references to be being buried near deceased spouses or children. Only in the case of William Perwyn (297) are there detailed instructions for a tomb which he wanted to be in marble and engraved with the images of himself, his wife and his ten sons and seven daughters.

Those who made these wills were not solely concerned that their earthly remains should be suitably interred and their resting place appropriately marked, it was of vital importance that they should enlist as many prayers as possible for the well being of their soul so that their time in Purgatory should be shortened. As far as the services are concerned the saying of Placebo on the night before the funeral and Dirige before the mass was customary e.g. Joan Ball (10) and occurs frequently in these wills. The trental of thirty consecutive masses on thirty consecutive days[67] is mentioned as are particular masses.

Those with sufficient funds might ask for a suitable chaplain to be found to say masses for a year. For example, John Hygham (18a) - £5, John Rycher (82) - £5 6 8d), Thomas Pepe (84) - £10, John Barnard (88) - 2 years, no sum stated, John Bukby (94) - 8 marks, Hugh Wodsall (336) - in return for pardoning a 60s debt; while Simon Brayfeld (347) left 40s to the fraternity of the Blessed Virgin Mary at All Saints for burial and that a priest should celebrate mass at the customary eight hour daily. The general sum for a priest to sing mass for a year has been reckoned at between £5 and £6.[68]

Bequests to people, both as individuals and corporately, are frequently linked with requests for prayers. Such as Alice Wynge (wife of William Wynge, weaver) (368) '... To St Thomas Hospital 20 ells of linen cloth price 4d the ell to be divided amongst them to pray for my soul'. In the will of Richard Harowdon (49) gifts to the clergy are stated to be '... that they may pray with greater devotion for the

67 Eamon Duffy, *The Stripping of the Altars*, Yale University Press, p. 369.
68 *Op. cit.*

health of my soul'. The poor, whose presence at the funeral might have been encouraged by the activities of the bellman,[69] could benefit in a number of ways - '. . . On the day of my burial 40 dozen of white bread to be distributed amongst the poor' (Margery Carter 22) or '. . . to eight poor people holding torches on the day of my death, to each of them a black gown' (John Colman 109).

The services of the Church were of course conducted in Latin and the degree to which the laity were actively involved in religious practices outside the routine observance of Mass has been the subject of much interest.[70] The mention of the 'wedding door' at All Saints (494) follows the pattern of Chaucer's Wife of Bath, 'Housbondes at chirche dore she hadde fyve'. From the tenth until the sixteenth century the marriage service was in two parts, the marriage itself, which took place at the door of the church, and the nuptial mass which was celebrated at the altar.[71]

If the religious views of the testators were conventional they seem to have been equally conventional in their religious practices. The most frequently mentioned devotional object is the rosary (12, 54, 107, 112, 341, 357), sometimes referred to as a pair of beads (101, 112, 130, 341, 364, 374, 389, 410). According to tradition the introduction of the rosary as an aid to worship is attributed to St Dominic in the early thirteenth century. It consists of either fifteen groups of ten small beads (or five for the lesser rosary) of ten small beads followed by one large bead or gaud. At each of the small beads the user recited an Ave Maria[72] and at the large bead a Paternoster[73] would be recited at the beginning and a Gloria[74] at the end of each set of Aves.

The rosaries mentioned in these wills were made of a variety of materials such as amber (John Kyng 357, jet (Ricardina Mose 12, Margaret Hancok 54), coral with gold and silver (Margaret Hancock 54), while Alice Peny (112) left two sets, one of amber and jet and the other of jet with paternosters of silver. These were obviously works of craftsmanship and beauty in their own right and objects of value, which is not to deny their devotional purpose nor the devotion of those who owned and presumably used them.

The religious work mentioned most frequently is the primer, a book of private devotions as distinct from a book of set church services.

69 *Op. cit.*
70 *Op. cit.*
71 F. N. Robinson (ed), *The Works of Geoffrey Chaucer,* 1957, note to line 460.
72 'Hail Mary full of grace, blessed art thou amongst women and blessed is the fruit of thy womb Jesus. Holy Mary Mother of God pray for us sinners, now and at the hour of our death'.
73 The Lord's Prayer - 'Our Father which art in Heaven . . .'.
74 'Glory be to the Father and to the Son and to the Holy Spirit as it was in the Beginning is now and ever shall be world without end Amen'.

It was used in the main by the laity and sometimes referred to as a Book of Hours. It has been said that by the early sixteenth century, in urban congregations at least, one was almost as likely to find a primer as a pair of beads in the hands of the worshippers in church. While ownership of such a book does not necessarily imply its use, it would be charitable to assume that some at least of these were used in private prayer outside the conventional church services. It would be equally true that lack of a book does not necessarily mean lack of private prayer.

These wills mention a number of books connected with Church Services. The breviary contained the ordinary and daily services of the church recited by those in Holy Orders, apart from the Mass itself which was contained in the Missal. Wealthier people such as Isabel Peche (born a Vaux and widow of William Tresham) who left '... to Richard Sadeler, clerk, my missal, my chalice and all other vestments and ornaments of the altar in my chapel' (45), had private chapels in their houses where the daily offices of the Church might be read. Certainly Isabel could have followed the psalms in the psalter which she left to St James Abbey.

In the centuries since their foundation the local religious houses had been accumulating property, some granted in return for their prayers. The Prior and convent of St Andrew's Priory in particular were major landowners in Northampton, and as Rectors of the churches were entitled to the tithes (tenths) of produce of the parishioners. It is therefore not surprising that the majority of the references to St Andrew's Priory in these wills relate to sums left '... for tithes forgotten or not well tithed' (78, 80, 87, 91 etc.). Taxation was clearly no more popular than it is today as there were only six actual bequests to St Andrew's, some leaving money with an explicit request for prayers (7, 334) and another specifying that the money should be equally divided among the convent (102) rather than to Priory funds. The Priory does not seem to have endeared itself to the people of Northampton.

St James Abbey was more popular with the townsfolk if we can judge by the eleven bequests made. The nunnery of Delapre, a much smaller foundation, received bequests in seven wills. In only one will, that of William Russhden, draper (7), are all three foundations mentioned. Far more popular were the Friaries, mentioned in 51 of the 147 wills.

The four major orders of Friars were all represented in Northampton in the fifteenth century. The Augustinian or Austin Friars in Bridge Street, the Dominican Friars in Horsemarket, Greyfriars to the north of the market place and the White Friars (The Carmelites or Friars of our Lady of Mount Carmel) in the north east of the town. In the early medieval period the cloistered religious orders had been the recipients of many gifts. This shift of benefactions to those who were active in the world has been recorded elsewhere - 'Thus the parish clergy were remembered in 41 percent of fifteenth century London wills, friars in 35 percent, monks in 15 percent, and nuns in 11 percent.'[75]

In addition to the greater tithes payable to the Rector and the lesser tithes due to the Vicar of the parish, there were other exactions which are mentioned in these wills. It was the custom for the church to receive a principal or mortuary payment of a jewel or animal. For example '... To the vicar of the aforesaid church my best jewel or horse in the name of mortuary' (Richard Haroweden 49).

The most popular destination, however, for religious bequests were the fraternities or guilds,[76] perhaps some of the clearest evidence of the entwining of secular civic life with the religious. Unlike the guilds that governed the operation of trades within the town, these fraternities were based in individual churches and drew their members from across the trades. However, since people of the same trade tended to live near each other certain fraternities appear to have been popular with specific occupations. For example the fraternity or Guild of Corpus Christi in All Saints Church included those connected to the textile trades. Open to both men and women, with a distinguishing livery of gown and hood (36, 110) these guilds fulfilled a social, religious and philanthropic purpose. Serjeantson suggests that the fraternity of St Katherine at All Saints was set up for the specific objective of assisting at the burial of those who died of the plague[77]. It was possible to be enrolled in a fraternity after one's death as William Prentice (365) bequeathed 20s to the fraternity of Our Lady in All Saints for him '... to be admitted a brother and my wife a sister at the same' and Alice Cutlerd (568) bequeathed 20s to the fraternity of Corpus Christi to be a sister there.

The original object of a fraternity was to maintain a light before a particular statue or support a priest to say mass for its members in their particular chapel within a parish church. It is not surprising that All Saints, the principal church of the town, should have the most fraternities: - St Cithe, Corpus Christi, Holy Cross, Holy Trinity, St George, St Katherine, St John, St Stephen and the Blessed Virgin.

---

75 Stephen Inwood, *A History of London*, London 1998, p. 40.

76 Details of a number of these guilds are given by Helen Cam, *ibid.*, and further guilds are listed by Serjeantson and Longden.

77 Serjeantson, *History of All Saints Church, 1901*. In consequence of the frequent visitations of the plague in Northampton, and the danger arising from burials round all Saint's Church in the very centre of traffic and business, a burial ground for such cases was enclosed on a vacant space between College Lane and Horsemarket. A chapel was built here, dedicated to St Katherine for mortuary purposes and for the use of those resident in infected houses.

The fraternity of Holy Trinity had four chaplains as well as three singing men and Corpus Christi had two chaplains.[78] These priests were in addition to the beneficed clergy who served the parish church. The College of All Saints was founded in the fifteenth century so that the priests attached to the various fraternities linked to the Church of All Saints could live a communal life.

There were only two fraternities in St Giles (St Clement and St Giles), two in St Sepulchre (Holy Sepulchre and St Martin) and three in St Gregory (Holy Sepulchre, Holy Cross in the Wall and the Virgin Mary). St Mary (St Katherine), St Michael (St Michael) and St Peter (St Ragener) all had one fraternity.

In other towns such as York and Wakefield we know that trade guilds were involved with the Miracle plays associated with the Feast of Corpus Christi (a festival which was officially recognised in 1311).[79] It seems that in Northampton the religious fraternities also played their part in civic entertainment. '. . . I bequeath my horn to the chapel of Corpus Christi there to remain for ever to the use of Robyn Hode to have every Whitson Monday and all other times when he need' (Thomas Symson 440).

Fraternities acquired their money not only from monetary bequests but also from rents (the best way to secure future income) and by the late fifteenth century some fraternities had already acquired land and a number of properties in the town and further gifts are recorded in these wills. For example the garden and meadow that William Harysson (26) left to the fraternity of the Holy Cross in the Wall in the church of St Gregory. The same fraternity was also left closes and gardens in the parish of St Gregory by Roger Butler (387).

Chaucer's five Guildsmen of a town famously travelled to Canterbury together but there are no references in these wills for funds for pilgrimages, or statements that someone had been on pilgrimage. There is a reference, however, to a maser of the Three Kings of Cologne (Richard Daffron 83). Was this a valued relic of a pilgrimage by the testator or a relative, or had it, more prosaically, been bought in the town from a visiting merchant?[80]

Reading these wills provides a number of questions to ponder - the sudden popularity of the fraternity of St Cithe for example. Was this St Osyth, the daughter of Frithewald and Walburga who were the first Christian rulers of East Anglia, or St Zita, the patroness of domestic

---

78 Serjeantson, *op. cit.*

79 A.C. Cawley (ed), *Everyman and Mediaeval Miracle Plays*, Everyman's Library, Dent 1956, reprinted 1965.

80 Serjeantson and Longden, *ibid.*, note a light of the Three Kings of Cologne at Middleton Cheney, p. 6.

servants, as assumed by the editor of St Albans wills of a similar date?[81] Eamon Duffy agrees with the latter and suggests that the appeal of saints like St Zita lay in their suitablility as patterns for imitation.[82] Perhaps the testators who invoked St Cithe hoped that this would influence their own servants to follow her example.

We may not be able to answer all questions but the wills remain an invaluable source of evidence for the religious practices of the citizens of Late Medieval Northampton.

81 Flood, *ibid.*

82 Duffy, p. 174. According to the *Dictionary of Saints,* Zita entered domestic service in the household of a weaver in Lucca. She was popularly acclaimed a saint at her death in 1278. Her Feast day is April 27th and her emblem is a bunch of keys.

The Wills

Transcriptions and translations

Notes on format

Each will has a dual identification. The numbers quoted are the original will numbers, but folio numbers have also been given to aid with the location of a specific will in the Northamptonshire Record Office volume. For any reader wishing to compare transcriptions with the original document, the line layout of each will has been retained. In addition to the actual transcriptions each will has been given a brief heading of name, date, and occupation (when given). Sometimes the occupation has been deduced from other wills and this is indicated by round brackets ( ).

Latin wills have been transcribed as fully and accurately as possible, with all contractions extended, but the arbitrary use of capital letters has been replaced by modern usage. The translations have been kept as close to the original Latin as is compatible with making sense of the content. Christian names have been changed to modern usage, except when they are very unusual, but surnames have been retained as written. Place names have been changed to modern usage when the place can be clearly identified. Some basic punctuation has been added to facilitate understanding and sums of money have been changed from Roman numerals to Arabic (but not to modern currency). For example vli vjs viijd in will 35 becomes £5 6s 8d.

English wills have been transcribed as written except for abbreviations being extended. Personal and place names have been retained as written, but modern place names have been inserted in round brackets ( ) where the present location might be unclear.

The original text of the wills is presented in standard typescript while translations are in italics.

For all of the wills, where the condition of the document or the handwriting renders a reading doubtful, this is indicated by square brackets [ ]. Angled brackets < > indicate that text was originally inserted above a line.

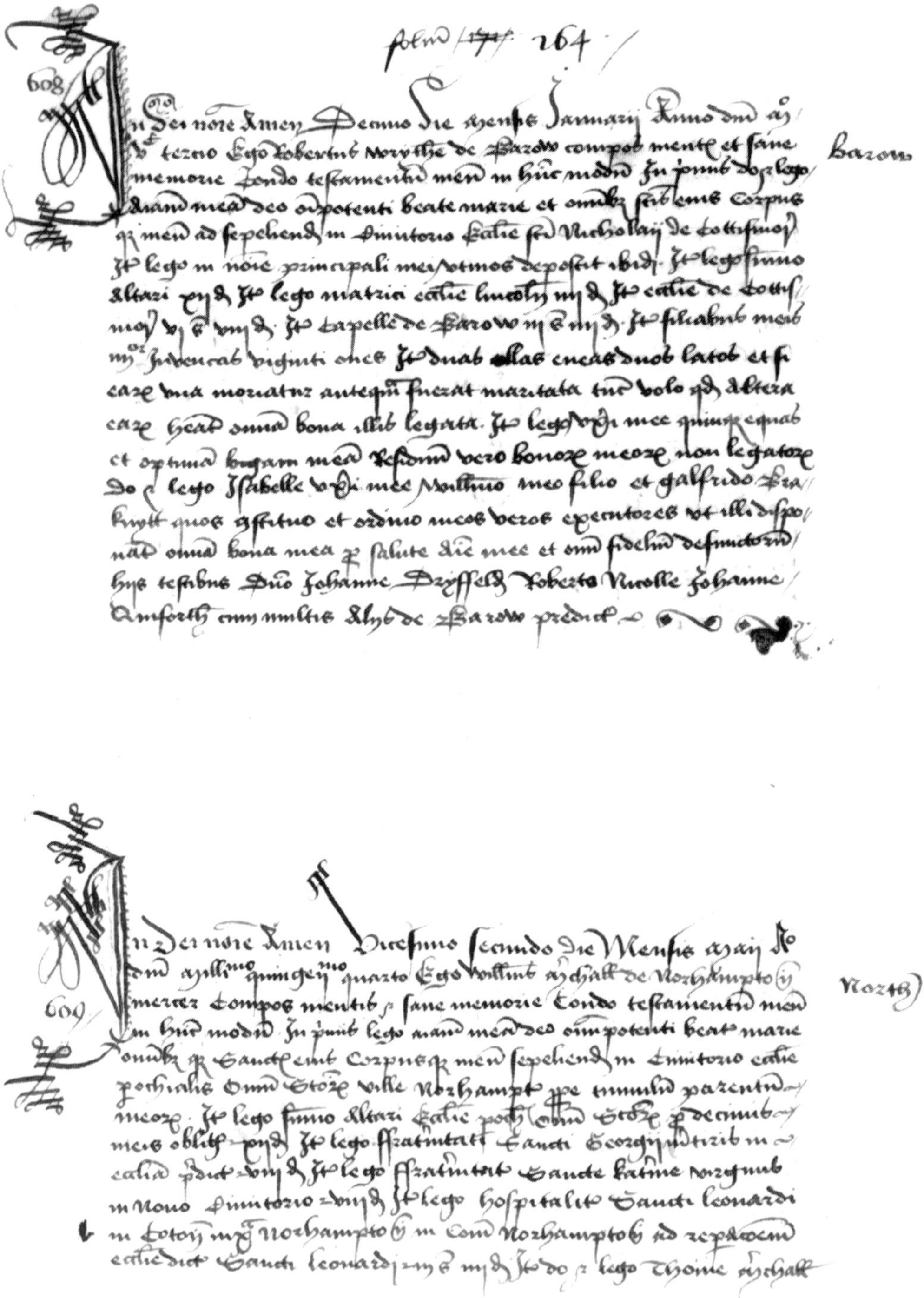

Fig. 6 Early Northamptonshire Wills, 1467-1510, folio 164. The lower text is the first part of the will of William Marchall of Northampton, mercer, 1504, (will 609). It continues over the page.

f1v 1 JOHN BYKYRSTON 26th October 1467 mercer

In Dei nomine Amen xxvj die mensis Octobris anno domini millesimo ccccIxvij Ego Johannes Bykyrston de Northampton mercer compos mentis et sane memorie condo testamentum meum in hunc modum In primis lego animam meam Deo Omnipotenti etcetera Beate Marie Virgini sue genitrici ei ac omnibus sanctis curie celestis corpusque meum sepiliendum in capella Sancti Johannes Baptiste infra ecclesiam Omnium Sanctorum ibidem Item lego summo
altari ecclesie predicte pro decimis meis non bene decimatis et oblationibus meis oblitis iijs.iiijd. Item lego sustentacioni dicte capelle Sancti Johannis Baptiste vjs.viijd. Item lego Johanni Rychard de Taunton in comitatu Somerset mercer fratri uxoris mee meam togam coloris rone russett Item lego Henrico Smyth de Northampton ffysher meam togam veridem Item lego Thome filio meo primarium meum ulteriusque do et lego Agneti uxori mee omnia et singula illa quinque cotagia mea sive stabula cum cameris supra gardinis adiacentibus et clausuris suis quondam Johannis Sprygg de Northampton armigeri et postmodum Thome Knygthley de Northampton et Emme uxoris situatana ad [...cem] in le Wollmonger Strete ville Northampton inter tenementum
prioris et conventus de Esshby Canorum ex parte orientali et tenementum Thome Smyth de Nothampton fflecher ex parte occidentali que quidam quinque cotagia sive stabula cum cameris supra gardinis adiacentibus et clausuris supra nuper perquisivi de predicte Emme uxore predicti Thome Knygthley in viduatate sua habendum et tenendum omnia et singula predicta quinque cotagia sive stabula cum cameris supra gardinis adiacentibus et clausuris suis ut predictum est prefate Agneti uxori mee heredibus et assignatis suis imperpetuum de capitalibus dominis feodi illius per servicia inde debita et de iure consueta Residuum vero omnium bonorum meorum superius non legatorum do et lego prefate Agneti uxori mee <ad disponendum pro anima mea> et animarum omnium amicorum meorum ac omnium fidelium defunctorum
prout ei melius videbitur expediri Et ad istud testamentum meum bene et fideliter exequendum
prefatam Agnetem uxorem meam ordino facio et constituo executricem meam Et de execucione eiusdem testamentum ordino facio et constituo Thomam Stewyn supervisorem et volo quod predictus Thomas habebit pro labore suo xld. per presentes

In the name of God Amen the 26th day of October 1467 I John Bykyrston of Northampton, mercer, in sound mind and good memory make my testament in this wise. First I bequeath my soul to Almight God etcetera to the Blessed Virgin Mary His mother and all the saints of the court of Heaven, my body to be buried in the chapel of St John the Baptist within the church of All Saints in the same place. Item I bequeath to the high altar of the aforesaid church for my tithes not well tithed and my oblations forgotten 3s 4d. Item I bequeath to the maintenance of the chapel of St John the Baptist 6s 8d. Item I bequeath to John Rychard of Taunton in the county of Somerset, mercer, brother of my wife, my gown of rone russet colour. Item I bequeath to Henry Smyth of Northampton, fisher, my green gown. Item I bequeath to Thomas, my son, my primer. Further I give and bequeath to Agnes, my wife, all and singular those five cottages or stables with rooms above and gardens adjoining and their closes, formerly of John Spryggy, esquire, of Northampton, and afterwards of Thomas Knygthley, of Northampton, and Emma his wife, situated at [...cem] in Woolmonger

Street in the town of Northampton between the tenement of the priory and convent of Canons Ashby on the east and the tenement of Thomas Smyth of Northampton, fletcher, on the west, and closes beyond formerly acquired by the aforesaid Emma, wife of the aforesaid Thomas Knygthley, in her widowhood, to have and to hold all and singular the aforesaid five cottages or stables with rooms above and gardens adjoining and their closes to the aforesaid Agnes, my wife, her heirs and assigns forever of the chief lords of the fee for services therefore due and by right accustomed. The residue of all my goods above not bequeathed I give and bequeath to the aforesaid Agnes, my wife, to dispose for the health of my soul and the souls of all my friends and all faithful departed as seems best to her. And that this my will be well and faithfully executed I ordain, make and constitute the aforesaid Agnes, my wife, my executrix. And concerning the execution of this will I ordain, make and constitute Thomas Stewyn supervisor and I will that the aforesaid Thomas have for his labour 40d by these presents.

f2v 4 THOMAS ARDERON 25th October 1469 tenant of Delapre

In Dei nomine Amen vicesimo quinto die mensis Octobris anno domini mccccl xix Ego Thomas Arderon mansum tenens infra claustra monasterii Beate Marie de Pratis iuxta Northampton compos
mentis et sane memorie condo testamentum meum in hunc modum In primis lego et comendo animam
Deo Patri Omnipotenti Jesu Christo eius unigenito meo creatori ac redemptori Beate Marie singulari
advocatrici et omnibus celestis curie ordinibus in illa tremenda hora pro me intercedentibus divine
clemencie ac suplicantibus corpus que meum tradendum ecclesiastice sepultura in basilica eiusdem
monasterii ex parte boreali prout me vivente amicis meis plenius patefeci Item lego nomine
mei mortuari j vaccam in custodia Thome Keynsham de Hardyngisthorn manentem Item
lego cuilibet sacerdoti de iiij ordinibus mendicancium et in die obitus mei pro salute anime mee
celebranti iiijd. in villa Northampton Item lego cuilibet pauperi interessenti obsequiis meis funera
libus j panem precii obuli et in pecunia jd. ad quantum quadraginta solidi sterlingorum se extendenter
et ultra secundum discrecionem executorum meorum Item lego Johanni Haynes capellano j peciam
argenti cum cooperterio et unum librum intitulatum Speculum Christianorum Item Johanni Liteley de

f3r

Donechurch in comitatu Warwici magnam ferraram laminam j veru et in pecunia xxs. Item lego Ricardo
Liteley j magnam lavacrum j magnum veru et in pecunia xxs. Item lego Elizabeth Lytley filie predicti
unam pelvem et j lavacrum Item lego Willelmo Heynes de Byfeld in pecunia xxs. Item lego Alicie

Litley servienti mee in pecunia xs. et vj cocliaria argenti Insuper volo quod dicta Alicia habeat cetera bona
fideliter et pacifice que preantea in vita mea eidem manibus meis propris dedi et deliberavi ac eciam
bona quod post decessum meum per executores meos eidem Alicie liberari assignavi Residuum vero omnium
bonorum meorum superius non legatorum do et lego Thome Cryspe de London mercer Johanni Chese capellani
ut ipse inde ordinent et disponant pro salute anime mee et amicorum meorum antecessorum prout illius melius
videbitur faciendi et eosdem Thomam Cryspe et Johannem Chese capellanum ordino facio et constituo
meos veros et legistimos executores per presentes ut ipsi deum pro occulis habentes presens testamentum meum fideliter exequantur et compleant cum effectu Date die et loco et anno domini supradicto
hiis testibus Ricardo Cryspe filio supranominato Thome Cryspe de London Johanne Egremond de
Northampton et aliis

Istud testamentum probatum fuit in ecclesia hospitali Sancti Johannis Baptiste Northampton primo die mensis Februari
anno supradicto comissaque et administratio ibidem bonorum

In the name of God Amen the 25th day of October 1469 I Thomas Arderon, house tenant inside the cloisters of the monastery of the Blessed Mary of Delapre near Northampton, in sound mind and good memory make my testament in this wise. First I bequeath and commend my soul to God the Father Almighty, Jesus Christ His only son, my Creator and Redeemer, to the Blessed Mary, my only advocate and all the orders of the courts of heaven, interceding and supplicating on my behalf at the day of judgment, my body to be committed for ecclesiastical burial in the basilica of the said monastery on the north side just as while I was alive I disclosed fully to my friends. Item I bequeath in the name of my mortuary one cow remaining in the custody of Thomas Keynsham of Hardingstone. Item I bequeath to each of the priests of the 4 orders of mendicants in the town of Northampton celebrating (mass) on the day of my funeral for the health of my soul 4d. Item I bequeath to each pauper taking part in my funeral rites 1 loaf worth a halfpenny and in money 1d as far as forty shillings sterling will stretch and further according to the discretion of my executors. Item I bequeath to John Haynes, chaplain, 1 piece of silver with a cover and one book called 'Speculum Christianorum'. Item to John Liteley of Dunchurch in the county of Warwick a large iron plate, 1 spit and in money 20s. Item I bequeath to Richard Litely 1 large ewer, 1 large spit and in money 20s. Item I bequeath to Elizabeth Lytley, daughter of the aforesaid one bowl and 1 ewer. Item I bequeath to William Heynes of Byfield in money 20s. Item I bequeath to Alice Litley, my servant, in money 10s and 6 silver spoons. Further I intend that the said Alice have faithfully and peaceably the other goods which I had given and delivered to the same by my own hands in my lifetime and also the goods which after my death I have assigned to be delivered to the same Alice by my executors. The residue of all my goods not bequeathed above I give and bequeath to Thomas Cryspe of London, mercer, John Chese, chaplain, and they to ordain and dispose for the health of my soul and my friends and ancestors as seems best to them to do and the said Thomas Cryspe and John Chese, chaplain, I ordain, make and constitute my true and legitimate executors by these presents that they, having God before their eyes, shall faithfully execute and carry into effect this present testament. Given the day and place and year abovesaid. With these witnesses Richard Cryspe, son of the aforenamed Thomas Cryspe of London, John Egremond of Northampton and others.

This testament was proved in the church of the Hospital of St John the Baptist, Northampton, on the first day of the month of February the year abovesaid and administration having been committed of the goods there.

f6r 7 WILLIAM RUSSHDEN 13th March 1466 draper

In Dei nomine Amen Die Jovis in festo Sancti Gregorii pape anno domini mcccclxvj Ego Willelmus Russhden de Northampton draper compos mentis licet in corpore non validus Deo in altissimo in omnibus regraciato condo testamentum meum in hunc modum In primis lego animam meam Deo Omnipotenti Beate Marie Virgini et omnibus sanctis corpusque meum sepiliendum in cimiterio ecclesie Omnium Sanctorum ville Northampton iuxta sepulturam Johanne uxoris mee et Katerine filie mee ibidem Item lego et volo quod xijcem torche quelibet earundem de pondere ix librarum ordinentur ad ardendum circa corpus meum in honore domini nostri Jesu Christi ad exequias meas ac missam et sepulturam meam et volo quod predicte torchie statim postquam exequis mee missa et sepultura mea plenarie compleantur immediate tunc per discrecionem executorum meorum ut melius viderint distribuantur et disponantur diversis ecclesiis et locis sanctis Item magistro Willelmo Breton vicario dicte ecclesie Omnium Sanctorum xxs. Item lego sacerdotibus et consortibus suis Collegii dicte ecclesie in generali recreatione inter eos habendum ad specialiter orandum pro salute anime mee et omnium fidelium defunctorum xiijs.iiijd. Item lego Ricardo Chandeler capellano ad celebrandum et specialiter orandum pro salute anime mee et omnium fidelium defunctorum xls. Item lego abbati et conventui Sancti Jacobi iuxta Northampton ad orandum pro salute anime mee xxvjs. viijd. Item lego pro funeralibus expensiis meis et sepultura mea ulterius honeste perficiendum videlicet in pane cibis et potabus ac aliis donis caritativis et elemosinis die sepulture mee disponendum secundum discrecionem et ordinacionem executorum meorum Item lego Priori et conventui Prioratus Sancti Andree ville Northampton ad orandum pro salute anime mee xxvjs.viijd. Item lego magistro hospitalis Sancti Johannis Baptiste ville Northampton et confratribus suis ad orandum pro salute anime mee xiijs.iiijd. Item lego abbatisse et conventui de Pratis iuxta Northampton ad orandum pro salute anime mee xiijs.iiijd. Item lego cuilibet ordini fratrum mendicancium ville Northampton ad specialiter orandum pro salute anime

mee vs. Item <lego> Willelmo Smyth de Stratford cognato meo xls. et eciam dimitto dicto Willelmo Smyth de moneta quam michi debet iijli.xiijs.iiijd. Residuum
vero omnium bonorum meorum superius non legatorum do et lego Roberto Tanfeld armigero Willelmo
Austyn de Northampton et Johanni Adam de eadem draper ad inde disponendum et ordinandum
per arbitrum predictorum Roberti Tanfeld Willelmi Austyn pro salute anime mee et omnium fidelium
defunctorum et ulterius ad presens testamentum meum ac ultimam voluntatem meam per me dictis
Roberto Willelmo et Johanni specificatis in omnibus fideliter exequendum et perimplendum adeo
plenarie prout ipsi vellent quod ego pro eis facerem in consimili casu et eosdem Robertum Willelmum et Johannem ordino facio et constituo executores meos per presentes In cuius rei testimonium sigillum officij mei apposui Date die loco et anno domini supradictis

Istud testum erat probatum et insumatum vij die mensis Julij anno domini mcccclxx in ecclesia hospitalis Sancti Johannis Baptiste Northampton per executores supradictos in forma iuris iuratos

In the name of God Amen Thursday in the Feast of St Gregory, Pope, 1466 I William Russhden of Northampton, draper, in sound mind although not strong in body, giving thanks to God on high in all things, make my testament in this wise. First I bequeath my soul to Almighty God, to the Blessed Virgin Mary and all saints, my body to be buried in the cemetery of the church of All Saints in the town of Northampton next to the grave of Joan, my wife, and Katherine, my daughter, there. Item I bequeath and will that 12 torches, each of them weighing 9 pounds, should be arranged to burn around my body in honour of Our Lord Jesus Christ, at my exequies and mass and my burial, and I wish that the aforesaid torches, immediately after my exequies, mass and burial are fully completed, are immediately distributed and disposed to diverse churches at the discretion of my executors as seems best. Item to Master William Breton, vicar of the church aforesaid of All Saints 20s. Item I bequeath to the priests and their fellows in the college of the said church to have between them for general recreation and to pray in particular for the health of my soul and all faithful departed 13s 4d. Item I bequeath to Richard Chandeler, chaplain, to celebrate and pray specially for the health of my soul and all faithful departed 40s. Item I bequeath to the Prior and convent of the Priory of St James near Northampton to pray for the health of my soul 26s 8d. Item I bequeath for my funeral expenses, further to perform honestly my burial, that is to say in bread and food and drink and other charitable gifts and alms on the day of my burial, to be disposed at the discretion and arrangement of my executors. Item I bequeath to the Prior and convent of St Andrew in the town of Northampton to pray for the health of my soul 26s 8d. Item I bequeath to the Master and brothers of the Hospital of St John the Baptist in the town of Northampton to pray for the health of my soul 13s 4d. Item I bequeath to the Abbess and convent of Delapre near Northampton to pray for the health of my soul 13s 4d. Item I bequeath to each of the orders of mendicant brothers in the town of Northampton for special prayers for the health of my soul 5s. Item I bequeath to William Smyth of Stratford, my relative, 40s and I also remit to the said William Smyth in money as much as he owes to me £3 13s 4d. The residue of all my goods not bequeathed above I give and bequeath to Robert Tanfield esq. William Austyn of Northampton and John Adam of the same, draper, to dispose and ordain by the judgment of the aforesaid Robert Tanfield, William Austyn for the health of my soul and all faithful departed and further by this my present testament and my last will to be faithfully executed in all things and fulfilled by Robert, William and John, specifically named by me, just as they will that I would act in like situation and the same Robert, William and John I ordain, make and constitute my executors by these presents. In testimony of which I have put the seal of my office. Given the day, place and year abovesaid.

This testament was proved and applied the 6th day of the month of July AD 1470 in the church of the Hospital of St John the Baptist, Northampton for the executors abovesaid and sworn in legal form.

f7r 10 JOHN PEDDER Wednesday after St James Apostle [28 July] 1462 weaver

In Dei nomine Amen die Mercurii proximo post festum Sancti Jacobi Apostoli anno domini mcccclxij Ego
Johannes Pedder de Northampton wever compos mentis condo testamentum meum in hunc modum In
primis lego animam meam Deo Omnipotenti Beate Marie Virgini et omnibus sanctis corpusque meum sepiliendum in ecclesia Omnium Sanctorum ville Northampton coram imagine Beate Marie Virginis
in corpore ecclesie predicte Item lego fabrice ecclesie predicte vjs.viijd. Item lego summo altari dicte ecclesie pro decimis meis et oblationibus oblitis iijs.iiijd. Item lego vicario dicte ecclesie iijs.iiijd. Item lego fraternitati Sancti Thome Martiris iijs.iiijd. Item lego Emme Smyth servienti mee xxs. Item lego Agneti servienti mee xs. Item do et lego Agneti uxori
mee totum illud tenementum meum cum suis pertinenciis in quo maneo situatum in le Wolmonger Strete
ville Northampton habendum et tenendum predictum tenementum cum suis pertinenciis prefate Agneti uxori mee ad
terminum vite ipsius Agnetis de capitalibus dominis feodi illius per servicia inde debita et consueta Et volo quod statim post decessum predicte Agnetis predictum tenementum cum suis pertinenciis remaneat
Johanni Mede de Northampton wever Roberto Bulcle de eadem wever et Willelmo Stevenes scryvener
heredibus et assignatis eorum imperpetuum tenendum de capitalibus dominis feodi illius per servicia inde
debita et consueta ea intentione tantum quod dicti Johannes Robertus et Willelmus heredes et assignati

eorum immediate post decessum predicte Agnetis uxoris mee quam cito tunc poterint rationabiliter
per supervisum et consilium Thome Merton predictum tenementum cum suis pertinenciis vendant et argentum
de eadem vendicione perveniens disponant in missis elemosinis et aliis donis caritatus
pro salute anime mee et eiusdem Agnetis uxoris mee ac pro salute animarum parentum nostrorum benefactorum
et omnium fidelium defunctorum prout melius viderint per eorum discreciones ad animarum nostrorum
fore salutes Residuum vero omnium bonorum meorum superius non legatorum do et lego
prefate Agneti uxori mee ac eisdem Johanni Mede Roberto Bulcle et Willelmo Stevenes
ad inde disponendum et ordinandum pro salute anime et omnium fidelium defunctorum prout eis
melius videbitur expediri et eosdem Agnetem Johannem Mede Robertum Bulcle et Willelmum
Stewenes ordino facio et constituo meos executores ac eundem Thomam Merton
huius presentis testamenti mei ordino facio et constituo fore supervisorem per presentes Date die loco et anno domini supradictis

Istud testamentum probatum fuit in ecclesia Omnium Sanctorum Northampton iiijto die Septembris anno domini m
cccclxij per predictos executores superius in eodem testamento specificatos in forma iuris iuratos et dimissi
fuernunt ab officio eodem Et registratum <fuit> hoc testamentum ultimo die Julij anno domini mccccclxxiij.

In the name of God Amen Wednesday after the Feast of St James the Apostle 1462 I John Pedder of Northampton, weaver, in sound mind make my testament in this wise. First I bequeath my soul to Almighty God, to the Blessed Virgin Mary and all saints, my body to be buried in the church of All Saints in the town of Northampton in front of the image of the Blessed Virgin Mary in the body of the church aforesaid. Item I bequeath for the fabric of the church aforesaid 6s 8d. Item I bequeath to the high altar of the said church 3s 4d. Item I bequeath to the fraternity of St Thomas the Martyr 3s 4d. Item I bequeath to Emma Smyth, my servant, 20s. Item I bequeath to Agnes, my servant, 10s. Item I bequeath to Agnes, my wife, all that tenement of mine with its appurtenances which is situated in Woolmonger Street in the town of Northampton to have and to hold the aforesaid tenement with its appurtenances to the aforesaid Agnes, my wife, for the term of her life of the chief lords of the fee by services therefore due and accustomed. And I wish that after the death of the aforesaid Agnes the aforesaid tenement with its appurtenances remain to John Mede of Northampton, weaver, Robert Bulcle of the same, weaver, and William Stevenes, writer, their heirs and assigns forever of the chief lord by services therefore due and accustomed with the intention that the said John, Robert and William, their heirs and assigns immediately after the death of the aforesaid Agnes, my wife, sell as quickly as they reasonably can, by the supervision and advice of Thomas Merton, the aforesaid tenement with its appurtenances, and the money coming from the same sale to dispose in masses, alms and other acts of charity for the health of my soul and the said Agnes, my wife, and for the health of the souls of our parents, benefactors and all faithful departed as seems best at their discretion to be for the health of our souls. The residue of all my goods not bequeathed above I give and bequeath to the aforesaid Agnes, my wife, and the said John Mede, Robert Bulcle and William Stevenes to then dispose and ordain for the health of my soul and all faithful departed as seems best to them and the same Agnes, John Mede, Robert Bulcle and William Stevenes I ordain, make and constitute my executors and the aforesaid Thomas Merton of this my present testament I ordain, make and constitute as supervisor by these presents. Given the day, place and year abovesaid.

This testament was proved in the church of All Saints, Northampton, the 4th day of September AD 1462 for the aforesaid executors above specified in the said testament in legal form and was handed over by officials of the same and this testament was registered the last day of July AD 1473.

f7v 11 JOAN BALL 7th February 1473 wife of Simon Ball, brasier

In Dei nomine Amen vij die mensis Februarij anno domini mccccIxxiij Ego Johanna Ball uxor Simonis Ball de Northampton brasyer sana memoria condo testamentum meum in hunc modum In primis lego animam meam Deo Omnipotenti Beate Marie eius genitrici ac omnibus sanctis curii celestis corpusque meum sepiliendum in capella Fraternitatis Corporis Christi in ecclesia Omnium Sanctorum Northampton iuxta tumulum Willelmi Wellys mercer nuper mariti mei Item lego Fraternitati dicte capelle vjs.viijd. Item lego summo altari dicte ecclesie iijs.iiijd. Item lego Fraternitati Sancti Georgii in eadem ecclesia xijd. Item lego Fraternitati Sancte Crucis in eadem ecclesia xijd. Item lego Fraternitati Sancti Johannis Baptiste in eadem ecclesia xijd. Item lego fabrice ecclesie Sancti Michaelis ville Northampton iijs. iiijd. Item lego Fraternitati Sancti Thome Martiris de domo elemosinaria iuxta portam australem ville Northampton duodecem ulnas panni linii Item lego cuilibet ordini fratrum mendicancium ville Northampton xxd. Item lego Abbatisse monasterii Beate Marie de Pratis iuxta Northampton xijd. et cuilibet monialium eiusdem domus iiijd.Item lego uno capellano ydoneo ad celebrandum in ecclesia Omnium Sanctorum ville Northampton pro salute anime mee et animarum dictorum Willelmi Wellys et Simonis Ball et Alicie nuper uxoris dicti Simonis viri mei et animarum parentum nostrorum et animarum omnium fidelium defunctorum xxli. bone et legalis monete Anglie Item lego Johanne Filie mee xx marcas bone et legalis monete Anglie Item lego Johanni filio meo decem libras legalis monete Item lego Katerine Monyngham uxori Willelmi Monyngham barbur vjs.viijd. Residuum vero omnium bonorum meorum superius non legatorum do et lego predicto Simoni Ball viro meo et eundem Simonem ordino facio et constituo executorem meum ut ipse disponat pro salute anime mee prout melius videbitur expediri Date die et anno supradictis hiis testibus Johanne Grenburgh capellano Omero Holme scryvener et aliis

Istud testamentum fuit probatum fuit xxiiij die Marcii anno domini mccccIxxiij in ecclesia hospitalis Sancti Johannis Northampton per supranominatum executorem et dismissus fuit xx die Maii anno domini mccccIxxiiij.

In the name of God Amen the 7th day of February 1473 I Joan Ball, wife of Simon Ball of Northampton, brasier, in sound mind and good memory make my testament in this wise. First I bequeath my soul to Almighty God, to the Blessed Mary His mother and all the saints of the court of heaven, my body to be buried in the chapel of the fraternity of Corpus Christi in the church of All Saints, Northampton, next to the grave of William Wellys, mercer, my late husband. Item I bequeath to the fraternity of the said chapel 6s 8d. Item I bequeath to the high altar of the said church 3s 4d. Item I bequeath to the fraternity of St George in the same church 12d. Item I bequeath to the fraternity of the Holy Cross in the same church 12d. Item I bequeath to the fraternity of St John the Baptist in the same church 12d. Item I bequeath to the fabric of the church of St Michael in the town of Northampton 3s 4d. Item I bequeath to the fraternity of St Thomas the Martyr of the almshouse near to the south gate of the town of Northampton twenty ells of linen cloth. Item I bequeath to each order of mendicant brothers in the town of Northampton 20d. Item I bequeath to the Abbess of the monastery of Delapre near Northampton 12d and each nun of the said house 4d. Item I bequeath to one suitable chaplain to celebrate in the church of All Saints in the town of Northampton for the health of my soul and the souls of the said William Wellys and Simon Ball and Alice, former wife of the said Simon, my husband, and the souls of our parents and the souls of all faithful departed £20 of good and legal English money. Item I bequeath to John, my son, 20 marks of good and legal English money. Item I bequeath to Joan, my daughter, ten pounds of legal money. Item I bequeath to Katherine Monyngham, wife of William Monyngham, barber, 6s 8d. The residue of all my goods not bequeathed above I give and bequeath to the aforesaid Simon Ball, my husband, and the same Simon I ordain, make and constitute my executor and he to dispose for the health of my soul as seems best to him. Given the day and year abovesaid. With these witnesses John Grenburgh, chaplain, Omero Holme, writer and others.

This testament was proved 23rd day of March 1473 in the church of the Hospital of St John, Northampton, by the abovenamed executors and was surrendered 20th day of May 1474.

f7v 12 RICARDINA MOSE 12th January 1473 wife of Robert Mose

In Dei nomine Amen xij die mensis Januarii anno domini mccccxxiij Ego Ricardina Mose uxor Roberti Mose de Northampton Lincoln' diocesis viam universe curans ingrediens ultimamque meam voluntatem exprimo in hunc modum In primis lego animam meam Deo Omnipotenti Beate Marie Virgini Matri Christi ac omnibus sanctis supercelestibus corpusque meum sepiliendum in cimiterio ecclesie Omnium Sanctorum Northampton ville Northampton sub capella Sancti Georgii eiusdem ecclesie Item lego summo altari eiusdem

f8r

ecclesie xijd. Item lego fraternitati Sancti Johannis in eadem ecclesia xijd. Item lego fraternitati Sancti Michaelis in ecclesia Sancti Michaelis ville Northampton viijd. Item volo et dono capelle Corporis Christi
in ville de Cranfeld unam acram terre jacentem in campis ville de Wyksyll Lincoln diocesis Item lego
et dono aliam acram terre capelle Sancti Laurencij <de Wroxhyll> jacentem in campis ville de Wroxhyll eiusdem
diocesis Item lego Johanne Dyve filie mee naturali unam togam de cremsyn ingrayne penulatam Item lego eidem Johanne aliam togam blodij coloris penulatam et aliam togam de russet
penulatam cum le blak shankys Item lego eidem Johanne Dyve filie mee unam fedyr
et unam matricem in una parte viridis coloris et alia parte albi coloris et aliud matricem album
Item lego et dono dicte Johanne Dyve filie mee duo cooperteria unam album et aliud veridem
et duo paria lodicum et quatuor paria linthiamentum unam bolster et quatuor pylowys
unam magnam arcam unam cistam et unum nigrum Focer. Item lego eidem unum par precum
de jete et pater nostor de argento et deaurato Item lego eidem Johanne Dyve unam magnam
ollam eneam et unam magnam paternam eneam cum ferro ligatam Residuum vero bonorum meorum
non legatorum sive dispositorum volo quod Robertus Moose maritus meus habeat et disponat
pro salute anime et animabus omnium fidelium defunctorum prout ei melius videbitur expediri

In the name of God Amen the 12th day of January 1473 I Ricardina Mose, wife of Robert Mose of Northampton, Lincoln diocese, about to die express my last will in this form. First I bequeath my soul to Almighty God, to the Blessed Virgin Mary Mother of Christ and all the saints in heaven above, my body to be buried in the cemetery of the church of All Saints in the town of Northampton below the chapel of St George in the same church. Item I bequeath to the high altar of the said church 12d. Item I bequeath to the fraternity of St John in the same church 12d. Item I bequeath to the fraternity of St Michael in the church of St Michael in the town of Northampton 8d. Item I will and give to the chapel of Corpus Christi in the town of Cranfield one acre of land next to the fields of Wyksyll in Lincoln diocese. Item I bequeath and give another acre of land to the chapel of St Lawrence of Wroxhill adjacent in the fields of the town of Wroxhill in the said diocese. Item I bequeath to Joan Dyve, my natural daughter, one gown of crimson dye furred. Item I bequeath to the same Joan another gown of blue colour furred and another gown of russet furred with 'le blak shankys'. Item I bequeath to the same Joan Dyve, my daughter, one feather(bed) and one mattress in one part green coloured and another part white coloured and another white mattress. Item I give and bequeath to the said Joan Dyve, my daughter, two covers, one white and the other green and two pairs of blankets and four pairs of sheets, one bolster and four pillows, one large money box, one chest and one black [ ]. Item I bequeath to the same one rosary of jet and a pater noster of silver and gilt. Item I bequeath to the same Joan Dyve one large brass pot and one large brass dish bound with iron. The residue of all my goods not bequeathed nor disposed I will that Robert Mose, my husband, have and dispose for the health of my soul and the souls of all faithful departed as seems best to him.

f8v 15 THOMAS STEPHEN 26th April 1474 mercer

In Dei nomine Amen anno domini mcccclxxiiij xxvj die Aprilis Ego Thomas Stephen de Northampton mercer compos mentis et sane memorie condo testamentum meum in hunc modum In primis lego animam meam Deo Omnipotenti Beate Marie et omnibus sanctis curie celestis corpusque meum sepiliendum in cimiterio ecclesie Omnium Sanctorum ville predicte Item lego summo altari pro decimis oblitis ijs. Item lego fraternitibus sanctorum Georgij Erasmi Crucis Johanis Baptiste et Sancte Katerine et cuilibet earum xvjd. Item lego Fabrice ecclesie predicte ijs. Item lego domui elemosinarie Sancti Thome Martiris ijs. Item lego Willelmo filio meo Elizabeth et Agneti filiabus meis cuilibet eorum x marcas Et si contingat aliquem eorum obire ante diem nupcialem tunc volo quod legate eiusdem distribuatur inter personas predictas supscriptas Item volo quod omnia tenementa mea post decessum Johanne uxoris mee remaneant predicto Willelmo filio meo Et si contingat illum decedere sine heredibus quod tunc dividere dictas sorores eiusdem Willelmi Et si contingat omnes predictos sine heredibus obire tunc volo ut vendantur et distribuantur pro salute anime mee Johanne uxoris mee Johannis of [Owr] et Johanne uxoris sue Item lego matri mee xls. Item lego honesto sacerdoti C solidos Residuum vero bonorum meorum superius non legatorum do et lego Johanne uxori mee et ipsam
facio et constituo executricem meam ut ipsa ordinet et disponat pro salute anime mee prout ei melius videbitur expediri supervisores ac huius testamentum facio et constituo Willelmum Austyn generosum et Johannem Grenburgh capellanum

In the name of God Amen the 26th day of April 1474 I Thomas Stephen of Northampton, mercer, in sound mind and good memory make my testament in this wise. First I bequeath my soul to Almighty God, to the Blessed Mary and all the saints of the court of heaven, my body to be buried in the cemetery of the church of All Saints in the town aforesaid. Item I bequeath to the high altar for tithes forgotten 2s. Item I bequeath to the fraternity of Saints George, Giles, Holy Cross, John the Baptist and St Katherine and to each of them 16d. Item I bequeath to the fabric of the church aforesaid 2s. Item I bequeath to the almshouse of St Thomas the Martyr 2s. Item I bequeath to William, my son, Elizabeth and Agnes, my daughters, to each of them 10 marks. And if it should happen anyone of them should die before their wedding day then I will that the legacy of the same be distributed between the persons aforesaid above written. Item I wish that all my tenements after the decease of Joan, my wife, remain to the aforesaid William, my son. And if it should happen that he dies without heirs that then be divided between the aforesaid sisters of the same William. And if it should happen that all the aforesaid die without heirs then I wish they are sold and (the money) distributed for the health of my soul, Joan, my wife, John of Owr? and Joan his wife. Item I bequeath to my mother 40s. Item I bequeath for an honest priest 100s.

The residue of all my goods not bequeathed above I give and bequeath to Joan, my wife, and she I make and constitute my executrix she to ordain and dispose for the health of my soul as seems best to her. As supervisors of this testament I make and constitute William Austyn, gentleman, and John Grenburgh, chaplain.

f11r 17b [RICHARD DAFFRON] 1473/4?

NOTE This will begins abruptly in the middle of a sentence.

faciant aut eorum aliquis solverit seu solvi fecerit ad huiusmodi tempus in quo seisina
et possessio de et in predictis terris tenementis domibus edificiis gardenis et suis pertinenciis supradictis
eis vel eorum alicui diliberatur fuerint Ricardo Daffron supranominato heredibus executoribus aut assignatis
suis x marcas bone monete secundum istam intencionem et formam quod dictus Ricardus heredes
executores seu assignati sui solverint et liberaverint aut eorum aliquis solverit et liberari fecerit de
predictis x marcis Alicie filie mee si se bene gubernet et honeste et laudabiliter vivat v marcas
bone monete et ecciam solvent et dabunt aut eorum aliquis solvet et dabit modo simile
alias quinque marcas postimo meo si[ ] predicta Alicia uxor mea de corpore meo impregnata
existat gracia favente divina de ipsa inposterum nascendo et si dicta Alicia uxor
mea non sit per me ut prefertur impregnata volo tunc quod predictem x marcas si prefate Alicie
filie mee si disponatur ut supradictum est solvantur et liberentur ad usum et opus eius imperpetuum
et si predicta filia mea antiquam solutio dictarum quinque marcarum et liberatio iuxta formam predictam
habeantur obierit et decesserit vivente dicto postimo meo volo quod ipse postimus percipiet
et habeat dictas x marcas ad usum et <pro> ficium suum prout dicta Alicia filia mea habuisset
si diutius ipse vivere potuisset Et si contingat dictam Aliciam filiam meam obire et nullum
postimum de uxore mea predicte sub forma antedicta nasci volo tunc quod dicte x marce
si nullo modo predicto solvantur et liberantur solvantur cuidam capellano ydoneo ad celebrandum et
orandum pro salute anime mee et anime uxoris mee predicte necnon animarum parentum amicorum
meorum et omnium fidelium defunctorum et in super volo quod post decessum dicte Alicie uxoris
mee Ricardus Daffron heredes et executores seu assignati sui gardinum meum situatum
in predicto vico vocato Flesshmonger Strete exparte australi eiusdem vici vendant et
pecunias inde receptas sub forma predictarum decem marcarum si Alicia filia mea et postimus
antidictus vivant et si econtra volo tunc quod dicte pecunie in missis elemosinis et
aliis donis caritatis disponantur pro salute anime et animarum supra specificatarum necnon volo post
decessum uxoris mee quod tenementum meum cum gardino adiacente nuper in tenura Thome
Swayayn situatum vocato Berker Strete infra parochiam Sancti Gregorii ville Northampton
Johanne filie mee intigre remaneat habendum et tenendum predictum tenementum cum gardino
adiacente et suis pertinenciis prefate Johanne heredibus et assignatis suis imperpetuum si se in gest[ ]
bono et gubernacione honeste trahat et sic continuet de capitalibus dominis feodi illorum

... pay or make payment at this time in that seisin and possession of and in the aforesaid tenement, house, buildings, gardens and their appurtenances aforesaid ....

Richard Daffron above named, his heirs, executors and assigns 10 marks of good money according to this intention and form that the said Richard, his heirs, executors, his assigns, pay and hand over, or any one of them pay and hand over from the said 10 marks to Alice, my daughter, if she governs herself well and honestly and lives a praiseworthy life, 5 marks of good money, and furthermore pays and owes in a similar way the other five marks to my posthumous child if the aforesaid Alice, my wife, is already pregnant by me by divine grace and favour and she herself afterwards gives birth, and if the said Alice, my wife, is not pregnant by me I wish then that the aforesaid 10 marks to the aforesaid Alice, my daughter be disposed as abovesaid and paid and handed over for her use and behoof forever. And if my aforesaid daughter should die and depart this life before the payment and delivery of the said 5 marks is made according to the form aforesaid with my posthumous child being alive, I will then that the same posthumous child himself receives and has the said ten marks for his use and profit just as the said Alice, my daughter, would have had if she herself had lived the longer. And if it happens that the said Alice, my daughter, dies and no child is born of my wife, I will then that the said 10 marks if in no way aforesaid paid and delivered should be paid and handed over to a certain suitable chaplain to celebrate and pray for the health of my soul and the soul of my aforesaid and also the souls of my parents, my friends souls and all faithful departed and furthermore I wish that after the death of the said Alice my wife, Richard Daffron his heirs and executors or assigns should sell my garden situated in the aforesaid street called Fleshmonger Street on the south side of the street and with the money received dispose of under the same form the aforesaid ten marks if Alice, my daughter, and posthumous child aforesaid are alive, and if otherwise then I wish that the said money be disposed in masses, alms and other charitable gifts for the health of my soul and the souls above specified and also I will after the death of my wife that my tenement with garden adjacent, lately in the tenure of Thomas Swayayn, situated in Berker Street in the parish of St Gregory in the town of Northampton, wholly remain to Joan, my daughter, to have and to hold the aforesaid tenement with garden adjacent and their appurtenances to the aforesaid Joan, her heirs and assigns forever of the chief lord of the fee if she behaves herself well and takes honest governance and continues so.

f11v 18a JOHN HYGHAM 31st May 1473 baker

In Dei nomine Amen [Ego Johannes] ultimo die mensis Maij anno domini mcccclxxiij Ego Johannes Hygham de Northampton bakar sane memoria condo testamentum

meum in hunc modum In primis lego animam meam Deo Omnipotenti Beate Marie eius genitrici et omnibus sanctis curie celestis corpusque meum sepiliendum in capella Beate Marie in ecclesia Sancti Sepulcri ville Northampton Item lego summo altari dicte ecclesie pro decimis meis oblitis vjs.viijd. Item lego fabrice dicte ecclesie vjs.viijd. Item lego ad invencionem unius novi vestmenti ad laudem Dei in dicta ecclesia servandum xxs. Item lego ordini hermitarum Sancti Augustinii ville Northampton iijs.iiijd. Item lego cuilibet ordini aliorum fratrum eiusdem ville xxd. Item lego Elizabet filie mee decem marcas in pecuniis muneratis cum apparatis camere sue convenientis Item lego Margeri filie mee decem marcas in pecuniis muneratis cum apparatis camere sue convenientis Et volo quod si altera filiarum mearum predictarum obierit infra legitimam etatem quod tunc pars superstes gaudeat et habeat partem illius discedentis Item lego Katerine Clerke unum coopertorium lecti unum lodicem unum linthiamen Item lego Thome <Cowper> de Hygham Feres togam meam rosetam Item lego Agneti sorori mee uxori eiusdem Thome unam togam viridis coloris Et volo quod executores mei conducant unum capellanum ydoneum ad [...] celebrandum pro salute anime mee per unum annum intigrum et volo quod habeat pro salario quinque libras bone monete Anglie Item do et lego Alicie uxori mee omnia et singula terras <et> tenementa mea cum omnibus eorum pertinenciis que habeo in villa et in campis Northampton Necnon do et lego prefate Alicie uxori mee omnes et omnimodas status possessiones et terminos quos habeo de et in omnibus et singulis terris et tenementis cum eorum pertinenciis in villa predicta prout in evidenciis inde confectis plenius apparet habendum et tenendum omnia predicta terras et tenementa status possessiones et terminos cum omnibus et singulis eorum
pertinenciis ut predictum est prefate Alicie uxori mee ad terminum vite ipsius Alicie de capitalibus
dominis ffeodi illius per servicia inde debita et de iure consueta Item volo quod Thomas filius meus inmediate post decessum predicte Alicie uxoris mee totum predictum tenementum meum in quo maneo cum pertinenciis suis habeat et gaudeat sibi heredibus et assignatis
suis imperpetuum de capitalibus dominis feodi illius per servicia inde debita et de iure consueta Item volo quod predictus Thoma habeat et teneat post decessum dicte Alicie totum statum et terminum quos habeo de et in tribus cotagiis situatis iuxta tenementum meum predictum tenendum de capitalibus dominis feodi illius per servicia inde debita et de iure consueta Item volo quod inmediate post decessum dicte Alicie Johannes filius meus habeat et teneat totum tenementum meum cum pertinenciis suis iuxta portam borialem ville predicte ex opposite fonti ibidem necnon
cum toto termino et statu <de> et in uno tenemento <modo> in tenure clerici maioris ville Northampton

f12r

simul cum statu et termino in aliis duobus cotagiis ibidem habendum et tenendum predictum tenementum cum suis pertinenciis simul cum predictis statu et termino prefato Johanni filio meo ac heredibus et assignatis suis imperpetuum de capitalibus dominis feodi illius per servicia inde debita
et de iure consueta Item volo quod Ricardus filius meus inmediate post decessum dicte Alicie matris sue habeat et teneat totum predictum tenementum cum pertinenciis suis situatum in
le Berward Strete ville predicte necnon totum gardinum cum tentura in eodum jacens in venilla Sancti Johannis ville predicte ac eciam illam parcellam qwarr' vocatam Le Delves in Kyngesthorp field habendum et tenendum predictum tenementum gardinum cum tentura
in eodem et predictam parcellam terre cum eorum pertinenciis ut predictum est prefato Ricardo heredibus et assignatis
suis imperpetuum tenendum de capitalibus dominis feodi illius per servicia inde debita et de iure consueta

Residuum vero omnium bonorum meorum superius non legatorum do et lego prefate Alicie uxori
mee et eandem Aliciam ac Thomam filium meum ordino <facio> et constituo executores meos ut ipse disponant pro salute anime mee prout eis melius videbitur expediri et
istius testamenti mei ordino facio et constituo magistrum Johannem Ilam ad supervidendum omnia premissa fideliter exequendum per presentes Date die et anno domini supradictis hiis testibus predicte Johannes Ilam Johannes Robyns Willelmo Philypp botcher et aliis

In the name of God Amen the 31st day of May 1473 I John Hygham of Northampton, baker, in good memory make my testament in this wise. First I bequeath my soul to Almighty God, to the Blessed Mary His mother and to all the saints of the court of heaven, my body to be buried in the chapel of the Blessed Mary in the church of Holy Sepulchre in the town of Northampton. Item I bequeath to the high altar of the said church for my tithes forgotten 6s 8d. Item I bequeath to the fabric of the said church 6s 8d. Item I bequeath to the provision of one new vestment to serve in the said church for the praise of God 20s. Item I bequeath to the order of Austin friars in the town of Northampton 3s 4d. Item I bequeath to each of the other orders of friars in that same town 20d. Item I bequeath to Elizabeth, my daughter, ten marks in good money with the suitable furnishings for her bedroom. Item I bequeath to Margery, my daughter, 10 marks in good money with the suitable furnishings for her bedroom. And I will that if either of my aforementioned daughters should die before she comes of age then the surviving daughter should have the benefit of the share belonging to the deceased. Item I bequeath to Katherine Clarke one bedspread, one blanket and one sheet. Item I bequeath to Thomas <Cowper> of Higham Ferrers, my rose gown. Item I bequeath to Agnes, my sister, wife of that same Thomas, one gown of green colour. And I will that my executors should instruct a suitable priest to celebrate [ ] for the health of my soul for one whole year and I will that he should have for his payment five pounds in good English money. Item I give and bequeath to Alice, my wife, each and every one of my lands and tenements with all their appurtenances, which I have in the town and fields of Northampton. And I also give and bequeath to the said Alice, my wife, all and every estate, possession and terms which I have coming from and in any of the lands and tenements with their appurtenances in the aforementioned town, as evidences thereof make more fully clear, to have and to hold all the said lands and tenements, incomes, possessions and settlements as is stated to Alice, my wife, to the end of her life of the chief lords of the fee by services therefore due and by right accustomed. Item I will that Thomas, my son, immediately after the death of the said Alice, my wife, should have and possess the whole of my aforesaid property, remaining with its appurtenances for himself, his heirs and assigns forever of the chief lords of the fee by services therefore due and by right accustomed. Item I will that the said Thomas should have and hold after the death of the said Alice, the whole estate and settlement which I have *coming from and within the three cottages situated next to my aforesaid property, holding from the chief lords of the fee for services therefore due and by right accustomed. Item I will that immediately after the death of the said Alice, my son John should have and hold the whole of my property with its appurtenances next to the north gate of the said town from the well opposite there, also with all the settlement and estate coming of and in the tenement lately in the tenure of the mayor's clerk of the town of Northampton, similarly with the estate and settlement in the other two cottages there, the said tenement with its appurtenances, and also with the aforementioned estate and settlement should be held and possessed by John, my son, and his heirs and assigns forever of the chief lords of the fee by services therefore due and by right accustomed. Item I will that Richard, my son, immediately after the death of the said Alice, his mother, should have and hold all the said tenement with its appurtenances situated in Berward Street in the said town, also all the garden with a tenter yard therein lying in St John's Lane in the said town and also that part of a quarry called Le Delves in Kingsthorpe field, having and holding the said tenement, garden with a tenter yard in it and the said plot of land with their appurtenances as previously stated to the said Richard, his heirs and his assigns forever of the chief lord of the fee by services therefore due and by right accustomed. The residue of all my goods not bequeathed above I give and bequeath to the said Alice, my wife, and I ordain, make and constitute the same Alice and Thomas, my son, my executors that they dispose for the health of my soul as seems best to them and I ordain, make and constitute Master John Ilam as supervisor of this my will, executing all promises faithfully by these presents. Given the day and year abovesaid.With these witnesses the aforesaid John Ilam, John Robyns, William Philypp, butcher, and others.*

f12v 20 THOMAS CARTER 16th May 1474 (baker)

In Dei nomine Amen sextodecimo die mensis Maij anno domini millesimo cccc septuagesimo quarto
Ego Thomas Carter sana memoria condo testamentum meum in hunc modum In primis lego animam meam Deo Omnipotenti Beate Marie eius genitrici et omnibus sanctis curie celestis corpusque
meum ad sepiliendum in cimiterio ecclesie Omnium Sanctorum ville Northampton Item lego summo altari
ibidem pro decimis meis oblitis duodecim denarios Item lego fraternitati Sancti Georgii Martiris in
eadem ecclesia xijd. Item lego fraternitati Sancte Crucis in eadem ecclesia xijd. Item lego fraternitati in
nova ecclesia existente in parochia Omnium Sanctorum xijd. denarios Item lego fraternitati Sancti Thome Martiris
de domo elemosinarum existenti parte australe eiusdem ville viijd. Item lego fraternitati Sancti **13r**
Clementis Martiris in ecclesia Sancti Egidii eiusdem ville viijd. Item lego fraternitati Sancte Crucis in Muro xijd.

Item lego fraternitati Sancti Johannis Baptiste in ecclesia Omnium Sanctorum ville predicte viijd. Item lego fraternitati Sancti
Sepulcri eiusdem ville viijd. Item lego cuilibet ordini fratrum mendicancium eiusdem ville xijd. Residuum vero omnium bonorum meorum superius non legatorum do et lego Margerie uxori mei
et eandem Margeriam ordino facio et constituo executricem meam ut ipsa disponat pro salute anime mee prout ei melius videbitur expediri et presentis testamenti ordino facio
et constituo Johannem Harrys corvisor supervisorem et volo quod habeat pro labore suo tres solidos sterlingorum per presentes date die et anno supradictis

In the name of God Amen the 16th day of May 1474 I Thomas Carter of good memory make my testament in this wise. First I bequeath my soul to Almighty God, to the Blessed Mary His mother and all the saints of the court of heaven, my body to be buried in the cemetery of the church of All Saints in the town of Northampton. Item I bequeath to the high altar there for tithes forgotten 12 pence. Item I bequeath to the fraternity of St George the Martyr in the same church 12d. Item I bequeath to the fraternity of the Holy Cross in the same church 12d. Item I bequeath to the fraternity in the new church existing in the parish of All Saints 12d. Item I bequeath to the fraternity of St Thomas the Martyr in the alms house existing in the southern part of the same town 8d. Item I bequeath to the fraternity of St Clement the Martyr in the church of St Giles in the same town 8d. Item I bequeath to the fraternity of the Holy Cross in the Wall 12d. Item I bequeath to the fraternity of St John the Baptist in the church of All Saints in the aforesaid town 8d. Item I bequeath to the fraternity of Holy Sepulchre in the same town 8d. Item I bequeath to each order of mendicant brothers in the said town 12d. The residue of all my goods not bequeathed above I give and bequeath to Margaret, my wife, and that same Margaret I ordain, make and constitute my executrix and she to dispose for the health of my soul as seems best to her and I ordain, make and constitute John Harrys, corvisor, supervisor of this present testament and I will that he should have for his labour three shillings in sterling by these presents. Given the day and year abovesaid.

f13r 21 JOHN BUCHER 16th December 1474 wiredrawer

In Dei nomine Amen anno domini mcccclxxiiij xvj die mensis Decembris Ego Johannes Bucher de Northampton wyredrawer compos mentis et sane memorie condo testamentum meum in hunc modum In primis lego animam meam Deo Omnipotente Beate Marie Sancto Egidio et omnibus celi sancti ac corpus meum sepiliendum in cimiterio ecclesie Sancti Egidii ville Northampton predicte Item lego summo altari ecclesie predicte pro decimis oblitis vjs. viijd. Item lego fabrice ecclesie prefate vjs.viijd. Item lego fraternitati
Sancti Clementis in eadem ecclesia unum torchium et xxd. Item lego lumini Sancti Sepulcri in eadem ecclesia xxd. Item lego Isabelle filie mee xls. Item
lego Agneti filie mee xls. Item lego Thome filio meo xls. Item lego
Johanni filio meo xls. Et si aliquis vel aliqui puerorum predictorum infra annos nubiles decesserit tunc volo quod pars ipsius decedentis dividatur inter alios superstites vel uni si plures non fuerint superstites si omnes decesserint tunc

volo quod Johanna uxor mea habeat predicta legata Item lego Thome Bucher fratri meo meam togam blodiam Item lego Ricardo Bucher cognato meo togam meam nigram Item lego Matildi Goldby de Castelasshby iijs.iiijd. Item lego Agneti Wodeouse servienti mee unum fultrum unum par lodicum unum par linthiamentium et unum coopertorium albi et <viridis> coloris et xs. argenti Item lego Johanni Gardiner servienti meo unum par linthiamentium novorum Residuum vero bonorum meorum in hoc testamento non legatorum do et lego Johanne uxori mee et ipsam constituo executricem meam ut ordinat et disponat pro salute anime cum assistencia supervisione et avisamento Johannis Clerke baker quem constituo huius testamenti supervisorem et eidem Johanni Clerke
lego pro labore suo xxs. Item lego cuilibet pueri spirituali xijd.

In the name of God Amen the 16th day of December 1474 I John Bucher of Northampton, wiredrawer, in sound mind and good memory, make my testament in this wise. First I bequeath my soul to Almighty God, to the Blessed Mary, to St Giles and to all the saints in heaven, my body to be buried in the cemetery of the church of St Giles in the town of Northampton aforesaid. Item I bequeath to the high altar of the said church for tithes forgotten 6s 8d. Item I bequeath to the fabric of the said church 6s 8d. Item I bequeath to the fraternity of St Clements in the same church one torch and 20d. Item I bequeath to the light of Holy Sepulchre in the same church 20d. Item I bequeath to Isabella, my daughter, 11s. Item I bequeath to Agnes, my daughter, 11s. Item I bequeath to Thomas, my son, 11s. Item I bequeath to John, my son, 11s. And if some or any of my said children should die whilst under age I will that the share of the deceased should be divided amongst the survivors or to the one if several should not survive. If all should die then I will that Joan, my wife, should have the said legacy. Item I bequeath to Thomas Bucher, my brother, my blue gown. Item I bequeath to Richard Bucher, my cousin, my black gown. Item I bequeath to Matilda Goldby of Castle Ashby 3s 4d. Item I bequeath to Agnes Woodhouse, my servant, one bed frame (or felt cover), one pair of blankets, one pair of sheets and one white and green coloured cover and 10s in silver. Item I bequeath to John Gardiner, my servant, one pair of new sheets. The residue of all my goods not bequeathed in this testament I give and bequeath to Joan, my wife, and I constitute her my executrice to ordain and dispose for the health of my soul with the assistance, supervision and advice of John Clerke, baker, whom I constitute supervisor of this testament and to the same John Clerke I bequeath for his labour 20s. Item I bequeath to each of my godchildren 12d.

f13v 22 MARGERY CARTER 16th March 1474 lately wife of Thomas Carter

In Dei nomine Amen sextodecimo die mensis Marcii anno domini millesimo cccclxxiiij Ego Margeria Carter nuper uxor Thome Carter de Northampton baker

sana memoria condo testamentum meum in hunc modum In primis lego animam meam
Deo Omnipotenti Beate Marie eius genitrici et omnibus sanctis curie celestis corpus-
que meum ad sepiliendum in cimiterio ecclesie Omnium Sanctorum ville Northampton iuxta tumulum
predicti Thome viri mei Item lego summo altari ibidem unum borcloth de
diapir wark et serecem Item lego reparacioni dicte ecclesie xijd. Item lego summo
altari de Richresthrop unum towell Item lego altari existenti in nova
capella Beate Katerine Virginis infra parochiam Omnium Sanctorum ville Northampton unum linthiamentum
Item lego ordini fratrum minorum Northampton xxd. Item lego cuilibet ordini alium trium
ordinum fratrum mendicancium eiusdem ville xijd. Item volo quod die sepulture mee
executores mei distribuant xl dosen de albo pane inter pauperes pro salute anime mee
et omnium fidelium defunctorum Residuum vero omnium bonorum meorum superius non legatorum
do et lego Johanni Essex seniori de Northampton fysshmongger et Johanni Harrys de
eadem corvisor et eosdem Johannem Essex et Johannem Harrys ordino facio et constituo
executores meos ut ipsi disponant pro salute anime mee prout eis melius videbitur
expediri et Johannem Grenburgh capellanum presentis testamenti ordino facio
et constituo esse supervisorem Et volo quod quilibet executorum meorum et supervisorum habeat
pro labore suo sex solidos et octo denarios bone et legalis monete Anglie adpremyssis
fideliter complendum per presentes Date die et anno supradictis

In the name of God Amen the sixteenth day of March 1474 I Margery Carter, lately wife of Thomas Carter of Northampton, baker, in good memory make my testament in this wise. First I bequeath my soul to Almighty God, to the Blessed Mary His mother and all the saints of the court of heaven, my body to be buried in the churchyard of All Saints in Northampton next to the grave of the aforesaid Thomas, my husband. Item I bequeath to the high altar there one boardcloth of diaper work and silk. Item I bequeath to the repair of the said church 12d. Item I bequeath to the high altar of Rothersthorpe one towel. Item I bequeath to the altar in the new chapel of Blessed Katherine the Virgin within the parish of All Saints in the town of Northampton one sheet. Item I bequeath to the order of Friars Minor in Northampton 20d. Item I bequeath to each of the other three orders of mendicant brothers in the same town 12d. Item I wish that on the day of my burying my executors will distribute 40 dozen of white bread amongst the poor for the health of my soul and all faithful departed. The residue of all my goods not bequeathed above I give and bequeath to John Essex, senior, of Northampton, fishmonger, and John Harrys of Northampton, corvisor, and the same John Essex and John Harrys I ordain, make and constitute my executors to then dispose for the health of my soul as seems best to them and I ordain, make and constitute John Grenburgh, chaplain, supervisor of this present testament. And I wish that each of my executors and supervisor have for his labour six shillings and eight pence of good and legal English money for faithfully completing these premises by these presents. Given the day and year abovesaid.

f13v 23 RICHARD WARDE 9th August 1474 chaplain

In Dei nomine Amen ix die mensis Augusti anno domini mcccclxxv Ego Ricardus Warde capellanus condo testamentum meum in hunc modum In primis lego animam meam Deo Omnipotenti Beate Marie Virgini ac omnibus sanctis curie celestis corpusque meum sepiliendum in capella Beate Marie Virginis in ecclesia Omnium Sanctorum ville Northampton Item lego ad sustentacionem et reparacionem dicte capelle xxs. Item lego ad reparacionem et novam picturacionem unius par panni linii existentis coram summo altari dicte ecclesie xiijs.iiijd. Item lego reparacione eiusdem capelle existentis in parte australi ecclesie parochiale de Banbery iijs.iiijd. Item lego ecclesie de Daventry iijs.iiijd. Item lego Fabrice ecclesie de Welton vjs. viijd. Item lego Fabrice ecclesie de Colde Asshby vjs.viijd. Item lego ecclesie de Hasylbyche iijs.iiijd. Item lego cuilibet fraternitati in ecclesia Omnium Sanctorum predicta xijd. Item lego magistro doctori vicario eiusdem ecclesie Omnium Sanctorum xxd. Item lego Ricardo Chandeler capellano xld. Item lego cuilibet presbytro celebranti in dicta ecclesia Omnium Sanctorum et pertinenti collegio ecclesie predicte xijd. Item lego Ricardo Warde cognato meo meam <longam> togam blodei coloris lynytt Item Katerine uxori eius xld. Item lego

f14r

Radulpho Warde de Dodford meam russetam togam longam et volo quod dictus Radolphus solvet ecclesie de Dodford predicte xijd. Item lego Edwardo Warde unum coopertorium lecti duas lodices unum par linthiamentium Item lego Thome Warde iijs.iiijd. Item lego Elizabeth filie sue xld. Item lego Roberto Conqwer' vjs.viijd. Item lego Katerine Roger iiijs. Item lego Willelmo Cooke iiijs. Item lego Matilde Pagett xxd. Item lego Henrico Warde meam longam veridem togam ij coopertoria et unum par linthiamentium Residuum vero omnium bonorum meorum superius [non] legatorum do et lego Willelmo Wymond capellano et Johanni Long taylor ad inde disponent pro salute anime mee et animarum omnium fidelium defunctorum prout ei melius videbitur expediri et ad istud testamentum meum bene et fideliter exequendum prefatum Willelmum Wymond et Johannem Long ordino facio et constituo executores meos ac Willelmum Austyn gentilman huius testamenti mei ordino esse supervisorem et volo quolibet predictorum Willelmo Austyn Willelmo Wymond et Johannis Long habeat pro labore sue ad premissa fideliter exequendum per presentes vjs.viijd.

In the name of God Amen the 9th day of August 1474 I Richard Warde, chaplain, make my testament in this wise. First I bequeath my soul to Almighty God, to the Blessed Virgin Mary and all the saints of the court of heaven, my body to be buried in the chapel of the Blessed Virgin Mary in the church of All Saints in the town of Northampton. Item I bequeath to the maintenance and repair of the said chapel 20s. Item I bequeath to the repair and new painting of one pair of linen cloths being before the high altar in the said church 13s 4d. Item I bequeath for the repair of the same chapel being on the south side of the parish church of Banbury 3s 4d. Item I bequeath to the church of Daventry 3s 4d. Item I bequeath to the fabric of the church of Welton 6s 8d. Item I bequeath to the fabric of the church of Cold Ashby 6s 8d. Item I bequeath to the church of

Hasilbech 3s 4d. Item I bequeath to each fraternity in the church of All Saints 20d. Item I bequeath to Richard Chandeler, chaplain, 40d. Item I bequeath to each priest celebrating in the said church of All Saints and belonging to the college of the church aforesaid 12d. Item I bequeath to Richard Ward, my kinsman, my long lined gown of blue colour. Item to Katherine, his wife, 40d. Item I bequeath to Ralph Ward of Dodford my long russet gown and I wish that the said Richard pay the church of Dodford aforesaid 12d. Item I bequeath to Edward Ward one bed cover, two blankets, one pair of sheets. Item I bequeath to Thomas Warde 3s 4d. Item I bequeath to Elizabeth, his daughter, 40d. Item I bequeath to Robert Conqwer' 6s 8d. Item I bequeath to Katherine Roger 4s. Item I bequeath to William Cooke 4s. Item I bequeath to Matilda Pagett 20d. Item I bequeath to Henry Warde my long green gown, 2 coverlets and one pair of sheets. The residue of all my goods not bequeathed above I give and bequeath to William Wymond, chaplain, and John Long, tailor, to then dispose for the health of my soul and the souls of all faithful departed as seems best to them and that this my testament be well and faithfully executed I ordain, make and constitute the aforesaid William Wymond and John Long my executors and William Austyn, gentleman, I ordain supervisor of this my testament and I will that the aforesaid William Austyn, William Wymond and John Long have for their labour in carrying out well these things mentioned before by these presents 6s 8d.

f15r 26 WILLIAM HARYSSON 8th December 1475 fuller

In Dei nomine Amen octavo die mensis Decembris anno domini millesimo ccccmo septuagesimo quinto Ego Willelmus Harysson de Northampton fuller sana memoria condo testamentum meum in hunc modum In primis lego animam meam Deo Omnipotenti Beate Marie
Virgini eius genitrici et omnibus sanctis curie celestis corpusque meum ad sepiliendum in cimiterio ecclesie Sancti Gregorii Pape ville Northampton Item lego Fabrice eiusdem ecclesie xxd. Item lego summo altari ibidem xxd. Item Agneti matri mee unum coopertorium duo paria linthiaminum unum par precum cum le pater nostris sive le gaudis de argento meam secundam
ollam eneam meam secundam pelvem cum lavacro de stagno j ollam de pewtyr continentem j quart j parapsidem et duos discos de pewter ij candelebra de laten iij cocliarios de argento quinque virgate panni lanei et <unam> ollam eneam continentem lagenam et j skelet cum manubrio
et j matras vocatas le cocher factam cum le draught flokkys j par blanketts duas pluminas vocatas le pelowes et unam parvam cofer Item lego Thome Harysson cognato meo iij cooperterios ij para linthiaminum j cocher factam de flokkys et bolster eiusdem cum tribus pe-
lowes meam optimam ollam eneam et meam optimam cawdron eneam ac aliam ollam eneam et unam patellam eneam continentem iiij lagenas j patell continentem j potell j chaffer

f15v

with ij eres ij iryn spyttes j par gobberdes ij ele spyttes de ferro
j skemur j fflesshhok j chargor de pewter iiij parapsides iiij discos

viij saucers de pewter j salt seler j chaffyng dysh de laton vij
candelabra de laton j ollam de pewter continentem j potell aliam ollam de
pewter continentem j mesurem servicia de obul ac aliam ollam de pewter continentem le
pynt pro vino et ij pelves cum duobus lavacris j grett coffer et j sprusse coffer
et quatuor cocliaria argenti Item lego Waltero Mayndow servienti meo ad opus
maritagii sui cum Elena Lodelay servienti Thome Norys togam meam de
violet j coopertorium j ollam eneam continentem j lagenem j par linthiaminum j
salsarium de pewter cum coopertorio et duas sausers de pewter et unum
candelabrum de laton Item lego Willelmo Benet servienti meo j
coopertorium j ollam eneam continentem j lagenam j candelabrum de laton j disch
de pewter et ij saucers de pewter Item lego Katerine cognate mee j
pelvem de laton ij candelabra de laton j saltserium de pewter cum
coopertorio ij ollas de pewter j veru de ferro ij gobbards et j ele spytt
de ferro Item lego Johanne Batman j coopertorium j patellam eneam continentem
j potell Item lego Johanni Bukby <seniori> iiij cocliarios de argento Item lego
Elene Welles nuper servienti mei iijs. argenti Item do et lego predicti Thome
Harysson cognato meo totum statum meum et terminum quos habeo de et in illo tenemento cum
pertinenciis suis in quo modo maneo necnon do et lego prefate Thome totum
gardinum meum cum clausuris suis iacens in quadam venilla vocata le Rye
in parochia Sancti Gregorii predicti quod quidam gardinum nuper habui cum pertinenciis
suis ex
dono et feoffomento Johannis Bussard de Northampton barbour per cartam suam simple
et feodi inde michi confectam plenius apparet habendum et tenendum predictum statum
meum et terminum meum predictum durante toto termino meo reddendo solvendo et
surportando prout inscriptis inde michi confectis plenius liquet nec non habendum
et tenendum predictum gardinum cum clausuris et pertinenciis suis in mediate post decessum
meum prefati Thome Harysson et assignatis suis durante tota vita ipsius Thome
de capitalibus dominis feodi illius per servicia inde debita et de iure consueta et sub hac
forma et condicione quod idem Thomas Harysson annuatim durante vita sua
teneat sive teneri facit diem anniversarii mei in ecclesia Sancti Gregorii predicti et
Roberti Harysson et Agnetis parentum meorum indicendis placebo et dirige et

f16r

in crastino celebrandum missam de requiem specialiter ad orandum pro salute anime mee
et animarum parentum meorum et omnium fidelium defunctorum Item volo quod immediate
post decessum predicte Thome Harysson predictum gardinum cum pertinenciis suis
descendum et integre vertatur confratribus et consororibus fraternitatis Sancte Crucis
in Muro existente in ecclesia Sancti Gregorii supradicta habendum et tenendum predictum
gardinum et pertinenciis suis prefatis confratribus et consororibus ac eorum successoribus
imperpetuum tenendum de capitalibus dominis per servicia inde debita et de iure
consueta et ultra tenendum annuatim diem anniversarii mei et parentum
meorum in ecclesia predicta in dicendis placcebo et dirige et in crastino
missam de requiem ut predictus est imperpetuum proviso semper quod si predictus
Thomas obient quousque et priusquam predictus status meus et terminum plenarie
sit compleantur tunc volo quod immediate post decessum Thome predicti
confratres et consorores habeant et teneant predictum statum et terminum durante
termino predicto et profitum inde perveniens distribuendum annuatim in missis
et donis caritativis prout eis melius videbitur expediri pro salute anime
mee et parentum meorum ac omnium fidelium defunctorum Residuum vero
omnium bonorum meorum superius non legatorum do et lego predicte Agneti
matri mee et eandem Agnetem et predictum Johannem Bukby ordino facio
et constituo executores meos ut ipsi disponant pro salute anime mee
Et istius testamenti ordino facio et constituo Henricum Colman de
Northampton deyster esse supervisorem per presentes et volo quod idem
Henricus habeat tria cocliaria argenti pro labore suo et volo quod predictus

Thomas Harysson sit sub gubernacione predicti Henrici Colman et Johannis Bukby ipsum in gubernandum habere quousque venit ad raccionabilem etatem se <ipsum> non gubernare per discreconem eorumdem Henrici et Johannis per presentes Date die et anno supradicto hiis testibus Johanne Grene de Northampton yoman Thoma Swayn de eadem Johanne Pepyn de eadem et aliis

In the name of God Amen the 8th day of December 1475 I William Harysson of Northampton, fuller, in good memory make my testament in this wise. First I bequeath my soul to Almighty God, to the Blessed Virgin Mary His mother and all the saints of the court of heaven, my body to be buried in the churchyard of the church of St Gregory the Pope in the town of Northampton. Item I bequeath to the fabric of the same church 20d. Item I bequeath to the high altar there 20d. Item I bequeath to Agnes, my mother, one coverlet, two pairs of sheets, one rosary with paternoster or beads of silver, my second brass pot, my second basin and ewer of tin, 1 pot of pewter holding 1 quart, one plate and two dishes of pewter, 2 candelabra of laten, 3 spoons of silver, five yards of woollen cloth and 1 brass pot containing 1 gallon, one skillet with a handle and one mattress called 'le cocher' made with 'le draught flokkys', one pair of blankets, two feather cushions called 'le pelowes' and 1 small coffer. Item I bequeath to Thomas Harysson, my kinsman, 3 coverlets, 2 pairs of sheets, 1 'cocher' made of flokkys and a bolster of the same with 3 pillows, my best brass pot, my best brass cauldron and another brass pot, one brass pan holding 4 gallons, one pan holding 1 pottell, 1 chaffer with two ears, 2 iron spits, one pair of gobberdes, 2 eel spits of iron, 1 skemer, 1 flesshook, 1 charger of pewter, 4 plates, 4 dishes, 8 saucers of pewter, 1 salt cellar, 1 chafing dish of laton, 7 candelabra of laton, 1 two quart jar, another pewter jar holding one half measure of ale and another pewter jar for wine holding 'le pynt' and two basins and two ewers, one large coffer and one spruce coffer and 4 silver spoons. Item I bequeath to Walter Mayndew, my servant, to further his marriage with Ellen Lodelay, servant of Thomas Norris, my gown of violet, one coverlet, one brass pot holding one gallon, one pair of sheets, one salt of pewter with a cover and 2 saucers of pewter and one candelabra of laton. Item I bequeath to William Benet, my servant, 1 coverlet, 1 brass pot holding 1 gallon, one candelabra of laton, one dish of pewter and 2 saucers of pewter. Item I bequeath to Katherine, my kinswoman, 1 basin of laton, 2 candelabra of laton, one salt of pewter with a cover, 2 jars of pewter, 1 spit of iron, two gobberdes and 1 eel spit of iron. Item I bequeath to John Batman 1 coverlet, one brass pan holding 1 potell. Item I bequeath to John Bukby senior 4 spoons of silver Item I bequeath to Ellen Welles, formerly my servant, 3 silver shillings. Item I give and bequeath to the said Thomas Harysson, my kinsman, all my estate and terms which I have from and in that tenement with its appurtenances in which I reside and also I give and bequeath to the aforesaid Thomas all my garden with its closes lying in that lane called 'le Rye' in the parish of St Gregory aforesaid, which same garden with its appurtenances I formerly had from the gift and feoffment of John Bussard of Northampton, barber, as fully appears by his charter of fee simple given to me to have and to hold my aforesaid estate and term during my whole term, giving, paying and conveying just as is fully apparent by the writing thereon made to me. And also to have and to hold the said garden with closes and its appurtenances immediately after my death the aforesaid Thomas Harysson and his assigns during the whole life of the same Thomas of the chief lords of the fee by services therefore due and by right accustomed, and under this form and condition, that the same Thomas Harysson, annually during his life shall hold or make to be held in the church of St Gregory aforesaid on the day of my anniversary and of my parents, Robert and Agnes Harysson, bringing in placebo and dirge and on the day after celebrate a special requiem mass for the health of my soul and the souls of my parents and all faithful departed. Item I wish that immediately after the death of the aforesaid Thomas Harysson the aforesaid garden with its appurtenances should descend and wholly revert to the brothers and sisters of the fraternity of the Holy Cross in the Wall being in the church of St Gregory abovesaid to have and to hold the aforesaid garden and its meadow land to the aforesaid brothers and sisters and their successors forever to hold of the chief lords by services therefore due and by right accustomed and further to hold a day of my anniversary and my parents in the church aforesaid including placebo and dirge and on the day after a requiem mass. In order that the aforesaid is forever provided for, if the aforesaid Thomas die as long as and before as much as my aforesaid estate and term are fully completed, then I will that immediately after the death of Thomas aforesaid, the brothers and sisters have and hold the aforesaid estate and term during the aforesaid term and the profit thereby arrived at be distributed annually in masses and charitable gifts as seems best to them for the health of my soul and my parents and all faithful departed. The residue of all my goods not bequeathed above I give and bequeath to the aforesaid Agnes, my mother, and the same Agnes and the aforesaid John Bukby I ordain, make and constitute my executors, they to dispose for the health of my soul. And of this will I ordain, make and constitute Henry Colman of Northampton, dyster, to be supervisor by these presents and I wish that the same Henry have three silver spoons for his labour and I wish that the aforesaid Thomas Harysson should be under the guidance of the aforesaid Henry Colman and John Bukby, himself to be governed until he come to reasonable age being able to govern himself, by the discretion of the same Henry and John by these presents. Given the day and year abovesaid. These being witness John Grene of Northampton, yeoman, Thomas Swayn of the same, John Pepyn of the same and others.

f16v 27 RALPH WEST 4th December 1475 barker (tanner)

In Dei nomine Amen quarto die mensis Decembris anno domini millesimo ccccmo septuagesimo quinto Ego Radulphus West de Northampton barker sana memoria condo testamentum meum in hunc modum In primis lego animam meam Deo Omnipotenti Beate Marie eius genitrici et omnibus sanctis curie celestis corpusque meum ad sepiliendum in capella Beate Marie Virginis existente in ecclesia parochia Sancti Petri ville Northampton Item lego reparacioni eiusdem capelle vjs. et viij denarios Item lego summo altari eiusdem ecclesie sex solidos octo denarios Item lego reparacione dicte ecclesie quadraginta solidos bone et legalis monete Anglie Item lego fraternitati Sancte Crucis in Muro existente in ecclesia Sancti Gregorii dicte ville iijs. iiijd. Item lego fraternitati Beate Katerine Virginis existente infra ecclesiam Beate Marie Virginis eiusdem ville sex solidos octo denarios Item lego reparacioni altaris Sancti Johannis in ecclesia Sancti Petri antedicta iijs. iiijd. Item lego <reparacioni ecclesie> Sancti Michaelis Archangeli ville Northampton iijs. iiijd. Item lego
reparacioni ecclesie Sancte Margarete Virginis infine Sancti Jacobi iuxta Northampton iijs. iiijd. Item lego reparacioni ecclesie parochiali de Brykksworth iijs. iiijd. Item lego reparacione ecclesie parochiali de Chirche Brampton iijs. iiijd. Item lego reparacioni ecclesie de Dalyngton iijs. iiijd. Item lego cuilibet ordini fratrum mendicancium ville Northampton decem solidos ita quod quilibet ordo dicti ordini dicat unum Trinomialem in mediate post decessum meum pro salute anime mee Item volo quod unus capellanus ydonius in mediate post decessum meum cotidie celebrat per unum annum integrum in capella Beate Marie in ecclesia dicti Sancti Petri pro salute anime mee et parentum meorum ac omnium fidelium defunctorum et volo quod dictus capellanus habeat pro salario suo centum solidos in pecuniis muneratis Item lego Ricardo filio meo centum solidos in pecuniis Item lego Alicie filie mee centum solidos in pecuniis muneratis Item lego Agneti filie mee centum solidos in pecuniis muneratis Item lego Avicie West consanguine mee viginti solidos in pecuniis muneratis Residuum vero omnium bonorum meorum superius non legatorum do et lego Alicie uxori mee et eandem Aliciam et Johannem Man de Northampton bocher ordino facio et constituo executores meos ut ipsi disponant pro salute anime mee prout ei melius videbitur expediri et presentis testamenti

f17r

mei ordino facio et constituo Johannem Bukby seniorem de Northampton barker et Johannem West fratrem meum esse supervisores Et volo quod uterque eorum habeat pro labore suo sex solidos
et octo denarios bone et legalis monete Anglie per presentes Date die et anno supradictis hiis testibus domino Ricardo Hyndeman capellano Willelmo Bate barker Willelmo Horpoll de Northampton et aliis

In the name of God Amen the fourth day of December 1475 I Ralph West of Northampton, barker, in good memory make my testament in this wise. First I bequeath my soul to Almighty God, to the Blessed Virgin Mary His mother and all the saints in the court of heaven, my body to be buried in the chapel of the Blessed Virgin Mary being in the parish church of St Peter, Northampton. Item I bequeath for the repair of the same chapel 6s 8d. Item I bequeath to the high altar of the said church 40s of good legal English money. Item I bequeath to the fraternity of the Holy Cross in the Wall being in the church of St Gregory of the said town 3s

4d. Item I bequeath to the fraternity of St Katherine the Virgin in the church of St Mary the Virgin in the same town 6s 8d. Item I bequeath for the repair of the altar of St John in the church of St Peter aforesaid 3s 4d. Item to the repair of the church of St Michael the Archangel of Northampton 3s 4d. Item I bequeath to the repair of the church of St Margaret in St James End by Northampton 3s 4d. Item I bequeath for the repair of the parish church of Brykkesworth 3s.4d. Item I bequeath for the repair of the parish church of Church Brampton 3s 4d. Item I bequeath for the repair of the parish church of Dallington 3s 4d. Item I bequeath to each of the orders of mendicant brothers in Northampton 10s so that each order of the said orders shall say one 'Trinomelis' immediately after my death for the health of my soul. Item I will that a suitable chaplain immediately after my death shall celebrate every day for one whole year after my death in the chapel of the Blessed Virgin Mary in the said church of St Peter for the health of my soul and the souls of my parents and all faithful departed and I will that the said chaplain shall have for his pay 100s in money. Item I bequeath to Richard, my son, 100s in money Item I bequeath to Alice, my daughter, 100s in money Item I bequeath to Agnes, my daughter, 100s in money. Item I bequeath to Avice West, my kinswoman 20s. in money. The residue of all my goods not bequeathed above I give and bequeath to Alice, my wife, and the same Alice and John Man of Northampton, butcher, I ordain, make and constitute my executors that they dispose for the health of my soul as seems best to them, and of this my present testament I ordain, make and constitute John Bukby senior of Northampton, barker, and John West, my brother, to be supervisors and I will that each of them have for their labour six shillings and eight pence of good, legal English money by these presents. Given the day and year abovesaid. With these witnesses Dom Richard Hyndeman, chaplain, William Bate, barker, and William Horpoll of Northampton and others.

f17r 28 RICHARD KNOTTYNG 1st December 1475

In Dei nomine Amen primo die mensis Decembris anno domini millesimo ccccmo septuagesimo quinto Ego Ricardus Knottyng de Northampton sana memoria condo testamentum meum in hunc modum

In primis lego animam meam Deo Omnipotenti Beate Marie eius genitrici et omnibus sanctis curie celestis

corpusque meum ad sepiliendum in cimiterio ecclesie Omnium Sanctorum ville Northampton coram hostio occidente

ibidem iuxta tumulum Agnetis quondam uxoris mee Item lego fraternitati Sancte Trinitatis in eadem ecclesia xxd. Item lego fraternitati Beate Marie Virginis in capella eiusdem ecclesie xxd. Item lego fraternitati Corporis Christi in eadem ecclesia xxd. Item lego fraternitati Sancti Thome Martiris iuxta portam australem eiusdem ville xijd. Item lego Thome Knotyng filio meo sex solidos et octo denarios in pecuniis muneratis Item lego Alicie Boteler filie mee xxd. Item lego Agneti Kydwyn filie mee xxd. Residuum vero omnium bonorum meorum superius non legatorum do et lego Emme uxori mee et eandem Emmam ordino facio et constituo executricem meam ut ipsa disponat pro salute anime mee prout ei melius videbitur expediri et presentis testamenti ordino facio et constituo Willelmum Heyrowe de Northampton deyster esse supervisorem per presentes in cuius rei testimonium huic presenti testamento meo sigillum meum apposui hiis testibus domino Johanne Grenburgh capellano Willelmo Palmer deyster Johanne Langton synger et aliis Date die et anno supradictis

In the name of God Amen the first day of December 1475 I Richard Knottyng of Northampton in good memory make my testament in this wise. First I bequeath my soul to Almighty God, to the Blessed Mary His mother and all the saints of the court of heaven, my body to be buried in the cemetery of the church of All Saints, Northampton, before the west door there next to the grave of Agnes, my late wife. Item I bequeath to the fraternity of the Holy Trinity in the same church 20d. Item I bequeath to the fraternity of the Blessed Virgin Mary in the chapel of the same church 20d. Item I bequeath to the fraternity of Corpus Christi in the same church 20d. Item I bequeath to the fraternity of St Thomas the Martyr next to the south gate of Northampton 12d. Item I bequeath to Thomas Knotyng, my son, 6s 8d in money. Item I bequeath to Alice Boteler, my daughter, 20d. Item I bequeath to Agnes Kydwyn', my daughter, 20d. The residue of all my goods not bequeathed above I give and bequeath to Emma, my wife, and I ordain, make and constitute the same Emma my executrix that she dispose for the health of my soul as seems best to her and by this present testament I ordain, make and constitute William Heyrowe of Northampton, deyster, to be supervisor by these presents. In testimony of which to this present testament I have put my seal. With these witnesses Dom John Grenburgh, chaplain, William Palmer, deyster, John Langton, synger, and others. Given the day and year abovesaid.

f17v 30 THOMAS CLARKE 22nd January 1475 mercer

In Dei nomine Amen xxij die mensis Januarii anno domini millesimo ccccIxxv Ego Thomas Clarke de Northampton mercer compos mentis et sane memorie condo testamentum meum in hunc modum In primis lego animam meam Deo Omnipotenti Beate Marie euis genitrici ac omnibus sanctis curie celestis corpusque meum sepiliendum in cimeterio ecclesie Omnium Sanctorum ville Northampton Item lego summo altari ecclesie predicte

pro decimis et oblationibus meis oblitis xijd. Item lego ad reparacionem ornamentum eiusdem altaris xxd. Item lego Fraternitati Sancte Trinitatis ibidem xxd. Item lego fraternitati Sancti Joahannis Baptiste in dicta ecclesia xxd. Item lego domui elemosinaris Sancti Thome Martiris iuxta portam australem xxd. Item lego fraternitati Sancte Sithe in dicta ecclesia Omnium Sanctorum xijd. Item lego Margarete Stanoton servienti mee xxd. Item lego Agneti Stacy servienti mee xxd. Item lego Katerine Wrygt servienti

mee xxd. Item lego Johanni Bernell fratri meo meam optimam togam cum le bevyr penulatem Item lego Johanne filie predicte Johannis Barnell unam flameolam precii xijd. Item lego Agneti filie mee j tapett de Tapstry wark

j magnam murram vocatam a fflatmaser et sex cocliaria de argento Item lego omnibus pueris meis tertiam partem omnium bonorum meorum superius non legatorum inter eos
et eas equaliter dividendum postquam omnia debita mea integre sunt soluta Residuum vero omnium bonorum meorum superius non legatorum do et lego Agneti uxori mee et Agneti filie nostre ad inde disponendum pro salute anime et animarum omnium fidelium defunctorum
prout eis melius videbitur expediri et ad istud testamentum meum bene et fideliter exequendum predictas Agnetem et Agnetem ordino facio et constituo executrices meas et magistrum Johannem Trentham doctorem et vicanum dicte ecclesie Omnium Sanctorum ordino facio et constituo fore supervisore per execucionem presentis testamenti mei fideliter fiend Item do et lego dicto vicario per labore suo vjs. viijd.

In the name of God Amen the 22nd day of January 1475 I Thomas Clarke of Northampton, mercer, in sound mind and good memory make my testament in this wise. First I bequeath my soul to Almighty God, to the Blessed Mary, His mother and all the saints of the court of heaven, my body to be buried in the cemetery of the church of All Saints in the town of Northampton. Item I bequeath to the high altar of the aforesaid church for my tithes and oblations forgotten 12d. Item I bequeath to the fraternity of Holy Trinity there 20d. Item I bequeath to the fraternity of St John the Baptist in the said church 20d. Item I bequeath to the almshouse of St Thomas the Martyr next to the south gate 20d. Item I bequeath to the fraternity of St Sithe in the said church of All Saints 12d. Item I bequeath to Margaret Stanoton, my servant, 20d. Item I bequeath to John Bernell, my brother, my best gown furred with le beaver. Item I bequeath to Joan, daughter of the aforesaid John Barnell, a kerchief worth 12d. Item I bequeath to Agnes, my daughter 1 carpet of tapestry work, 1 large maser called a flatmaser and six spoons of silver. Item I bequeath to all my children a third part of all my goods not bequeathed above between them equally divided after all my debts are wholly paid. The residue of all my goods not bequeathed above I give and bequeath to Agnes my wife, and Agnes our daughter, to then dispose for the health of my soul and the souls of all faithful departed as seems best to them and that this my testament be well and faithfully executed I ordain, make and constitute the aforesaid Agnes and Agnes my executrixes and Master John Trentham, Doctor and vicar of the said church of All Saints I ordain, make and constitute supervisor of the faithful execution of this my present testament. Item I bequeath the said vicar 6s 8d for his labour.

f18r 31 ISABEL PARMYNTER 23rd May 1476 widow

In Dei nomine Amen xxiij die mensis Maii anno domini millesimo ccccl xxv Ego Isabella Parmynter
de Northampton vidua et relicta nuper Rogeri Parmynter de eadem compos mentis et sane memorie

condo testamentum meum in hunc modum In primis commendo animam meam Deo Omnipotenti etcetera
corpusque meum sepiliendum in cimiterio ecclesie parochie Sancti Petri ville Northampton iuxta sepulcrum
viri mei Item lego ecclesie Beate Marie pro decimis meis oblitis xxd. Item lego reparacioni dicte eecclesie Beate Marie xxd. Item lego fabrice ecclesie Sancti Petri xxd. Item lego fraternitati Sancte Katerine in ecclesia Beate Marie predicte unam magnam ollam eneam Item lego luminibus Sancte Marie in
ecclesia de Dalyngton unam vaccam disponendum secundum discrecione custodium dicti luminis Item
do et lego pro anniversario observando per terminum x annorum post decessum [meum] immediate sequencium
et complendum pro animabus Rogeri Parmynter et mee parentum nostrorum et amicorum antecessorum xiijs.iiijd.
annuatim percipiendum de duobis tenementis meis quorum unum est situatum in parochia Sancti Petri
in le Barkersyend ville predicte et aliud in parochia Sancte Marie in quo nunc maneo distribuandum
in die obitus mariti mei sacerdotibus et Deo devotis secundum discrecionem executoris mei annuatim durante termino predicto x annorum et si contingat executorem <meum> predictum infra
terminum prefixum decedere etcetera quod tunc bene licebit per presens testamentum meum prepositus dicte ecclesie
in pro tempore fierunt percipere de dictis duobis tenementis meis prefatam summam pecunie secundum consuetudinem et libertatem eiusdem ville ab antiquo usitate ad predictum anniversarium bene et fideliter perimplendum durante termino prefixo ita quod quilibet prepositus
habendum pro labore sue etcetera reservet annuatim sibi ipsi de prefata pecunia viijd. Residuum vero
omnium bonorum meorum superius non legatorum do et lego Thome Parmynter in artibus magistro et eundem
magistrum Thomam ordino facio et constituo meam verum et legitimum executorem ut ipse ordinat et disponat pro salute anime mee et amicorum meorum prout ei melius videbitur expediri Datum ut supra

In the name of God Amen the 23rd day of May 1476 I Isabel Parmynter of Northampton, widow and lately relict of Roger Parmynter of the same, in sound mind and good memory make my testament in this wise. First I commend my soul to Almighty God etcetera, my body to be buried in the cemetery of the parish church of St Peter of the town of Northampton near the grave of my husband. Item I bequeath to the church of St Mary for tithes forgotten 20d. Item I bequeath for the repair of the said church of St Mary 20d. Item I bequeath to the fabric of the church of St Peter 20d. Item I bequeath to the fraternity of St Katherine in the church of St Mary aforesaid one great brass pot. Item I bequeath to the lights of St Mary in the church of Dallington one cow to be disposed of according to the discretion of the keeper of the said lights. Item I give and bequeath for observing the anniversary for the term of ten years immediately following after my death and including for the souls of Roger Parmynter, of me and our parents and friends and ancestors to be fulfilled from 13s

4d received annually from my two tenements of which one is situated in the parish of St Peter in le Barkersyend of the said town, and the other in the parish of St Mary in which I now live, to be distributed annually on the day of my husband's death to the priests and faithful to God according to the discretion of my executor during the aforesaid term of ten years and if it should happen that my executor aforesaid should die during term of ten years aforesaid etcetera that then it shall be lawful by this present testament for the churchwarden of the said church at that time to receive from the two tenements the aforesaid sum of money according to the custom and liberty of the same town from ancient usage to well and faithfully fulfil the said anniversary during the term arranged so that the said churchwarden should have for his pains etcetera reserved for him annually from the aforesaid money 8d. The residue of all my goods not bequeathed above I give and bequeath to Thomas Parmenter, Master of Arts, and the same Master Thomas I ordain, make and constitute my true and legitimate executor that he may ordain and dispose for the health of my soul and my friends as seems best to him. Given as above.

f19v 35 THOMAS MAUTEBY 10th April 1477 esquire

In Dei nomine Amen x die Aprilis anno domini mccccլxxvij Ego Thomas
Mauteby de Northampton armiger compos mentis et sane memorie condo testamentum
meum in hunc modum In primis lego animam meam Deo Omnipotenti Gloriose
Virgini Marie ac omnibus sanctis corpusque meum sepiliendum in capalla Alme
matris Dei infra ecclesiam Sancti Egidii ville Northampton predicte Item lego pro
mortuario meo ad quod ius requirit in ea parte Item lego summo altari pro
negligenciis meis preteritis et ignoranciis expiandis xxs. Item lego ffabrice ecclesie
saltem pro uno vestimento ad Dei honorem et Sancti Egidii emendo xxs. et pro

f20r

loco sepulture mee lego vjs. viijd. Item lego fraternitati Sancti Clementis in eadem
ecclesia vjs. viijd. Item lego uni sacerdoti honeste ad celebrandum per unum annum in capella
predicta pro anima mea et animabus parentum meorum et omnium fidelium defunctorum
vli. vjs. viijd.
ita quod incipiet infra annum post obitum meum. Item volo quod lumen coram ymagine
Beate Marie in capella predicta inveniatur ex sumptibus bonorum meorum per unum annum
post decessum meum Item lego pauperibus domus Sancti Thome Martiris ville predicte
xxs. Item lego pauperibus infra hospitale Sancti Johannis Baptiste eiusdem ville vjs. viijd.
Item volo quod sex torticia ordinentur ad comburendum tempore exquiarum mearum et
missa ac
postea quod quatuor remaneant ad serviendum autentico altari in ecclesia Sancti Egidii
predicta et unum ad altare Sanctissime Marie Virginis et aliud ad altare Sancti Clementis
in eadem ecclesia Residuum vero omnium bonorum meorum non legatorum do et lego
Margarate Harowden sorori mee Thome Hunnt draper et Johanni Ilam clerico
ipsos quam constituo et facio meos executores ut ipsi disponant et distribuant
bona mea cum illis relicta et ad manus eorum devenienda pro salute anime mee
in pios usus et pro anniversario meo observando secundum meliorem eorum discrecionem
sicut ipsi volunt coram summo Deo in die tremendi judicii redere racionem
et cuilibet ipsorum executorum meorum pro labore <lego> xxs Date Northampton die
et anno domini supradictis

In the name of God Amen the 10th day of April 1477 I Thomas Mauteby of Northampton, esquire, in sound mind and good memory make my testament in this wise. First I bequeath my soul to Almighty God, to the glorious Virgin Mary and all the saints, my body to be buried in the chapel of the sweet Mother of God within the church of St Giles in the town of Northampton aforesaid. Item I bequeath for my mortuary what right requires in that part. Item I bequeath to the high altar for the expiation of my past neglects and omissions 20s. Item I bequeath to the fabric of the church for a vestment to the honour of God and to amending St Giles 20s and for my place of burial I bequeath 6s 8d. Item I bequeath to the fraternity of St Clement in the same church 6s 8d. Item I bequeath for an honest priest to celebrate for one year in the aforesaid chapel for my soul and the souls of my parents and all faithful departed £5 6s 8d. so that he begins within a year after my death. Item I will that a light be found before the image of the Blessed Mary in the same chapel for a year after my death from the sale of my goods. Item I bequeath to the poor of the house of St Thomas the Martyr in the said town 20s. Item I bequeath to the poor in the Hospital of St John the Baptist in the same town 6s 8d. Item I will that six torches be found to burn at the time of my exequies and mass and afterwards that four remain to serve the high altar in the church of St Giles aforesaid and one at the altar of the most holy Virgin Mary and another at the altar of St Clement in the same church. The residue of all my goods not bequeathed I give and bequeath to Margaret Harrowden, my sister, Thomas Hunnt, draper, and John Ilam, clerk, whom I make and constitute my executors that they may dispose of and distribute my goods left with them and coming into their hands for the health of my soul in pious uses and for observing the anniversary of my death just as they would wish to answer before the high God at the dread day of judgment. And to each of these my executors I bequeath for their labour 20s. Given in Northampton the day and year abovesaid.

f20r 36 JOHN HANCOK 25th April 1478 dyer

In Dei nomine Amen xxv die Aprilis anno domini mccccIxviij Ego Johannes Hancok de Northampton,
deyster sana memoria condo testamentum meum in hunc modum In primis lego animam Deo Omnipotenti
Beate Marie et omnibus sanctis curie celestis corpusque meum sepiliendum in capella Corporis Christi in ecclesia Omnium Sanctorum ville Northampton Item lego fraternitati dicte capelle pro sepultura mea ibidem vjs. viijd. Item lego fraternitati Sancte Trinitatis in eadem ecclesia iijs. iiijd. Item lego fraternitati Beate Marie in eadem ecclesia iijs. iiijd. Item lego fraternitati Sancti Johannis
Baptiste in eadem ecclesia xijd. Item lego fraternitati Sancte Crucis in eadem ecclesia xijd. Item lego fraternitati Sancti Georgii in eadem ecclesia xijd. Item lego reparacioni dicte ecclesie ijs. Item lego cuilibet ordinii fratrum mendicancium ville Northampton iijs.iiijd. ad orandum pro salute anime mee Item volo quod die sepulture mee xl xijcem de albe pane

distribuantur inter pauperes per discrecionem executricis mee Item lego Thome filio meo unum salsarium cum coopertorio de argento unam murram argentem ligatam et xij cocliaros
argenti unum craterum de argento ac meam optimam zonam argenti harnesatam Item lego dicto Thome togam meam vocatam Corpus Christi lyvery cum penula in eadem Item lego eidem Thome
togam meam de vyolett cum penula in eadem Residuum vero omnium bonorum meorum superius
non legatorum do et lego Margarate uxori mee et eandem Margaratam ordino facio et constituo executricem meam ut ipsa disponat pro salute anime mee prout ei melius videbitur expediri Et presentis testamenti ordino et constituo Willelmum Mylle de Northampton deyster fore supervisorem
per presentes hiis testibus Doctore Willelmo Melton capellano Willelmo Wynger wever Johanne Hygham baker et
aliis Date die et anno supradictis

In the name of God Amen the 25th day of April 1478 I John Hancok of Northampton, dyster, in good memory make my testament in this wise. First I bequeath my soul to Almighty God, to the Blessed Mary and all the saints of the court of heaven, my body to be buried in the chapel of Corpus Christi in the church of All Saints in the town of Northampton. Item I bequeath to the fraternity of the Holy Trinity in the same church 3s 4d. Item I bequeath to the fraternity of St John in the same church 3s 4d. Item I bequeath to the fraternity of the Holy Cross in the same church 3s 4d. Item I bequeath to the fraternity of St George in the same church 3s 4d. Item I bequeath to the repair of the said church 2s. Item I bequeath to each of the orders of mendicant brothers in the town of Northampton 3s 4d. to pray for my soul. Item I will that on the day of my burial forty dozen of white bread be distributed among the poor at the discretion of my executors. Item I bequeath to Thomas, my son, one salt with a cover of silver, one maser bound with silver and 12 silver spoons, one silver bowl and my best girdle ornamented with silver. Item I bequeath to the said Thomas my gown called Corpus Christi livery with a hood in the same. Item I bequeath to the same Thomas my gown of violet with a hood in the same. The residue of all my goods not bequeathed above I give and bequeath to Margaret, my wife, and the same Margaret I ordain, make and constitute my executrix that she dispose for the health of my soul as seems best to her. And of this present testament I ordain and constitute William Mylle of Northampton, dyster, to be supervisor by these presents. With these witnesses Doctor William Melton, chaplain, William Wynger, weaver, John Hygham, baker, and others. Given on the day and year abovesaid.

f21v 39 ROBERT GYBSON 31st July 1477 roper

In Dei nomine Amen ultimo die mensis Julii anno domini mcccclxxvij Ego Robertus Gybson de Northampton roper compos mentis et in bona me-

moria existens condo testamentum meum in hunc modum In primis lego
animam meam Deo Omnipotenti Beate Marie et omnibus sanctis corpusque
meum sepiliendum in capella Beate Marie parochialis ecclesie Omnium Sanctorum ville Northampton
coram sede mea ibidem Item lego dicte capelle pro sepultura mea xij[d.]
Item lego fraternitati Sancte Trinitatis in eadem ecclesia xiijs. iiijd. Item
lego fraternitati Corporis Christi in eadem ecclesia iijs. iiijd.
et unam torchiam Item lego fraternitati Sancti Georgii ibidem xijd.Item lego
fraternitati Sancte Crucis in dicta ecclesia xijd.Item lego fraternitati Sancte
Katerine iuxta Collegium xijd. Item lego fraternitati Sancti Thome Martiris ad portam
australem ville Northampton xxd. Residuum vero omnium bonorum meorum do
et lego Isabelle uxori mee ut ipsa inde ordinet et disponat pro salute
anime mee et eandem Isabellam ordino facio et constituo executricem
et Johannem Artylburgh supervisorem

In the name of God Amen the last day of July 1477 I Robert Gybson of Northampton, roper, still in good memory make my testament in this wise. First I bequeath my soul to Almighty God, to the Blessed Virgin Mary and all the saints, my body to be buried in the chapel of the Blessed Mary in the parish church of All Saints in the town of Northampton before my seat there. Item I bequeath to the said chapel for my burial 12d. Item I bequeath to the fraternity of Holy Trinity in the same church 13s 4d. Item I bequeath to the fraternity of Corpus Christi in the same church 3s 4d and one torch. Item I bequeath to the fraternity of St George there 12d. Item I bequeath to the fraternity of the Holy Cross in the said church 12d. Item I bequeath to the fraternity of St Katherine next to the college 12d. Item I bequeath to the fraternity of St Thomas the Martyr at the south gate of the town of Northampton 20d. The residue of all my goods I give and bequeath to Isabel, my wife, that she should ordain and dispose of the same for the health of my soul and the same Isabel I ordain, make and appoint executrix and John Artylburgh supervisor.

f22v 43 AGNES RYNGLOND 24th July 1479 widow

In Dei nomine Amen in vigilia Sancti Jacobi apostoli anno domini mcccclxxix Ego Agnes
Rynglond de Northampton vidua compos mentis et sane memorie condo testamentum
meum in hunc modum In primis commendo animam meam Deo Beate Marie
et omnibus sanctis eius corpusque meum sepiliendum in cimiterio ecclesie parochialis
Sancti Egidii in ville Northampton iuxta sepulcrum Johannis Rynglond nuper mariti mei
Item lego summo altari pro decimis meis oblitis xs. Item lego pro ornament-
as summum altare unam mappam de dyaper Item lego lumini Sancte Crucis in dicta
ecclesia xld. Item lego abbatisse et conventui monalium de pratis iuxta Northampton
xiijs. iiijd. distribuendum inter abbissam conventum per discrecionem executorum
meorum. Item lego pauperibus domus Sancti Thome Martiris vjs. viijd. distribuendum
inter eosdem cum necesse fuerint secundum discrecionem executorum meorum Item pauperibus
hospitali Sancti Johannis Northampton xld distribuendum simili modo Item lego Johanni Faux
mercer unam honestam mensam plicabilem et optimum superlectale et sex cocliaria
argenti de mediis Item Johanne uxori eius meam optimam togam Item lego
Willelmo Faux unam cistam cum evidenciis et optimam ollam et optimam chafor

cum duobus auribus j pelvim cum lavacro et unum hangyng laver Item Thome Faux unum brode towell de dyaper cum duobis cocliariis argenti Item Agneti Faux iij qwyshyns j towell de dyaper unam ollam vocatam sonday pott et unum chafurn Item lego magistro Johanni Roberts meam optimam murram unum parvum chafum
Item domino Johanni Lynn alias Clarke unum armariolum unum chafum pro igne aularia cum ymagine Sancte Dorothee i banker iij pulvinaria de optimis et duo de aliis Item lego domino Johanni Palmer j ollam eneam vocatam kerchyf pott unum cervicall Item lego Johanne Ratt meam parvam murram et bona secundum discrecionem executorum meorum Item Johanni Clerke baker meam magnam cistam Item lego uxori Johannis Clerke meam brasyn morter Residuum vero omnium bonorum meorum superius non legatorum do et lego domino Johanni Lynn alias Clerke Johanni Clerke baker et Johanni Faux et eosdem dominum Johannem Clerke Johannem Clerke baker et Johannem Faux ordino facio et constituo meos veros executores per presentes ut ipse ordinent et disponant pro salute anime mee prout eis in posterum melius videbitur expediri Date die loco et anno domini supradictis

In the name of God Amen the eve of St James the Apostle 1479 I Agnes Rynglond of Northampton, widow, in sound mind and good memory make my testament in this wise. First I commend my soul to God, the Blessed Mary and all His saints, my body to be buried in the cemetery of the parish church of St Giles in the town of Northampton next to the grave of John Rynglond, my late husband. Item I bequeath to the high altar for my tithes forgotten 10s. Item I bequeath for the adornment of the high altar one cloth of diaper. Item I bequeath to the light of the Holy Cross in the said church 40d. Item I bequeath to the Abbess and convent of nuns of Delapre near Northampton 3s 4d to be distributed between the Abbess and convent at the discretion of my executors. Item I bequeath to the poor of the house of St Thomas the Martyr 6s 8d to be distributed among them as they need according to the discretion of my executors. Item to the poor of the Hospital of St John, Northampton 40d distributed in similar manner. Item I bequeath to John Faux, mercer, one sound folding table and the best cover and six silver spoons of the middle sort. Item I bequeath to Joan, his wife, my best gown. Item I bequeath to William Faux one chest with the evidences and the best pot and the best chafer with two handles, 1 jug and ewer and one hanging laver. Item to Thomas Faux one broad towel of diaper with two silver spoons. Item to Agnes Faux 3 cushions, 1 towel of diaper, one pot called Sunday pot and one chafer. Item I bequeath to Master John Roberts my best maser one small chafer. Item to Dom John Lynn, alias Clarke, one small chest, one chafer for the fire, one with an image of St Dorothy, 1 baker, 3 best cushions and two others. Item I bequeath to Dom John Palmer 1 brass pot called kerchief pot, one pillow. Item I bequeath to Joan Ratt my small maser and other goods according to the discretion of my executors. Item to John Clerke, baker, my large chest. Item I bequeath to the wife of John Clerke my brass mortar. The residue of all my goods not bequeathed above I give and bequeath to Dom John Lynn, alias Clerke,

John Clerke, baker, and John Faux and the same Dom John Clerke, John Clerke, baker, and John Faux I ordain, make and constitute my true executors by these presents that they to ordain and dispose for the health of my soul as seems best to them hereafter. Given the day, place and year abovesaid.

f23r 44 HUGH HOPWOD 22nd August 1479 fuller

In Dei nomine Amen xxij die mensis Augusti anno domini millesimo cccclxxix. Ego Hugo Hopwod
de Northampton fuller sana memoria condo testamentum meum in hunc modum In primis lego
animam meam Deo Omnipotenti Beate Marie eius genitrici ac omnibus sanctis curie celestis corpus-
que meum sepiliendum in ecclesia Sancti Petri ville Northampton Item lego summo altari ibidem xld.
Item lego domino Roberto Alcok confessori meo iijs.iiijd. Item lego Willelmo filio meo
Cs. Item lego Thome filio meo Cs. Item lego Henrico filio meo Cs. Item lego
Johanne filie mee Cs. Item lego Gregorio filio meo Cs. Item lego Roberto filio
meo Cs. Item lego unum craterem de argento deauratum precii sex librarum inter dictos
pueros meos equaliter dividend' proviso semper quod Alicia uxor mea habeat et custodiat
predictum craterem in sua gubernacione durante vita sua ad usum et proficium dictorum puerorum
Residuum vero omnium bonorum meorum superius non legatorum do et lego predicte Alicie uxori
mee et eandem Aliciam ac Willelmum Hayrow de Northampton ordino facio et constituo execu-
tores meos ut ipsi ordinent et disponant pro salute anime mee prout eis melius videbitur
expediri Date die et anno supradictis

In the name of God Amen the 22nd day of August 1479 I Hugh Hopwod of Northampton, fuller, in good memeory make my testament in this wise. First I bequeath my soul to God Almighty, to the Blessed Mary His mother and all the saints of the court of heaven, my body to be buried in the church of Saint Peter in the town of Northampton. Item I bequeath to the high altar of the same 40d. Item I bequeath to lord Robert Alcok my confessor 3s 4d. Item I bequeath to William my son 100s. Item I bequeath to Thomas my son 100s. Item I bequeath to Henry my son 100s. Item I bequeath to Joan my daughter 100s. Item I bequeath to Gregory my son 100s. Item I bequeath to Robert my son 100s. Item I bequeath one bowl of silver gilt worth six pounds between the said children equally divided providing always that Alice my wife holds the custody of the aforesaid bowl in her governance for the duration of her life to the use and profit of the said children. The residue of all my goods not bequeathed above I give and bequeath to the aforesaid Alice my wife and the same Alice and William Hayrow of Northampton I ordain, make and constitute my executors that they ordain and dispose for the health of my soul as seems best to them. Given the day and year abovesaid.

f23r 45 ISABEL PECHE November 1st 1479 widow

In Dei nomine Amen primo die mensis Novembris anno domini mcccclxxix Ego domina Isabella Peche vidua compos mentis et sane memorie condo testamentum meum in hunc modum In primis lego animam meam Deo Omnipotenti Beate Marie Virgini Dei genitrici ei ac omnibus sanctis curie celestis corpusque meum sepiliendum in ecclesia monasterii Sancti Jacobi iuxta Northampton per tumulum Willelmi Tresham armigeri nuper viri mei Item lego dicto monasterio spalterium meum Item lego Ricardo Sadeler clerico missale meum et calicem meum ac omnia alia vestumenta et ornamenta altari in capella mea spectantes et pertinentes Item lego Margarete Haroweden sorori mea togam meam coloris crymyssyn penulatam cum lez martrons j payer lez tyrys de albo cerico unam zonam de auro et unum ffyrkyn de Ossey Item lego Joanne Kyghtley meam nigram togam cum bordura de blak velwett j par de tyres de rubio cerico Item lego Philippe Shukborugh meam togam coloris de tawney penulatam cum lez shankys et unam par de tyres de cerico murrey Item lego Alicie Torey servienti mee togam meam nigram Item Alicie Johonson alii servienti mee togam meam veridem duplicatam cum lez bukram et circa collam cum nigro velwett Residuum vero omnium bonorum meorum superius non legatorum do et lego predicto Ricardo Sadeler clerico ac Johanni
Robyns de Hoghton Magna ad inde disponendum pro salute anime animarum amicorum et benefactorum meorum necnon omnium fidelium defunctorum prout eis melius videbitur expediri et ad istud testamentum meum bene et fideliter exequendum prefatos Ricardum Sadeler et Johannem Robyns ordino facio et constituo executores meos ac magistrum Johannem Tresham
sup-
ervisorem per presentes

In the name of God Amen the first day of the month of November 1479 I Lady Isabel Peche, widow, in sound mind and good memory make my testament in this wise. First I bequeath my soul to God Almighty, to the Blessed Virgin Mary, God's mother, and all the saints of the court of heaven, my body to be buried in the church of the monastery of Saint James near Northampton by the grave of William Tresham esquire, my late husband. Item I bequeath to the said monastery my psalter. Item I bequeath to Richard Sadler, cleric, my missal and my chalice and all other vestments and ornaments belonging and pertaining to the altar in my chapel. Item I bequeath to Margaret Harrowden, my sister, my gown of crimson colour furred with marten, 1 pair of headresses of white silk, one girdle of gold and one firkin of Ossy. Item I bequeath to Joan Knightley my black gown with a border of black velvet, 1 pair of headresses of red silk Item I bequeath to Philippa Shukburgh my gown of tawney colour furred with shankys and one pair of headresses of mulberry silk. Item I bequeath to Alice Torey, my servant, my black gown. Item I bequeath to Alice Johnson, also my servant, my green gown lined with buckram with black velvet around the collar. The residue of all my goods not bequeathed above I give and bequeath to the aforesaid Richard Sadler, cleric, and John Robins of Great Houghton to then dispose for the health of my soul and the souls of my friends and benefactors and also all faithful departed as seems best to them and to that this my testament be well and faithfully executed I ordain, make and constitute the aforesaid Richard Sadler and John Robins my executors and Master John Tresham supervisor by these presents.

f24r 49 RICHARD HAROWEDON 29th september 1479 esquire

In Dei nomine Amen xxix die mensis Septembris anno domini mcccclxxix Ego Ricardus Harowedon armiger compos mentis et sane memorie condo testamentum meum in hunc modum In primis commendo animam meam Deo Omnipotenti Beate Marie et omnibus sanctis et corpus meum sepiliendum in capella Sancti Petri infra ecclesiam Sancti Egidii ville Northampton coram ymagine Sancti Petri in eadem capella Item lego vicario predicto ecclesie meum optimum jocale sive equum nomine mortuarii Item lego predicte vicario vjs.viijd. Item lego domino Rogero Barnard iijs.iiijd. Item lego domino Johanni Palmer iijs.iiijd. ut ipse et dictus vicarius cum domino Rogero magis devote orent pro salute anime mee Item lego Thome Veysy iijs.iiijd. Item lego Ricardo Cowper servo meo iijs.iiijd. Item lego Elizabeth Bovy xxd. Item lego predicte ecclesia pro novis vestimentis emendis xxs. Item lego fraternitati Sancti Clementis in eadem ecclesie vjs.viijd. Item lego capella Sancti Petri predicti pro loco sepulture mee vjs.viijd. Residuum vero bonorum meorum superius non legatorum do et lego Margarete Harowedon uxori mee et Willelmo Catesby filio Willelmi Catesby militis ad disponendum pro salute anime mee et omnium fidelium Deo commendatorum prout eis melius videbitur expediri et ut ipsi vellent quod ego pro eis disponendum in casu simili contingent Et eosdem Margaretem et Willelmum ordino facio et constituo executores <meos> per presentes Date die et anno supradictis

In the name of God Amen the 29th day of September 1479 I Richard Harowedon, esquire, in sound mind and good memory make my testament in this wise. First I bequeath my soul to Almighty God, to the Blessed Mary and all saints and my body to be buried in the chapel of Saint Peter in the church of Saint Giles in the town of Northampton before the image of Saint Peter in the said chapel. Item to the vicar of Saint Giles my best jewel or a horse in the name of mortuary and 6s 8d. Item I bequeath to Dom Roger Barnard 3s 4d. Item I bequeath to Dom John Palmer 3s 4d that he and the said vicar and Dom Roger may pray with greater devotion for the health of my soul. Item I bequeath to Thomas Veysy 3s 4d. Item I bequeath to Richard Cowper, my servant, 3s 4d. Item I bequeath to Elizabeth Bovy xxd. Item 20s. to the church to buy new vestments. Item I bequeath to the fraternity of Saint Clement in the church of Saint Giles 6s.8d. Item I bequeath to the chapel of Saint Peter for a burial place 6s 8d. The residue of my goods not bequeathed above I give and bequeath to Margaret Harowedon, my wife, and William Catesby, son of William Catesby, knight, to dispose for the health of my soul and all faithful departed in God as seems best to them and they wish that I would dispose in similar circumstances. And the same Margaret and William I ordain, make and constitute my executors by these presents. Given the day and year abovesaid.

f24v 50 JOHN BUKK 10th March 1479

In Dei nomine Amen x die mensis Marcii anno domini mcccclxxix Ego Johannes Bukk de Northampton compos mentis et sane memorie condo testamentum meum in hunc modum In primis commendo animam Deo Omnipotenti Beate Marie et omnibus sanctis corpusque meum sepiliendum in cimiterio ecclesie Sancti Egidii ville Northampton iuxta sepulturam matris mee Item lego summo altari dicte ecclesie pro decimis meis oblitis iijs. iiijd. Item lego reparacioni capelle Sancte Marie predicte ecclesie ijs. Item lego reparacioni capelle Sancti Petri in eadem ecclesia ijs. Item lego fraternitati Sancti Clementis in eadem ecclesia ijs. Item lego Roberto Bukk filio meo Cs. Item lego Johanne filie mee Cs. Item lego Elizabeth filie mee Cs. Item lego postimo meo Cs. Item lego Willelmo Wytwell xxs. Item lego Agneti Wytwell <famule mee> xxs. Item volo quod Margareta uxor mea habeat disposicionem predicte pecunie Roberto Bukk Johanne Elizabethe et postimo meo superius legate quousque predicti pueri adveniant etatem annorum discrecionis et si contingat aliquem vel aliquos predictorum Roberti Bukk Johanne Elizabeth et postimi obire quo antiquam ad etatem annorum discrecionis attingant sive aliquis eorem attingat volo tunc quod predicta Margareta Bukk uxor mea habeat illam porceonem pecuniarum illi sive illie superius legatorum ad disponendum pro salute anime mee Item volo quod eadem Margareta Bukk uxor mea habeat illud tenamentum in quo inhabito ad terminum vite sue sub hac condicione videlicet quod si ipsa Margareta Bukk sola et inmaritata permaneat Ita quod statim post decessum sive maritagium dicte Margarete volo quod predictum tenementum remaneat predicto Roberto Bukk filio meo et heredibus de corpore suo legitime procreatis imperpetuum et si contingat predictus Robertus Bukk obire sine herede de corpore suo legitime procreato volo tunc quod dictum tenementum cum suis pertinenciis remaneat prefatis Johanne Bukk Elizabeth et postimo meo et heredibus de corporibus <eorum> legitime procreatis imperpetuum Et si contingat dictam Johannam Bukk Elizabeth' et postimum meum obire sine heredibus de corporibus eorum legitime procreatis quod absit volo tunc quod illud tenementum cum pertinenciis suis remaneat heredibus executoribus et assignatis predicti Roberti Bukk Johanne Elizabeth' et postimi mei qui vel que diucius vixerit ea intencione ut ipsi meliore modo quo sciverint aut poterint vendant et argentum <inde> perveniens fideliter disponant et distribuant in forma premissa prout inde coram Deo rendere voluerunt Et ad istud testamentum meum fideliter exequendum prefatam Margaretam Bukk uxorem meam ordino facio et constituo executricem meam ac Johannem Clerke de Northampton baker presentis testamenti mei supervisorem per presentes Date die et anno supradictis

In the name of God Amen the 10th day of March 1479 I John Bukk of Northampton in sound mind and good memory make my testament in this wise. First I commend my soul to Almighty God, to the Virgin Mary and all the saints, my body to be buried in the cemetery of the church of St Giles in the town of Northampton next to the grave of my mother. Item I bequeath to the high altar of the said church for my tithes forgotten

3s 4d. Item I bequeath to the repair of the chapel of St Mary in the aforesaid church 2s. Item I bequeath to the repair of the chapel of St Peter in the same church 2s. Item I bequeath to the fraternity of St Clements in the same church 2s. Item I bequeath to Robert Bukk, my son, 100s. Item I bequeath to Joan, my daughter, 100s. Item I bequeath to Elizabeth, my daughter, 100s. Item I bequeath to my future offspring 100s. Item I bequeath to William Wytwell, my servant, 20s. Item I bequeath to Agnes Wytwell, my servant, 20s. Item I will that Margaret, my wife, should have the administration of the aforementioned money bequeathed above, to Robert Bukk, Joan, Elizabeth and my posthumous child, until the said children reach the age of discretion and if it should happen that one or others of the said Robert Bukk, Joan, Elizabeth or future offspring should die before reaching the age of discretion I wish then that the said Margaret Bukk, my wife, should have that portion of the money bequeathed formerly to them to dispose for the health of my soul. Item I will that the same Margaret Bukk, my wife, should have that property in which she lives to the end of her life under this condition, namely that the same Margaret Bukk should remain single and unmarried. Thus in this state after the death or marriage of the said Margaret I will that the said property should belong to the aforementioned Robert Bukk, my son, and to the heirs of his body legitimately begotten forever, and if it should happen that the said Robert Bukk should die without heirs of his body legitimately begotten then I will that the said property with its appurtenances should remain to the aforesaid Joan Bukk, Elizabeth and my posthumous child and to their legitimate heirs of their bodies forever. And if it should happen that the said Joan Bukk, Elizabeth and my posthumous child should die without heirs of their bodies legitimately begotten remaining I will then that the property with its appurtenances should remain to the heirs, executors and assigns of the said Robert Bukk, Joan, Elizabeth and my poshumous child or whoever should be most fit for this intention so that they, in the best way they know or are able to, should sell and the money thus ensuing they should dispose of and distribute in the form as mentioned, as they would wish thence to render before God. And that this my testament be well and faithfully executed I ordain, make and constitute the aforementioned Margaret Bukk, my wife, my executrix and John Clerke of Northampton, baker, as supervisor of my present will by these presents. Given the day and year abovesaid.

f25r 51 THOMAS BUKKE 20th March 1479

In Dei nomine Amen vicesimo die Marcii anno domini mcccclxxix Ego Thomas Bukke de Northampton compos mentis et sane memorie condo testamentum in hunc modum In primis lego animam meam Deo Omnipotenti Beate Marie et omnibus sanctis eius corpus-
que meum sepiliendum in cimiterio Sancti Egidii ville Northampton iuxta sepulturam Johanne Bukke nuper uxoris mee Item lego summo altari eiusdem ecclesie vjs.viijd.

Item lego capelle Beate Marie in eadem ecclesia vjs.viijd. Item lego capelle Beate Petri ex parte australi eiusdem ecclesie vjs.viijd. Item lego fraternitati Sancti Cle- -mentis in dicta ecclesia xiij.iiijd. Item lego reparacionibus ecclesie predicte ubi necessitas magis requirit xls. Item lego cuilibet presbytero interessento misse et exequiis meis viijd. Item lego clerico parochie dicte ecclesie viijd. Item lego sacriste eiusdem ecclesie viijd. Item lego cuilibet clerico interessenti misse et exequiis meis ijd. Item lego cuilibet pauperi in dicta villa Northampton paralitice iacentem et necessitatem habenti xijd. Item lego uni presbitero ydoneo ad celebrandum pro salute anime mee et anime uxoris mee et omnium fidelium defunctorum per terminum trium annorum inmediate sequentum post decessum meum xvjli. Item lego cuilibet filiolo meo xijd. item lego xiijcem pauperibus xiij togas de panno vocato Frese. Item lego Roberto Bukke nepoti meo xl marcas Item lego Johanne Bukke nepti mee xxti marcas Item lego Elizabeth <Bukk> nepti mee xxti marcas. Item lego postimo Johannis Bukke nuper defuncti xxti marcas Et si contingat aliquem vel aliquos predictorum Roberti Johanne Elizabeth et postimo Johannis Bukk obire antiquam maritati fuerint tunc volo quod illa porcio pecuniarum illi sive illis in forme predicte legate equaliter distribuatur viventi sive viventibus Et si contingat omnes illos obire antiquam maritati fuerint sive ad etatem xviij annorum pervenerint quod absit extunc volo quod executores mei habeant omnes denarios et summas supra dictas prefatis Roberto Johanne Elizabeth et postimo Johannes Bukk in forma predictorum legatorum ad ea pro salute anime mee fideliter disponendum et distribuendum in elemosinis et aliis donis caritatis prout eis melius videbitur Item volo quod executores mei in omnibus perimpleant voluntatem meam indentatam signo meo manuali signatam quam quidem voluntatem volo quod huic testamento meo sit annexa. Item volo quod ffeoffati mei faciant sufficientem statum Margarete Bukke nuper uxori predicte Johannis Bukke ad terminum vite sue sub hac condicione sequenti quod si eadem Margareta sola et immaritata permaneat de et in omnibus illis terris et tenementis redditus et servicio que dicti ffeoffati mei habent ad usum mei dicti Thome Bukke in villis et campis de Wylberston Brynghurst Eston Northampton Stokedaubeney Asshley Suttonbassett et Desburgh in comitate Northampton et Laicester habendum et tenendum omnia predicta terras et tenementa et cetera premissa cum pertinenciis

f25v

ut prefertur prefate Margarete ad totam vitam suam sub condicione predicte libere quiete bene et in pace de capitalibus dominis feodi illorum per servicia inde debita et de iure consueta Ita quod statim post decessum seu maritagium dicte Margarete volo quod omnia predicta terras tenementa redditus
et servicia cum pertinenciis intigre remaneant predicto Roberto Bukk filio predicti Johannis Bukk et heredibus de corpore suo legitime procreatis imperpetuum tenendum de capitalibus dominis feodi
illius per servicia predicta Et si contingat dictum Robertum Bukk obire sine heredibus de corpore suo legitime procreatis volo quod tunc omnia predicta terra et tenementa redditus et servicia cum
pertinenciis integre remaneant prefatis Johanne Bukk Elizabeth Bukk et postimo Johannis Bukk et heredibus de corporibus eorum legitime procreatis imperpetuum tenendum de
capitalibus dominis feodis illius per servicia prolibate Et si contingat predictos Johannem Elizabeth et postimo Johanni Bukk obire sine heredes de corporibus eorum legitime procreatis quod absit volo quod tunc omnia predicte terre tenementa redditus et servicia cum pertinenciis
integre remaneant Willelmo Brayfeld nepoti mei et heredibus de corpore suo legitime procreatis imperpetuum <tenendum> de capitalibus dominis feodi illius per servicia prenotata proviso
semper quod si dicti Robertus Johanna Elizabeth, postimus Johannes Bukk et Willelmus

Brayfeld obierint nullo legitimo exitu de corporibus nec de corporibus cuiuslibet
eorum tunc vivente volo quod tunc statim post mortem ultimi eorumdem Roberti Johanne
Elizabeth postimi Johannis Bukk et Willelmi Brayfeld omnia predicta terra tenementa redditus
et servicia cum pertinenciis ut prefertus integre remaneat dictis ffeoffatis meis habendum eis
eis heredibus et assignatis eorum imperpetuum de capitalibus dominis ffeodi illius per servicia
supradicta
sub hac condicione sequente videlicet quod dicti ffeoffati mei omnia predicta terra tenementa
redditus et servicia cum pertinenciis tunc vendant quamcito poterint et totam argen-
-tum inde perveniens disponantur in missis elemosinis et aliis donis caritatis
pro salute anime mee et anime uxori mee ac animarum parentum amicorum benefactorum
meorum
et omnium fidelium defunctorum necnon pro animabus omnium illorum de quibus aliqua bona
seu
catalla in vita mea quoismodo recepi prout eis melius videbitur expediri er prout
coram summo judice voluerint respondere Residuum vero omnium bonorum meorum non
legatorum
do et lego Thome Parmenter clerico Johanni Clerke baker dicte Margarete Bukk
et Roberto Bukk ad ulterius disponendum pro salute anime mee prout eis magis
expediens fuerit et necesse et eosdem Thomam Parmenter Johannem Clerke Margaretam
Bukk et Robertum Bukk ordino facio et constituo executores meos per
presentes

In the name of God Amen the twentieth day of March 1479 I Thomas Bukke of Northampton in sound mind and good memory make my testament in this wise. First I bequeath my soul to Almighty God, to the Blessed Mary and all His saints, my body to be buried in the churchyard of St Giles of the town of Northampton next to the grave of Joan Bukke my late wife. Item I bequeath to the high altar of the same church 6s 8d. Item I bequeath to the chapel of the Blessed Mary in the same church 6s 8d. Item I bequeath to he chapel of the Blessed Peter on the south side of the same church 6s 8d. Item I bequeath to the fraternity of St Clement in the said church 13s 4d. Item I bequeath to the repairs of the aforesaid church where greater need requires 40s. Item I bequeath to each priest taking part at my mass and exequies 8d. Item I bequeath to the clerk of the said parish church 8d. Item I bequeath to the sacrist of the same church 8d. Item I bequeath to each clerk taking part at my mass and exequies 2d. Item I bequeath to each poor person in the town of Northampton lying paralysed and having need 12d. Item I bequeath to a suitable priest to celebrate [mass] for the health of my soul, my wife's soul and the souls of all faithful departed for three years immediately following after my death £16. Item I bequeath to each godchild 12d. Item I bequeath to 13 poor men 13 gowns of the cloth called frese [frieze]. Item I bequeath to Robert Bukke, my nephew, 40 marks. Item I bequeath to Joan Bukke, my niece, 20 marks. Item I bequeath to Elizabeth Bukk, my niece, 20 marks. Item I bequeath to the posthumous child of John Bukke, now deceased, 20 marks. And if it happens that any one or ones of the aforesaid Robert, Joan, Elizabeth and the posthumous child of John Bukk die before they are married then I will that his or their portions of money in the aforesaid form of legacy be distributed equally to those living. And if it happens that they all die before they are married or come to the age of 18, which God forbid, then I will that my executors shall have all the money and sums abovesaid to the aforesaid Robert, Joan, Elizabeth and the posthumous child of John Bukk in the form of the aforesaid legacies and that to be faithfully disposed and distributed in alms and other charitable gifts just as seems best to them. Item I will that my executors shall fulfil in all ways my will indented, signed with my manual sign, which will I wish be annexed to this my testament. Item I will that my feoffees shall make a sufficient state to Margaret Bukke, wife of the aforesaid late John Bukke, for the term of her life under the following condition, that if the same Margaret remains single and unmarried, of and in all those lands and tenements, rents and services which my said feoffees have to the use of me, the said Thomas Bukke, in the towns and fields of Wilbarston, Bringhurst, Eston north, Stoke Albany, Ashley, Sutton Basset and Desborough in the counties of Northampton and Leicester, to have and to hold all the aforesaid lands and tenements to the aforesaid Margaret for her whole life under the aforesaid condition - freely, quietly, well and in peace of the chief lords of the fee by services therefore due and by right accustomed, so that immediately after the death or marriage of the said Margaret I will that all the aforesaid lands, tenements, rents and services with appurtenances shall remain wholly to the aforesaid Robert Bukk, son of the aforesaid John Bukk, and the heirs of his body lawfully begotten for ever to hold of the chief lords of the fee by services aforesaid. And if it happens that the said Robert Bukk die without heirs of his body lawfully begotten then I will that all the aforesaid land and tenements, rents and services with their appurtenances shall remain wholly to the aforesaid Joan Bukk, Elizabeth Bukk and the posthumous child of John Bukk and the heirs of their bodies lawfully begotten forever to hold of the chief lords of the fee by willing? service. And if it happens that the aforesaid Joan, Elizabeth and the posthumous child of John Bukk die without heirs of their bodies lawfully begotten, which God forbid, I will then that all the aforesaid lands, tenements, rents and services with their appurtenances shall wholly remain to William Brayfeld, my nephew, and the heirs of his body lawfully begotten forever to hold of the chief lords of the fee by services before noted. Always with the proviso that if the said Robert, Joan, Elizabeth, the posthumous child of John Bukk and William Brayfeld die with no legitimate issue of their bodies, not even of any of their bodies, then living I will then that the interest in the property after the death of the last of the same Robert, Joan, Elizabeth, the posthumous child of John Bukk and William Brayfeld all the aforesaid lands, tenements, rents and services with the appurtenances of the same shall wholly remain to my said feoffees to have to them, their heirs and assigns forever of the chief lords of the fee by services abovesaid under this following condition that my said feoffees shall then sell the aforesaid lands, tenements, rents and services with appurtenances as quickly as they can and dispose all the silver arising in masses, alms and other charitable gifts for the health of my soul and the soul of my wife and the souls of my parents, friends, benefactors and all faithful departed and also for the souls of all others from whom I have received any goods of chattels whatsoever in my life, just as they would wish to answer before the high judge. The residue of all my goods not bequeathed I give and bequeath to Thomas Parmenter, clerk, John Clerke, baker, the said Margaret Bukk and Robert Bukk to dispose for the health of my soul just as seems most expedient and necessary and I ordain, make and constitute the same Thomas Parmenter, John Clerke, Margaret Bukk and Robert Bukk my executors by these presents.

f26r 52 THOMAS BUKKE

Thys indenture wytnesseth that this ys the laste wylle of me Thomas Bukke of Northampton to be done and performed after the discrecon of myn executors and the surveyor of thys my laste wylle as here after folowyth. First I bequeth to the hygh awter of the churche of Wylberston vjs.viijd. Item to the reparacon of the same churche xxd. Item to the pore folke of the same town vjs.viijd. Item to the church of Stokedawbeney xs. Item to the pore folke of same town iijs.iiijd. Item to the churche of Carleton iijs.iiijd. Item to the pore folke of the same town iijs.iiijd. Item to the churche of Cotyngham iijs.iiijd. Item to the pore folke of the same town iijs.iiijd. Item to the bruge of the same town iijs.iiijd. Item to the churche of Rokyngham iijs.iiijd. Item to the pore folke of the same town iijs.iiijd. Item to the bruge of the same town iijs.iiijd. Item to the churche of Haryngworth vjs.viijd. Item to the pore folke of the same town vjs.viijd. Item to the bruge of the same town iijs.iiijd. Item to the churche of Corby vjs.viijd. Item to the pore folke of the same town iijs.iiijd. Item to the churche of Mykyll Okeley iijs.iiijd. Item to the pore folke of the same town iijs.iiijd. Item to the churche of Lytyll Okeley vjs.viijd. Item to the pore folke of the same town xxd. Item to the West churche of Rushton iijs.iiijd. Item to the pore folke of the same town xxd. Item to the Este churche of the same town iijs.iiijd. Item to the pore folke of the same paryssh xxd. Item to the churche of Rowell vjs. viijd. Item to the pore folke of the same town vjs. viijd. Item to the bruge of the same town iijs.iiijd. Item to the nunnes of the same town vjs.viijd. Item to the church of Desburgh xs. Item to the pore folke of the same town iijs.iiijd. Item to the bruge of the same town iijs.iiijd. Item to the churche of Haryngton iijs.iiijd. Item to the pore folke of the same town iijs.iiijd. Item to the church of Braybroke vjs.viijd. Item to the pore folke of the same town iijs.iiijd. Item to the churche of Arthyngworth iijs.iiijd. Item to the pore folke of the same town iijs.iiijd. Item to the churche of Keymarssh iijs.iiijd. Item to the pore folke of the same town iijs.iiijd. Item to the churche of Oxton iijs. iiijd. Item to the pore folke of the same towne iijs.iiijd. Item to the church of Farndon iijs.iiijd. Item to the pore folke of the same town iijs.iiijd. Item to the church of Lubbynham iijs.iiijd. Item to the pore folke of the same town iijs.iiijd. Item to the church of Thedyngworth iijs.iiijd. Item to the

f26v

pore folke of the same iijs.iiijd. Item to the church of Harburgh vjs.viijd. Item to the pore folke of the same town vjs.viijd. Item to the chapell of the same town iijs.iiijd. Item to the church of Mykyll Bowden iijs.iiijd. Item to the pore folke of the same town iijs. iiijd. Item to the churche of Langton vjs.viijd. Item to the pore folke of the same paryssh vjs.viijd. Item to the chapell of Sutton iijs.iiijd. Item to the pore folke of the same town xxd. Item to the churche of Weston iijs.iiijd. Item to the pore folke of the same town xxd. Item to the bruge of the same town xxd. Item to the church of Welham iijs.iiijd. Item to the pore folke of the same town xxd. Item to the bruge of the same town xxd. Item to the churche of Asshton iijs.iiijd. Item to the pore folke of the same town iijs.iiijd. Item to the bruge of the same town iijs.iiijd. Item to the church of Brampton iijs.iiijd. Item to the pore folke of the same town iijs.iiijd. Item to the church of Dyngley iijs.iiijd. Item to the pore folke of the same town iijs.iiijd. Item to the church of Lytell Bowden iijs.iiijd. Item to the pore folke of the same town iijs. iiijd. Item to the churche of Medburn iijs.iiijd. Item to the pore folke of the same town iijs.iiijd. Item to the bruge of the same town iijs.iiijd. Item to the churche of Brynghyrste iijs.iiijd. Item to the pore folke of the same town & Drayton iijs.iiijd. Item to the churche of Eston iijs.iiijd. Item to the pore folke of the same town iijs.iiijd. Item iiij orders of ffrerys in Stamford to every order vjs.viijd. Item to the nonnes of the same town vjs.viijd. Item to the iiij orders of ffrerys in Northampton to every order xiijs.iiijd. Item to the nonnes of Delapray be syde Northampton vjs.viijd. Item to the churche of Brafeld iijs.iiijd. Item to the pore folke of the same town iijs.iiijd. Item to the chapell of Saynt Edmund withowte est gate of Northampton iijs.iiijd. Item to the pore men of Saynt Thomas howse nexte withowte the south gate of Northampton iijs.iiijd. Item to the pore men in the bedehowse of Saynt Johnys of Northampton iijs.iiijd. Item to Agnes Whytwell of Stoke Dawbeney xxs. Item to William Whytwell xls. Item to Agnes Whytwell the younger xxs. Item to Agnes Elyott of Wylberston vjs.viijd. Item to Robert Miller servant to Symon Brayfeld xxs. Item to Robert Fyssher [vjs.viijd.] Item to Johan Gyfe vjs.viijd.

f27r 54 MARGARET HANCOK 20th August 1480 widow

In Dei nomine Amen xx die Augusti anno domini mcccclxxx Ego Margareta Hancok vidua compos mentis et sane memorie condo testamentum meum in hunc modum In primis lego animam meam Deo Omnipotenti et Beate Marie sue genitrici ac omnibus sanctis curie
celestis corpusque meum sepiliendum in capella Corporis Christi in ecclesia Omnium Sanctorum
ville Northampton iuxta tumulum Johannis Hancok deyster nuper viri mei Item lego summo altari eiusdem ecclesie pro decimis <meis> oblitis et non bene decimatis et oblationibus eciam oblitis
xijd. Item lego fraternitati Corporis Christi in dicta ecclesia iijs.iiijd. Item lego domui elemosinis Sancti Thome Martiris extra portam australem xijd. Item lego ffraternitati Sancte Crucis in Muro in ecclesia Sancti Gregorii Pape xijd. et unam torchiam Item

f27v

Item lego altari Corporis Christi unam torchiam Item lego altari Sancte Crucis in dicta ecclesia Omnium Sanctorum unam torchiam Item lego fraternitati Sancti Michaelis Archangeli unam torchiam et iijs.iiijd.

Item lego hospitali Sancti Johannis Baptiste unam torchiam et iijs.iiijd. Item lego Agneti uxori Thome
Hancok meam zonam coloris blodii cum argento et auro harnesiato et deaurato et
unum par precum de corall gaudytt cum auro et argento Item lego Agneti
Byrde consanguine mee unum par precium de rounde geet cum gaudiis de argento,
unam zonam cum argento harnesiato unam ollam eneam continentem quattuor lagenas unam
aliam ollam eneam continentem unam lagenam unam patellam eneam continentem xviij
lagenas unum pelvin cum lavacro de laten unam hallyng picturatum cum ymaginibus
istorum sanctorum videlicet Sancti Johannis Baptiste Sancti Christoferi et Johannis Evangeliste Item
lego ffermario hospitali Sancti Johannis Baptiste predicte unam partem panni mei
picturatam cum angelis et aliis lez garlands ac rebus pendentis in aula mea ad
pendendum ibidem super totam illam partem in quam communis cominus est Item lego predicte
ecclesie Sancti Michaelis aliam partem eiusdem panni Item lego Jacobo Smyth servienti
meo unam ollam eneam continentem tres lagenas unum vetus plumbum et unum
wodefatte Item lego cancello predicte domus elemosinaris Sancti Thome Martiris terciam
partem dicti panni Item lego predicte Agneti Birde unum lavacrum de
laten vocatum a hangyng laver unam cistam et duo paria linthiamentium Item Johanni
Harlok aprenticio meo unam ollam eneam continentem duas lagenas et unam patellam
eneam continentem duas lagenas Item magistro Johanni Trentham doctori et vicario perpetuo
ecclesie Omnium Sanctorum supradicte ijs. Item lego collegio dicte ecclesie unam mappam
de plano panno lineo Item lego domino Willelmo Melton capellano xxs. Residuum
vero omnium bonorum meorum superius non legatorum do et lego predicto Thome
Hancok ad inde disponendum per discrecionem et supervisorum Thome Hunt <hic rasura fuit in testamento> de Northampton
draper et non aliter prout eis melius videbitur expediri pro salute anime mee
anime predicti Johannis Hancok nuper viri mei et animarum amicorum nostrorum et animarum omnium
fidelium defunctorum Et ad istud testamentum meum bene et fideliter exequendum prefatum
Thomam Hancok ordino facio et constituo executorem meum et prefatum Thomam
Hunt supervisorem Et volo quod predictus Thomas Hancok habeat pro labore suo in exequendum
istam voluntatem <meam> in forma prinotatam <xls>. Et quod dictus Thomas Hunt habeat pro labore suo
in supervivendo execucionem predictam xxs. per presentes ulterius quo lego sustentac-
eoni capelle Beate Marie Virginis in dicta ecclesia Omnium Sanctorum iijs.iiijd.

In the name of God Amen the 20th day of August 1480. I Margaret Hancock, widow, in sound mind and good memory make my testament in this wise. First I bequeath my soul to Almighty God and to the Blessed Mary His mother and all the saints of the court of heaven, my body to be buried in the chapel of Corpus Christi in the church of All Saints in the town of Northampton next to the grave of John Hancock, dyster, my late husband. Item I bequeath to the high altar of the same church for tithes forgotten and not well tithed 12d. Item I bequeath to the fraternity of Corpus Christi in the said church 3s 4d. Item I bequeath to the almshouse of St Thomas outside the south gate 12d. Item I bequeath to the fraternity of the Holy Cross in the Wall in the church of St Gregory the Pope 12d and one torch. Item I bequeath to the altar of Corpus Christi one torch.

Item I bequeath to the fraternity of the Holy Cross in the said church of All Saints one torch. Item I bequeath to the fraternity of St Michael the Archangel one torch and 3s 4d. Item I bequeath to the Hospital of St John the Baptist one torch and 3s 4d. Item I bequeath to Agnes, the wife of Thomas Hancock, my gown of blue colour ornamented with silver and gold and gilt and one set of coral rosary beads with gold and silver. Item I bequeath to Agnes Byrde, my cousin, one set of round jet rosary beads with silver, one girdle ornamented with silver, one brass pot holding four gallons, one other brass pot holding one gallon, one brass bowl holding 18 gallons, one basin with a metal ewer, one hallyng painted with pictures of these saints, namely St John the Baptist, St Christopher, and John the Evangelist. Item I bequeath to the infirmary of the Hospital of St John the Baptist aforementioned one share of my cloth, painted with angels and other garlands and items, hanging in my hall, to be hung there above all that part which is the common fireplace. Item I bequeath to the said church of St Michael the other share of the said cloth. Item I bequeath to Jacob Smyth, my servant, one brass pot holding three gallons, one old leaden vessel, one wooden vat. Item I bequeath to the said chancel of the almshouse of St Thomas the Martyr the third share of the said cloth. Item I bequeath to the aforesaid Agnes Byrd one metal ewer called a hanging laver, one chest and two pairs of sheets. Item to John Harlock, my apprentice, one brass pot holding two gallons and one brass bowl holding two gallons. Item I bequeath to Master John Trentham, Doctor and perpetual vicar of the church of All Saints above mentioned 2s. Item I bequeath to the college of the said church a covering of plain linen cloth. Item I bequeath to Dom William Melton, chaplain, 20s. The residue of all my goods not bequeathed above I give and bequeath to the said Thomas Hancock to then dispose at his discretion with the supervision of Thomas Hunt (this was erased in the testament) of Northampton, draper, and none other, as seems best to them for the health of my soul, the soul of the aforesaid John Hancock, my late husband, and the souls of all our friends and of all faithful departed. And that this my testament be well and faithfully executed I ordain, make and constitute the aforesaid Thomas Hancock my executor and the aforesaid Thomas Hunt supervisor. And I will that the aforesaid Thomas Hancock have for his labour in executing this my testament in the manner previously noted 40s. And that the said Thomas Hunt should have for his labour in supervising the aforesaid execution 20s by these presents. In addition to which I bequeath for the support of the chapel of the Blessed Virgin Mary in the said church of All Saints 3s 4d.

f28r 56 AGNES CHAMBRE 31st October 1480 widow

In Dei nomine Amen ultimo Octobris anno domini mccccclxxx Ego Agnes nuper uxor Thome Chambre quondam uxor Willelmi Nuncourte in pura viduatate mea compos mentis

et sane memorie condo testamentum meum in hunc modum In primis lego animam meam Deo Omnipotenti Beate Marie sue genitrici ac omnibus sanctis corpusque meum sepiliendum in cimiterio ecclesie Omnium Sanctorum Northampton Item lego capelle Beate Marie Virginis in eadem
ecclesia unam torchiam Item lego hospitali Sancti Johannis Baptiste ville Northampton predicte unam torchiam
Item lego ecclesie Sancti Egidii eiusdem ville unam torchiam Item lego Willelmo Austyn et Johanne uxori eius gardinum meum situatum iuxta lee Dernyate infra parochiam Sancti Egidii ville Northampton inter gardinum et clausum Willelmi Catesby armigeri ex parte occidentali ac gardinum
dicte hospitali ex parte australi necnon gardinum quondam Thome Tressham militis ex parte boriali
habendum et tenendum totum predictum gardinum meum cum omnibus suis pertinenciis ut predictum est prefato
Willelmo Austyn et Johanne uxori eius ad terminum vite eorum et utriusque eorum diucius viventis
de capitalibus dominis feodi illius per servicia inde debita et de iure consueta ita quod inmediate post ultimum eorumdem Willelmi Austyn et Johanne uxori sue dictum gardinum meum cum omnibus suis
pertinenciis integre remaneatt Johanni Wellys senior ville predicte mercer et Matilde uxori eius heredibus et assignatis suis imperpetuum de capitalibus dominis feodi illius per servicio inde debita
et de iure consueta
sub ista condicione quod prefatus Johannes et Matilda distribuent inmediate post meum decessum
xiijs.iiijd. pro salute anime mee et animarum omnium amicorum et benefactorum meorum necnon
omnium fidelium defunctorum Item do et lego domui elemosinario Sancti Thome Martiris extra portam
australem ville predicte pro sustentacione et relevio pauperum ibidem existencium librum <redditum> meum
ijs. quem habeo de toto illo tenemento cum suis pertinenciis quondam Willelmi Russhden nuper in [tenura]

f28v

Roberti Stele baker situatum in Abyndon Strete inter tenementum Alicie Waren vidua nuper in tenura Willelmi Wrygth corvyser ex parte orientali et tenementum Abbatis Sancti Jacobi quondam
Johannes Gobyon corvysur ex parte occidentali habendum et tenendum totum predictum librum
redditum ijs. de et in predicto tenemento quondam Willelmi Russhden cum suis pertinenciis et
in quolibet <inde> parcella annuatum percipienda in eadem forma prout ego prefata Agnes percipere et recipere
consueta sum pro sustentacione pauperum ibidem existencium quamdiu alii pauperes ibidem inhabitantes
sustentanti ac relivati existentes in casu quo nulli pauperes et egeni in domo elemosinario in forma antedicta residentes et inhabitantes non fuerint volo tunc quod predictus reditus ijs.
integre remaneat capella Beate Marie Virginis in dicta ecclesia Omnium Sanctorum imperpetuum tenendum
de capitalibus dominis ffeodi illius per servicia inde debita et de iure consueta sub hac condicione videlicet ut capella et ministri euisdem capelle pro tempore existentes orabunt cotidie annuatim pro salute anime mee et animarum predicti Willelmi Nuncourt amicorum meorum

et omnium fidelium defunctorum secundum illum morem et consuetudinem prout pro aliis fratribus
et sororibus ac benefactoribus dicte capelle orare et precare tenentur imperpetuum Item lego cuilibet domui fratrium mendicancium dicte ville xijd. Residuum vero omnium bonorum meorum superius non legatorum do et lego predicto Willelmo Austyn ad inde disponendum pro salute anime mee animarum predicti Willelmi Nuncourte et omnium fidelium defunctorum pro ut ei
melius videbitur expediri et ad istud testamentum bene et fideliter exequendum predictum Willelmum
Austyn ordino facio et constituo executorem meum per presentes hiis testibus Roberto Waren capellano Johanne Wellys seniore Thoma Malpase et aliis

In the name of God Amen the last day of October 1480 I Agnes Chambre, late wife of Thomas Chamber, once the wife of William Nuncourt, in chaste widowhood, in sound mind and good memory make my testament in this wise. First I bequeath my soul to Almighty God, to the Blessed Mary His mother and all the saints, my body to be buried in the cemetery of the church of All Saints Northampton. Item I bequeath to the chapel of the Blessed Virgin Mary in the same church one torch. Item I bequeath to the Hospital of St John the Baptist in the town of Northampton aforesaid one torch. Item I bequeath to the church of St Giles in the same town one torch. Item I bequeath to William Austyn and Joan, his wife, my garden situated next to the Derngate in the parish of St Giles between the garden and close of William Catesby esquire on the west side and the garden of the said hospital on the south side and also the garden once belonging to Sir Thomas Tresham on the north side, to have and to hold all my aforesaid garden with all its appurtenances in order that the aforesaid and proclaimed William Austyn and Joan, his wife, may have and hold for the term of both their lives and whichever of them lives the longest of the chief lords of the fee by services therefore due and by right accustomed and that immediately after the death of William Austyn and Joan, his wife, my garden aforesaid with all its appurtenances shall remain entirely to John Wellys senior of the said town, mercer, and Matilda, his wife, their heirs and assigns forever to hold of the chief lords of the fee by services therefore due and by right accustomed, on this condition that the said John and Matilda shall distribute immediately after my death 13s 4d for the health of my soul and the souls of all my friends and benefactors and also all faithful departed. Item I bequeath to the masters of the almshouse of St Thomas the Martyr outside the south gate of the said town for the sustenance and relief of the poor living there, that freehold rent of 2s which I have from all that tenement with its appurtenances, formerly in the possession of William Rushden and now held by Robert Stele, baker, situated in Abingdon Street, between the tenement of Alice Waren, widow, formerly in the tenure of William Wrigth, corvisor, on the east side and the tenement of the Abbey of St James formerly held by John Gobion, corvisor, on the west side, to have and to hold the whole aforesaid freehold rent of 2s from and in the aforesaid tenement, formerly held by William Russhden, with its appurtenances, and in whatsoever parcel received annually in the same form which I, the aforesaid Agnes, am accustomed to draw and receive it, for the sustenance of the poor people living there as long as any poor people are living there being sustained and relieved. In the case that no poor or indigent people shall be residing in or inhabiting the almshouse then I will that the said yield of 2s shall remain wholly to the chapel of the Blessed Virgin Mary in the said church of All Saints forever to hold of the chief lords of the fee by services therefore due and by right accustomed, under this condition, that is to say that the chaplains and ministers of the same chapel at that time shall pray daily for a year for my soul and the souls of the said William Nuncourt, my friends and all faithful departed, according to the manner and custom they hold, and to pray and praise for other brothers and sisters and benefactors of the said chapel for ever. Item I bequeath to every house of mendicant friars in the said town 12d. The residue of all my goods not bequeathed above I give and bequeath to the said William Austyn to then dispose for the health of my soul and the souls of the said William Nuncourt and all faithful departed as seems best to him and that this testament be well and faithfully executed I ordain, make and constitute the aforesaid William Austyn my executor by these presents. With these witnesses Robert Waren, chaplain, John Wellys senior, Thomas Malpase and others.

f28v 57 JOHN STANBRYGE senior 7th April 1481 baker

In Dei nomine Amen vij die Aprilis anno domini mccccclxxxj Ego Johannes Stanbryge senior
de Northampton baker compos mentis et sane memorie condo testamentum meum in hunc modum
In primis lego animam meam Deo Omnipotenti Beate Marie sue genitrici ac omnibus sanctis corpus-
que meum sepiliendum in cimiterio ecclesie Omnium Sanctorum ville Northampton predicte Item lego summo
altari dicte ecclesie pro decimis meis non bene decimatis et oblationibus oblitis xxd. Item lego
fabrice dicte ecclesie xijd. Item lego fraternitati Beate Marie Virginis in dicta ecclesia vjs.viijd.
Item lego fraternitati Sancte Cithe ibidem xijd. Item lego fraternitati Sancte Trinitatis in eadem ecclesia
iijs.iiijd. Item lego fraternitati Sancti Georgii Martiris ibidem xijd. Item lego fraternitati Sancte Crucis
ibidem xijd. Item lego fraternitati Sancte Katerine in novo cimiterio xijd. Item lego fraternitati Sancti
Clementis in ecclesia Sancti Egidii ville Northampton viijd. Item lego fraternitati Sancte Crucis in Muro
in ecclesia Sancti Gregorii in eadem villa xijd. Item lego domui elemosinario Sancti Thome
Martiris extra portam australem pro sustentacione pauperum ibidem existencium xld. Item lego
lego fraternitati Sancti Michaelis viijd. Item lego Johanni Stanbryge filio meo x marcas Item
lego Isabelle Byngham filie mee x marcas Residuum vero omnium bonorum meorum superius
non legatorum do et lego Johanne uxori mee ad inde disponendum pro salute anime mee

animarum parentorum et amicorum meorum ac omnium fidelium defunctorum prout ei melius videbitur expediri et ad istud testamentum bene et fideliter exequendum prefatam Johannam uxorem meam
ordino facio et constituo executricem ac dominum Willelmum Melton capellanum eiusdem testamenti mei supervisorem
Et volo quod habeat pro labore suo in supervidendo premisse vjs.viijd. per presentes hiis testibus Willelmo Austyn Willelmo Flowre Willelmo Dyssy et aliis

In the name of God Amen the 7th day of April 1481 I John Stanbryge senior of Northampton, baker in sound mind and good memory make my testament in this wise. First I bequeath my soul to Almighty God to the Blessed Mary His mother, and to all the saints, my body to be buried in the cemetery of All Saints, Northampton. Item I bequeath to the high altar of the said church for tithes not well tithed and oblations forgotten 20d. Item I bequeath for the fabric of the same church 12d. Item I bequeath to the fraternity of the Blessed Virgin Mary in the said church 6s 8d. Item I bequeath to the fraternity of the Holy Trinity in the same church 3s 4d. Item I bequeath to the fraternity of St George the Martyr there 12d. Item I bequeath to the fraternity of St Katherine in the new cemetery 12d. Item I bequeath to the fraternity of St Clement in the church of St Giles, Northampton 8d. Item I bequeath to the fraternity of the Holy Cross in the Wall in the church of St Gregory, Northampton 12d. Item I bequeath to the almshouse of St Thomas the Martyr outside the south gate for the sustenance of the poor living there 40d. Item I bequeath to the fraternity of St Michael 8d. Item I bequeath to John Stanbryge, my son, 10 marks. Item I bequeath to Isabel Byngham, my daughter, 10 marks. The residue of all my goods not bequeathed above I give and bequeath to Joan, my wife, to then dispose for the health of my soul, the souls of my parents and the souls of my friends and all faithful departed as seems best to her and that this testament be well and faithfully executed I ordain, make and constitute Joan, my wife, executrix and Dom William Melton, chaplain as supervisor of this my said testament and I will that he shall have for his labour in supervising these premises 6s 8d by these presents. With these witnesses William Austyn, William Flowre, William Dyssy and others.

f29r 58 AGNES CLERKE 2nd May 1481 widow

In Dei nomine Amen ij die Maii anno domini millesimo cccclxxxj Ego Agnes Clerke de Northampton vidua compos mentis et sane memorie condo testamentum meum in hunc modum In primis
lego animam meam Deo Omnipotenti et Beate Marie Virginie sue genitrici ac omnibus sanctis curii
celestis corpusque meum sepiliendum in cimiterio ecclesie Omnium Sanctorum ville Northampton predicte iuxta tumulum
Thome Clerke mercer nuper viri mei et puerorum meorum defunctorum Item lego summo altari ecclesie predicte pro decimis meis oblitis et non bene decimatis vjs viijd. Item lego fabrice

dicte ecclesie iijs iiijd. Item lego fraternitati Beate Marie Virginis in ecclesia predicta xxd. Item lego fraternitati Corporis Christi in eadem ecclesia xxd. Item lego fraternitati Sancte Trinitatis ibidem xxd
Item lego fraternitati Sancti Johannis Baptiste in eadem ecclesia xxd. (Item fraternitati) Item lego fraternitati Sancte Crucis
in ecclesia predicta xijd. Item lego fraternitati Sancti Georgij ibidem xijd. Item lego fraternitati Sancte Cithe ibidem xijd
Item lego cuilibet domui fratrum mendicancium in dicta villa Northampton xxd. Item lego fraternitati Sancte Katerine
in nova capella iuxta collegium ecclesie predicte xxd. Item lego fraternitati Sancti Thome Martiris extra portam
australem ville Northampton predicte xxd. Item lego sustentacioni le condite xs. Item lego Elizabeth
uxori Thome Wyseman fratris mei unam plitam de lande de optima elecione Item lego Cicilie Rutter
sorori mee tunicam meam vocatam (vocatam) a curtyll coloris sanguenii yngreyn et unam plitam de launde de optima elecione Item lego Emmote filie dicte Thome Wyseman fratris mei zonam meam secundam de serice coloris blodij cum argento harnesiato Item Ricardo Wyseman filio eiusdem Thome fratris mei unam parvam peciam de argento Item lego cuilibet aliorum puerorum dicte Thome Wyseman unum cocliar de argento. Item lego Willelmo Russell filio dicte Cicilie Rutter sororis mee vjs viijd. Item lego Agneti filie predicte sororis mee sorori dicti Willelmi Russell vjs viijd. Item lego Johanne Benett alii sorori mee togam meam coloris
le blakaleyr penulatam cum le blakboge Item lego cuilibet puerorum dicte Johanne xxd. Item lego
Willelmo filio Ricardi Floure et Agnetis uxoris eius nuper filie mee defuncte in valore bonorum meorum quinque marcas Item lego sorori dicte Willelmi filie dictorum Ricardi et Agnetis filie mee
de bonis meis predictis quinque marcas summa dicte duarum partium in valore de bonis meis supra legatis x marcas quamquidam summam x marcarum in valore bonorum meorum executores
mei inferius nominati prefatis Willelmo et Agneti sorori sue in forma sequente deliberabunt videlicet volo quod predictus Willelmus habeat partam suam dicte summe x marcas et gaudebit eadem imperpetuum
in valore bonorum meorum superius sibi legatorum quandoncumque idem Willelmus sit in plena etate
annorum discrecionis et modo simili volo quod dicta Agnes soror eiusdem Willelmi habeat partem
suam eiusdem summe x marcaram in valore bonorum meorum sibi supra legatorum si sit in plena
etate annorum discrecionis et si contingat dictum Willelmum obire antequam sit de plena etate annorum discrecionis dicte Agnete sorore sue vivente et de plena etate annorum discrecionis volo tunc quod predicti executores mei solvent et liberabunt eidem Agneti sorori eiusdem Willelmi
partem dicti Willelmi superius sibi legatam habendum et gaudendum eidem Agneti una cum parte
sua propria eidem Agneti superius legate imperpetuum et econtra si contingat predictam Agnetem
sororem dicti Willelmi obire predicto Willelmo vivente et de plena etate
annorum discrecionis tunc volo quod predicti executores <mei> predictem partem eiusdem Agnetis sibi in forma predicte legate
prefato Willelmo deliberabunt habendum et gaudendum eidem Willelmo una cum parte sua propria sibi superius
in forma preliberate legate imperpetuum et si contingat tam predictum Willelmum quam dictam Agnetam sororem

suam obire ante quam fuit de plena etate annorum discrecionis volo tunc quod dicti executores mei dictam summam x marcarum in valore bonorum meorum secundum eorum discreciones distribuant

f29v

et disponant in donis caritatis et aliis elemosinis ad maximum commodium et proficium pro salute anime mee animorum predictorum Willelmi et Agnetis sororis sue et omnium fidelium defunctorum
Item lego Henrico Wyseman filio Johannis Wyseman fratris mei vjs viijd. Item lego Alicie filie eiusdem Johannis fratris mei vjs viijd. Item lego Johanni Barnell fratri predicti Thome Clerke nuper viri mei j materas j par lodicum j par linthiamentum et unum cooperterium rubij coloris Item lego cuilibet filiolorum meorum et filialarum mearum de bonis meis ad valorem xijd deliberandum per discreciones executorum meorum. Item lego collegio ecclesie Omnium Sanctorum unam mappam lineam de playn cloth Item lego Margarete Stanton
unam materas viij ulnas pannii linii pro uno par linthiamentum inde fiendum precii cuiuslibet ulni vijd unum par lodicum j coopertorium j ollam eneam et unam patellam eneam Item lego cuilibet servienti mee unam materas Item volo quod unus capellanus ydoneus conduattur
per executores meos predictos per spacium unius anni integri proximo sequente decessum meum
ad celebrandum in dicta ecclesia Omnium Sanctorum pro salute anime mee et animarum predicte Thome Clerk
nuper viri mei et omnium puerorum nostrorum defunctorum necnon omnium fidelium defunctorum et
lego in pecuniis muneratis pro salario et stipendio dicti capellani Cs si bona mea premissis plenie perimpletis extendere poterint Residuum vero omnium bonorum meorum superius non legatorum do et lego domino Roberto Waryn capellano et predicto Thome Wyseman fratri meo
ad inde disponendum pro salute anime mee et animarum predicti Thome Clerke nuper viri mei et puerorum nostrorum defunctorum prout eis melius videbitur expediri et ad istud testamentum bene et fideliter exequendum prefatum dominum Robertum Waryn et Thomam Wyseman fratrum
meum ordino facio et constituo executores meos per presentes hiis testibus Johanni Johanne Barnell Cicilie Rutter et aliis

In the name of God Amen the 2nd day of May 1481 I Agnes Clerke of Northampton, widow, in sound mind and good memory make my testament in this wise. First I bequeath my soul to Almighty God and the Blessed Virgin Mary His mother and all the saints of the court of heaven, my body to be buried in the cemetery of the church of All Saints of the aforesaid town of Northampton next to the graves of Thomas Clerke, mercer, my late husband, and my deceased children. Item I bequeath to the high altar of the said church for my tithes forgotten 6s 8d. Item I bequeath to the fabric of the said church 3s 4d. Item I bequeath to the fraternity of the Blessed Virgin Mary in the aforesaid church 20d. Item I bequeath to the fraternity of Corpus Christi in the same church 20d. Item I bequeath to the fraternity of Holy Trinity there 20d. Item I bequeath to the fraternity of St. John the Baptist in the same church 20d. Item I bequeath to the fraternity of the Holy Cross in the aforesaid church 12d. Item I bequeath to the fraternity of St. George there 12d. Item I bequeath to the fraternity of St. Cithe there 12d. Item I bequeath to each of the houses of mendicant friars in the said town of Northampton 20d. Item I bequeath to the fraternity of Saint Katherine in the new chapel next to the college in the aforesaid church 20d. Item I bequeath to the fraternity of St. Thomas the Martyr outside the south gate of the aforesaid town of Northampton 20d. Item I bequeath to the maintenance of the conduit 10s. Item I bequeath to Elizabeth, wife of Thomas Wyseman my brother, one fold of lawn of the best quality. Item I bequeath to Cicely Rutter, my sister, my tunic called a curtyll dyed ingreyn sanguine colour and a fold of lawn of the best quality. Item I bequeath to Emmotte, daughter of the aforesaid Thomas Wyseman, my brother, my second silk girdle of blue colour ornamented with silver. Item I bequeath to Richard Wyseman, son of the said Thomas Wyseman, my brother, one small piece of silver. Item I bequeath to each of the children of the said Thomas Wyseman one silver spoon. Item I bequeath to William Russell, son of the aforesaid Cicely Rutter, my sister, 6s 8d. Item I bequeath to Agnes, daughter of my said sister and sister of the said William Russell, 6s 8d. Item I bequeath to Joan Bennett, my other sister, my gown of the colour of blakaleyr furred with blakboge. Item I bequeath to each of the children of the said Joan 20d. Item I bequeath to William, son of Richard Floure and Agnes his wife, formerly my daughter now deceased, my goods to the value of 5 marks. Item I bequeath to the sister of the said William, son of the said Richard and Agnes my daughter, of my goods to the value of said five marks. The sum of the said two parts of my goods above bequeathed being 10 marks, which said sum of 10 marks in goods my executors below named shall deliver to the aforesaid William and Agnes his sister in the following manner. That is to say that the aforesaid William should have his share of the said 10 marks in value of my goods and enjoy the same above legacy forever when the same William comes to the age of discretion and in a similar way I will that the said Agnes, sister of the same William, have her part of the said sum of 10 marks in value of my goods above bequeathed when she comes to the age of discretion. And if it should happen that the said William should die before he comes to the age of discretion with the said Agnes, his sister, living and of the age of discretion, then I will that my aforesaid executors shall release and free to the said Agnes, sister of the said William, that part that the said William was above bequeathed to hold and to enjoy forever to the said Agnes, together with her share that the said Agnes was above bequeathed and similarly if it should happen that the aforesaid Agnes, sister of the said William, should die with the said William living and of the age of discretion then I will that my aforesaid executores shall deliver the aforesaid share that the said Agnes was left in form aforesaid to the aforesaid William to have and enjoy forever. And if it should happen that both the aforesaid William and the aforesaid Agnes his sister should die before coming to the age of discretion then I will that my aforesaid executors should distribute and dispose the said sum of 10 marks in value of my goods in charitable gifts and alms at their discretion and maximum advantage and profit for the health of my soul, the souls of the aforesaid William and Agnes his sister, and of all faithful departed. Item I bequeath to Henry Wyseman, son of John my brother, 6s 8d. Item I bequeath to Alice, daughter of the same John my brother, 6s 8d. Item I bequeath to John Barnell, brother of the aforementioned Thomas Clarke my late husband, 1 mattress, 1 pair of blankets, 1 pair of linen sheets and 1 red coverlet. Item I bequeath to each of my godsons and goddaughters 12d from the value of my goods to be handed over at the discretion of my executors. Item I bequeath to the college of the church of All Saints 1 linen cloth of plain material. Item I bequeath to Margaret Stanton 1 mattress, 8 ells of linen cloth to make a pair of sheets, the price of each ell to be 7d, 1 pair of blankets, 1 coverlet, 1 brass pot and 1 brass bowl. Item I bequeath to each of my servants one mattress. Item I will that a suitable chaplain be chosen by my named executors for some years after my death to celebrate in the said church of All Saints for the health of my soul and the souls of the aforesaid Thomas Clerke, my late husband, and all our deceased children and also all faithful departed and I bequeth in cash for the salary and stipend of the said chaplain 100s if my goods mentioned before will extend to carrying this out. The residue of all my goods not bequeathed above I give and bequeath to Dom Robert Waryn, chaplain, and Thomas Wyseman, my brother and to then dispose from thence for the health of my soul and the souls of the aforesaid Thomas Clerke, my late husband, and our deceased children as seems best to them and that this testament be well and faithfully executed I ordain, make and constitute the aforesaid Dom Robert Waryn and Thomas Wyseman my executors by these presents. With these witnesses John Barnell, Cicely Rutter and others.

f29v 59 JOHN ASPLOND 1st December 1472

In Dei nomine Amen Primo die mensis Decembris anno domini mlcccclxxij Ego Johannes Asplond
de Northampton compos mentis condo testamentum in hunc modum In primis lego animam Deo
Omnipotenti etcetera corpusque sepiliendum in cimiterio ecclesie Sancti Michaelis ville Northampton
Item lego fabrice eiusdem ecclesie vjd. Item volo quod Thomas Clarell de Lyllyngston Lovell gentilman Robertus Ryselley de eadem gentilman Thomas Carter de Northampton baker et Johannes Essex de eadem senior chandeler ffeoffati mei predicti Johannis Asplond et Margarete uxori mee omnium terrarum et tenementum meorum cum eorum pertinenciis in ville Northampton videlicet unius capitale
mesuagium cum gardino adiacente et unius cotagium situatum iuxta dictum mesuagium exparte
australi cum omnibus eorum pertinenciis invicem adiacentibis in le Neweland ville Northampton
inter croftum quondam Georgii Longvyle senioris armigeri ex parte boriali et tenementum Sancti Johannis Baptiste modo in tenura Johannis Asplond filii mei ex parte australi et dictum

capitale mesuagium extendit se a via regia ex parte occidentali usque clausum fratrum ordinis Carmeletarum ex parte orientali faciant seu fieri faciant prefato Willelmo Asplond filio meo et Juliane uxori sue bonum et securum statum in lege de et in predicto mesuagio gardino et cotagio cum omnibus eorum pertinenciis <habendum> et tenendum predictum capitale
mesuagium gardenum
cum cotagio predicto et eorum pertinenciis ut predictum est prefato Willelmo Asplond et Juliane uxori sue ac heredibus de corporibus eorum inter eos procreatis imperpetuum de capitalibus dominis feodi
illius per servicia inde debita et consueta et si contingat prefatum Willelmum Asplond obire sine herede de corpore sue legitime procreato Tunc volo quod dicti Feoffati mei et

f30r

eorum heredes et executores predicti Willelmi Asplond vendent predictum capitale mesuagium gardinum et
cotagium cum eorum pertinenciis et pecunie inde provenientur per prefatos ffeoffatos heredes eorum
ac executores predicti Willelmi Asplond per eorum discreciones distribuantur in missis elemosiniis
ac aliis donis caritativiis videlicet pro salute animarum Roberti Gylford Johannis Asplond et Margarete
uxoris sue Willelmi Asplond et Juliane uxoris sue et omnium fidelium defunctorum per presentes
Residuum vero omnium bonorum meorum superius non legatorum do et lego predicto Willelmo filio
meo et eundem Willelmum ordino facio et constituo executorem meum ut ipse disponat pro salute anime mee prout ei melius videbitur expediri Date die et anno supradictis hiis testibus Johanne Essex seniore Johanne Sutton baker Johanne Eydon et aliis

In the name of God Amen the first day of December 1472 I John Asplond in sound mind make my testament in this wise. First I bequeath my soul to Almighty God etcetera my body to be buried in the cemetery of the church of St. Michael in the town of Northampton. Item I bequeath for the fabric of that church 6d. I will that Thomas Clarell of Lillingstone Lovell, gentleman, Robert Ryselley of the same place, gentleman, Thomas Carter of Northampton, baker, and John Essex senior of the same place, chandler, feoffees of me the aforesaid John Asplond and Margaret my wife for all my lands and tenements with their appurtenances in the town of Northampton that is to say one capital messuage with adjacent garden and a cottage situated next to the said messuage on the south side with all their appurtenances in the Neweland in the town of Northampton between the croft once belonging to George Longvyle senior, esquire, on the north side and the tenement of St. John the Baptist, in the tenure of John Asplond, my son, on the south side and the said capital messuage extending from the king's road on the west side and as far as the close of the Carmelite brothers on the east side. They should make or cause to be made to the aforesaid William Asplond and Juliana, his wife, a good and secure title in law in the said messuage, garden and cottage with all their appurtenances, to have and to hold the aforesaid capital messuage, garden with cottage aforesaid and their appurtenances as aforesaid to

William and Juliana, his wife, and the heirs of their bodies between them begotten forever of the chief lords of the fee by services therefore due and accustomed. And if it should happen that the the aforesaid William should die without heirs of his body legitimately begotten then I will that my said feoffees and their heirs and the executors of the aforesaid William Asplond should sell the aforesaid capital messuage, garden and cottage with their appurtenances and with the money therefore coming should be distributed by the aforesaid feoffees, their heirs and executors of the aforesaid William Asplond in masses, alms and other charitable gifts by their discretion for the health of the souls of Robert Gylford, John Asplond and Margaret his wife, William and Juliana Asplond and all faithful departed. The residue of all my goods not bequeathed above I give and bequeath to the aforesaid William, my son, and the same William I ordain, make and constitute my executor and he to dispose for the health of my soul as seems best to him. Given the day and year abovesaid. With these witnesses John Essex senior, John Sutton, baker, John Eydon and others.

f30v 62 THOMAS MERTON July 1481 [fuller]

In Dei nomine Amen dominica proxime ante festum Sancti Jacobi Apostoli anno domini mlccccIxxxj regni vero
regis Edwardi quarti xxj. Ego Thomas Merton de Northampton compos mentis sane memorie et in sanitate corporis condo testamentum meum in hunc modum In primis lego animam meam Deo Omnipotenti per intercessionem Beate Marie Virginis Beati Nicholi Episcopi ac omnium sanctorum Dei corpusque meum ad sepiliendum infra capellam Beate Katerine Virginis in ecclesie parochiali Sancti Gregorii ibidem Item lego summo altari dicte ecclesie pro decimis meis oblitis vjs viijd. Item lego prepositis eiusdem ecclesie pro sepultura mea ibidem vjs viijd. Item lego octo presbytris exequiis meis interessentibus ijs viijd
inter eos equaliter dividendum Item lego iiij clericis simili modo interessentibus cuilibet eorum ijd. Item lego fodenti puteum meum vjd. Item lego pulsantibus campanas in dicta ecclesia ad exequias meas xijd. Item lego per vastacione
torchiarum circa premissa xld. Item lego fratribus et sororibus fraternitatis
Sancte Crucis in Pariete in dicta ecclesia Sancte Gregorij unum annualem redditum
sex solidorum et octo denariorum percipiendum annuatim de et in tenemento cum pertinenciis et tentura ffullonium in eadem iacentem in parochia eiusdem ecclesie nuper in
tenura Johannis Pykeryng de London modo in tenura Nicholi Bowker
ffuller habendum et percipiendum predictum annualem redditum eidem fraternitati et successoribus ad terminos ibidem usuales annualem post decessum meum dicti Thome Merton durante termino xxti annorum completorum <ad> exerandum pro anima mea Item do et lego fratribus et sororibus fraternitatis Beate Marie Virginis in ecclesia Omnium Sanctorum ville Northampton unum annualem redditum decem solidarum et quattuor denariorum percipiendum annuatim
ad terminos ibidem usuales de et in tenemento cum pertinenciis in vico pontis eiusdem ville nuper in tenura Thome Hancok habendum et percipiendum dictum annualem redditum xs et iiijd. dicte fraternitati Beate Marie et successoribus suis durante termino xx
annorum inmediate post decessum mei Thome Merton predicti ad terminos ibidem usuales

f31r

ad exorandum pro anima mea amicorum meorum et omnium fidelium defunctorum. Item do et lego fratribus pauperibus

ordinis Augustiniencis eiusdem ville vjs.viijd. Residuum vero omnium bonorum antea non legatorum
do et lego Alicie uxori mee et eandem Aliciam ordino facio et constituo solam executricem meam ad ea
disponendum et ministrandum pro salute anime et amicorum meorum parentium meorum et omnium fidelium defunctorum
in missis elemosinis et operibus caritatis prout ei melius videbitur expediri Deo placenti

In the name of God Amen the Sunday next before the Feast of St. James 1481 in the 21st regnal year of Edward IV I Thomas Merton of Northampton in sound mind, good memory and healthy body make my testament in this wise. First I leave my soul to Almighty God by the intercession of the Blessed Virgin Mary, the Blessed Bishop Nicholas and all the saints of God, my body to be buried inside the chapel of the Blessed Katherine the Virgin in the parish church of St. Gregory. Item I bequeath to the high altar of the said church for my tithes forgotten 6s 8d. Item I bequeath to the Churchwardens of the same church for my burial there 6s 8d. Item I bequeath to the eight priests saying prayers at my exequies 6s 8d to be shared equally between them. Item I bequeath to the 4 clerks praying in the same way to each 2d. Item for digging my grave 6d. Item for ringing the bells in the same church at my exequies 12d. Item I bequeath for burning surrounding torches 40d. Item I bequeath to the brothers and sisters of the fraternity of the Holy Cross in the Wall in the said church an annual rent of six shillings and eight pence every year for twenty years of and in the tenements with appurtenances, tenter yard and fulling house in the same, lying in the parish of the said church, formerly held in the tenure of John Pykeryng of London, mercer, now in the tenure of Nicholas Bowker, fuller, to have and receive the aforesaid annual rent to the same fraternity and its successors at the usual annual fixed dates after my death, the aforesaid Thomas Merton, for the complete term of 20 years to pray for my soul. Item I bequeath to the brothers and sisters of the fraternity of the Blessed Virgin Mary in the church of All Saints in Northampton an annual rent of ten shillings and four pence every year to receive annually at the usual fixed dates of and in a tenement with appurtenances in Bridge Street in the said town, formerly in the tenure of Thomas Hancock, to have and receive the said annual rent of 10s 4d annually immediately after my death, the said Thomas Merton, at the usual fixed dates to pray for my soul, my friends and all faithful departed. Item I bequeath to the poor brothers of St. Augustine of the same town 6s 8d. The residue of all my goods not bequeathed above I give and bequeath to Agnes, my wife, and the same Agnes I ordain, make and constitute my sole executrix and she to dispose and administer for the health of [my] soul and my friends, my parents and all faithful departed in charitable masses and works of charity as my seem best to her and pleasing to God.

f32v 68 WILLIAM GOLDWYRE 1482 fishmonger

In Dei nomine Amen in vigilia Sancti Thome Apostoli anno domini millesimo cccclxxxij Ego Willelmus Goldwyre
de Northampton ffyshmonger compos etcetera condo testamentum in hunc modum In primis lego
animam mee (sic) Omni potenti etcetera Beate Marie etcetera corpusque meum sepiliendum in cimiterio ecclesie
Omnium Sanctorum ville Northampton predicte Item lego summo altari eiusdem ecclesie pro decimis oblitis
etcetera xijd. Item lego fabrice eiusdem ecclesie iijs.iiijd. Item domui elemosinario Sancte Thome Martiris extra portam australem ad sustentacionem pauperum ibidem xxs. solvendum in forma subscripta videlicet quolibet anno trium annorum proxima sequencium vjs viijd etcetera Item
do et lego Johanne uxori mee scamellas meas existentes in foro piscatorum
habendum et tenendum totas predictas scamellas cum suis pertinenciis ut predictum est prefate Johanne
uxori mee heredibus et assignatis suis imperpetuum de capitalibus dominis feodi illius per servicia inde
debita et de iure consueta Item do et lego Johanni Goldewyre filio meo totum statum meum et terminum quos habeo in illo tenemento in quo modo maneo habendum et tenendum totum
predictum terminum et statum meos de et in predicto tenemento cum suis pertinenciis prefato Johanni
filio meo heredibus executoribus et assignatis suis secundum vim et formam indenturarum inde factarum
reddendo inde annuatim et faciendo omnia illa onera que predictus Willelmus Goldwyre virtute
earundem indenturarum reddere et facere debee et volo quod predicta Johanna uxor mea habeat infra tenementum meum predictum quandem mansionem pro se ipsa cum libere ingressu et egressu
si sit vidua et non nupta ibidem moraturur et si predicta Johanna uxor non ultra expertitur(?) infra dictum tenementum mansionem sibi assignatis volo tunc quod predictus Johannes filius meus
heredes et executores et assignati sui reddent et solvent eidem Johanne uxori mee vel suis assignatis annuatim ad quatuor anni terminos usuales equis porcionibus viijs bone monete Anglie pro redditu alicuius alterius domus mansionis ad libitum dicte Johanne uxoris mee habendum durante tota vita dicte Johanne uxoris mee Residuum
vero omnium bonorum meorum superius non legatorum do et lego prefatis Johanne uxori mee et Johanni filio meo ad inde disponendum pro salute anime mee et animarum amicorum ac omnium
fidelium defunctorum prout eis melius videbitur expediri et ad istud testamentum meum bene et fideliter exequendum predictos Johannam uxorem meam et Johannem filium meum
ordino facio et constituo executores meos per presentes

In the name of God Amen on the eve of St. Thomas the Apostle 1482 I William Goldwyre of Northampton, fishmonger, in possession of etcetera make my testament in this wise. First I bequeath my soul to the Almighty etcetera to the Blessed Mary etcetera my body to be buried in the cemetery of the church of All Saints in the town of Northampton aforesaid. Item I bequeath to the high altar of the same church for tithes forgotten etcetera 12d. Item I bequeath to the fabric of the same church 3s 4d. Item to the almshouse of St Thomas the Martyr outside the south gate to the sustenance of the poor there 20s to be paid in the form below, that is to say for each year in the following three years 6s 8d. Item I give and bequeath to Joan my wife my stalls that are in the fishmarket to have and to hold all the aforesaid stalls with their appurtenances as aforesaid to Joan, my wife, her heirs and assigns forever of the chief lord of the fee for services therefore due and by right accustomed. Item I give and bequeath to John Goldwyre, my son, my whole estate and terms that I have in which I have in that tenement in which I now dwell to have and to hold all my aforesaid terms and estate of and in the aforesaid tenement with its appurtenances to the aforesaid John, my son, his heirs, executors and assigns according to the force and form of indentures made giving thence annually and doing all those charges which the aforesaid William Goldwyre should pay or do and I will that the aforesaid Joan, my wife, shall have for herself free entry and exit in my tenement that aforesaid mansion if she remain a widow and virtuous there. And if the aforesaid Joan [my] wife, does not wish to live in the house assigned to her then I wish that the aforesaid John, my son, his heirs and executors and assigns shall give to the said Joan or her assigns a yearly sum of 8s of good English money at the usual four terms in equal proportions for her to rent such other house or home of her choice during her lifetime. The residue of all my goods not above bequeathed above I give and bequeath to the aforesaid Joan, my wife, and John, my son, to then dispose for the health of my soul and my friends and all faithful departed as seems best to them and that this my testament be well and faithfully executed I ordain, make and constitute the aforesaid Joan, my wife, and John, my son, my executors by these presents.

f36r 74 JOHN LEYCESTR' alias Atylburgh 6th April 1490 mercer & apothecary

In Dei nomine Amen vj die mensis Aprilis anno domini mccccIxxxx Ego John Leycestr' alias Atylburgh de Northampton
mercer et potycary compos mentis et sane memorie infirmus tamen in corpore condo testamentum meum in
hunc modum In primis commendo animam meam Deo Beate Marie et omnibus celestis curie ordinibus corpusque
meum sepiliendum in capella Beate Marie ecclesie Omnium Sanctorum ville Northampton predicte Item lego pro sepultura
predicte capella vjs viijd. Item volo quod Amya uxor mea habeat omnes redditus exitus et proventus
omnium terrarum tenementorum redditum servicium homagium ward' relevium et reversionum ac omnia et singula predictis pertinenciis
sue concernenc' cum acciderint quousque Henricus Leycestr' filius et heres meus perveniat ad legalem etatem

et si contingat quod Deus avertat dictum Henricum filium et heredem meum obire antequam devenieat ad completam
etatem ex tunc volo quod dicta Amya uxor mea habeat omnia terras et tenementa redditus et servicia simplicia
feodi cum omnibus eorum pertinenciis in comitatu Northampton et Leic(ester) ad terminum vite sue et post decessum eius volo
quod predicta tenementa cum omnibus eorum pertinciis per executores meos vendantur et debitis meis ex integro per solutis proventus
eorundem tenementorum sic disponantur quod fiat meria pro salute anime et amicorum meorum antecessorum in quodem monaster-
io sive alibi secundum discreciones executorum meorum imperpetuum duraturis si commodo fieri poterit insuper volo quod
si contingat predictam Amyam uxorem meam maritari tali viro qui sibi scilicet uxoris mee predicte et suis benevolus
bene consencies ac bene morigeratus fuerit et simul cum hoc emere voluerit et ad hoc et sic faciendum sufficiens
repertus fuerit quod tunc omnia predicta terre et tenementa mea in feodo simplici remaneant eisdem viro et
uxori mee sub minori precie per decem marcas sterlingorum quoque alicui alteri de regno Anglie hec omnia et
singula volo perimpleri et perfici secundum discrecionem executorum meorum meliore modo quo industria eorum executorum
nolerit[sic] perimplendum Item lego Alicie Rudde servienti mee unam vaccam unam ollam unam patellam
dimidiam garnyssh de pewter vessell lectum integrum cum toto apparatu j basen et j laver Residuum vero
omnium bonorum meorum superius non legatorum etcetera
Executores magister Johannes Palady Amya uxor mea dominus Willelmus Grene rector de Pysford <et> Thomas
Edward mercer hiis testibus magistro Johanne Roberd Ricardo Grene notario publico comuni scriba et registrario domini archidiaconi
Northampton domino Roberto Waryn domino Roberto Cornwale Thome Henke et aliis

In the name of God Amen the 6th day of April 1490 I John Leycestr' alias Atylburgh, mercer and apothecary, of sound mind and good memory though weak in body make my testament in this wise. First I commend my soul to God, to the Blessed Mary and all the orders of the court of heaven, my body to be buried in the chapel of the Blessed Mary in the church of All Saints in the aforesaid town of Northampton. Item I bequeath for the burial place in the said chapel 6s 8d. Item I will that Amy, my wife, should have all revenue, profits and income of all lands, tenements, rents, services, homages, wards, levies, returns concerning and falling due and all and singular their aforesaid appurtenances until Henry Leycestr', my son and heir, should come of legal age and if it should happen that God wills that the said Henry, my son and heir, should die before he comes of age then I will that the said Amy, my wife, should have all lands and tenements, rents and services in fee simple with all their appurtenances in the counties of Northampton and Leicester to the end of her life and after her death I will that the said tenements with all appurtenances be sold by my executors and that my

debts should be paid in full from the proceeds of the same tenements and the rest of the money should be used for the health of [my] soul and of my deceased friends, in a monastery or other place, according to the discretion of my executors, forever if it can be arranged in such a way. Furthermore I will that if it should happen that the aforesaid Amy, my wife, should be married to a man who is benevolent to her and hers and is of good character, and at the same time is willing to buy and has sufficient funds to do this, I will that all my aforesaid lands and tenements should remain in fee simple to this man and to my wife at a price lesser by ten marks of sterling than anywhere else in the realm of England and I will that all of this should be arranged and completed at the discretion of my executors as best they can. Item I bequeath to Alice Rudde, my servant, one cow, one pot, one pan, half a garnish of pewter vessels, one complete bed with all its bedding, 1 basin and 1 laver. The residue of all my goods not bequeathed above etcetera.
Executors Master John Palady, Amy my wife, Dom. William Grene, rector of Pitsford, and Thomas Edward, mercer. With these witnesses - Master John Roberd, Richard Grene, public notary, town clerk and registrar to the Dom Archdeacon of Northampton, Dom Robert Waryn, Dom Robert Cornwale, Thomas Henke and others.

f36r 75 JOHN LEYNHO 7th May 1483 glover

In Dei nomine Amen septimo die mensis Maii anno domini millesimo ccccIxxxiij. Ego Johannes Leynho de Northampton glover compos
mentis et sane memorie condo testamentum meum in hunc modum In primis lego animam meam Deo Omnipotente
Beate Marie Virgini sue genitrici ac omnibus sanctis curie celestis corpusque meum sepiliendum in capella Beate
Marie Virginis in ecclesia Omnium Sanctorum ibidem Item lego summo altari dicte ecclesie pro decimis meis et oblationibus
non bene decimatis et oblitis xxd. Item lego capella Beate Marie ibidem unam torchiam Item lego ffraternitati
Sancti Johannis ibidem xxd. Item lego domui elemosinario Sancti Thome Martiris extra portam australem Northampton predicta
xijd. Item lego fabrice dicte ecclesie Omnium Sanctorum xxd. Item lego sustentacioni collegii dicte ecclesie
xxd. Item lego fraternitati Sancte Crucis in eadem ecclesia iijs.iiijd. Item lego ad le coundyte xxd.
Item lego Simoni filio meo x marcas Item lego Johanni seniori filio x marcas Item lego Thome filio
meo x marcas Item lego Johanni juniori filio meo x marcas Item lego Agneti filie mee v marcas
bone monete Anglie Residuum vero omnium bonorum meorum superius non legatorum do et lego Elizabeth
uxori mee ad inde disponendum pro salute anime mee et animarum amicorum meorum ac omnium fidelium defunctorum
prout ei melius videbitur expediri et ad istud testamentum meum bene et fideliter exequendum prefatam Elizabeth

ordino facio et constituo executricem meam necnon dominum Willelmum Melton capellanum pro premissis exequendis in forma
predicta ordino facio supervisorem per presentes sigillo meo signatas die et anno superius specificatis etcetera
hiis testibus Willelmo Mylly de Northampton deyster Willelmo Ferrer de eadem baker Thome Malpas et aliis

In the name of God Amen the seventh day of May 1483 I John Leynho of Northampton, glover, of sound mind and good memory make my testament in this wise. First I bequeath my soul to Almighty God, to the Blessed Virgin Mary His mother and all the saints of the court of heaven, my body to be buried in the chapel of the Blessed Virgin Mary in the church of All Saints in the same town. Item I bequeath to the high altar of the said church for tithes forgotten 20d. Item I bequeath to the chapel of the Blessed Mary one torch. Item I bequeath to the fraternity of St John 20d. Item I bequeath to the almshouse of St Thomas the Martyr outside the south gate of the aforementioned Northampton 12d. Item I bequeath to the fabric of the said church of All Saints 20d. Item I bequeath to the maintenance of the College of the said church 20d. Item I bequeath to the fraternity of the Holy Cross in the same church 3s 4d. Item I bequeath to the conduit 20d. Item I bequeath to Simon my son 10 marks. Item I bequeath to John my eldest son 10 marks. Item I bequeath to Thomas my son 10 marks. Item I bequeath to John my youngest son 10 marks. Item I bequeath to Agnes my daughter 5 marks in good English money. The remainder of all my goods not bequeathed above I give and bequeath to Elizabeth my wife to then dispose for the health of my soul and the souls of my friends and all faithful departed as seems best to her and that this testament be well and faithfully executed I ordain, make and constitute the aforesaid Elizabeth my executrix and also I ordain and make Dom William Melton, chaplain, as supervisor for these premises to be executed in the form aforesaid by these presents. Sealed and signed by me on the day and year above specified etcetera. With these witnesses William Mylly of Northampton. deyster, William Ferrer, baker, of the same, Thomas Malpas and others.

f37r 77 THOMAS MORE 8th June 1484 cook

In Dei nomine Amen viij die mensis Junii anno domini mcccclxxxiiij. Ego Thomas More de Northampton cooke compos
mentis et sane memorie condo testamentum meum in hunc modum In primis lego animam meam Deo Omnipotenti
Beate Marie Virgini sue genitrici ac omnibus sanctis curie celestis corpusque meum sepiliendum in cimiterio
ecclesie parochiali Omnium Sanctorum ville Northampton Item lego fraternitati Sancte Trinitatis in eadem ecclesia ijs.iiijd.
et unam torcheam precii iijs. Item fraternitati Corporis Christi ijs. et unam torcheam Item lego

fraternitati
Beate Marie Virginis in eadem ecclesia ijs. et unam torcheam Item fraternitati Sancti Georgii Martiris ijs. et unam
torcheam Item lego fraternitati Sancte Crucis in eadem ecclesia unam torcheam Item fraternitati Sancte Katerine in novo
cimiterio unam torcheam Item lego Stephano Omore patri meo xls. meam togam coloris vyolett meum
optimum deployedem et optimam par galigarum meum optimam pylvum et optimam meam caleptram Item lego
ad sustentacionem pauperum existentium in domo elemosinario Sancti Thome Martiris extra portam australem
iijs.iiijd. et unam torcheam Residuum vero omnium bonorum meorum superius non legatorum do et lego Elizabeth
uxori mee ad inde disponendum pro salute anime mee ac omnium fidelium defunctorum prout ei melius
videbitur expediri Et ad istud testamentum bene et fideliter exequendum prefatam Elizabeth uxorem meam ordino facio et
constituo executricem meam et ordino facio et constituo Henricum Humfrey similiter pro executione eiusdem
testamenti mei fore supervisorem Et volo quod ibidem Henricus habeat pro labore sue in supervivendum executione
eiusdem testamenti mei xiijs.iiijd. bone monete Anglie etcetera Date ut supra

In the name of God Amen the 8th day of June 1484 I Thomas More of Northampton, cook, in sound mind and good memory make my testament in this wise. First I bequeath my soul to Almighty God, to the Blessed Virgin Mary His mother and all the saints of the court of heaven, my body to be buried in the cemetery of the parish church of All Saints in the town of Northampton. Item I bequeath to the fraternity on the Holy Trinity in the same church 2s 4d and one torch valued at 3s. Item to the fraternity of Corpus Christi 2s and one torch. Item I bequeath to the fraternity of the Blessed Virgin Mary in the same church 2s and one torch. Item to the fraternity of St George the Martyr 2s and one torch. Item I bequeath to the fraternity of the Holy Cross in the same church one torch. Item to the fraternity of St Katherine in the new cemetery one torch. Item I bequeath to Stephen Omore, my father, 40s and my gown of violet colour, my best doublet and my best pair of hose, my best cap and my best hat. Item I bequeath for the sustenance of the poor living in the almshouse of St Thomas the Martyr outside the south gate 3s 4d and one torch. The remainder of all my goods not bequeathed above I give and bequeath to Elizabeth, my wife, to then dispose for the health of my soul and all faithful departed as seems best to her. And that this testament be well and faithfully executed I ordain, make and constitute the aforesaid Elizabeth, my wife, my executrix and similarly I ordain, make and constitute Henry Humfrey supervisor for the execution of my said testament. And I will that the said Henry Humfrey shall have for his labour in supervising the execution of this my said testament 13s 4d of good English money etcetera. Given as above.

f37r 78 WILLIAM FERROUR 20th July 1484 baker

In Dei nomine Amen xx die Julii anno domini mcccclxxxiiij Ego Willelmus Ferrour de Northampton
baker compos mentis et sane memorie condo testamentum meum in hunc modum In primis lego
animam meam Deo Omnipotente Beate Marie Virgini sue genitrici ac omnibus sanctis curie celestis
corpusque meum sepiliendum in capella Beate Marie Virginis in ecclesia Omnium Sanctorum ville Northampton
predicte Item lego priori Sancti Andree pro decimis meis non bene decimatis et oblationibus oblitis iijs. iiijd.
Item lego ffraternitati Sancte Katerine in novo cimiterio ijs. Item lego ad reparacionem summi altaris in
dicta ecclesia Omnium Sanctorum xijd. Item lego fraternitati Sancte Trinitatis in eadem ecclesia xijd. Item lego fraternitati
Beate Marie Virginis in eadem ecclesia xijd. Item lego fraternitati Corporis Christi in eadem ecclesia xijd.
et unam torchiam Item lego fraternitati Sancte Johannis Baptiste xijd. Item lego fraternitati Sancti Georgii ibidem
xijd. Item lego fraternitati Sancte Crucis ibidem xijd. Item lego fraternitati Sancte Cithe ibidem xijd.
Item lego fabrice ecclesie de Bryngton xld. Item lego eidem ecclesie unam torchiam
ad serviendum summo altari tempore levacionis Sancti Sacramenti ibidem Item lego Margate Shawe
filie mee xxs. Item lego Johanne filie mee xls. unam matricem unam par lodicum
unam par lintheamentum unum coopertorium Anglice a coverlett meam optimam secundam ollam eneam
et unam petellam eneam continentem xvj lagenas mensur' Item lego Margerie filie mee
xls. unum matricum unum par linthiamentum par lodicum et unum coverlett unam ollam eneam vocatam
the thryd potte unam patellam eneam Item lego Agneti More filiole mee duo coclearia
argenti Item lego Willelmo Shawe filiolo meo duo coclearia argenti Item volo quod Alicia
uxor mea dabit et deliberabit inmediate post decessum meum Thome Shawe unam murram
ligate cum argento deaurato videlicet de illis duabus murris suis michi per ipsum liberatis pro
plegiis dicta Alicia uxore mea aliquam summam pecunie pro eadem murram non petente
f37v
ulterius lego Johanni filio meo unam matricam unam par linthiamentum unam par lodicum unum
coopertorium vocatum a coverlett unam ollam eneam et unam patellam eneam Residuum vero omnium
bonorum meorum superius non legatorum do et lego Alicie uxori mee ad inde disponendum
pro salute anime mee animarum omnium amicorum meorum ac omnium fidelium defunctorum prout
ei melius videbitur expediri et ad istud testamentum bene et fideliter exequendum prefatam
Aliciam ordino et constituo meam executricem et Willelmum Sabyn ordino et facio pro
executione premissorum supervisorem per presentes

In the name of God Amen the 20th day of July 1484 I William Ferrour of Northampton, baker, of sound mind and good memory make my testament in this wise. First I bequeath my soul to Almighty God, to the Blessed Virgin Mary His mother and all the saints of the court of heaven, my body to be buried in the chapel of the Blessed Virgin Mary in the church of All Saints, Northampton. Item I bequeath to the Prior of St Andrew's for my tithes not well tithed and oblations forgotten 3s 4d. Item I bequeath to the fraternity of St Katherine in the new churchyard 2s. Item I bequeath to the repair of the high altar in the said church of All Saints 12d. Item I bequeath to the fraternity of the Blessed Virgin Mary 12d. Item I bequeath to the fraternity of Corpus Christi 12d and one torch. Item I bequeath to the fraternity of St John Baptist 12d. Item I bequeath to the fraternity of St George 12d. Item I bequeath to the fraternity of the Holy Cross 12d. Item I bequeath to the fraternity of St Cithe 12d. Item I bequeath to the fabric of Brington Church 40d. Item I bequeath to the same church one torch to serve at the high altar at the time of the elevation of the Holy Sacrament there. Item I bequeath to Margate Shawe, my daughter, 20s. Item I bequeath to Joan, my daughter, 40s, one mattress, one pair of blankets, one pair of sheets, one covering, one coverlet, my second best brass pot and one brass pot holding 16 gallons measure. Item I bequeath to Marjorie, my daughter, 40s, one mattress, one pair of sheets, one pair of blankets, one coverlet, one brass pot called the third pot, one brass bowl. Item I bequeath to Agnes More, my granddaughter, two silver spoons. Item I bequeath to William Shaw, my grandson two silver spoons. Item I will that Alice, my wife, will give and deliver to Thomas Shaw immediately after my death, one maser bound with silver gilt, that is to say from those two masers of his given to me as a pledge, not seeking from Alice, my wife, any other sum of money for the same maser. Further I bequeath to my son John one mattress, one pair of sheets, one pair of blankets, one cover called a coverlet, one brass pot and one brass dish. The residue of all my goods not bequeathed above I give and bequeath to Alice, my wife, to then dispose then for the health of my soul, the souls of all my friends and the souls of all faithful departed as seems best to her and that this testament be well and faithfully executed I ordain and constitute the aforesaid Alice my executrix and I ordain and make William Sabyn supervisor for the execution of these premises by these presents.

f37v 80 RICHARD COTELERD 16th July 1484

In Dei nomine Amen xvj die mensis Julii anno domini mccccIxxxiiij Ego Ricardus Cotelerd de Northampton compos mentis et sane memorie condo testamentum meum in hunc modum In primis lego animam
meam Deo Omnipotenti et Beate Marie Virgini sue genitrici ac omnibus sanctis curie celestis corpusque meum sepiliendum in capella Beate Marie Virginis in ecclesia Omnium Sanctorum ibidem
Item lego priori Sancti Andree ville Northampton predicte pro decimis meis oblitis non bene decimatis
et oblationibus meis oblitis xld. Item lego fabrice ecclesie predicte xxd. Item fraternitati Sancte Trinitatis in eadem ecclesia ijs. Item lego fraternitati Corporis Christi in eadem ecclesia xijd.

Item lego fraternitati Beate Marie in eadem ecclesia xijd. Item lego fraternitati Sancti Georgii in eadem ecclesia martiris in eadem ecclesia xijd. Item lego fraternitati Sancti Johannis Baptiste ibidem xijd.
Item lego fraternitati Sancte Crucis ibidem xijd. Item lego fraternitati Sancte Cithe ibidem xijd. Item lego
fraternitati Sancte Katerine in novo cimiterio xijd. Item lego domui elemosine Sancti Thome Martiris
extra portam australem ijs. Residuum vero omnium bonorum meorum superius non legatorum
do et lego Alicie uxori mee et Willelmo Cuttelard filio meo ad inde disponendum pro salute anime et animarum omnium amicorum meorum ac omnium fidelium defunctorum prout eis melius
videbitur expediri et ad istud testamentum meum bene et fideliter exequendum prefatos Aliciam et Willelmum ordino executores meos per presentes

In the name of God Amen the 16th day of July 1484 I Richard Cotelerd of sound mind and good memory make my testament in this wise. First I bequeath my soul to Almighty God, to the Blessed Virgin Mary His mother and all the saints of the court of heaven, my body to be buried in the chapel of the Blessed Virgin Mary in the church of All Saints, Northampton. Item I bequeath to the priory of St Andrew in the aforesaid town of Northampton for tithes forgotten or not well paid and oblations forgotten 40d. Item I bequeath to the fabric of the aforesaid church 20d. Item to the fraternity of the Holy Trinity in the aforesaid church 2s. Item I bequeath to the fraternity of Corpus Christi in the same church 12d. Item I bequeath to the fraternity of Blessed Mary in the same church 12d. Item I bequeath to the fraternity of St George the Martyr in the same church 12d. Item I bequeath to the fraternity of St John the Baptist also 12d. Item I bequeath to the fraternity of the Holy Cross also 12d. Item I bequeath to the fraternity of St Cithe also 12d. Item I bequeath to the fraternity of St Katherine in the new cemetery 12d. Item I bequeath to the almshouse of St Thomas the Martyr outside the south gate 2s. The residue of all my goods not bequeathed above I give and bequeath to Alice, my wife, and William Cottelerd, my son, to then dispose for the health of my soul, and the souls of all my friends and all faithful departed as seems best to them and that this testament be well and faithfully executed I ordain the aforesaid Alice and William as my executors by these presents.

f37v 82 JOHN RYCHERE 10th May 1485 innholder

In Dei nomine Amen x die mensis Maii anno domini mcccclxxxv Ego Johannes Rychere de Northampton inholder compos mentis etcetera condo testamentum meum in
hunc modum In primis lego
animam Deo Omnipotenti Beate Marie etcetera corpusque meum sepiliendum in cimiterio ecclesie parochialis
Omnium Sanctorum ville Northampton predicte Item do et lego rectori dicte ecclesie pro decimis et oblationibus

negligenter detentis seu subtractis vjs.viijd. Item lego summo altari in eadem ecclesia pro reparacione
eiusdem altaris iijs.iiijd. Item lego fraternitati Sancte Crucis in eadem ecclesia xxd. Item lego fraternitati Sancti Georgii
infra eandem ecclesiam xxd. Item lego fraternitati Sancti Johannis Baptiste in eadem ecclesia xxd. Item lego fraternitati
Sancte Trinitatis in dicta ecclesia xxd. Item lego fraternitati Sancte Katerine vocate le pardon churche infra parochiam
Omnium Sanctorum predictam iijs.iiijd. Item lego cuilibet ordino fratrum infra villam predictam ad orandum pro anima mea
xxd. Item lego pauperibus infra domum Sancti Thome Martiris in ville predicte disponendum inter
eosdem iijs.iiijd. Item lego capellanis ydoniis ad dicendum unum trentale missarum pro salute anime mee
xs. Item lego capellano ydoneo ad dicendum missam per unum annum <integrum> etcetera vli.vjs.viijd.
Item lego le condyte ville Northampton xxd. Item lego cuilibet servienti meorum infra domum
meam tam masculem quam femine pro suis bonis serviciis unam cocliare argenti Item lego Willelmo
Swayne servienti meo pro suo bono servicio michi impense unam togarum mearum de le russett
Item lego cuilibet puerorum meorum masculorum infra domum meam serviencium unam togarum mearum
de le russett pro suis bonis et diligentis laboribus et serviciis michi impensis Residuum vero omnium
bonorum meorum non legatorum do et lego totaliter Agneti uxori mee et Roberto Shefford de
Northampton aurifabro ad inde ordinandum et disponendum pro salute anime mee prout eis melius
videbitur et facio et ordino dictam Agnetem uxorem meam et Robertum Shefford meos executores
presentis testamenti mei et Robertum Waren capellanum esse supervisorem eiusdem hiis testibus Simone
Rowland Johanne ap Ryce Thoma Williamson et aliis

In the name of God Amen the 10th day of May 1485 I John Rychere, innholder, in sound mind etcetera make my testament in this wise. First I bequeath my soul to Almighty God, to the Blessed Mary etcetera my body to be buried in the churchyard of the parish church of All Saints. I bequeath to the rector of the said church for tithes and oblations negligently detained or withheld 6s 8d. Item I bequeath to the high altar in the same church for the repair of the same altar 3s 4d. Item I bequeath to the fraternity of the Holy Cross in the same church 20d. Item I bequeath to the fraternity of St George 20d. Item I bequeath to the fraternity of St John Baptist 20d. Item I bequeath to the fraternity of the Holy Trinity 20d. Item I bequeath to the fraternity of St Katherine called le Pardon Church within the aforesaid parish of All Saints 3s 4d. Item I bequeath to each of the friars in the said town to pray for my soul 20d. Item I bequeath to the poor people within the house of St Thomas the Martyr in the aforesaid town to be distributed among the same 3s 4d. Item I bequeath to suitable chaplains to say a trental of masses for the health of my soul 10s. Item I bequeath to a suitable chaplain to say mass for a full year etcetera £5 6s 8d. Item I bequeath to the conduit of the town of Northampton 20d. Item I bequeath to each of my servants within my house both male and female for their good service one silver spoon. Item I bequeath to William Swayne, my servant, for his devoted service to me one gown of mine of le russet. Item I bequeath to each of the boys serving within my house one gown of mine of le russet for their good and diligent labour and devoted service to me. The residue of all my goods not bequeathed above I give and bequeath totally to Agnes, my wife, and Robert Shefford of Northampton, goldsmith, to then ordain and dispose for the health of my soul as seems best to them and I make and ordain the said Agnes, my wife, and Robert Shefford my executors of this my present testament and Robert Waren, chaplain, to be supervisor of the same. With these witnesses, Simon Rowland, John ap-Ryce, Thomas Williamson and others.

f38r 83 RICHARD DAFFRON 20th July 1485 butcher

In Dei nomine Amen xx die Julii anno millesimo cccclxxxv Ego Ricardus Daffron de Northampton bocher compos mentis et sane memorie condo testamentum meum in hunc modum
In primis lego animam meam Deo Omnipotenti Beate Marie et omnibus sanctis curie celestis corpusque
meum sepiliendum in cimiterio ecclesie parochialis Omnium Sanctorum ville Northampton predicte Item lego summo
altari eiusdem ecclesie pro decimis meis oblitis non bene decimatis et oblationibus oblitis xxs. Item lego ad reparacionem dicte altaris iijs.iiijd. Item lego fraternitati Corporis Christi ijs. Item lego fraternitati Beate Marie Virginis ibidem iijs.iiijd. Item lego fraternitati Sancti Georgii Martiris ibidem xld.
Item lego fraternitati Sancte Crucis ibidem ijs. Item lego fraternitati Sancte Trinitatis ibidem iijs.iiijd. Item lego
fraternitati Sancti Johannis ibidem xxd. Item lego fraternitati Sancte Katerine in novo cimiterio ijs. Item lego
fraternitati Sancte Cithe ibidem xijd. Item lego ad le cawsee in Westcotton iuxta crucem ibidem vocatis le Oxford Waye iijs.iiijd. Item lego domino Willelmo Daffron filio meo meam togam coloris le Blakalyre penulatam cum le oter meam zonam de cerico sanguinii coloris cum argento arnasiato unam murram cum nominibus trium regum de Colen circa le bonde eiusdem scriptis unam ollam eneam in mensuris quattuor lagenarum unam petellam
eneam continentem xvj lagenas in mensuris vj cocliaria argenti Item lego Anne sorori mee xs. bone monete Anglie Item lego Johanni Gylby togam meam de murrey Item lego Sibell nuper servienti mee vjs.viijd. Item lego fabrice ecclesie Sancti Sepulcri in eadem villa Northampton iijs.iiijd. Item lego cuilibet filiorum et filiolarum meorum xijd. Residuum vero bonorum meorum non legatorum do et lego Alicie uxori mee predicte domino Willelmo Daffron filio meo et Thome Henke yoman ad inde disponendum pro salute anime et animarum omnium amicorum meorum ac omnium fidelium defunctorum prout eis melius
videbitur expediri Et ad istud testamentum bene et fideliter exequendum prefatos Aliciam dominum
Willelmum et Thomam Henke ordino facio et constituo executores meos et Willelmum Austyn supervisorem huius presentis testamenti mei Et volo quod quilibet dictorum domini Willelmi Daffron filii mei et Thome Henke habeat pro labore suo in exequendum istud testamentum meum et ultimam voluntatem in predicta forma xxs. ac eciam volo quod predictus

Willelmus Austyn habeat pro labore suo in supervidendo execucionem eiusdem testamenti mei xxs. per presentes hiis testibus Ricardo Marsebroke Thome Malpas et aliis

In the name of God Amen the 20th day of July 1485 I Richard Daffron, butcher, in sound mind and good memory make my testament in this wise. First I bequeath my soul to Almighty God, to the Blessed Mary and all the saints of the court of heaven, my body to be buried in the cemetery of the parish church of All Saints in the town of Northampton aforesaid. Item I bequeath to the High Altar in the same church for tithes forgotten and not well paid and forgotten oblations 20s. Item I bequeath for the repair of the same altar 3s 4d. Item I bequeath to the fraternity of Corpus Christi 2s. Item I bequeath to the fraternity of the Blessed Virgin Mary also 3s 4d. Item I bequeath to the fraternity of St George the Martyr 40d. Item I bequeath to the fraternity of the Holy Cross 2s. Item I bequeath to the fraternity of the Holy Trinity 3s 4d. Item I bequeath to the fraternity of St John 20d. Item I bequeath to the fraternity of St Katherine in the new cemetery 2s. Item I bequeath to the fraternity of St Cithe 12d. Item I bequeath to the causeway in Westcotton next to the cross there, called the Oxford Way, 3s 4d. Item I bequeath to Master William Daffron, my son, my gown the colour of Blackalyre and furred with otter, my silk girdle of sanguine colour ornamented with silver, one maser with the names of the three kings of Cologne written around the band, one brass pot containing four gallons, one brass pottle containing a measure of 16 gallons and 6 silver spoons. Item I bequeath to Anne, my sister, 10s in good English money. Item I bequeath to John Gylby my mulberry gown. Item I bequeath to Sybil, formerly my servant, 6s 8d. Item I bequeath to the fabric of the church of St Sepulchre in the aforesaid town of Northampton 3s 4d. Item I bequeath to each grandson and granddaughter 12d. The residue of my goods not bequeathed I give bequeath to Alice, my wife, the aforesaid Dom William Daffron, my son, and Thomas Henke, yeoman, to then dispose for the health of my soul and the souls of all my friends and all faithful departed as seems best to them. And that this testament be well and faithfully executed I ordain, make and constitute as my executors the said Alice, Dom William and Thomas Henke, and William Austyn as supervisor of this my present testament. And I will that the said William Daffron, my son, and Thomas Henke each to have for their labour in executing this testament 20s and the aforesaid William Austyn to have for his labour in supervising the execution of this my testament 20s by these presents. With these witnesses Richard Marsebroke, Thomas Malpas and others.

f39r 84 THOMAS PEPE 20th June 1485 grazier

In Dei nomine Amen xx die mensis Junii anno domini mcccclxxxv Ego Thomas Pepe de Northampton
grasier compos mentis et sane memorie condo testamentum meum in hunc modum In primis lego animam

meam Deo Omnipotenti Beate Marie et omnibus sanctis eius corpusque meum sepiliendum in ecclesia pariochiali
Sancti Egidii ville Northampton predicte Item lego summo altari <eiusdem ecclesie> pro decimis meis oblitis xxs. Item
lego reparacioni altaris <Sancti Petri> eiusdem ecclesie vjs.viijd. Item lego fraternitati Sancti Clementis ibidem
vjs.viijd. Item lego reparacioni dicte ecclesie ubi necessitas maxime requirit vjs.viijd. Item lego Johanne Pope uxori mee xlli. Item lego eidem Johanne dimidium utensilium domus mee per modum illius exceptis rebus argenteis Item lego predicte Johanne tres vaccas cum panno de rone rosett Item lego domino Willelmo Pope iiijli. Item lego ydoneo capellano celebranturo pro salute anime mee et parentum meorum post decessum meum xli. Item lego reparacioni ecclesie de Lytyll Bowden xxs. Item lego reparacioni ecclesie de Bryngeste xxs. Item
lego Thome Colfox filiolo meo xxs. Item lego Johanni Pepe fratri meo lx oves Item
lego Agneti Pope lx oves Item lego Johanni Coleor lxxxvj shepe Residuum vero
omnium bonorum meorum superius non legatorum do et lego Willelmo Pope filio meo quem ordino
facio et constituo meum verum et legitimum executorem per presentes ut ipse ordinet disponat pro salute anime mee prout ei videbitur in posterum melius expediri Date die loco et anno domini supradictis

In the name of God Amen the 20th day of June 1485 I Thomas Pepe, grazier, in sound mind and good memory make my testament in this wise. First I bequeath my soul to Almighty God, to the Blessed Mary and all His saints, my body to be buried in the parish church of St Giles in the town of Northampton aforesaid. Item I bequeath to the High Altar of the same church for my forgotten tithes 20s. Item to the repair of the altar of St Peter of the same church 6s 8d. Item I bequeath to the fraternity of St Clement 6s 8d. Item I bequeath to the repair of the said church where it is most needed 6s 8d. Item I bequeath to Joan Pope, my wife, £40, to the same Joan half of my household utensils except the silver things. Item I bequeath to the said Joan three cows with cloth of rone russet. Item I bequeath to Dom William Pepe £4. Item I bequeath to a suitable chaplain celebrating for the health of my soul and my parents after my death £10. Iem I bequeath to the repair of the church of Little Bowden 20s. Item I bequeath to the repair of the church of Bringhurst 20s. Item to Thomas Colfox my grandson 20s. Item I bequeath to John Pepe my brother 60 sheep. Item I bequeath to Agnes Pepe 60 sheep. Item I bequeath to John Coleor 86 sheep. The residue of all my goods not bequeathed above I give and bequeath to William Pope, my son, whom I ordain, make and constitute my true and legal executor by these presents that he shall ordain and dispose for the health of my soul as seems henceforth best to him. Given the day, place and year abovesaid.

f39r 86 EDWARD ATWELL junior 28th September 1485 butcher

In Dei nomine xxviij die mensis Septembris anno domini mccccl xxxv Ego Edwardus Atwell junior de Northampton bucher compos mentis et sane memorie condo testamentum meum

in hunc modum In primis lego animam meam Deo Omnipotenti Beate Marie et omnibus sanctis curie celestis corpusque meum sepiliendum in cimiterio ecclesie Omnium Sanctorum ville Northampton Item
lego priori Sancti Andree eiusdem ville pro decimis meis oblitis et oblationibus eceam oblitis xijd.
Item lego rectori ecclesie Beate Marie iuxta Castrum Regis pro decimis et oblacionibus non decimatis seu oblitis
xijd. Item lego Cicilie uxori mee vijxx oves Item lego Edmundo fratri meo ix^{no} oves Item lego Thome Atwell fratri meo ix oves Item lego Agneti filie mee tria cocliaria argentea

f39v

Item lego Ricardo Atwell filiolo meo ij oves Residuum vero omnium bonorum superius non legatorum do et lego predicte Cicilie uxori mee ad inde disponendum pro salute anime mee et animarum
omnium fidelium defunctorum prout ei melius videbitur expediri et ad istud testamentum meum
bene et fideliter exequendum prefatam Ciciliam ordino facio et constituo executricem meam et dominum Robertum Waren capellanum ac Johannem Wodward de execucione premissorum supervisores
et volo quod quilibet predictorum domini Roberti Waren et Johannis Wodward habeat pro labore suo xld. per presentes
hic est voluntas mea that my ij pese hovelles be putto the churche behoveth of Whyston to Saynt Marget chapell of Deventon [Denton] ij quarter of malte or ellis vjs.viijd. to the chirch of Emerton
vjs.viijd. to Byllyng bryge iijs.iiijd. to Olney bryge iijs.iiijd. to my modyr in
money x marke a matrasse iiij blanketts iiij flaxon shetys and ij hempyn shetis my wyte
wolen coverlet my beste rede coverlet and my best bolster ij pyllowse and the seler over my bed
Item to Wanden churche iijs.iiijd. Item to Tyryngham churche iijs.iiijd. Item to Olney churche
iijs.iiijd. Item to William by broder my best shedde carte Item to the sidyd William
my beste horse next my principall Item to the sayd William ij oxen to hys plogh
a blak garye and a brentis Item to the sayde William xl ewys and xxti hogerellys
Item to the sayde William my rede cowe with the whyte face Item iij of my beste bacon
oggyes Item j payer of yerne harowys and my vyrly plowe ij of my beste sythys
my beste yron spete and all my bords in the woll howse my beste bereloy my ffan
of wykers my bankor and my qwysshons Item to John Pruey my brothyr son xxti ogerellys
and my rede kowe that was Chapmannys of Daventon and my beste brasse potte and my best
brasse pan and my hanhyng laver and my laton basen and the ewer and my ij beste laton
candylstykks and my chafyng dyssh for eelys my water chafer and my fyre forke of
yern my fodyn tabull and xxs of money to by and sell with qwen he hys xviij yere
of age Item to Jane Pruey my brothir doghter whan schewe comyth to lawfull age
xls in money Item to John Brerege my kosyn my second shedd carte and a harowe
of yron and a nothyr of tre and my rede godryd oxe and my blake oxe hys felowe
wyth her yog and chaynes and my oxe plowe my bushell and [. . .]estotyls and my redall
and ryeng sefe and oon of my wyndowyng clothys my haye and quarter stak a
sex stryke sak and a bakk of iiij stryke my masshyng tubb and my newe ale
tubb my grete botell and my ij lesse bottells my grettes yron spete save one my
cobards of yern Item to the sayde John xxti shepe Item to John Pruey myn yern
bond coffer and vj sylver sponys of the beste Item to Richard Lampney my
dunkarte my sterryd horse my thyll gerys for the carte and the carte sadyll a payer
of mydell gerys color (collar) and all and my blak herfar and x ewys Item to Margery my cosyn
a materas a payer of flaxen shetis and a payer of hardyn shetis my second
rede coverlett my lytill brasee potte my second brasse panne vj platers of pewter

f40r
vj pewter dysshys and vj sawcers ij candyllstykks and a salt seler my brown kowe and hyr caffe sex sylver spones of the medyl sorte and x shepe Item to Jon Bolbek of Bosezate my ij stere bullokks the oon ys rede the odyr ys blak and my thyll horse and x schepe and iij quarter of barly Item to Margery a borde cloth of flex Item to John Henyk my bryndyd cowe and a payer of flaxen shetes a koverlett vi shepe iij quartere of berly Item to William Conwyn an whyte cowe and ij quarter of barly and a payer of shetes Item to George Dobb of Olney iiij schepe and iiij buschell of malte Item to William Bayle iiij shepe Item to Alice Kydyer iiij stryke of berly Item to William my lytill matress and a payer of fflaxen shetes a payer of hardyn shetes and my second brasse pott and my thryd brasse pann ij candylstykks ij quarter sakks a sak of vj stryke and a sak of iiij stryke vj grete platers of pewter and my iij quarte botell Item to Amye Brerage iiij chayer in the hall vj pewter dysshys and vj sawcers a salt seler and a payer of schetes a lytil brasse pan a long borde clothe of flex vj sylver sponys a shorte borde clothe of flex a lytill spete of yern and a bacon hogg Item to yche of my godschylder a shepe and iiijd. Item to every howse of frerys Northampton iijs.iiijd. Item to every man of qwyshton tha holdyth a plowe xijd. Item to every cotyer in the same vjd. Item syr John of Dewinton my portowse and all my bokys my foldyng

(bottom of page)
sylver spon and my odyr sylver sponys and vjs.viijd. The resydewe of my gods nott afore beqwest I kyffe to Sir John Carter preste of Doventyn to William Pruey my brothyr and to John Brerhege qwo I ordeyn myn executors to dyspose for the helthe of my sowle in beste wyse they can acordybg to my wyll

In the name of God Amen the 28th day of September 1485 I Edward Atwell junior, butcher, in sound mind and good memory make my testament in this wise. First I bequeath my soul to Almighty God, to the Blessed Mary and all the saints of the court of heaven, my body to be buried in the cemetery of the church of All Saints in the town of Northampton. Item I bequeath to the priory of St Andrew of the same town for debts and tithes forgotten 12d Item I bequeath to the rector of the church of the Blessed Mary near the King's Castle for unpaid tithes or forgotten debts 12d. Item I bequeath to Cicily my wife 140 sheep. Item I leave to Edmund my brother 90 sheep. Item I bequeath to Thomas Atwell my brother 9 sheep. Item I bequeath to Agnes my daughter three silver spoons. Item I bequeath to Robert Atwell my grandson 2 sheep. The residue of all goods not bequeathed above I give and bequeath to the aforesaid Cicily, my wife, to then dispose for the health of my soul and the souls of all faithful departed as seems best to her and that this my testament be well and faithfully executed I ordain, make and constitute the said Cicily my executrix and Dom Robert Waren and John Woodward supervisors of the execution of these premises and I wish that each of the aforesaid Robert Waren and John Woodward should have for his labour 40d by these presents.

f40r 87 WILLIAM ATWELL 24th September 1485 butcher

In Dei nomine Amen xxiiij die mensis Septembris anno domini mcccclxxxv Ego Willelmus Atwell de Northampton bucher compos mentis et sane memorie condo testamentum meum in hunc

modum In primis lego animam meam Deo Omnipotenti Beate Marie et omnibus sanctis curie celestis
corpusque meum sepiliendum in cimiterio ecclesie Omnium Sanctorum ibidem Item lego priori Sancti Andree
pro decimis oblitis et oblationibus xxs. Item lego fraternitati Sancte Trinitatis fraternitati Beate Marie et fraternitati
Corporis Christi in dicta ecclesia Omnium Sanctorum totum merennium meum iacens ante hostum meum
inter eas equaliter dividendum Item lego Johanne uxori mee CC oves existentes in Grafton
Wydwyle Item lego Willelmo filio meo CC oves existentes in Estcote Et si contingat
dictum Willelmum filium obire antequam debitam deliberacionem predictum CC ovium in Estcote predictam factam fuerint
predicte Johanna uxori mea supervivente volo tunc quod dicta Johanna uxor mea
habeat predictos CC oves in Estcote habeat ad usum suum proprium imperpetuum Item lego lumini
Sancti Martini in ecclesia Sancti Sepulcri ibidem ij torchias de precio xiijs iiijd. Item lego
ecclesie de Patsyll vjs.viijd. Item lego ecclesie de Grafton vjs.viijd. Item lego ecclesie
de Byttelswell vjs.viijd. Item lego Elizabeth Hayle Cs. et viginti
oves matrices et xxti agnellos Item lego dompno Johanni fratri meo monacho Sancti Andree
meam optimam togam Item lego conventui Sancti Andree xld. Item lego sustenacionem
pauperum existentes in domo elemosine Sancti Thome Martiris extra portam australem xijd. Item
lego cuilibet domui fratrum mendicancium ibidem xxd. Residuum vero omnium bonorum meorum
superius non legatorum do et lego predicte Johanne uxori mee Edwardo Atwell patri meo
et Thome Pyncard ad inde disponendum pro salute anime mee et animarum omnium fidelium
defunctorum prout eis melius videbitur expediri et ad istud testamentum meum bene et fideliter exequendum
prefatos Johannam uxorem meam, Edwardum Atwell patrum meum et Thomam Pyncard ordino
facio et constituo executores meos et de execuciones premissorum Johannem Hayle de Stonystrat-
ford ordino et facio supervisorem per presentes

In the name of God Amen the 24th day of September 1485 I William Atwell, butcher, in sound mind and good memory make my testament in this wise. First I bequeath my soul to Almighty God, to the Blessed Mary and all the saints of the court of heaven, my body to be buried in the cemetery of the church of All Saints. Item I bequeath to the priory of St Andrews for my tithes forgotten and oblations 20s. Item I bequeath to the fraternity of Holy Trinity, the fraternity of the Blessed Mary, the fraternity of Corpus Christi in the said church of All Saints all my timber lying in front of my house to be divided equally between them. Item I bequeath to Joan, my wife, 200 sheep to be found at Grafton Woodville. Item I bequeath to William, my son, 200 sheep at present in Eastcote and if it happens that the said William, my son, should die before his dues be delivered then the aforementioned sheep should be handed over to my wife Joan if she is still living. I wish then that the said Joan, my wife, should have the aforementioned 200 sheep for her own use from then on. Item I bequeath for St Martin's light in the church of Holy Sepulchre 2 torches sharing 13s 4d. Item I bequeath to the church of

Pattishall 6s 8d. Item I bequeath to the church of Grafton 6s 8d. Item I bequeath to the church of Bittlesewell 6s 8d. Item I bequeath to Elizabeth Hayle 100s and 20 ewes and 20 lambs. Item I bequeath to Dom John, my brother, monk of St Andrews, my best gown. Item I bequeath to the convent of St Andrews 40d. Item I bequeath for the sustenance of the poor people living in the almshouse of St Thomas the Martyr outside the south gate 12d. Item I bequeath to each house of mendicant brothers there 20d. The residue of all my goods not bequeathed above I give and bequeath to the said Joan, my wife, to Edward Atwell, my father, and to Thomas Pincard to then dispose for the health of my soul and the souls of all faithful departed as seems best to them and to and that this testament be well and faithfullyexecuted I ordain, make and constitute the said Joan, my wife, Edward Atwell, my father, and Thomas Pincard as my executors and as for the execution of these premises I ordain and make John Hayle of Stony Stratford as supervisor by these presents.

f40v 88 JOHN BARNARD 17th September 1485 esquire

In Dei nomine Amen xvij die mensis Septembris anno domini mcccclxxxv Ego Johannes Barnard armiger de Northampton compos mentis et sane memorie condo testamentum meum in hunc modum In primis lego animam meam Deo Omnipotenti Beate Marie Virgini et omnibus sanctis curie celestis corpusque meum sepiliendum in loco illo cui Deo Omnipotenti placuerit Item lego domui sive hospitali Sancte Johannis Baptiste ville Northampton pro uno trentali ibidem pro salute anime dicendo xs. Item volo quod executrix inferius nominata conducat unum presbytrum ydoneum ad cotidie celebrandum et orandum pro salute anime et animarum omnium fidelium defunctorum per spacium duorum annorum inmediate post decessum ulterius volo quod Thomas Barnard filius meus habebit et gaudebit ad suum proprium usum omnia et singula proficia exitus et reveniencia exeuncia de dominio meo cum suis pertinenciis in Bryngton in comitatu Northampton annuatim ibidem percipiendum durante minore etate Johannis Barnard filii et heredis mei Residuum vero omnium bonorum meorum superius non legatorum do et lego Margarete uxori mee ad inde disponendum pro salute anime et animarum omnium fidelium defunctorum prout ei melius videbitur expediri et ad istud testamentum bene et fideliter exequendum prefatam Margaretam uxorem meam ordino facio et constituo executricem meam Et de execucione premissorum Walterum Mancyll militem dominum Ricardum Sherd clericum Johannem Pekk generosum ordino et facio supervisores per presentes in cuius rei testimonium huic testo sigillum meum Die et anno supradicto apposui hiis testibus domino Henrico Clyff domino Roberto Bell capellano Willelmo Raynton et aliis

In the name of God Amen the 17th day of September 1485 I John Barnard, esquire, in sound mind and good memory make my testament in this wise. First I bequeath my soul to Almighty God, to the Blessed Virgin Mary and all the saints of the court of heaven, my body to be buried wherever it shall please Almighty God. Item I bequeath to the Hospital of St John the Baptist in Northampton for a trental to be said there for the well being of my soul 10s. Item I will that my below named executrix should appoint a suitable priest to celebrate daily and pray for my soul and the souls of all faithful departed for the space of 2 years after my death. Further I will that Thomas Barnard, my son, shall have and enjoy to his own use all and singular profits, issues and revenues arising from my demesne with its appurtenances in Bryngton in the county of Northampton to be received during the minority of John Barnard, my son and heir. The residue of all my goods not bequeathed above I give and bequeath to Margaret, my wife, to then dispose for the health of my soul and the souls of all faithful departed as seems best to her and that this testament be well and faithfully executed I ordain, make and constitute Margaret, my wife, my executrix. And for the execution of these premises I ordain and make Walter Mancyll, knight, Dom Richard Sherd, clerk, John Peck, gentleman, supervisors by these presents. In testimony of which matter I have placed my seal the day and year as above. With these witnesses Dom Henry Clyff, Dom Robert Bell, chaplain, William Raynton and others.

f40v 89 WILLIAM MORETON (probably late 1485)

I William Moreton beqweth my sowle to God Almyghty and to the Blessed
Virgin Ower Lady Saynt Mary and to all the company of hewyn and my
body to be beryed in Saynt Mary paryssh within Saynt Katerine chapell
Item I beqweth to Saynt Katerine chapell j torche and to the Holy Rode
a torche also emenges pore folke in brede and mete xxxs. Also
to the iiij howsys of Freres every howse xijd. Also I make my
wyfe and my son to be myn executors and also my wyfe & my son
to be myn ayres and my wyfe to have Brayfeld and North-
ampton for her feftement and Herry my son to have Moreton & Godds
blessyng and myn and my maister officiall and Teryngham to be myn
over sears and as for all other matteres to be att my wyfes disposicon
and gydyng and that shee do for me as shee wold I shulde do for
hyr yf shee had departyt before mee etcetera

f41v 90 WILLIAM MULTON 31st December 1485 innholder

In Dei nomine Amen ultimo die mensis Decembris anno domini mcccclxxxv Ego Willelmus
Multon de Northampton inholder compos mentis et sane memorie condo testamentum meum
in hunc modum In primis lego animam meam Deo Omnipotenti Beate Marie Virgini
et omnibus sanctis curie celestis corpusque meum sepiliendum in cimiterio ecclesie Omnium
Sanctorum ibidem iuxta tumulum Johanne nuper uxoris Item lego summo altari ecclesie
predicte

pro decimis meis non bone decimatis et oblationibus meis oblitis xxd. Item lego Fabrice ecclesie predicte xijd. Item lego fraternitati Sancte Trinitatis in eadem ecclesia xijd. Item lego fraternitati Corporis Christi in eadem ecclesia xijd. Item lego fraternitati Beate Marie in eadem ecclesia xijd. Item lego fraternitati Sancti Johannis Baptiste ibidem xijd. Item lego fraternitati Sancti Georgii in eadem ecclesia xijd. Item lego fraternitati Sancte Crucis in eadem xijd. Item lego fraternitati Sancte Cithe ibidem xijd. Item lego fraternitati Sancte Katerine in novo cimiterio xijd. Item lego fraternitati Sancte Crucis in Muro in ecclesia Sancti Gregorii xijd. Item lego Simoni Multon filio meo optimam meam plumale unum par linthiamenti unum par lodicum et meam optimam togam coloris de violett penulatam cum lee Fuches Item lego Margate Roose filie mee unum matricum unum par linthiamenti unum par lodicum unum coopertorium et unam vaccam Item lego Willelmo filio meo unam murram vocatam a standyng maser cum una coopertura Residuum vero omnium bonorum meorum superius non legatorum do et lego Isabelle uxori mee ad inde disponendum pro salute anime mee et animarum omnium fidelium defunctorum prout ei melius videbitur expediri et ad istud testamentum meum fideliter exequendum prefatam Isabellam ordino facio et constituo executricem meam et pro executione premissorum dominum Willelmum Melton capellanum ordino et facio supervisorem per presentes hiis testibus Johanne Barre vyntener Wilelmo Monyngham Thome Malpase et aliis

In the name of God Amen the 31st day of December 1485 I William Multon, innholder, in sound mind and good memory make my testament in this wise. First I bequeath my soul to Almighty God, to the Blessed Virgin Mary and all the saints of the court of heaven, my body to be buried in the cemetery of All Saints church next to the grave of Joan, my late wife. Item I bequeath to the high altar of the said church for tithes not fully paid and forgotten oblations 20d. Item I bequeath to the fabric of the said church 12d. Item I bequeath to the fraternity of Holy Trinity in that same church 12d. Item I bequeath to the fraternity of Corpus Christi in that same church 12d. Item I bequeath to the fraternity of Blessed Mary in that same church 12d. Item I bequeath to the fraternity of St John the Baptist in that same church 12d. Item I bequeath to the fraternity of St George in that same church 12d. Item I bequeath to the fraternity of the Holy Cross in that same church 12d. Item I bequeath to the fraternity of St Cithe in that same church 12d. Item I bequeath to the fraternity of St Katherine in the new cemetery 12d. Item I bequeath to the fraternity of the Holy Cross in the Wall in St Gregory's church 12d. Item I bequeath to Simon Multon, my son, my best feather bed, one pair of sheets, one pair of blankets and my best gown of violet colour furred with polecat. Item I bequeath to Margat Roose, my daughter, one mattress, one pair of sheets, one pair of blankets, one bedspread and one cow. Item I bequeath to William, my son, one bowl called a standing maser with a cover. The residue of all my goods not bequeathed above I give and bequeath to Isabel, my wife, to then dispose for the health of my soul and the souls of all faithful departed as seems best to her and that this testament be well and faithfully executed I ordain, make and constitute the said Isabel, my wife, as my executrix and for the execution of these premises I ordain and make Dom William Melton, chaplain, supervisor by these presents. With these witnesses John Barre, vintner, William Monyngham, Thomas Malpas and others.

f41v 91 THOMAS WYLLIAMSON 20th September 1485 barber

In Dei nomine Amen xx die mensis Septembris anno domini mcccclxxxv Ego
Thomas Wylliamson de Northampton barber compos mentis et sane memorie condo
testamentum meum in hunc modum In primis lego animam meam Deo Omnipotenti
et Beate Marie Virgini sue genitrici ac omnibus sanctis curie celestis corpusque meum sepili-
endum in novo cimiterio iuxta collegium ecclesie Omnium Sanctorum ville Northampton Item
lego priori Sancti
Andree ville predicte pro decimis meis non bone decimatis et oblationibus meis oblitis
iijs. iiijd. Item lego fraternitati Sancte Crucis ibidem j torcheam Item lego fraternitati Sancte
Trinitatis ibidem
j torcheam Item lego fraternitati Sancti Johannis Baptiste ibidem j torcheam Item lego fraternitati
Sancte Cithe ibidem j torcheam Item lego fraternitati Sancte Katerine in novo cimiterio j
torcheam
Item lego Alicie filie mee v marcas bone monete Anglie unam murram vj cocliaria argenti
zonam meam de rubeo serico Item lego Margate filie mee v marcas bone monete Anglie
f42r
Anglie unam murram vj cocliaria argentea meam zonam powred cum argento et zonam
meam nigram de cerico harnesiatam cum argento Residuum vero omnium bonorum meorum
superius non
legatorum do et lego Agneti uxori mee ad inde disponendum pro salute anime mee et omnium
fidelium
defunctorum prout ei melius videbitur expediri et ad istud testamentum [testamentum] bene et
fideliter exequendum
prefatam Agnetem ordino facio et constituo executricem meam et de execucionem premissorum
Dominum Robertum
Waren capellanum et Johannem Dyssy ordino et facio supervisores per presentes et volo quod
quilibet super-
visorum predictorum pro labore suo xld. sterlingorum

In the name of God Amen the 20th day of September 1485 I Thomas Wylliamson, barber, in sound mind and good memory make my testament in this wise. First I bequeath my soul to Almighty God and the Blessed Virgin Mary His mother and all the saints of the court of heaven, my body to be buried in the new cemetery by the college at the church of All Saints, Northampton. Item I bequeath to the Prior of St Andrews for tithes and oblations forgotten 3s 4d. Item I bequeath to the fraternity of the Holy Cross there 1 torch. Item I bequeath to the fraternity of Holy Trinity there 1 torch. Item I bequeath to the fraternity of St John Baptist there 1 torch. Item I bequeath to the fraternity of St Cithe there 1 torch. Item I bequeath to the fraternity of St Katherine in the new cemetery 1 torch. Item I bequeath to Alice, my daughter, 5 marks of good English money, one maser, 6 silver spoons and my girdle of red silk. Item I bequeath to Margat, my daughter, 5 marks of good English money, one maser, 6 silver spoons, my girdle powred with silver and my girdle of black silk ornamented with silver. The residue of all my goods not bequeathed above I give and bequeath to Agnes, my wife, to then dispose for the health of my soul and all faithful departed as seems best to her and that this testament be well and faithfully executed I ordain, make and constitute the said Agnes as my executrix and for the execution of these premises I ordain and make Dom Robert Waren, chaplain, and John Dyssy as supervisors and I wish that each shall have for his labour 40d sterling.

f42v 93 THOMAS HAROWDON 21st August 1485 esquire

In the name of God Amen the xxj day of Auguste the yere of ower Lord God mcccc lxxxv I Thomas Harowdon esqwyer in the counte of Northampton beyng in clere mynde sadly consyderyng the unstabulness of this transiterye lyfe dyspose my testament in manner folowyng Fyrst I beqweth my sowle to God Almyghty Ower Lady Saynt Marye and to al the company of hewyn my body also to be buryed qwere God hath provided Also I bequeth in the name of my principall that ryghth requiryth Also I beqwethe to the he awter of Saynt Gyles churche in Northampton xxd. Also I beqweth and devyse to Elen my wyfe almy landes tenements rentes and reversions with theyr apurtenances asswele suche as I am sole seasyd of and all othyr wyche eny othyr persone ys seasyd of to my use to have and to hold and also to perceyve all the premysses to the same Elen and to hyr assignes duryng hyr lyfe except a place in Northampton called Castylons and ij othyr places adioynyng to the same qwyche iij places I wyll that the sayde Elene or her assignes do sell after my decese to thentent that shee shall content my dettes and the resydew of the money receyvyd if eny be after my dettes payed remayn to the sayde Elene wyth all my godes and catelles the whyche sayde Elene I ordeyn and make myn executrice of this my present laste wyll and testament In wytnes wherof I required Thomas Grene esqwyer Robert Pemberton esqwyer Thomas Hasylwodd gentilman John Chauncy and diverse othyr to testyfye the same

f42v 94 JOHN BUKBY junior 8th March 1485 barker (tanner)

In Dei nomine Amen viij die mensis Marcii anno domini mcccclxxxv Ego Johannes Bukby junior de fano Sancti Jacobi iuxta Northampton barker compos mentis et sane memorie condo testamentum meum in hunc modum In primis lego animam meam Deo Omnipotenti Beate Marie Virgini sue genitrici ac omnibus sanctis curie celestis corpus que meum sepiliendum infra ecclesiam monasterii Sancti Jacobi iuxta Northampton predicte Item lego abbati et conventui eiusdem monasterii in pecuniis muneratis xls. Item lego summo altari ecclesie Sancte Margarate in predicto fano pro decimis oblitis et obla-cionibus xd. Item lego fabrice eiusdem ecclesie xd. Item lego reparacioni altaris Sancte Katerine in eadem ecclesia xxd. Item lego reparacioni et sustentacioni summi altaris in ecclesia Sancti Petri ville Northampton predicte ijs.vjd. Item lego Fabrice dicte ecclesie Sancti Petri ijs.vjd. Item lego reparacioni stansil' existente in cimiterio eiusdem ecclesie Sancti Petri unam fraxinam Item lego Lucie uxori mee in plenam satisfacionem solucionem et contentacionem omnium legacionum sibi per istam voluntatem meam ultimam ullo modo legato in pecuniis muneratis xl li. bone monete Anglie et omnia utensilia domisilia et

f43r

mea iocalia ac medietatem omnium catallorum meorum vivorum ubicumque fuerint infra regnum Anglie Item
lego Roberto filio meo in pecuniis muneratis x li. x dyker of ledder vocatam tam over ledyr quam
soleledyr x carectatus de le barke et alterium medietatem catallorum meorum vivorum Item lego Ricardo Wylson
meam togam veridem et vjs.viijd. in pecuniis muneratis Item lego Elizabeth uxori eiusdem Ricardi duas virgas
panni lanei pro una toga sibi fiend et iijs.iiijd. in pecuniis muneratis Item Lucie servienti mee duas
virgas panni lanei pro una toga sibi fiend et xxs. in pecuniis muneratis ad suum maritagium solvendum
Item lego Ricardo Walker servienti mee duas virgas panni lanei et vjs.viijd. in pecuniis muneratis
Item lego Elizabeth uxori eiusdem Ricardi Walker duas virgas panni lanei ulterius volo quod executrix
mea inferius nominata ordinabit et conducet unum presbyterium ydoneum ad celebrandum pro salute anime mee
et omnium fidelium defunctorum in dicta ecclesia Sancte Margarete per spacium unius anni inmediate post decessum
meum Item do et lego eidem prebytero sic conduct' pro salario suo viij marcas bone et legalis monete
Anglie solvend fieri ad terminos usuales equis porceonibus Item volo quod dicta executrix mea
disponat et distribuat in domus caritatis et elemosinis in die sepulture mee et in die
vocata my monythmynd day secundum discrecionem suam xij marcas bone monete Anglie Residuum
omnium bonorum meorum non legatorum do et lego prefate Lucie uxori mee ad inde disponendum pro
salute anime et animarum omnium fidelium defunctorum prout ei melius videbitur expediri et ad istud
testamentum meum bene et fideliter exequendum prefatam Luciam uxorem meam ordino facio et constituo executricem
meam et Johannem Bukby seniorem fratrum meum et Ricardum Horpoll pro execucione premissorum ordino et
constituo supervisores et volo quod dictus Johannes Bukby
habeat pro labore suo xxxiijs.iiijd. Et similiter dictus Ricardus Horpoll habeat pro labore suo xxvjs.viijd. per presentes

In the name of God Amen the 8th day of March 1485 I John Bukby junior, barker, of the district of St James by Northampton in sound mind and good memory make my testament in this wise. First I bequeath my soul to Almighty God, to the Blessed Virgin Mary His mother and all the saints of the court of heaven, my body to be buried within the church of the monastery of St James by Northampton aforesaid. Item I bequeath to the Abbot and convent of the same monastery 40s in money. Item I bequeath to the high altar of the church of St Margaret in the aforesaid district for tithes and oblations forgotten 10d. Item I bequeath to the fabric of the same church 20d. Item I bequeath to the repair and maintenance of the high altar in the church of St Peter of Northampton 2s 6d. Item I bequeath to the fabric of the said church of St Peter 2s 6d.

Item I bequeath to the repair of the stansil in the cemetery being in the churchyard of the same church of St Peter one ash tree. Item I bequeath to Lucy, my wife, in full satisfaction of all legacies in any way left to her by my last will £40 of good English money and all the household utensils and my jewels and half of all my living cattle wherever they may be within the realm of England. Item I bequeath to Robert, my son, £10 in money, 10 dyker of leather cloth called both over leather and sole leather, 10 cartloads of bark and the other half of my living cattle. Item I bequeath to Richard Wilson my green gown and 6s 8d in money. Item I bequeath to Elizabeth, the wife of the said Richard, two yards of woollen cloth to be for a gown and 3s 4d in money. Item I bequeath to Lucy, my servant, two yards of woollen cloth for a gown and 20s in money. Item I bequeath to Richard Walker two yards of woollen cloth for a gown and 6s 8d in money. Item I bequeath to Elizabeth, the wife of the said Richard Walker, two yards of woollen cloth. And in addition I will that my executors named below should ordain and find a suitable priest to celebrate for the health of my soul and all faithful departed in the said church of St Margaret for one year following my death. Item I bequeath to the same priest 8 marks of good and legal money of England for his salary to be paid at the usual terms in equal portions. Item I wish that my said executrix should dispose and distribute in charitable gifts on the day of my burial and on the day called my month mind day according to her discretion 12 marks of good English money. The residue of all my goods not bequeathed above I give and bequeath to Lucy, my wife, to then dispose for the health of my soul and the souls of all faithful departed as seems best to her and that this testament be well and faithfully executed I ordain, make and constitute the said Lucy as my executrix and for the execution of these premises I ordain and make John Bukby, senior, my brother, and Richard Harpole as supervisors and I wish that the said John Bukby to have for his labour 33s 4d and similarly the said Richard Harpole to have for his labour 26s 8d by these presents.

f44v 99 THOMAS POUNCE 27th June 1486 fisher

In Dei nomine Amen xxvij die mensis Junii anno domini mccccclxxxvj Ego Thomas Pounce de Northampton ffyssher compos mentis et sane memorie condo testamentum meum in hunc modum In primis lego animam meam Deo Omnipotenti Beate Marie Virgini sue genitrici ac omnibus sanctis curie celestis corpusque meum sepiliendum in cimiterio ecclesie Omnium Sanctorum

ville Northampton Item lego fabrice dicte ecclesie xld. Item lego Priori Sancti Andree ville predicte pro decimis et oblationibus non bene solutis xld. Item lego fraternitati Sancte Trinitatis in eadem ecclesia xld. Item lego fraternitati Beate Marie Virginis ibidem xijd. Item lego fraternitati Sancte

Crucis ibidem xijd. Item lego fraternitati Sancti Georgii Martiris ibidem xld. Item lego fraternitati Sancte Cithe ibidem xijd. Item lego ecclesie de Abyndon duas oves precii xld. Item lego

fraternitati Sancte Katerine in novo cimiterio xijd. Item lego domui elemosinarii Sancti Thome Martiris
extra portam australem iiijd. Item lego Willelmo filio meo C oves Item lego Jacobo filio meo C oves Item lego Elizabeth filie mee quinquagenta oves. Item lego Margarete
filie mee quinquagenta oves Item lego Henrico fratri meo togam meam longam coloris

f45r

blodii penulatam cum lez whyte lambe skynnes Item lego cuilibet servienti servientis ....
meum xijd. ulteriusque do et lego Alianore uxori mee totam illam peciam terre arabilis quam de Johanne Wellys seniore mercer nuper emi et perquisivi que quodem pecia terre arabilis iacet in campis ville Northampton predicte extra muram orientalem eiusdem ville vocatam le town wall iuxta
parvam portam nuncupatur le postern yate prope cimiterium ecclesie Sancti Egidii infra quadem croftam
vocatam le fayer crofte et iacet inter via regiam ex parte occidentali et terras quondam Willelmi Lucy militis et Thome Mulso armigeri ex parte orientali habendum et tenendum totam predictam peciam terre
arabilis cum omnibus suis pertinenciis ut predictum est prefate Alianore uxori mee ad terminum vite sue
de capitalibus dominis feodi illius per servicio inde debita et de iure consueta ita quod immediate post decessum
dicte Alianore uxoris mee volo quod tota predicta pecia terre arabilis cum omnibus suis pertinenciis
ut prefertur predicte Jacobo filio meo et heredibus de corpore suo legitime procreatis remaneat imperpetuum
tenendum de capitalibus dominis feodi illius per servicio inde debita et de iure consueta et si contingat
dictum Jacobum filium meum sine heredibus de corpore suo legitime procreatis obire volo tunc quod predicta
pecia terre arabilis cum suis pertinenciis ut prefertur predicto Willelmo filio meo heredibus et assignatis
suis integre remaneat imperpetuum tenendum de capitalibus dominis feodi illius per servicio inde debita et de
iure consueta Residuum vero omnium bonorum meorum superius non legatorum do et lego predictis
Alianore uxori mee et Willelmo filio meo ad inde disponendum pro salute anime et animarum omnium
fidelium defunctorum prout eis melius videbitur expediri et ad istud testamentum meum bene et fideliter exequendum prefatam Alianoram et Willelmum ordino facio et constituo executores meos et Ricardum
fratrum meum huius testamenti mei supervisorem et volo quod idem Ricardus habeat pro labore suo vjs.viijd.
per presentes

In the name of God amen the 27th day of June 1486 I Thomas Pounce, fisher, in sound mind and good memory make my testament in this wise. First I bequeath my soul to Almighty God, to the Blessed Virgin Mary His mother and all the saints of the court of heaven, my body to be buried in the cemetery of the church of All Saints, Northampton. Item I bequeath to the fabric of the said church 40d. Item I bequeath to the Prior of St Andrews for tithes and oblations not well paid 40d. Item I bequeath to the fraternity of the Holy Trinity in the same church 40d. Item I bequeath to the fraternity of the Blessed Virgin Mary 12d. Item I bequeath to the fraternity of the Holy Cross 12d. Item I bequeath to the fraternity of St George the Martyr 40d. Item I bequeath to the fraternity of St Cithe 12d. Item I bequeath to the church of Abington two sheep worth 40d. Item I bequeath to the fraternity of St Katherine in the new churchyard 12d. Item I bequeath to the almshouse of St Thomas the Martyr outside the south gate 4d. Item I bequeath to William, my son, 100 sheep. Item I bequeath to James, my son, 100 sheep. Item I bequeath to Elizabeth, my daughter, fifty sheep. Item I bequeath to Margaret, my daughter, fifty sheep. Item I bequeath to Henry, my brother, my long gown of blue colour furred with white lambskins. Item I bequeath to each of my servants serving with me 12d. Further I bequeath to Alianore, my wife, all that piece of arable land which I formerly bought from John Wells senior, mercer, which lies in the fields of the town of Northampton outside the east wall of the town called the Town Wall, next to a little gate called Postern Gate and next to the cemetery of St Giles, with a certain croft called le Fair Croft which lies between the king's highway on the west and lands formerly of Sir William Lucy and Thomas Mulso esquire on the east, for the term of her life, and immediately after the decease of the said Alianore the aforesaid piece of arable land with all its appurtenances shall remain to the aforesaid James, my son, and to the heirs of his body legitimately begotten forever. And if James, my son, dies without heirs of his body legitimately begotten then I will that the said land remain to the aforesaid William, my son, and heirs and assigns forever to hold of the chief lords of the fee by services therefore due and by right accustomed. The residue of all my goods not bequeathed above I give and bequeath to the aforesaid Alianore, my wife, and William, my son, to then dispose for the health of my soul and the souls of all faithful departed as seems best to them and that this my testament be well and faithfully executed I ordain, make and constitute the said Alianore and William my executors and my brother Richard as supervisor of this my testament and I wish that Richard should have 6s 8d for his labour by these presents.

f46r 101 MARGARET HAROWEDON 2nd September 1485 widow

In the name of God Amen etcetera the seconde day of September the
yere of ower lorde Jeshu Cryste mccccclxxxv I Margeret Harowedon wedowe
beyng in hole mynd and feythfull belefe of holy churche dysposyde to make
me redy to the mercy of the moste gracyus lord ower savour Jeshu Cryste qwen yt
shal please hym to call me owte of this mortall lyfe declare ordeyne and make
my laste wyll and testament in maner and form that folowth Fyrste I commend
my soule to the mercy of All mygthy God my body to be beryed in the churche
of Al Halowys of Haroweden the more in the shyre of Northampton Also I beqweth
to the vycar of Saynt Gyles of Northampton qwer I am dwellyng for my mortuary
my best jewell after the custome of the same town of Northampton Also I beqweth
to Thomas Praty a premour a federbedd a payer of shetys a coverlet for
a bedd Also I beqweth to John Mutt my servaunt a feder bed a payer of

shetes a coverlet for a bed Also to Margeret Awdeley my roset gown Also I beqweth to my dogthyr Margery Garnam my crosse of golde and a ryng of golde Also I beqweth to Margett my doghtyr the wyfe of George Longvyle my capp furryt with armyns (ermine) Also I beqweth to Johan Chaney the wyfe of John Chaney my bedys of awmber Also I beqweth to Richard Knyghtley a gown of skarlet Also to Jane the wyfe of the same Richard a gyrdyll Also to Richard the son of the same Richard Knyghtley a spone of sylver Also to Thomas the son to the same Richard a sylver spone Also to Edmund the son of the same Richard a spone of sylver and as for my plate that was layde to pleage to the vicary of Sulgrave be my son Thomas Harowdon I wyll that my sayde dogthyr Margery feche the same plate and pay for yt suche as ytt lyth fore and the resydewe of yt to be done for my sowle helth be the discrecoun of the sayde Margery my doghter And for all suche dettes as lyth owyng to me be my sayde son Thomas or be any othir persone or persones I wyll my sayde doghter Margery shall have and receyfe hem to dispose them for the wele of my sowle be hyr discrecoun Also qwere I have infeoffed Nicholas Vause Thomas Grene Richard Knyghtley and othir in the maner of Plompton with ther apurtenunce in the counte of Northampton to the entent that they shuld make sale of wodde there to performe my laste wyll with suche money as they shall recyve for the same wodd be them or any of them there sold

f46v

That not withstandyng I wyl ordeyn dispose and declare be thys my last wyll that my sayde Feoffes shall immediatly after my discease suffer my doghter Margery peasbully to enter to the sayde maner of Plompton with the apurtenances with owte interrupcoun of them or ony of them in theyr names for shee ys rygthfull heyr and suffer hyr to take the issues and the profettes therof as they wyl answer a fore ower saveor Jeshu Cryst at the dredefull day of dome for I chearge them and disgearge me agyenst God for my last wyll that my sayde doghter Margery in no wyse be hurte nor dyshered be the sayd feoffment Also I wyll that my seyd Feoffes make no ferther sale in the woddes ther but be the advyse and assent of my sayde doghter Margery and suche wod as ys fellyd and solde ther I wyll that my doghter Margery receyve the money of ytt then to berye me with All the resydewe of my godys not beqwethyt I wyll that they be at the disposicoun of my sayde doghter Margery Garnam and the sayd Margery Garnam I wyll ordeyn and make myn executrice for to dyspose my godes not beqwethyt for the helth of my sowle and of my husbandes and for all Crystyn sowles In wytnes of thys my last wyll I have sett my seale the day and yere above sayd in the presens of John Clerke baker William Lyne marchaunt John Pasty Nicholas Wodd Richard Jonys and othyr moo

f46v 102 WILLIAM BAYLE 11th July 1486 corvisor

In Dei nomine Amen xj die mensis Julii anno domini mcccclxxxvj Ego Willelmus Bayle de Northampton corvesur compos mentis et sane memorie condo testamentum meum in hunc modum In primis lego animam meam Deo Omnipotenti Beate Marie Virgini sue genitrici ac omnibus sanctis curie celestis corpusque meum sepiliendum in cimiterio ecclesie parochiali Omnium Sanctorum ville Northampton predicte iuxta murum capelle Sancti Johannis Baptiste
ibidem versus borialem Item lego priori Sancti Andree apostoli Northampton pro decimis et oblacionibus
meis subtractis seu oblitis vjs.viijd. Item lego fraternitati Sancte Trinitatis et Beate Marie Virginis ibidem xxd. Item lego fraternitati Sancte Crucis ibidem xxd. Item lego fraternitati Sancte Katerine in novo cimiterio xxd. Item lego fraternitati Sancti Johannis Baptiste in

dicta ecclesia Omnium Sanctorum xxd. Item lego fraternitati Sancte Cithe ibidem xxd. Item cuilibet
domui fratrum mendicancium ville Northampton xxd. Item lego fraternitati Sancti Michaelis in eadem ville xxd. Item lego Firmario hospitali Sancti Johannis Northampton xxd. equaliter inter pauperes ibidem distribuendum Item lego leproso domus Sancti Leonardi iuxta Northampton
(via) ibidem existenti viijd. Item lego fabrice ecclesie de Weston Favell xijd.

f47r

Item lego fabrice ecclesie Omnium Sanctorum predicte iijs.iiijd. Item lego reparacioni de Russhmyl cawse
iijs.iiijd. Item lego conventui prioratus Sancti Andree ville Northampton inter eos equaliter dividendum
vjs.viijd. Item lego monasterio Sancti Jacobi iuxta Northampton vjs.viijd. secundum formam predictam distribu-
endum Item lego fabrice ecclesie de Ekton xxd. Item lego monasterio de Launde inter conventum
ibidem dividendum vjs.viijd. Item lego fabrice ecclesie de Wolde ijs. ulteriusque (volo) do et lego
ad usum domus elemosinarii Sancti Thome Martiris extra portam australem ville Northampton pro sustentacione
et confortacione ac releva[min]e pauperum nunc et infuturum ibidem residencium imperpetuum durati
unum annualem redditum xijd. bone monete Anglie percipiendum annuatim de tenemento meo
in vico Magistrali ville Northampton predicte modo in tenura Johannis Cappam wever habendum
et tenendum totum predictum annualem redditum xijd. de et in predicto tenemento cum suis pertinenciis ut predictum est dicte domui elemosinarie imperpetuum percipiendum annuatim ad festum
Michaelis Archangeli et si contingat predictum annualem redditum xijd. aretro fore in parte vel in toto non soluto per sex septimanas post festum predictum si petatur volo tunc quod licitum erit magistris sive custodibus domine fraternitatis Sancti Thome Martiris pro tempore existentis
ac eorum successoribus vel assignatis in predicto tenemento cum suis pertinenciis et quolibet eorumdem parcella distringere districtiones que sic captas licite asportare abducere et effugare et penes se retinere quousque de predicte redditu et eius arreragiis eis plenarie fuerint satisfactum et persolutum ac sic tociens casus huiumodi contigerit ac in super volo per presentes
quod si contingat Ricardum filium meum et heredem me supervivere quod tunc ibidem Ricardus super
benedicionem meam causabit fiere securi et legalem statum de predicte annuali redditu xijd. habendum et percipiendum informa prenotata imperpetuum absque perturbacione aliqui Residuum
vero bonorum meorum superius non legatorum do et lego Johanni Marchall de Northampton seniori
corvesur et prefato Ricardo filio meo ad inde disponendum prosalute anime mee et animarum omnium
amicorum meorum necnon omnium fidelium defunctorum prout eis melius videbitur expediri
et ad istud testamentum bene et fideliter exequendum prefatum Johannem et Ricardum ordino facio
et constituo executores meos Et pro debita execucione premissorum dominum Willelmum Melton capellanum ordino et facio supervisorem Et volo quod idem dictus Willelmus habeat

pro labore suo vjs.viijd. Et similiter quod predictus Johannes Marchall senior habeat pro labore suo
xs. bone monete Anglie per presentes Date die et anno supradictis

In the name of God Amen the 11th day of July 1486 I William Bayle, corvisor, in sound mind and good memory make my testament in this wise. First I bequeath my soul to Almighty God, to the Blessed Virgin Mary His mother and all the saints of the court of heaven, my body to be buried in the churchyard of the parish church of All Saints in the said town of Northampton next to the chapel wall of St John the Baptist there facing the the north. Item I bequeath to the Prior of St Andrew the Apostle in Northampton for tithes and offerings underpaid by me or forgotten 6s 8d. Item I bequeath to the fraternity of Holy Trinity and Blessed Virgin Mary there 20d. Item I bequeath to the fraternity of the Holy Cross there 20d. Item I bequeath to the fraternity of St Katherine in the new churchyard 20d. Item I bequeath to the fraternity of St John the Baptist in the same church of All Saints 20d. Item I bequeath to the fraternity of St Cithe there 20d. Item to each house of mendicant brothers in the town of Northampton 20d. Item I bequeath to the fraternity of St Michael in the same town 20d. Item I bequeath to the infirmary of the Hospital of St John in Northampton 20d to be distributed equally amongst the poor there. Item I bequeath to the leprosy house of St Leonard next to the Northampton Road there 8d. Item I bequeath to the fabric of the church of Weston Favell 12d. Item I bequeath to the fabric of the church of All Saints aforesaid 3s 4d. Item I bequeath to the repair of Rushmill Cawse 3s 4d. Item I bequeath to the convent and priory of St Andrew in the town of Northampton to be divided equally amongst them 6s.8d. Item I bequeath to the monastery of St James next to Northampton to be distributed according to the manner above stated 6s 8d. Item I bequeath to the fabric of the church of Ecton 20d. Item I bequeath to the monastery of Launde to be shared there amongst the convent 6s 8d. Item I bequeath to the fabric of the church of Old 2s. Moreover I give and bequeath for the benefit of the almshouse of St Thomas the Martyr outside the south gate of Northampton for the sustenance, comfort and relief of the poor now and in the future for the duration of their residence, an annual rent of 12d in good English money to be received from my tenement in Masters Street in Northampton aforesaid, now in the tenure of John Cappam, weaver. To have and to hold to the aforesaid almshouse forever the whole of the aforesaid annual rent of 12d of and in the aforesaid tenement with its appurtenances aforesaid to be received annually at the Feast of St Michael the Archangel and if it should happen that the said annual rent of 12d. should be in unpaid arrears either in part or the whole amount for 6 weeks after the said feast day, I will then that it should be lawful for the masters or guardians for the time being of the said fraternity of St Thomas the

Martyr, or their designated successors or assigns, to distrain on the aforesaid tenement with its appurtenances whatsoever parcel of the same and lawfully to carry, load and drive away the distraints thus taken until full satisfaction and payment is met concerning the aforesaid rent and arrears and thus it shall happen as many times in this way. And further I will by these presents that if it happens that Richard, my son and heir, survives me that then the said Richard, upon my blessing, shall cause to be made a secure and legal estate concerning the aforesaid annual rent of 12d to be had and received in form above noted for ever without any disruption. The residue of my goods not bequeathed above I give and bequeath to John Marshall senior of Northampton, corvisor, and the said Richard, my son, to then dispose for the health of my soul and the souls of all my friends and also all faithful departed as seems best to them and that this testament be well and faithfully executed I ordain, make and constitute the said John and Richard my executors. And for the due execution of these premises I ordain and make Dom William Melton, chaplain, as supervisor and I wish that the same William should have for his labour 6s 8d. And similarly that the said John Marshall, senior, should have for his labour 10s in good English money by these presents. Given the day and year abovesaid.

f47r 103 WILLIAM GEORGE 14th August 1485

In the name of God Amen xiiij day of August the yere of ower lorde mcccclxxxv I William George in myn hole and clere mynd thankyt beyth Jeshu make ordeyn this my testament in manner and forme folowyng Fyrst I beqwethe my sowle to All mygthy God my creator and to hys blessyt moder Saynt Marye and to all the payntes of heweyn my body to be beryed qwer yt shall please God Item I beqweth to the vycar of my paryssh churche* for my tythes and offeryngs forgoton xld. Also I beqweth to the fraternite of Saynt Clement ther to be prayed for xld. Item I woll that my Feoffes make unto Gylys Swayn my modyr a swire astate in and of that tenement curtelage and crofte in Warmynster late in the tenure of Amye Whyte and now in the holde of John Freland To have and to holde to hyr hyr heyres and assignes for ever more provided alway that the saide John Freland be not interrupt

f47v

noe hurte be my sayde modyr of the yerys that he hath in the premisses as long as he payth and performe hys covenantes acordyng to hys indentures and also that myn executryce delyver unto my sayde modyr all syche evydens as covereth the same Also I wyll that my sayde executrice immediately after the discease of my sayde modyr delyver unto my nexte heyr all othyr evydences concernyng all othyr landes and tenementes that I have in Warmynster afore sayde The residewe of all my godes after my dettes payde I geve and bequeth unto Johanne Chauncy my maisteres and hyr I ordeyn and make myn executryce be this presentes In wytnes qwerof to this my laste wyll I have putte my seale the day and yere above sayde

* *This must be St. Giles as it is the only church to have a fraternity of St. Clement.*

f48r 106 RICHARD HORPOLL 29th March 1487 tanner

In Dei nomine Amen xxix die Marcii anno domini mccccl xxxvij Ego Ricardus Horpoll de Northampton tanner compos mentis et sane memorie sponte et non coactus condo testamentum meum
in hunc modum In primis lego animam meam Deo Omnipotenti Beate Marie et omnibus sanctis corpus-
que meum sepiliendum in ecclesia Sancti Petri ville Northampton Item lego imagino crucifixe iijs.iiijd. Item
lego summo altari xijd. Item lego altari Beate Marie xijd. Item lego altari Sancti Johannis Baptiste xijd.
Item lego altari Sancti Nicholi (Sancti Nicholi) xijd. Item lego altari Sancte Katerine xijd. Item lego Alicie
uxori mee unam domum cum molendino et orto cum aliis pertinenciis ad terminum vite sue excepte
quod Willelmus Horpoll frater meus habeat liberum aditum et exitum pro suo aisamento ad stagna
sicut in vita mea et post obitum predicte Alicie volo ut frater meus habeat predictam domum cum molendino et orto sibi et assignatis suis durante termino dimissionis illius Item
lego unum gardinum jacens inter terras Willelmi Sabyn et tenementum Roberti Baldwyn in parochia
Sancti Petri ad sustentacionem fraternitati Sancti Riginarii in ecclesia predicta Sancti Petri Item lego Willelmo
Hayrowe vjs.viijd. Item Willelmo Davys vjs.viijd. Item lego Isabelle Dowton sorori mee vjs.viijd.
Item Roberto Baldwyn vjs.viijd. Residuum vero omnium bonorum meorum non legatorum do et lego
predicte Alicie uxori mee et ad istud testamentum meum bene et fideliter exequendum predictam Aliciam ordino executricem
meam et Willelmum Hayrowe supervisorem die et anno supradictis hiis testibus domino Willelmo Aythrope Willelmo Hayrowe et
Willelmo Horpoll cum aliis

In the name of God Amen the 29th day of March 1487 I Richard Horpoll, tanner, in sound mind and good memory, freely and without compulsion make my testament in this wise. First I bequeath my soul to Almighty God, to the Blessed Mary and all the saints, my body to be buried in the church of St Peter in the town of Northampton. Item I bequeath to the image of the cross 3s 4d. Item I bequeath to the high altar 12d. Item I bequeath to the altar of the Blessed Mary 12d. Item I bequeath to the altar of St John the Baptist 12d. Item I bequeath to the altar of St Nicholas 12d. Item I bequeath to the altar of St Katherine 12d. Item I bequeath to Alice, my wife, one house with a mill and a garden with all appurtenances for the term of her life, except that William Horpoll, my brother, shall have the free access and egress for his easement to the pond as in my lifetime, and after the death of the aforesaid Alice I will that my brother shall have the said house with mill and garden for himself and his assigns during the term of these demises. Item I bequeath one garden lying between the lands of William Sabyn and the tenement of Robert Baldwin in the parish of St Peter for the support of the fraternity of St Ragener in the said church of St Peter. Item I bequeath to William Hayrowe 6s 8d. Item to William Davys 6s 8d. Item I bequeath to Isabel Dowton, my sister, 6s 8d. Item to Robert Baldwin 6s 8d. The residue of all my goods not bequeathed I give and bequeath to the said Alice, my wife, and that this my testament be well and faithfully executed I ordain the aforesaid Alice my executrix and William Hayrowe supervisor. Day and year abovesaid. With these witnesses Dom William Aythrope, William Hayrowe and William Horpoll with others.

f48v 107 JOHN WELLYS 24th August 1487 mercer

In Dei nomine Amen xx quarto die Augusti anno domini mccccIxxxvij
Ego Johannes Wellys de Northampton mercer compos mentis et sane memorie condo testamentum meum in hunc modum In primis lego et commendo animam Deo Omnipotenti Beate Marie matri eius ac omnibus celi sanctis corpus que meum sepiliendum in cimiterio ecclesie Omnium Sanctorum ville Northampton predicte in platea processionaria ex parte boriali eiusdem ecclesie Item lego rectori eiusdem ecclesie pro decimis et oblationibus oblitis xjs.vd. quos michi debet pro diversis rebus a me emptis ad proficium loci sui pro servienti eiusdem tempore Willelmi Breknok ibidem existenti prout patet per billam paupiri parcellatam Item lego fraternitati Sancte Trinitatis in eadem ecclesia ad orandum pro anima mea xxd. et unam torche cere Item lego fraternitati Corporis Christi eiusdem ecclesie xxd. Item lego fraternitati Beate Marie in eadem ecclesia xxd. Item lego fraternitati Sancte Crucis in eadem ecclesia xijd. et unam torche Item lego fraternitati Sancti Johannis Baptiste infra eandem ecclesiam xxd. et unam torche Item lego fraternitati Sancti Georgii in eadem ecclesia xijd. Item lego fraternitati Sancte Katerine
in le pardon church yerd xxd. et unam torche cere Item lego reparacione capelle Sancte Katerine in le pardon churche yerd predicto iijs.iiijd. Item lego reparacionibus ecclesie Omnium Sanctorum iijs.iiijd. Item lego reparacionibus ecclesie Sancti Michaelis ville Northampton
iijs.iiid. Item lego quattuor ordinibus fratrum infra villam predictam ad orandum cuilibet eorum xxd. Item lego pauperibus domus Sancti Thome Martiris ad portam australem ville predicte ad orandum pro anima mea iijs.iiijd. Item lego reparacionibus ecclesie parochali de Cranfeld vjs.viijd. Item lego reparacionibus ecclesie parochali de Maldon iijs.iiijd. Item lego Margate filie mee ad suam maritagium vel ad etatem legitimam Cs. et unum lectum videlicet a materasse cum le bolster par linthiamentum unum par lodicum unum coopertorium unum par precium unam missam cum argento deaurato ligatam quatuor cocliaria argentea et unam zonam argento arnesiatam Item lego Johanne sorori mee iijs.iiijd.
Item lego cuilibet puerorum eiusdem Johanne sororis mee ijd. et unam pileam
Item lego Johanni Godfrey, bocher de suo debito michi pertinente ad orandum pro anima mea vjs.viijd. Item lego Willelmo Hylles fratri meo ad orandum pro anima mea iijs.iiijd. Item lego Thome Wellys mercer xxd. Item lego Willelmo Wellys xxd. Item lego servientibus meis mecum modo existentibus cuilibet eorum xxd. Item do et lego Agneti uxori mee meum magnum tenementum cum omnibus suis pertinenciis situatumm in vico vocato Abyndon Strete ville Northampton predicte ex parte australi eiusdem vici inter tenementum Sancti Georgii ibidem ex parte orientali habendum et tenendum totum predictum tenementum cum omnibus
suis pertinenciis prefate Agneti et assignatis suis durante vita sua et inmediate post decessum predicte Agnetis volo quod predictum tenementum cum omnibus suis pertinenciis

f49r

totaliter remaneant predicte Margate filie mee habendum et tenendum sibi et heredibus de corpore suo legitime
procreatis imperpetuum de capitalibus dominis feodi illius per servicia inde debita et de iure consueta
Et si contingat predictam Margaretam filiam meam sine heredebus de corpore legitime procreatis
obire quod absit tunc volo quod totum predictum tenementum cum suis pertinenciis totaliter remaneat
proximis heredibus meis habendum et tenendum eis heredibus et assignatis suis imperpetuum de capitalibus
dominis feodi illius etcetera Item do et lego predicte Agneti uxori mee alia duo tenementa
mea situata in venella vocata Whyte Freres Lane infra villam Northampton antedictam
cum omnibus suis pertinenciis habendum et tenendum predicta duo tenementa cum omnibus suis pertinenciis
sibi et assignatis suis custodiendum vel vendendum pro solucione debitorum meonum in exoneracionibus
anime mee prout ei melius videbitur expediri sine aliquo contradiccione interruptione vel
impedimento alicuius alterius sive aliquorum aliorum quorumcumque in futurum Residuum
vero omnium bonorum meorum superius non legatorum debitis meis solutis totaliter do et lego
predicte Agneti uxori mee ad inde ordinandum et disponendum pro salute anime mee et
animarum omnium parentum et amicorum meorum ac filiorum meorum prout ei melius videbitur
expediri Et facio et ordino presentis testamenti mei predictam Agnetam meam executricem
simull cum domino Roberto Waren capellano Et volo ac similiter rogo Henricum Umfrey
mercer si sibi placuerit esse supervisorem

In the name of God Amen the 24th day of August 1487 I John Wellys, mercer, in sound mind and good memory make my testament in this wise. First I bequeath and commend my soul to Almighty God to the Blessed Mary His mother and all the saints of heaven, my body to be buried in the cemetery of the church of All Saints in the town of Northampton aforesaid, in the processional place on the north side of the same church. Item I bequeath to the rector of the same church for tithes and oblations forgotten 11s 5d which he owes me for various things bought from me for the profit of his place by his servant for the time being there, William Breknok, just as appears by a detailed bill of paper. Item I bequeath to the fraternity of Holy Trinity in that same church to pray for my soul 20d and one wax candle. Item I bequeath to the fraternity of Corpus Christi in that same church 20d. Item I bequeath to the fraternity of the Blessed Mary in that same church 20d. Item I bequeath to the fraternity of the Holy Cross in that same church 20d and one torch. Item I bequeath to the fraternity of St John the Baptist within the same church 20d and one torch. Item I bequeath to the fraternity of St Katherine in the pardon churchyard 20d and one wax torch. Item I bequeath to the repairs of the chapel of St Katherine in the pardon churchyard aforesaid 3s 4d. Item I bequeath to the repairs of the church of All Saints 3s 4d. Item I bequeath to the repairs of the church of St Michael in the town of

Northampton 3s 4d. Item I bequeath to the four orders of brothers within the aforesaid town to pray, to each of them 20d. Item I bequeath to the poor of the house of St Thomas the Martyr at the south gate of the said town to pray for my soul 3s 4d. Item I bequeath to the repairs of the parish church of Cranfield 6s 8d. Item I bequeath to the repairs of the parish church of Maldon 3s 4d. Item I bequeath to Marget, my daughter, on her marriage or her coming of legal age 100s and one bed, namely one mattress with the bolster, one pair of sheets, one pair of blankets, one coverlet, one rosary, one missal bound with silvergilt, four silver spoons and one girdle ornamented with silver. Item I bequeath to Joanne, my sister, 3s 4d. Item I bequeath to each child of that same Joanne, my sister, 2d and a cap. Item I bequeath to John Godfrey, butcher, from his debt to me to pray for my soul 6s.8d. Item I bequeath to William Hylles, my brother, to pray for my soul 6s 8d. Item I bequeath to Thomas Wellys, mercer, 20d. Item I bequeath to William Wellys 20d. Item I bequeath to my servants at present working for me, to each one of them 20d. Item I give and bequeath to Agnes, my wife, my large tenement with all its appurtenances situated in Abington Street in the aforementioned town of Northampton on the south side of that street between the property of St George's there on the east side, for Agnes and her assigns to have and to hold the whole of that property and its appurtenances, to the aforesaid Agnes for the duration of her life and immediately after the death of the said Agnes I will that the aforementioned property should remain in its entirety to Marget, my aforementioned daughter, to have and to hold to her and to the heirs of her body legitimately begotten forever, to hold of the chief lords of the fee for services therefore due and by right accustomed. And if it happens that Marget, my daughter, die without heirs of her body lawfully begotten (which God forbid) then I will that the whole aforesaid tenement with its appurtenances remain totally to my next heirs to have and to hold to them, their heirs and assigns for ever of the chief lords of the fee by services therefore due and by right accustomed. Item I give and bequeath to the aforesaid Agnes, my wife, my other two tenements situated in the lane called Whyte Friars Lane, within Northampton aforesaid, with all their appurtenances, to have and to hold the aforesaid two tenements with all their appurtenances to her and her assigns to keep or sell for the payment of my debts and exoneration of my soul as seems best to her, without any contradiction, interruption or impediment of any other or any others whatsoever in the future. The residue of all my goods not bequeathed above, my dues and total payments I give and bequeath to the aforesaid Agnes, my wife, to then ordain and dispose for the health of my soul and all the souls of my parents and my friends and my children as seems best to her. And I make and ordain the aforesaid Agnes, my wife, my executrix of this my present testament together with Dom Robert Waren, chaplain. And I will and similarly ask Henry Umfrey, mercer, if it would please him to be supervisor.

f50r 109 JOHN COLMAN 22nd October 1487

In Dei nomine Amen xxij die Otobris anno domini mccccLxxxvij Ego Johannes Colman de Northampton compos mentis etcetera condo testamentum meum in hunc modum In primis lego
animam meam Deo Omnipotenti etcetera corpusque meum sepiliendum in capella Corporis Christi infra ecclesiam Omnium Sanctorum ville Northampton iuxta sepulturam Henrici Colman patris
mei Item lego pro sepultura mea ibidem vjs.viijd. Item lego fraternitati Corporis Christi ibidem vjs.viijd. Item lego fraternitati Sancte Trinitatis in eadem ecclesia xxs. Item
lego fraternitati Sancte Marie in eadem ecclesia xxs. Item lego summo altari ibidem pro decimis
et oblationibus oblitis xxs. Item lego fraternitati Sancte Crucis in eadem ecclesia iijs.iiijd. Item lego fraternitati
Sancti Johannis Baptiste in eadem ecclesia iijs.iiijd. Item lego fraternitati Sancte Cithe in eadem ecclesia
iijs.iiijd. Item lego fraternitati Sancti Georgii Martiris in eadem ecclesia iijs.iiijd. Item lego fraternitati Sancte Katerine
in le newe churche yerde iijs.iiijd. Item lego reparacionibus ecclesia Omnium Sanctorum predicte xs.
Item lego quattuor ordinibus fratrum mendicancium infra ville predicte cuilibet videlicet eorum vs. Item
lego abbati et conventui Sancti Jacobi iuxta Northampton ad orandum pro anima mea xxs. Item lego
ad sustentacionem collegii infra parochiam Omnium Sanctorum ville Northampton predicte xs. Item lego
abbitesse et conventui de Pratis iuxta Northampton ad orandum pro anima mea xs. Item lego ad sustentacionem
domus Sancti Thome Martiris extra portam australem ville predicte xls. Item lego priorisse et conventui
de Rothwell ad orandum pro anima mea xs. Item lego fraternitati Sancti Michaelis in ecclesia Sancti Michaelis eiusdem
ville Northampton iijs.iiijd. Item lego octo pauperibus tenentibus torchias die obitus mei cuilibet
eorum unam togam nigram Item lego dictas octo torchias diversis ecclesiis sive fratribus ubi executrici
mee melius videbitur expediri Item lego pauperibus die obitus mei inter ipsos distribuendum in
pecuniis xxli. Item lego domino Willelmo Melton capellano xls. Item lego Katerine filie
mee ad suum maritagium vel ad suam legitimam etatem per deliberaciones executrice mee xl.li. et
si contingat dictam Katerinam filiam meam obire infra etatem legitimam tunc volo quod predictas xl.li.
totaliter distribuantur per discrecionem executrice mee pro salute anime mee et animarum parentum
meorum et amicorum meorum prout ei melius videbitur expediri Item lego Elizabeth nuper
servienti mee vjli.xiijs.iiijd. Item lego ydoneo capellano per tres annos post obitum meum
ad celebrandum servicium infra ecclesiam Omnium Sanctorum ville Northampton predicte quolibet anno vli.vjs.viijd.
Item lego Willelmo Colman avunculo meo ad orandum pro anima mea xxs. Item lego Ricardo Fawcer
avunculo meo xs. Item lego Willelmo Palmer dyer xxs. Item lego <Thome> Palmer fratri suo xxs.

f50v

Item lego Alicie Morwood uxori Roberti Morwood vjs.viijd. Item lego Johanni Reus de Kyngesthorp xls. Item lego Willelmo Jakelyn alias Willelmo Clerke vyntener xls.
Item lego Agneti Palmer vidue xiijs.iiijd. Item lego Agneti Palmer filie eiusdem Agneti ad suum maritagium xs. Item lego Johanni Wem ad orandum pro anima mea vjs.viijd.
Item lego cuilibet serviencium meorum [nunc] mecum existencium vjs.viijd. Item lego Margarete
Legge ijs. Item lego reparacione pontis occidentalis prope villam Northampton predictam xxs.
Item lego Johanni Palmer filio predicto Willelmi Palmer duo cocliaria argenti Item lego Agneti
Chylde de Dalyngton ad orandum pro anima mea iijs.iiijd. Item lego Johanne filie predicte Agnetis Palmer vidue vjs.viijd. Item lego Johanne Drewry unum panii et unum laver precii vjs.viijd. Item lego Johanne Smarte ijs. Item lego Margerie London iijs.
Item lego pauperibus in firmaria domus Sancti Johannis ville predicto equaliter inter eos distribuendum xiijs.iiijd. Residuum vero omnium bonorum meorum superius non legatorum totaliter do et lego Agneti Isaak matri mee ad inde ordinandum
et disponendum pro salute anime mee et animarum parentum et amicorum meorum prout ei melius videbitur expediri et facio et ordino eandem Agnetem matrem meam executricem etcetera.

In the name of God Amen the 22nd Day of October 1487 I John Colman of Northampton in sound mind etcetera make my testament in this wise. First I bequeath my soul to Almighty God etcetera, my body to be buried in the chapel of Corpus Christi within the church of All Saints, Northampton next to the grave of Henry Colman my father. Item I bequeath for my burial there 6s 8d. Item I bequeath to the fraternity of Corpus Christi there 6s 8d. Item I bequeath to the fraternity of Holy Trinity in the same church 20s. Item I bequeath to the fraternity of St Mary in the same church 20s. Item I bequeath to the high altar there for tithes and oblations forgotten 20s. Item I bequeath to the fraternity of the Holy Cross in the same church 3s 4d. Item I bequeath to the fraternity of St John Baptist in the same church 3s 4d. Item I bequeath to the fraternity of St Cithe in the same church 3s 4d. Item I bequeath to the fraternity of St George the Martyr in the same church 3s 4d. Item I bequeath to the fraternity of St Katherine in the new churchyard 3s 4d. Item I bequeath for the repair of the said church of All Saints 10s. Item I bequeath to the four orders of mendicant brothers in the said town, that is to say to each of them 5s. Item I bequeath to the Abbot and convent of St James near Northampton to pray for my soul 20s. Item I bequeath to the support of the college in the parish of All Saints of the town of Northampton 10s. Item I bequeath to the Abbess and convent of Delapre near Northampton to pray for my soul 10s. Item I bequeath for the sustenance of the house of St Thomas the Martyr outside the south gate of the said town 40s. Item I bequeath to the Prioress and convent of Rothwell to pray for my soul 10s. Item I bequeath to the fraternity of St Michael in the church of St Michael in the same town of Northampton 3s 4d. Item I bequeath to eight poor people holding torches on the day of my death, to each of them a black gown. Item I bequeath the said eight torches to various churches and brothers as it seems best to my executrix. Item I bequeath £20 to be distributed among the poor on the day of my death. Item I bequeath to Dom William Melton, chaplain, 40s. Item I bequeath to Katherine, my daughter, at her marriage or at her coming of legal age at the judgment of my executrix £10 and if it should happen that Katherine, my daughter, should die before coming of age then I will that the said £10 should be totally distributed at the discretion of my executrix for the health of my soul and the souls of my parents and friends as may seem best to her. Item I bequeath to Elizabeth, formerly my servant, £6 8s 4d. Item I bequeath to a suitable chaplain for three years after my death to conduct services in the church of All Saints each year £5 6s 8d. Item I bequeath to William Colman, my uncle, to pray for my soul 20s. Item I bequeath to Richard Fawcer, my uncle, 10s. Item I bequeath to William Palmer, dyer, 20s. Item I bequeath to Thomas Palmer, his brother 20s. Item I bequeath to Alice Morwood, wife of Robert Morwood, 6s 8d. Item I bequeath to John Reus of Kingsthorpe 40s. Item I bequeath to William Jakelyn also known as William Clerk vintner 40s. Item I bequeath to Agnes Palmer, widow, 13s 4d. Item I bequeath to Agnes Palmer, daughter of the said Agnes at her marriage 10s. Item I bequeath to John Wem to pray for my soul 6s 8d. Item I bequeath to each of my servants then living with me 6s 8d. Item I bequeath to Margaret Legge 2s. Item I bequeath for the repair of the west bridge near the said town of Northampton 20s. Item I bequeath to John Palmer, son of the said William Palmer, two silver spoons. Item I bequeath to Agnes Chylde of Dallington to pray for my soul 3s 4d. Item I bequeath to Joan, daughter of the said Agnes Palmer widow 6s 8d. Item I bequeath to Joan Drewry one measure of cloth and a laver to the value of 6s 8d. Item I bequeath to Joan Smart 2s. Item I bequeath to Margery London 3s. Item I bequeath to the poor in the infirmary of the house of St John in the said town 13s 4d. to be equally distributed amongst them. The residue of all my goods not above bequeathed I give and bequeath entirely to Agnes Isaak, my mother, to then dispose for the health of my soul and the souls of my parents and friends as seems best to her and I make and ordain the said Agnes, my mother, my executrix etcetera.

f50v 110 WILLIAM MAY 28th August 1487 mercer

In Dei nomine Amen xxviij die Augusti anno domini millesimo cccclxxxvij Ego Willelmus May de Northampton mercer compos mentis et sane memorie condo testamentum meum in hunc

modum In primis lego animam meam Deo Omnipotenti Beate Marie Virginis eius genitrici et omnibus sanctis curie celestis corpus meum sepiliendum in capella Beate Marie virginis in ecclesia Omnium Sanctorum ville Northampton iuxta sepulturam Elizabethe nuper uxoris mee Item lego

Priori Sancti Andree pro decimis meis oblitis vjs.viijd. Item lego vicario ecclesie Omnium Sanctorum xvjd. Item lego cuilibet presbytero exequiis meis et missis interessenti iiijd. Item lego cuilibet clerico parochali ijd. Item lego fraternitati Sancte Trinitatis xvjd. Item lego fraternitati Beate Marie Virginis pro sepultura mea in capella predicta vjs.viijd. Item lego fraternitati Corporis Christi xvjd. Item lego fraternitati Sancti Georgii xijd. Item lego fraternitati Sancte Crucis xijd. Item lego fraternitati Sancti Johannis Baptiste xvjd. Item lego fabrice ecclesie Omnium Sanctorum xijd. Item lego fratribus minoribus Northampton xxd. Item lego cuilibet alio ordini fratrum mendicancium infra eandem villam xijd. Item lego Margarete uxori mee xxli. percipiendum tam de vendicacione tenementi mei iuxta collegiam quam de debitis meis Item lego <Willelmo May> filio meo et herede meo omnia terras tenementa redditus et servicia cum pertinenciis suis que michi discendebant iure hereditario post decessum Ricardi May patris mei tam infra villam Northampton quam infra villam de Holcote Item lego Ricardo May filio meo xxs. et similiter pro legacione quondam sibi factam per Simonem Draper de Lyn avum suum xxs. Item lego Agneti

f51r

filie mee cum xxs. de consimile legacione ave sui predicti xls. Item lego eidem Agneti filie mee duas ollas eneas videlicet maiorem et minorem et unam patellam eneam et unam pelvim de masslyn cum lavacro secundum discrecionem executorum meorum liberandum Item lego Willelmo Chanterell meam optimam togam de skarlett penulatam Item lego Ricardo filio meo unam togam meam de liberatura Gilde Corporis Christi cum furrura eiusdem Item lego Willelmo Holcote consanguino meo meam togam coloris violett et unam cistam secundum discrecionem exe-cutorum meorum liberandum Item lego Thome Holcote filio eiusdem Willelmi unam ollam eneam et unam pelvim cum lavacro secundum discrecionem executorum meorum Item volo quod omnia jocalia mea in custodia alicuius persone existencia replegiantur per executores meos et residuum pecunie valoris eorundem disponetur per eosdem executores meos in bonis operibus et aliis donis caritativis Item volo quod reversio tenementi mei iacentis iuxta collegiam infra ville Northampton vendatur per executores meos meliori modo quo poterint ad perficiendum legata predicta salve jure cuiuslibet Item volo quod aliud tenementum meum iacens in parochia Sancti Petri quod nuper habui ex dono et feoffamento Petri Flaxman et Alicie uxoris suo vendatur per dicte executores meos et disponatur tam pro salute anime mee quam pro salute animarum eorundem Petri et Alicie secundum discrecionem dictorum executorum meorum

Item lego Margarete uxori mee duo tenementa mea cum omnibus suis pertinenciis in villa et campis de Holcote habendum et tenendum sibi et assignatis suis ad terminum vite sue secundum vim formam et effectum cuiusdem carte mee sibi inde confectam Item lego eidem Margarete uxori mee duo cotagia mea situata infra portam orientalem ville Northampton habendum et tenendum sibi et assignatis suis ad terminum vite sue et post decessum eiusdem Margarete remaneant duo cotagia predicta cum suis pertinenciis Agneti May filie mee habendum et tenendum sibi heredibus et assignatis suis imperpetuum Et pro defectu talium

heredum predictorum duo tenementa vedantur et disponantur per dictos executores meos
in missis et aliis donis caritativis pro salute anime mee uxoris parentum et benefactorum meorum ac omnium fidelium defunctorum Residuum vero omnium bonorum meorum superius
non legatorum debitis meis persolutis do et lego Margarete uxori ac Willelmo Chanterell filio meo quos ordino facio et constituo executores meos ac Willelmum Austyn
et Willelmum Mylly supervisores huius testamenti ut ipsi executores disponant pro salute anime
mee sicut coram summo judice respondere voluerint

In the name of God Amen the 28th day of August 1487 I William May of Northampton, mercer, in sound mind and good memory make my testament in this wise. First I bequeath my soul to Almighty God, to the Blessed Virgin Mary His mother and all the saints of the court of heaven, my body to be buried in the chapel of the Blessed Virgin Mary in the church of All Saints in the town of Northampton, next to the grave of Elizabeth my late wife. Item I bequeath to the Prior of St Andrews for tithes forgotten 6s 8d. Item I bequeath to the Vicar of All Saints church 16d. Item I bequeath to each of the priests acting at my funeral and mass 4d. Item I bequeath to each of the parish clerks 2d. Item I bequeath to the fraternity of the Holy Trinity 16d. Item I bequeath to the fraternity of the Blessed Virgin Mary for my grave in the aforementioned chapel 6s 8d. Item I bequeath to the fraternity of Corpus Christi 16d. Item I bequeath to the fraternity of St George 12d. Item I bequeath to the fraternity of the the Holy Cross 12d. Item I bequeath to the fraternity of St John Baptist 16d. Item I bequeath to the fabric of All Saints church 12d. Item I bequeath to the Friars Minor of Northampton 20d. Item I bequeath to each of the four orders of mendicant brothers within the same town 12d. Item I bequeath to Margaret, my wife, £20 to oversee both the sale of my property next to the College and my debts. Item I bequeath to William May, my son and heir, all land, tenements, rents and services with their appurtenances which came down to me as an inheritance after the death of Richard May, my father, both within the town of Northampton and the town of Holcote. Item I bequeath to Richard May, my son, 20s. and similarly his legacy of 20s. which came to him from Simon Draper of Lyn, his grandfather. Item I bequeath to Agnes, my daughter, with 20s. and a similar legacy from her aforesaid grandfather of 40s. Item I bequeath to the same Agnes, my daughter, two brass pots, that is to say one big one and one small one, and one brass bowl and a brass basin and ewer, to be given to her according to the discretion of my executors. Item I bequeath to William Chanterell my best gown trimmed with scarlet. Item I bequeath to Richard, my son, my Corpus Christi livery gown with fur trimming of the same. Item I bequeath to William Holcote, my cousin, my gown of violet colour and a chest according to the discretion of my executors. Item I bequeath to Thomas Holcote, son of the said William, one brass pot and one basin with ewer according to the discretion of my executors. Item I wish that all my jewels, in the custody of whichever person, should be redeemed by my executors and the residual monetary value from them should be disposed in good works and other charitable gifts. Item I will that the reversion on my tenements lying in the parish of St Peter, which I had formerly from a gift and feoffment from Peter Flaxman and Alice his wife, should be sold by my said executors and they should dispose of it for the health of my soul and the health of the souls of the said Peter and Alice according to the discretion of my executors. Item I bequeath to Margaret, my wife, my two tenements with all their appurtenances in the town and fields of Holcote to have and to hold to her and assigns to the end of her life according to the will, form and effect of a certain charter made to her concerning this. Item I bequeath to that same Margaret, my wife, my two cottages situated within the east gate of the town of Northampton to have and to hold to her and her assigns to the end of her life and after the death of that same Margaret the two aforementioned cottages with their appurtenances should belong to Agnes May, my daughter, to have and to hold to her, her heirs and assigns for ever. And in default of heirs aforesaid the two tenements are to be disposed of by my said executors in masses and other charitable gifts on behalf of my soul and that of my wife, parents, my benefactors and all faithful departed. The residue of all my goods not above bequeathed, my debts having been paid I give and bequeath to Margaret, my wife, and to William Chanterell, my son, whom I ordain, make and constitute as my executors, and William Austyn and William Mylly as supervisors of this testament, such that the executors themselves should settle for the health of my soul just as they will wish to answer before the high judge.

f51v 111 THOMAS WHYTE 30th July 1487 (clothier)

In Dei nomine Amen penultimo die mensis Julii anno domini millesimo ccccIxxxvij
Ego Thomas Whyte de Northampton sana memoria condo testamentum meum in
hunc modum In primis lego animam meam Deo Omnipotenti Beate Marie eius genitrici
et omnibus sanctis curie celestis corpusque meum sepiliendum in cimiterio ecclesie Sancti Sepulcri
ville predicte iuxta parentos meos Item lego summo altari ibidem iijs. iiijd. Item
lego to the rode lofte ibidem xiijs.iiijd. Item lego reparacione ecclesie Sancti Sepulcri
vjs.viijd. Item lego fraternitati Sancte Katerine in ecclesia Beate Marie Virginis eiusdem
ville ijs. Item lego fraternitati Sancti Georgii in ecclesia Omnium Sanctorum eiusdem ville ijs. Item
lego fraternitati Sancte Crucis in ecclesia Omnium Sanctorum predicta ijs. Item lego campane fratrum
Carmelitarum Northampton vjs.viijd. Item volo quod executores mei distribuant die sepulture
mee decem dosen in pane albo inter pauperes utriusque generis secundum discrecionem
executorum meorum Item lego cuilibet domui fratrum mendicancium infra ville North-ampton

iijs.iiijd. Item lego to the pavyng of the Northyate in Northampton iijs.iiijd.
Item lego vicario ecclesie Sancti Sepulcri de Northampton unum gown clothe coloris viridis
Item lego Henrico Thonger de Dalyngton unam togam de russet furryd with blak
lambe Item lego Thome Whyte de Saynt Albanys unam blodiam togam furryd
et unam togam de violet lynyd unum potte et unam panne eneam et unum red
corse gyrdyll hernest with sylver unam materasse unam par lodicum unam par
linthiamentum et unum superlectile Item lego Edwardo Hunne de Elvestowe
j grene corse gyrdyll harnest with sylver Item lego Thome Hunne filio
predicti Edwardi unam ollam eneam ac unam pelvim cum lavacro Item lego
Isabelle Rooche unam pelvim cum lavacro et unam par linthiamentum Item lego
Margarete Cobbe pelvim cum lavacro et unam ollam eneam unam materasse unam par
linthiamentum et unam superlectile Residuum vero bonorum meorum superius
non legatorum do et lego Emmote uxori mee et eandem Emmotam ordino
facio et constituo executricem meam̄ ut ipsa disponat pro salute anime mee
prout sibi videbitur melius expediri Et Edwardum Hunne de Elvestowe
et Thomam Mulso de Northampton ordino et facio presentes testamenti mei supervisores
Date die et anno domini supradictis Item lego dompno Johanni Bulwyk
monacho prioratus Sancti Andree de Northampton xxd. Item lego dompno Thome
Roche monacho eiusdem prioratus xxd. Item lego ecclesie Sancti Sepulcri
duas torchias ad valorem vjs.viijd. Item lego fraternitati Sancti Martini ibidem xijd.

In the name of God Amen the penultimate day of July 1487 I Thomas Whyte of Northampton of sound memory make my testament in this wise. First I bequeath my soul to Almighty God, to the Blessed Virgin Mary His mother and all the saints of the court of heaven, my body to be buried in the churchyard of Holy Sepulchre next to my parents. Item I bequeath to the high altar 3s 4d. Item I bequeath to the Rood loft of the same 13s 4d. Item 1 bequeath to the repair of the church of St Sepulchre 6s 8d. Item I bequeath to the fraternity of St Katherine in the church of the Blessed Virgin Mary in the said town 2s. Item I bequeath to the fraternity of St George in the church of All Saints in the said town 2s. Item I bequeath to the fraternity of the Holy Cross in the aforesaid church of All Saints 2s. Item I bequeath to the bell of the Carmelite Friars of Northampton 6s 8d. Item I will that my executors distribute on the day of my burial ten dozen white loaves among the poor of both kind according to their discretion. Item I bequeath to each house of mendicant brothers within the town of Northampton 3s.4d. Item I bequeath to the paving of the North gate in Northampton 3s 4d. Item I bequeath to the vicar of Holy Sepulchre a gown of green coloured cloth. Item I bequeath to Henry Thonger of Dallington one gown furred with black lamb. Item I bequeath to Thomas Whyte of St Albans a gown of blue colour furred and one gown with violet lining, one pot and one brass pan and one red corse girdle ornamented with silver, one mattress, one pair of blankets, one pair of sheets and one coverlet. Item I bequeath to Edward Hunne of Elvestowe a green corse girdle ornamented with silver. Item I bequeath to Thomas Hunne, son of the aforesaid Edward, one brass pot and one basin with ewer. Item I bequeath to Isabelle Rooche one basin with ewer and one pair of sheets. Item I bequeath to Margaret Cobbe one basin with ewer, one brass pot, one pair of sheets and one coverlet. The residue of all my goods not above bequeathed I give and bequeath to Emmotte, my wife, and the same Emmotte I ordain, make and constitute my executrix to then dispose for the health of my soul as seems best to her and Edward Hunne of Elvestwe and Thomas Mulso of Northampton I ordain and make supervisors of this my present testament. Given the day and year above said. Item I bequeath to Dom John Bulwyk, monk of the priory of St Andrew 20d. Item I bequeath to Dom Thomas Roche, monk of the same priory 20. Item I bequeath to the church of Holy Sepulchre two torches to the value of 6s 8d. Item I bequeath to the fraternity of St Martin there 12d.

f52r 112 ALICE PENY 3rd November 1487 widow

In Dei nomine Amen tercio die mensis Novembris anno domini mcccclxxxvij
Ego Alicia Peny de Northampton vidua sana memoria condo testamentum meum in hunc modum In primis lego animam meam Deo Omnipotenti Beate Marie eius genitrici ac omnibus
sanctis corpusque meum sepiliendum in ecclesia Sancti Egidii ville predicte Item lego summo
altari ibidem iijs.iiijd. Item lego fraternitati Sancti Clementis Martiris ibidem xijd. Item lego reparacione de Medylton xxd. Item lego reparacione Via Regis in Cotton xxd. Item lego domui fratrium Carmelitorum Northampton xxd. Item lego vicario Sancte Sepulcri viijd. Item
lego ydoneo capellano celebraturo in ecclesia Sancti Egidii predicte pro salute anime mee et anime Johannis Peny nuper viri mei centum solidos Item lego Agneti Dawes filie mee unam togam unam zonam et unam vacam ac unam pelvi. Item lego Alicie filie predicte Agnetis unam togam unum cocliarum argenti unum plater unum discum et unum sawcer de pewter Item lego Margarete Hay filie mee unam togam unam zonam et unam vaccam Item lego Thome Haye filio predicte Margarete unum cocliarum argenti unum plater unum discum et unum sawcer de pewter Item lego Johanni filio dicte Margarete unum cocliarum argenti unum plater unum discum et unum sawcer de pewter. Item Johanne filie dicte Margarete unum cocliarum argenti unum plater unum discum et unum sawcer de pewter Item lego Alicie Peny filie mee unum lectum in le hall chamber
cum omnibus pertinenciis suis ibidem que continatur in hac camera et unum lectum in le medyl chamber ac unum panum de triginta virgas vocatum a rono russet
et in pecuniis quattuor libras bone monete Anglie ac duos crateros
argenti unum unius est standyng cum le cover et alium vocatum a playn pece
ac duos ciphos vocatos masers j saltseler argenti et xij cocliarios argenti
ac meam optimam zonam coloris de sangwyn et aliam zonam rubei coloris ac
unum magnum lavacrum duo paria de bedes unum unius par est de gete et le paternoster de argento et aliud par de coral et jette et unum garnyssh de pewter vessell et quattuor ollas eneas et tres pelves cum duobus lavacris electri ac omnia vasa in le yelyng howse et duas chafyngdisshys et duas optimas togas
octo candelabra octo par linthiamenti sex manntergia longa et vj curta et ij
cistas depictas Item quatuor mappas Item secundum hallyng Item ciphorium coloris rubei Item unam mensam duplicatam Item omnia vasa pertinentes ad le brewehows
et duo cotylis Item unam mensam cum duobus trestyllis unum stanum unum verum de. . . .
de le cobards et duas patellas eneas et duas ollas de pewter. Residuum vero
omnium bonorum meorum superius non legatorum do et lego Thome filie mee [sic] et ipse disponat

ea pro salute anime maritorum meorum et omnium amicorum meorum ac omnium fidelium defunctorum
et dictum Thomam filium ordino et constituo meum executorem et magistrum Thomam Permynter vicarium ecclesie Sancti Egidii predicte supervisorem istius ultime voluntatis mee perficiendum
et volo quod predictus magister Thomas habeat pro labore suo decem solidos hiis testibus Willelmo
Lynde mercatore Johanne Weste pistore Johanne ffolyott cum aliis

In the name of God Amen the third day of November 1487 I Alice Peny of Northampton, widow, of good memory make my testament in this wise. First I bequeath my soul to Almighty God, to the Blessed Mary His mother and all the saints, my body to be buried in the church of St Giles in the town aforesaid. Item I bequeath to the high altar there 3s 4d. Item I bequeath to the fraternity of St Clement the Martyr there 12d. Item I bequeath to the repair of the king's highway at Middleton 20d. Item I bequeath to the house of the Carmelite Friars, Northampton 20d. Item I bequeath to the vicar of Holy Sepulchre 8d. Item I bequeath for a suitable chaplain to celebrate in the church of St Giles for the good of my soul and the soul of John Peny, my late husband, 100s. Item I bequeath to Agnes Dawes, my daughter, one gown, one girdle, one cow and one bowl. Item I bequeath to Alice, daughter of the aforesaid Agnes, one gown, one silver spoon, one platter, one dish and one saucer of pewter. Item I bequeath to Margaret Hay, my daughter, one gown, one girdle and one cow. Item I bequeath to Thomas Hay, son of the aforesaid Margaret, one silver spoon, one platter, one dish and one saucer of pewter. Item I bequeath to John, son of the said Margaret, one silver spoon, one platter, one dish and one saucer of pewter. Item I bequeath to Joan, daughter of the said Margaret, one silver spoon, one platter, one dish and one saucer of pewter. Item I bequeath to Alice Peny, my daughter, one bed in the hall chamber with everything belonging to it which is contained in that chamber and one bed in the middle chamber, and one piece of cloth of thirty yards called a rone russet and in money four pounds of good English money and two silver bowls, one of them a standing one with the cover and another called a 'playn' piece and two bowls called masers, one silver salt cellar and 12 silver spoons and my best girdle of red colour and another girdle of ruby colour and a large bowl, two pairs of beads, one pair of jet with the paternoster of silver, and the other pair of coral and jet, and one complete set of pewter vessels and four brass pots and three bowls with two ewers of latten and all the vessels in the 'yelyng' house and two chafing dishes and two best gowns, eight candlesticks, eight pairs of sheets, six long towels and 6 short ones and 2 painted chests. Item four tablecloths. Item the second halling. Item one goblet of red colour. Item one folding table. Item all the vessels pertaining to the brewhouse and two cups. Item a table with two trestles, one bench, one iron pot for the cob-irons and two brass pans and two pots of pewter. The residue of all my goods not above bequeathed I give and bequeath to Thomas, my son, to then dispose for the health of the souls of my husband and all my friends and all faithful departed and the said Thomas, my son, I ordain and constitute my executor and Master Thomas Permynter, vicar of the church of St Giles aforesaid, to be supervisor of this my last will to be performed and I will that the aforesaid Master Thomas to have for his labour ten shillings. With these witnesses William Lynde, merchant, John Weste, baker, and John Folyott with others.

f53r 114 MARGARET BRAFELD 20th December 1487 widow

In Dei nomine Amen xx die mensis Decembris anno domini millesimo cccclxxx septimo
Ego Margareta Brafeld quondam uxor Thome Brafeld de Northampton deyster defuncti condo
testamentum meum in hunc modum In primis lego animam meam Deo Omnipotenti Beate Marie et omnibus
sanctis curie celestis corpusque meum sepiliendum in capella Corporis Christi in ecclesia Omnium Sanctorum ville
Northampton iuxta tumulum dicte Thome Brayfeld nuper mariti mei Item lego summo altari in
dicta ecclesia vjs.viijd. Item lego fraternitati Corporis Christi in eadem ecclesia vjs.viijd. Item
lego fraternitati Sancte Trinitatis in eadem ecclesie vjs.viijd. Item lego fraternitati Beate Marie Virginis
in eadem ecclesia vjs.viijd. Item lego fraternitati Sancti Johannis Baptiste ibidem iijs.iiijd. Item lego fraternitati
Sancti Georgii Martiris ibidem iijs.iiijd. Item lego fraternitati Sancte Crucis in eadem ecclesia iijs.iiijd. Item lego
fraternitati Sancte Cithe ibidem iijs.iiijd. Item lego fraternitati Sancte Katerine in novo cimiterio iuxta collegium
dicte ecclesie iijs.iiijd. Item lego cuilibet domui ordinum fratrum mendicancium in dicta villa Northampton
vjs.viijd. Item lego fabrice ecclesie de Bowden Magna iijs.iiijd. Item lego pueris Simonis
Brayfeld filii mei v marcas equaliter inter eos distribuendum Item lego pueris Thome Brayfeld
filii mei v marcas bone monete Anglie inter ipsos equaliter dividendum. Item volo quod unus capella-
nus ydonius conducator per executorem meum inferius nominatum per spacium vigenti annorum proximo
sequencium post decessum meum ad celebrandum ad altarem Corporis Christi in predicta ecclesia Omnium Sanctorum
ville Northampton pro salute anime mee Thome Brayfeld nuper mariti mei animarum parentum et
amicorum meorum ac animarum omnium fidelium defunctorum et pro condicione predicti capellani in
forma predicta celebranturi durante dicto spacio xx annorum lego centum libras in pecuniis muneratis bone monete
Anglie pro salario eiusdem capellani etcetera ulterius volo quod dictus executor meus ordinabit sumptibus
meis propriis xiij torchias cere quolibet eorum continente in pondere xiili cere ad ardendum
circa corpus meum in die sepulture mee dum exequie et missa de requiem cantentur
et legantur. Item volo quod idem executor meus provideat et ordinat pro xiij pauperibus ad

tenendum dictas torchias tam ad exquias quam ad missam et sepulturam meam xiij togas in usus
illorum pauperum imperpetuum applicandum et habendum ac eciam volo quod idem executor meus inmediate
post predictas exquias missam et sepulturam meas et servicium finitum dabit et deliberavit
pro salute anime mee omnes predicta torchias sub forma sequenti videlicet fraternitati Sancte Trinitatis
in predicta ecclesia Omnium Sanctorum unam torchiam fraternitati Corporis Christi ibidem unam torchiam fraternitati Sancti
Johannis Baptiste ibidem unam torchiam fraternitati Sancte Katerine in capella novi cimiterii unam torchiam
fraternitati Sancte Cithe in dicta ecclesia Omnium Sanctorum unam torchiam capelle Sancti Thome Martiris extra
portam australem eiusdem ville Northampton unam torchiam fraternitati Sancte Crucis in Muro in ecclesia
Sancti Gregorii eiusdem ville unam torchiam fraternitati Beate Marie Virginis in ecclesia Omnium Sanctorum predicta
unam torchiam fraternitati Sancti Georgii ibidem unam torchiam fraternitati Sancte Crucis ibidem unam torchiam
ecclesie hospitalis Sancti Johannis Baptiste ville Northampton predicte xs. bone monete et unam torchiam
ecclesie de Bowden predicte unam torchiam et ecclesie Sancti Michaelis Archangeli ville Northampton unam
torchiam Item lego domino Willelmo Melton capellano iijs.iiijd. Item lego domino Ricardo Algude capellano iijs.iiijd.
Residuum vero omnium bonorum meorum superius non legatorum do et lego predicti Simoni Brafeld filio meo
ad inde disponendum pro salute anime mee ac Thome Brafeld nuper viri mei et animarum parentum meorum et amicorum
ac omnium fidelium defunctorum prout ei melius videbitur expediri et ad istud testamentum meum fideliter ex-
equendum prefatum Simonem ordino executorem meum et volo quod habeat pro labore suo in execucionem voluntatis
mee xls. etcetera hiis testibus domino Willelmo Melton et Ricardo Algude capellanis Willelmo Mylle deyster et Thome Malpas

In the name of God Amen the 20th day of December 1487 I Margaret Brafeld, former wife of the late Thomas Brafeld of Northampton, deyster, deceased, make my testament in this wise. First I bequeath my soul to Almighty God, to the Blessed Mary and all the saints of the court of heaven, my body to be buried in the chapel of Corpus Christi in the church of All Saints in the town of Northampton next to the grave of the said Thomas Brafeld, my late husband. Item I bequeath to the high altar of the said church 6s 8d. Item I bequeath to the fraternity of Corpus Christi in the same church 6s 8d. Item I bequeath to the fraternity of Holy Trinity in the same church 6s 8d. Item I bequeath to the fraternity of the Blessed Virgin Mary in the same church 6s 8d. Item I bequeath to the fraternity of St John Baptist there 3s. 4d. Item I bequeath to the fraternity of St George the Martyr there 3s 4d. Item I bequeath to the fraternity of the Holy Cross in the same church 3s 4d. Item I bequeath to the fraternity of St Cithe there 3s. 4d. Item I bequeath to the fraternity of

St Katherine in the new cemetery next to the College of the said church 3s 4d. Item I bequeath to each of the houses of the orders of mendicant brothers in the same town, Northampton, 6s 8d. Item I bequeath to the fabric of the church of Gt Bowden 3s 4d. Item I bequeath to the children of Simon Brafeld, my son, 5 marks equally divided between them. Item I bequeath to the children of Thomas Brafeld, my son, 5 marks of good English money to be shared equally between them. Item I wish that a chaplain be suitably appointed by my executor below named for the period of twenty years following after my death to celebrate at the altar of Corpus Christi in the said church of All Saints in the town of Northampton for the health of my soul and the souls of Thomas Brafeld, my late husband, and the souls of my parents and friends and the souls of all faithful departed, and on condition that the said chaplain celebrates in the said form during the said space of 20 years I bequeath a hundred pounds in good English money for the salary of the said chaplain etcetera, moreover I will that my said executor should order at my own expense 13 wax torches, each of them containing 13 lbs of wax in weight, to be burnt around my body on the day of my burial during my exequies and sung and spoken requiem mass as bequeathed. Item I will that my same executor should provide and ordain for 13 poor people to hold the said torches both at my exequies and also at my mass and burial, 13 gowns to be had and applied to the use of those poor people for ever and also I will that my same executors, immediately after my said funeral, mass and burial and the end of the service, should give and deliver for the health of my soul all the said torches in the following manner, that is to say to the fraternity of the Holy Trinity in the aforesaid church of All Saints one torch, to the fraternity of Corpus Christi there one torch to the fraternity of St John Baptist there one torch to the fraternity of St Katherine in the chapel in the new cemetery one torch to the fraternity of St Cithe in the said church of All Saints one torch, to the chapel of St Thomas the Martyr outside the south gate of the same town of Northampton one torch, to the fraternity of the Holy Cross in the Wall in the church of St Gregory in the same town one torch, to the fraternity of the Blessed Virgin Mary in the same church of All Saints aforesaid one torch, to the fraternity of St George there one torch to the fraternity of the Holy Cross there one torch, to the hospital church of St John the Baptist in the town of Northampton aforesaid 10s of good money and one torch, to the church of Bowden aforesaid one torch, and to the church of St Michael the Archangel in the town of Northampton one torch. Item I bequeath to Dom William Melton, chaplain, 3s 4d. Item I bequeath to Dom Richard Algude, chaplain, 3s 4d. The residue of all my goods not above bequeathed I give and bequeath to the aforesaid Simon Brafeld, my son, to then dispose for the health of my soul and Thomas Brafeld, my late husband, and the souls of my parents and friends and all faithful departed as seems best to him, and that this testament be well and faithfully executed I ordain the aforesaid Simon as my executor and I will that he should have for his labour in the execution of my will 40s and with these witness Dom William Melton and Richard Algude, chaplains, William Mylle, deyster, and Thomas Malpas.

f53v 115 JOHN WILKOKKES 12th May 1488 gentleman

In Dei nomine Amen xij die mensis Maii anno domini mcccclxxx octavo Ego
Johannes Wilkokkes de Northampton gentilman compos mentis et sane memorie condo
testamentum meum in hunc modum In primis lego animam meam Deo Omnipotenti Beate
Marie
sue genitrici ac omnibus sanctis curie celestis corpusque meum sepiliendum in capella
Beate Marie Virginis infra ecclesiam Omnium Sanctorum ville Northampton Item lego
sustentacioni
capelle predicte vjs.viijd. Item lego reparacioni ecclesie Beate Marie Virginis in ville
de Everdon vjs.viijd. Item lego reparacione ecclesie Sancti Egidii in Northampton predicte
vjs.
viijd. Item lego cuilibet domui fratrum mendicancium eiusdem ville inter fratres
in eisdem domibus tempore mortis mee equaliter dividendum et distribuendum iijs.iiijd.
bone monete Anglie Item lego sustentacioni capelle Sancti Georgii Martiris in dicta ecclesia
Omnium Sanctorum iijs.iiijd. Item lego pauperibus existentes in domo elemosinario Sancti
Thome
Martiris extra portam australem ville Northampton predicte tempore mortis mee equaliter in
ipsos
distribuendum iijs.iiijd. Item lego reparacioni ecclesie Sancti Michaelis Archangeli in
Newenham
iuxta Daventr' vjs.viijd. ac in super do et lego Thome Hasylwodd
generoso totum statum meum et terminum quos habeo in uno crofto et columbari in eodem
crofto situato cum suis pertinenciis iacente in parochia Sancti Egidii ville Northampton
predicte
inter croftum quondam mei predicti Johannis Wylkokkes modo dicti Thome Hasylwodde ex
parte occidentali et Viam Regiam subtus murum ville Northampton predicte ex parte
orientali
ac cimiterium ecclesie Sancti Egidii predicte ex parte australi et lez delvys iuxta portam
orientalem
ex parte boriali habendum et tenendum totum predictum statum et terminum de et in
predicto
crofto et columbari in eodem situato cum omnibus eorum pertinenciis ut predictus est
prefato Thome
Hasilwodde heredibus et assignatis durante vita mei Johannis Wilkokkes ac ultra per
tregenta xxx
tres annos proximo sequente immediate post decessum meum reddendo inde annuatim
eiusdem
fratribus et sororibus fraternitatis sive gilde Beate Marie Virginis in ecclesia Omnium
Sanctorum ville
predicte aut eorum successoribus vel assignatis octo solidos bone monete Anglie ad iiijor
anni terminos videlicet festum Nativitatis Sancti Johannis Baptiste Sancti Michaelis
Archangeli Natalis Domini
et Pasche equis porcionibus ac eciam faciendo reparendo supportando et mauntendo
et simile modo custodiendo ex sumptibus suis propriis et expensis omnia alia huius modi
que predicto Johanni Wilkokkes heredibus et executores mei secundum tenorem
quarumdem indenturarum

inter Willelmum Austyn et Rogerum Maydeston ad tunc custodes predicte fraternitatis ex parte et me dictum Johannem Wilkokkes coniunctim cum Agnete nuper uxore mee ex parte inde factis facere reparare supportare mauntenere et custodire tenemur de statu et termino predictis per presentes Residuum vero omnium bonorum meorum superius non
legatorum do et lego Matilde uxori mee ad inde disponendum pro salute anime mee ac animarum parentorum meorum et amicorum meorum ac omnium fidelium defunctorum prout ei
melius videbitur expediri et ad istud testamentum bene et fideliter exequendum eam Matildam uxorem meam ordino facio et constituo executorem meam per presentes

In the name of God the 12th day of May 1488 I John Wilkokkes of Northampton, gentleman, in sound mind and good memory make my testament in this wise. First I bequeath my soul to Almighty God, to the Blessed Mary His mother and all the saints of the court of heaven, my body to be buried in the chapel of the Blessed Virgin Mary within the church of All Saints, Northampton. Item I bequeath to the maintenance of the chapel aforesaid 6s 8d. Item I bequeath to the repair of the church of the Blessed Virgin Mary in the town of Everdon 6s 8d. Item I bequeath to the repair of the church of St Giles in Northampton aforesaid 6s 8d. Item I bequeath to each house of mendicant brothers of the same town to be equally divided and distributed between the brothers in the same houses at the time of my death 3s 4d of good money of England. Item I bequeath to the maintenance of the chapel of St George the Martyr in the said church of All Saints 3s 4d. Item I bequeath to the poor being in the almshouse of St Thomas the Martyr outside the south gate of the town of Northampton aforesaid at the time of my death to be equally divided between them 3s 4d. Item I bequeath to the repairs of the church of St Michael the Archangel in Newnham by Daventry 6s 8d and further I give and bequeath to Thomas Hasylwodd, gentleman, all my state and term which I have in one croft and the dovecote in the same croft, lying with its appurtenances in the parish of St Giles in the town of Northampton between the croft formerly mine, the said John Wylkokkes, now of the said Thomas Hasylwodde on the west part, and the king's road under the wall of the town of Northampton aforesaid on the east, and the churchyard of the church of St Giles aforesaid on the south, and 'les delvys' by the east gate on the north, to have and to hold all the aforesaid state and term of and in the aforesaid croft and dovecote situated in the same with all their appurtenances as is aforesaid to the aforesaid Thomas Hasylwodde, his heirs and assigns during the life of me John Wilkokkes and further for thirty three years next after my death, paying therefrom annually to the same brothers and sisters of the fraternity or gilde of the Blessed Virgin Mary in the church of All Saints of the town aforesaid, or their successors and assigns, eight shillings of good money of England at four terms of the year, that is to say the Feast of the Nativity of St John the Baptist, St Michael the Archangel, the birth of the Lord and Easter, in equal portions and also to do, repair, sustain and maintain and likewise to keep, at his own proper cost and expense according to the tenor of certain indentures made between William Austyn and Roger Maydston, at that time wardens of the aforesaid fraternity, on the one part and me the said John Wilkokkes together with Agnes, my late wife, on the other part, by which presents we are bound to make, repair, support, maintain and keep concerning the state and term aforesaid. The residue of all my goods not above bequeathed I give and bequeath to Matilda, my wife, to then dispose for the health of my soul and the souls of my parents and my friends and all faithful departed as seem best to her and that this testament be well and faithfully executed, I ordain, make and constitute Matilda, my wife my executrix by these presents.

f55v 130 AGNES MULSO 22nd August 1488 widow

In Dei nomine Amen anno domini mccccLxxxxviij mensis Augusti die xxij Ego Agnes
Mulso de Northampton vidua compos mentis condo testamentum meum in hunc modum In
primis
lego animam Deo Omnipotenti etcetera corpusque meum sepiliendum in cimiterio ecclesie
Omnium
Sanctorum ville Northampton Item lego Johanni filio meo tria paria linthiamentum Item lego
Agneti
filie mee tria paria linthiamentum meam optimam tunicam meam blodiam togam unum
par precarum de lez amber et meam optimam zonam Item lego Willelmo Abrey notiare
togam
russett coniugis mei defuncti Item lego Johanni Abrey uxori dicti Willelmi meam veridem
togam Residuum vero omnium bonorum meorum non legatorum do et lego Rogero
Hayward quem
ordino et constituo executorem meum ad disponendum prout sibi melius videbitur expediri
Item ordino dictum Willelmum Abrey supervisorem huius testamenti mei Hiis testibus
Roberto
Mydelham curato meo Katerina Mulso Emma Skydmor Alicia Pratt et
Margareta Stafford cum aliis

In the name of God Amen the 22nd day of August 1488 I Agnes Mulso of Northampton, widow, in sound mind make my testament in this wise. First I bequeath my soul to Almighty God etcetera my body to be buried in the cemetery of the church of All Saints in the town of Northampton. Item I bequeath to John, my son, three pairs of sheets. Item I bequeath to Agnes, my daughter, three pairs of sheets, my best tunic, my blue gown, one set of amber beads and my best girdle. Item I bequeath to William Abrey, notary, one gown of russet cloth on my death. Item I bequeath to Joan Abrey, wife of the said William, my green gown. The residue of all my goods not bequeathed above I give and bequeath to Roger Hayward whom I ordain and constitute my executor to then dispose as seems best to him. Item I ordain the said William Abrey as supervisor of this my testament. With these witnesses Robert Mydlham, my curate, Katherine Mulso, Emma Skydmor, Alice Pratt and Margaret Stafford with others.

f57r 139 JOHN LONGE 20th June 1488 tailor

In Dei nomine Amen xx die mensis Junii anno domini mccccl xxxxviij Ego Johannes Longe de Northampton tailor in sana memoria existens condo testamentum meum in hunc modum In primis
lego animam meam Deo Omnipotenti etcetra corpusque meum sepiliendum in cimiterio ecclesie
Omnium Sanctorum ville Northampton Item lego rectori eiusdem ecclesie pro decimis oblitis xijd. Item lego
reparacione dicte ecclesie xijd. Item lego fraternitati Sancti Johannis Baptiste in eadem ecclesia xijd.
Item lego fraternitati Sancti Georgii in eadem ecclesia xijd. Item fraternitati Sancte Crucis ibidem xijd. Item
fraternitati Sancte Katerine in novo cimiterio xijd. Item fraternitati Sancti Thome xijd.
Item lego cuilibet domui fratrum mendicancium eiusdem ville xxd. Item lego Roberto
filio meo meam magnam murram et meam magnam ollam eneam unam pelvim cum lavacro
et unum lectum completum cum aliis rebus seu pecuniarum summis ad valenciam in toto
decem macaram Item lego Willelmo filio meo unam ollam eneam tria cocliaria argentea unam
pelvim cum lavacro unum cornu harnesatum cum argento et coopertorium eiusdem cornu
et unum lectum completum cum aliquis bonis in toto ad valorem quinque marcarum Item lego
Johanne filie mee unam ollam eneam unam pelvim cum lavacro et unam murram vocatam
the brown maser et unum lectum completum cum aliis rebus vel pecuniis ad valenciam
quinque marcarum in toto Residuum vero omnium bonorum meorum non legatorum do et lego
Katerine uxori mee et Roberto filio meo ad inde disponendum pro salute anime mee et
animarum omnium fidelium defunctorum prout illis videbitur melius expediri et prefatos
Katerinam et Robertum ordino facio et constituo executores meos hiis testibus magistro Roberto
Mydelham vicario ecclesie Omnium Sanctorum predicte Johanne Holwell Jacobo Pynchester
et Thoma Fyssher de eadem

In the name of God Amen the 20th day of June 1488 I John Longe of Northampton, tailor, still in good memory make my testament in this wise. First I bequeath my soul to Almighty God etcetera, my body to be buried in the churchyard of the church of All Saints, Northampton. Item I bequeath to the Rector of the same church for tithes forgotten 12d. Item I bequeath to the repair of the said church 12d. Item I bequeath to the fraternity of St John the Baptist in the same church 12d. Item I bequeath to the fraternity of St George in the same church 12d. Item I bequeath to the fraternity of the Holy Cross there 12d. Item I bequeath to the fraternity of St Katherine in the new churchyard 12d. Item I bequeath to the fraternity of St Thomas 12d. Item I bequeath to the each of the houses of mendicant brothers of the same town 20d. Item I bequeath to Robert, my son, my great maser, my large brass pot, one basin with ewer and one complete bed with all its fittings and a sum of money of total value ten marks. Item I bequeath to William, my son, one brass pot, three silver spoons, one basin with ewer, one drinking horn chased with silver and the cover of the same horn, one complete bed with all its goods, in total to the value of five marks. Item I bequeath to Joan my daughter, one brass pot, one basin with ewer and one maser called the brown maser and a complete bed with all its fittings or money to the value in total five marks. The residue of all my goods not above bequeathed I give and bequeath to Katherine, my wife, and Robert, my son, to then dispose for the health of my soul and the souls of all faithful departed as seem best to them and the said Katherine and Robert I ordain, make and constitute my executors. With these witnesses Master Robert Mydelham, vicar of the church of All Saints aforesaid, John Holwell, Jacob Pynchester and Thomas Fisher of the same.

f60r 154 JOHN NUTMAN 10th September 1487

In Dei nomine Amen decimo die Septembris anno domini mcccclxxxxvij Ego Johannes Nutman de Northampton compos mentis etcetera condo testamentum meum in hunc modum In primis
lego animam meam Deo Omnipotenti et corpus sepiliendum in cimiterio ecclesie Omnium Sanctorum ville predicte
Item do et lego ad usum summi altaris eiusdem ecclesie unum manutergium Item lego Johanni Nutman filio meo
togam meam optimam et cathedram meam meliorem Item lego Matildi Style filie mee a postnett
Item do et lego Johanne filie mee unum linthiamen et unum candelabrum Item lego Thome filio meo unam
magnam cistam Item lego et unum veru ad usum Thome et Johannis filiorum meorum predictorum alterius vicbus
in necessibus eorum et volo quod remaneat alteri eorum diucius viventi Item do et lego Johanne uxori
mee annuam porconem sex solidos et octo denarios durante vita sua solvendum per manus Thome filii mei
predictis de integris terris redditibus meis in possessionibus Thome et Johannis filiorum meorum predictorum existentis
Residuum vero et bonorum meorum superius non legatorum do et lego Johanne uxori mee predicte et ipsam
et Thomam filium meum predictum executores meos constituo et facio per presentes Hiis testibus Johannes Nortman
et Matilda Stele cum multis aliis circumstantibus

In the name of God Amen the 10th day of September 1487 I John Nutman of sound mind etcetera make my testament in this wise. First I bequeath my soul to Almighty God and my body to be buried in the cemetery of the church of All Saints in the said town. Item I give and bequeath for the use of the high altar in the same church one towel. Item I bequeath to John Nutman, my son, my best gown and my best chair. Item I bequeath to Mathilda Style, my daughter, one posnet. Item I give and bequeath to Joan, my daughter, one sheet and one candlestick. Item I bequeath to Thomas, my son, one large chest. Item I bequeath one [veru] for the mutual use of Thomas and John, my sons aforesaid, to either of them according to their need and I wish that it remains to who lives longest. Item I give and bequeath to Joan, my wife, an annual portion of six shillings and eight pence during her life to be paid through the hands of Thomas, my aforesaid son, from the returns of my entire lands being in the possession of Thomas and John, my sons aforesaid. The residue of my goods not bequeathed above I give and bequeath to Joan, my aforesaid wife, and she and Thomas, my aforesaid son, I constitue and make my executors by these presents. With these witnesses John Mortman and Mathilda Stele with many others standing around.

f69v 224(a) RICHARD TAILOUR 20th April 1499

In Dei nomine Amen xx die Aprilis anno domini mccccIxxxxix Ego Ricardus Tailour compos mentis et sane memorie condo testamentum meum in hunc modum In primis lego animam meam Deo
Omnipotenti etcetera corpusque meum sepiliendum in cimiterio ecclesie parochiali Omnium Sanctorum ville Northampton.
Item lego reparacionibus ecclesie Omnium Sanctorum predicte xijd. Item lego capelle Sancte Katerin xijd. Item lego
capelle Sancti Georgii xijd. Residuum vero omnium bonorum meorum do et lego Johanne uxori mee
ut illa disponat pro salute anime mee ut ipsa disponat etcetera quam ordino meam executricem
hiis testibus magistro Roberto Mydellham doctore curato meo ecclesie Omnium Sanctorum Thoma Shepard
Barnardo Marshall et multis aliis

In the name of God Amen the 20th day of April 1499 I Richard Tailour of sound mind and good memory make my testament in this wise. First I bequeath my soul to Almighty God and my body to be buried in the churchyard of the parish church of All Saints in the town of Northampton. Item I bequeath to the repairs of the church of All Saints aforesaid 12d. Item I bequeath to the chapel of St Katherine 12d. Item I bequeath to the chapel of St George 12d. The Residue of all my goods I give and bequeath to Joan, my wife, whom I ordain my executrix to then dispose for the health of my soul as she herself is inclined etcetera. With these witnesses Master Robert Mydelham, Doctor, my curate of the church of All Saints, Thomas Shepard, Bernard Marshall and many others.

f69v 224 THOMAS FYSSH 8th June 1499 barber

In the name of God Amen the yere of our lorde God mccccIxxxxix the viijth day of month of Juny I Thomas Fyssh of Northampton barbor hole of mynde etcetera make my testament
in this maner Firste I bequeth my soule to Almyghty God etcetera my body to be buryed in the
chyrche yerd of All Halowes in the town of Northampton Also I bequeth to hygh auter of

the same chyrche for my tythes forgoten iiijd. Also to the mother chyrche of Lincoln ijd. Item I bequeth to my son John j basen j ewer of laton j pott and j panne of brasse Item I bequeth to my son William j basen j ewer of pewter j pott j panne of brass syche as my wyfe will dyliver them to whom I truste shoo wylbe gude mother or ellys I wold more largely bequeth them Item I bequeth my brothyr William ij bassenes and j ewer of laton with the pouche and al the knyfees therin as he ys wonte to were Also I bequeht to my servant
Annes the owte syde of my roset gown j pewter plater ij pewter dysshes j sawcer and j candyllstyk The resydue of my gods not bequethed I wyll that Kateryn my wyfe use them paying my dettes as shoo thynke moste expedyent for the elthe of my soule whom I make myne executryce Also I wyll that Christofer Messenger have oversight that this my testament and laste wyll may be performed Theys bering wytnes Sir John Brydgeman and Roger Hancok

f70v 231 WILLIAM ADAMS 19th June 1498 ironmonger

In Dei nomine Amen xix die mensis Junii anno domini mccccIxxxxviij Ego Willelmus Adams de Northampton yrnemonger compos mentis condo testamentum meum in hunc modum In primis
lego animam meam Deo Omnipotenti etcetera corpusque meum sepiliendum in cimiterio ecclesie
parochiali Omnium Sanctorum Northampton Item lego rectoribus eiusdem ecclesie pro decimis oblitis xxd. Item
lego fraternitati Sancte Trinitatis in eadem ecclesia xvjd. Item lego fraternitati Corporis Christi in eadem ecclesia
xvjd. Item fraternitati Beate Marie Virginis in ecclesia predicta xvjd. Item lego fraternitati Sancte Crucis ibidem
xijd. Item fraternitati Sancti Georgii ibidem xijd. Item fraternitati Sancti Johannis Baptiste in eadem
ecclesia xijd. Item lego fraternitati Sancte Katerine Virginis in le pardon chyrche yerd xijd. Item lego
pauperibus domus Sancti Thome Martiris extra portam australem ville Northampton xijd. Item lego Sancte
Sepulcre infra ecclesiam Sancti Sepulcri ville predicte xxd. Item lego Sancto Laudo in ecclesia predicta
xijd. Residuum vero omnium bonorum meorum superius non legatorum post debita mea soluta totaliter do et lego Elizabeth uxori mee ad inde disponendum pro salute anime mee et pro
animabus omnium parentum et amicorum meorum et omnium fidelium defunctorum prout ei melius videbitur
expediri ac eciam ordino eandem Elizabeth executricem meam et magistrum Ricardum Adams filium supervisorem
Date die et anno predictis

In the name of God Amen the 19th day of June 1498 I William Adams of Northampton, ironmonger, in sound mind make my testament in this wise. First I bequeath my soul to Almighty God etcetera, my body to be buried in the churchyard of the parish church of All Saints, Northampton. Item I bequeath to the rectors of the same church for tithes forgotten 20d. Item I bequeath to the fraternity of the Holy Trinity in the same church 16d. Item I bequeath to the fraternity of Corpus Christi in the same church 16d. Item I bequeath to the fraternity of the Blessed Virgin Mary in the aforesaid church 16d. Item I bequeath to the fraternity of the Holy Cross there 12d. Item I bequeath to the fraternity of St George there 12d. Item I bequeath to the fraternity of St John Baptist in the same church 12d. Item I bequeath to the fraternity of St Katherine in le pardon chyrche yerd 12d. Item I bequeath to the poor people of the house of St Thomas the Martyr outside the south gate of the town of Northampton 12d. Item I bequeath to the Holy Sepulchre within the church of the Holy Sepulchre of the aforesaid town 20d. Item I bequeath to St [Laudo] in the aforesaid church 12d. The residue of all my goods not bequeathed above and after my debts are fully paid I give and bequeath to Elizabeth, my wife, to then dispose for the health of my soul and for the souls of all my parents and friends and all faithful departed as seems best to her and in addition I ordain the same Elizabeth my executrix and Master Richard Adams, (my) son as supervisor. Given the day and year abovesaid.

f75v 257 ISBELL GEFFRON 25th December 1489

In Dei nomine Amen the yere of our lord God mccccIxxxxix the xxv day of December Ibeyng in perfyte mynd etcetera make my testament in this forme Fyrste I bequeth my soule to Almyghty God etcetera my body to beryed in the chyrche of Saynt Gyle in the town of Northampton Also I bequeth to my principall as the custom requireth Item I bequeth to the chyrche of Lincoln xijd. Also to the fraternity of Saynt Clement in the chyrche of Saynt Gylys xijd. Also to my servant John Walthew j hole bed j materas j payre of shets and a coverlett Also to Alys Hunt xxs in money or ellys in money worth Also to Annes my servant j pott j cawdron that was takyn for j soress? at the north yat j narke standyng in the chese chamber and oon of the newe small cheyers Also I bequeth to iij chylder of my doghter Margaret Hartwell yche one of them to have sum whatt owthyr pott pan or beddyng at the syght of myn executors Also to my god doghter at John Walkers wever j sylver spone Also to Alys Lambert j sylver spone The resydue of all my gods moveabull or un moveabull after my detts payed and the chearge of my berying I gyffe and bequeth to Thomas my son Also I ordeyng The sayd Thomas John Adams of the Swan and William Lambard myn executors for to dispose and ordeyn for the helthe of my soule as yt may be beste sene to them Theys witnes Thomas Flowre fuller and John Walker wever

f81v 296 JOHN BREKNOK 20th June 1500

In Dei nomine Amen xx die mensis Junii anno domini millesimo quingentisimo Ego Johannes Breknok compos mentis etcetera condo testamentum meum in hunc modum In primis lego animam meam Deo Omnipotenti etcetera corpusque meum sepiliendum in monasterio Sancti Andree Apostoli Northampton legando summo altari eiusdem monasterii vjs.viijd. Item lego Sancte Sepulcri suum mortuarium Item constituo

Jacobum filium meum verum et legitimum heredem meum omnium terrarum et tenementorum
meorum post decessum Sibille uxoris mee Item lego eidem filio meo unum olla'
eneam cum cista Item lego Johanne filie mee duas ollas eneas et unam patell'
cum una pelvim et lavacro et una cista. Item do et lego fabrice ecclesie Sancte
Sepulcri xijd. Residuum vero omnium bonorum meorum superius non legatorum lego
Sibille uxori mee et Hugoni filio meo ut ipsi inde disponant pro salute
anime mee ut eis melius expediri videbitur et ipsos Sibillam et Hugonem
constituo meos executores ad istud testamentum meum fideliter exequendum
Istud testamentum probatum fuit coram nobis etcetera xxiiij die mensis Julii <anno [..xx]> et comissa
est administracio etcetera executoribus in eodem testamento nominatis in hospitali Sancti Johannis Northampton

In the name of God Amen the 20th day of June 1500 I John Breknok in sound mind etcetera make my testament in this wise. First I bequeath my soul to God Almighty etcetera my body to be buried in the monastery of St Andrew the Apostle, Northampton, leaving to the high altar of that same monastery 6s 8d. Item I bequeath to Holy Sepulchre the mortuary money. Item I constitute that James, my true and legitimate son, should inherit all my lands and properties after the death of Sybil, my wife. Item I bequeath to the same son one brass jar with chest. Item I bequeath to Joan, my daughter, two brass pots and one pan with one basin and ewer and one chest. Item I give and bequeath to the fabric of the church of Holy Sepulchre 12d. The residue of all my goods not bequeathed above I bequeath to Sybil, my wife, and to Hugh, my son, to then dispose for the health of my soul as seems best to them and the same Sybil and Hugh I constitute my executors that this my testament be faithfully executed.

This testament was proven before us on the 24th July [1500] in the Hospital of St John, Northampton. Administration was granted to the executors named in the same testament.

f81v 297 WILLIAM PERWYN 25th July 1500

In Dei nomine Amen xxv die mensis Junii anno millesimo quingentisimo Ego Willelmus Perwyn
de parochia Omnium Sanctorum ville Northampton compos mentis etcetera condo testamentum meum
in hunc modum In primis lego animam meam Deo Omnipotenti etcetera corpus-
que meum sepiliendum in capella Corporis Christi in predicta ecclesia iuxta sedem
meam in eadem Insuper volo quod Elizabeth uxor mea provideat lapidem marmorem
ad tumulum meum precii vli. in quo lapide volo quod sculpantur ymagines
mei et uxoris mee et filiorum filiarum que meorum quorum decem filiorum ponantur
ex parte patris et septem filiarum ex parte matris Item do et lego fraternitati Corporis
Christi in ecclesia predicta vjs.viijd. Item lego quatuor ordinibus fratrum mendicancium
in villa predicta ad precedendum corpus meum quando ad ecclesiam die sepulture
mee deportabitur et ad orandum pro anima mea vjs.viijd. Item volo quod distri-
buantur pauperibus xijcem duodene panis venul' Item do et lego Johanni filio
meo xxli. Item do Roberto filio meo xiijli.vjs.viijd. Item do Edwardo

filio meo xiijli.vjs.viijd. Item do et lego Johanne filie mee xiijli.vjs.viijd. Et si contingerit aliquem filiorum meorum predictorum decedere ante etatem octodecem annorum tunc volo quod bona ipius [ipius] sic decedentis dividantur per equales porciones inter ceteros filios superviventes et si casu accederit omnes filios meos predictos obire ante etatem predictam volo tunc quod bona illorum disponantur pro animabus illorum a quibus originatur provenieruntur Item volo quod dictus Johannes filius meus habeat porcionem sibi assignatam in brevi diliberatam Et si predicta Elizabeth iterum nupserit ex tunc volo quod relique porciones trium filiorum meorum predictorum ponantur extra manus suas in salva custodia pro securitate illorum Residuum vero omnium bonorum meorum non legatorum do predicte Elizabeth et ipsam ordino et facio executricem huius ultime voluntatis mee et predictum Johannem filium meum constituo cum ea supervisorem ut voluntas mea predicta maturii impleatur et ad adiuvandum matrem suam pro viribus suis etcetera ut debita mea persolvantur Teste Roberto Mydelham presencium scriptore

Istud testamentum probatum fuit in ecclesia Hospitalis Sancti Johannis Northampton <v die Augusti>
anno predicte et commissa et administracio etcetera executrice in eodem testamento nominate

In the name of God Amen the 25th day of June 1500 I William Perwyn of the parish of All Saints, Northampton in sound mind etcetera, make my testament in this wise. First I bequeath my soul to Almighty God etcetera and my body to be buried in the chapel of Corpus Christi in the church aforesaid next to my seat in the same. Further I wish that Elizabeth, my wife, shall provide a marble stone for my tomb £5 in value, on which stone I will that it shall be engraved in the image of me, my wife and my sons and daughters of whom ten of my sons shall be placed on the father's side and seven of my daughters on the mother's side. I give and bequeath to the fraternity of Corpus Christi in the same church 6s 8d. I bequeath to the four orders of mendicant brothers in the town aforesaid to go before my body when it is buried in the church on the day of my burial and to pray for my soul 6s 8d. I will that 12 dozen [venal] bread be distributed to poor people. I give and bequeath to John my son £20. I give and bequeath to Robert my son £13 6s 8d. I give and bequeath to Edward my son £13 6s 8d. I give and bequeath to Joan my daughter £13 6s 8d and if it happens that any of my sons aforesaid die before the age of eighteen then I will that the goods of the same deceased be divided by equal portions amongst the other sons surviving and if by chance it happens that all my sons aforesaid die before the age aforesaid I will then that their goods be disposed for the good of those from whom they originally came. I will that the said John, my son, have the portion assigned to him to come to him delivered by writ. And if the aforesaid Elizabeth marry again than I will that the remaining portions of my three sons aforesaid be placed out of her hands in safe custody for their security. The residue of all my goods not bequeathed I give to the aforesaid Elizabeth and the same I ordain and make executrix of this my last will and my aforesaid son John I constitute as supervisor with her that my aforesaid will may be fulfilled and to help his mother by his strength etcetera that my debts be paid. Witness Robert Mydelham, writer of these presents.

This testament was proved in the church of the Hospital of St John, Northampton 5th August of the year aforesaid and administration was granted etcetera to the executrix named in the same testament.

f82r 298 GEORGE DYK 16th June 1500

In the name of God Amen the xvjth day of Juny in the yere of our lorde mccccc I George Dyk of Northampton hole of mynde make my testament in this wyse First I bequeth my soule to Allmyghty God etcetera my body to be buryed in the churche yerd of All Halowes of the town of Northampton nygh to the chapell of Saynt George Item I bequeth to thygh awter for tythis forgoten iiijd. Item I bequeth to the fraternite of Saynt George in the same chyrche vjd. Item to the mothyr chyrche of Lincoln iiijd. Item I wyll that Thomas my son have all syche thyngs as was bequethed <to hym> by the gyfte of my mothyr as hyr testament more playnly showith that ys to say j brasse pott j brasse panne j basen j lavor of laten and vis.viijd. in money that is in my lady Saxby handes also j ffetherbed j bolster j payer of shetis j coveryng of a bed with barrs of blewe in hyt j copbord j spruse cheste and j chayer And over this my mothyrs bequests I bequeth to the same Thomas my son j cownter tabull j hanging lavor a iiij fotet cheste j yern beem and j weghte of dimidium hundreth j weght of xiiijlb with othyr smale weghtys Item I bequeth to Agnes Dyk my doghter all syche thynges as my mothyr bequethed to hyr that ys to say j brasse pott j brasse panne j bason j lavor of laten and vjs viijd whiche money is in my sayde lady Saxby handes also j red gyrdyll harneset with sylver and gylte And over this my sayde mothyr bequeste I bequeth to the same Agnes my doghter ij materesse ij payer of shetes Item I wyll that Marget Dyk my doughter have all syche thynges as was bequethed to hyr by my mothyr that ys to say j brasse pott j brasse pann j basen j lavor of laten and vis viij whyche ys my sayde lady Saxby handes also j red gyrdyll harneset with sylver And over this my sayde mothers wyll I bequeth to the same Marget my doghter ij materesse ij payer of shetes Item I bequeth to Elizabeth my wyfe j grete spruce cheste in the chamer j foldyn tabull and ij chestes in the lytyll parlor with all othyr moveabull stuffe excepte the standards of the houce and the hanginges in the hall The residue of all my godes not above bequethed I gyffe to the sayde Elizabeth and Thomas my son and the same Elizabeth and Thomas I ordeyng and make myn executors as they may se beste to please God to do for my soule and all Crysten soules Also I gyffe my sayde wyfe xijs towardes hyr houce rente for one yere nexte after my decesse Theys men beyng wittnes Master John Cokkes parson of the chyrche of Saynt Gregory in Northampton Syr John Brygeman preste and William Mownford notary

Istud testamentum probatum fuit in ecclesia Hospital Sancti Johannis Northampton vij die Augusti anno
predicte et comissa et administracionem etcetera Elizabeth executricem et superius nominate altera executor non comperen

This testament was proven in the church of the Hospital of St John, Northampton on the 7th day of August in the year aforesaid and administration etcetera was granted to Elizabeth the executrix and above named other executors who did not appear.

f84r 312 RICHARD BRUESTER 14th October 1500

In the name of God Amen <xiiij day of October> the yere of our Lord God mlccccc I Richard Bruester of hole mynd make my testament in this manner with this that peraventur sum thynges I may change in mynd after and subscribe them yf I lefe and yf I do not I wyll this become for my laste wyll In primis I bequeth my soul to Almyghty God etcetera my body to be beryed in the chyrche yerd of All Hallowys of Northampton Item I bequeth to hygh awter for tythis forgoten ijs. Item to the chapell of Corpus Christi ijs. Item to the chapell of Saynt Kateryne ijs. Item to the chapell of Saynt John ijs. Item I bequeth to my brothyr Jamys Bruster my beste gown The residue of my gods I gyffe and bequeth to my wife Alyce whom I make myne executrix and my brothyr Jamys they to dispose parte of them for the moste profett of my soule as my speciall treste ys in them by the councell of my fathyr John Rushden wytness this beyng record Sir Richard Cranfeld and Sir Thomas Gudechyld prests with moo

f84v 314 RICHARD BRUESTER 14th October 1500 mercer

In the name of God Amen the yere of our Lord God mlccccc the xiiij day of October. I Richard Bruester of Northampton mercer in hole mynd not knowyng the ower of my dethe thus dispose me when yt shall please God to cal me with this peraventur from thynges I may cheange in mynd and wryte them yf I lefe and yf I do not I wyll this stand for my laste wyll Fyrste I bequeth my soul to Almyghty God etcetera my body to be buryed in the chyrche of All Hallows within the town of Northampton Item I bequeth to hygh awter for tythynges forgotten ijs. Item to the chapell of Corpus Christi ijs. Item to the chapell of Saynt Kateryne ijs. Item to the chapell of Saynt John ijs. Item I bequeth to my brothyr Jamys my beste gown The residue I gyffe and bequeth to Alyce my wife whom I make myn executrix and my brothyr Jamys they to dispose parte of them for helthe of my soule etcetera as my specall treste ys in them thorowe the concell of my fathyr John Rushden whiche I make surveyor of my gods to odur them as yt ys before rehersed theys witnes Sir Richard Cranfeld Sir Thomas Gudechild with moo

f86r 321 [William] AUSTYN 6th September 1488 gentleman

In Dei nomine Amen vi die mensis Septembris anno domini millesimo cccclxxxviij Ego [William] Austyn de Northampton gentilman compos mentis et sane memorie condo testamentum meum in hunc modum In primis lego animam meam Deo Omnipotenti et Beate Marie Virgini sue genitrici ac omnibus sanctis curie celestis corpusque meum sepiliendum infra capellam Beate Marie Virginis in ecclesie parochia Omnium Sanctorum ville Northampton in illo loco ubi choriste eiusdem capelle stant durante et [..] ad missam dicte Beate Marie Virginis et ad antiphonam vocatam le Salve Item lego abbati et conventui monasterii Sancti Jacobi iuxta Northampton predictam in pecuniis muneratis xls. bone monete Anglie distribuendum in forme sequenti videlicet predicti abbati vjs.viijd. et omnibus dicte conventus viventi tempore sepulture mee xijd. Et Residuum dicte xls. [..]

distribuatur volo quod distribuatur inter dictos canonicos pro recreaceone eorum ad eorum libitum ut orandum
pro anima mea et anima Johanne nuper uxoris mee et animarum omnium fidelium defunctorum Item lego
cuilibet domui fratrum mendicancium eiusdem ville vjs. Item volo quod executores mei [...] nominati disponent et distribuent inter pauperes die seputure mee Cs. in pecuniis muneratis Residuum vero omnium bonorum meorum non legatorum do et lego Johanni Holwell et
Ricardo Gregory ad inde disponendum pro salute anime et anime predicte Johanne uxoris mei et animarum omnium fidelium defunctorum prout eis melius videbitur expediri et ad istud testamentum meum bene et fideliter exequendum prefatos Johannem Holwell et Ricardem Gregory constituo
et facio executores meos Et de execucione eiusdem Johannem Chauncy generosum ordino et constituo supervisorem Et volo quod quilibet executorum meorum habeat pro labore suo xiijs.iiijd.
ac insuper volo quod predictus Johannis Chauncy habeat pro labore suo in supervidendo execucionem
firmiter et debite fiendum a coppe et stanter in aula mea

In the name of God Amen the 6th day of September 1488 I [William] Austyn, gentleman, in sound mind and good memory make my testament in this wise. First I bequeath my soul to Almighty God and to the Blessed Virgin Mary His mother and all the saints of the court of heaven, my body to be buried in the chapel of the Blessed Virgin Mary in the parish church of All Saints in the town of Northampton in that place where the choir of that same chapel stand during and [ ] at the Mass of the said Blessed Virgin Mary and at the Antiphon called le Salve. Item I bequeath to the Abbot and convent of the monastery of St James next to the aforesaid Northampton in money 40s of good English money to be distributed in the following form, that is to say to the aforesaid Abbot 6s 8d and to all the said canons living at the time of my burial 12d. And the rest of the said 40s to be distributed I will that it be distributed amongst the aforesaid canons for their recreation at their pleasure as they pray for the good of my soul, the soul of Joan my late wife and the souls of all faithful departed. Item I bequeath to each house of mendicant brothers in the said town 6s. Item I will that my named executors should dispose and distribute among the poor on the day of my burial 100s in moneys. The residue of all my goods not bequeathed I give and bequeath to John Holwell and Richard Gregory to then dispose for the health of my soul and the soul of the aforesaid Joan my wife and the souls of all faithful departed as seems best to them, and that this testament be well and faithfully executed I constitute and make the aforesaid John Holwell and Richard Gregory my executors. And for the execution of the same I ordain and constitute John Chauncy, gentleman, as supervisor. And I will that each of my executors have for his labour 13s 4d. And moreover I will that the said John Chauncy have for his labour in supervising the execution to see it firmly and duly done a cup and stanter in my hall.

N.B. *The right hand page edge is torn which makes some line endings impossible to read.*

f86v 324 JOHN ROBARDES 4th July 1489 innholder

In Dei nomine Amen iiij die mensis Julii anno domini mcccclxxxix Ego Johannes Robardes de Northampton
innholder compos mentis et sane memorie condo testamentum meum in hunc modum In primis lego animam
Deo Omnipotenti Beate Marie Virgini sue genitrici ac omnibus sanctis curie celestis corpusque
meum sepiliendum in capella Beate Marie Virginis in ecclesia Omnium Sanctorum Northampton predicte
Item lego summo altari ecclesie predicte pro decimis oblacionibus oblitis non bene decimatis iijs. iiijd. Item lego cuilibet fraternitati eiusdem ecclesia xijd. Item lego Willelmo Roberdes fratri mee togam meam coloris sanguinum penulatem cum le calabur Item lego cuilibet filiorum Georgii Dyke iam viventi unum coclear de argento et unam pelvim
de laten Item do et lego prefato Georgio Dyke reversionem omnium terrarum et tenementorum
meorum immediate post decessum meum et decessum Agneti uxoris mei habendum et tenendum totam
predictam reversionem omnium terrarum et tenementorum meorum predictorum cum omnibus suis pertinenciis ut predictum
est prefato Georgio Dyke heredibus et assignatis suis inperpetuum de capitalibus dominis feodi illius per servicia
inde debita et de iure consueta Residuum vero omnium bonorum meorum superius non legatorum do et lego prefate
Agneti uxori mee et Georgio Dyke ad inde disponendum pro salute anime mee et animarum omnium fidelium defunctorum
prout eis melius videbitur expediri et ad istud testamentum meum bene et fideliter exequendum predictos Agnetam et Geogium
ordino facio et constituo executores meos per presentes hiis testibus Magistro Roberto Mydylham clerico domino
Willelmo Daffron clerico Thoma Malpas et aliis

In the name of God Amen the 4th day of July 1489 I John Robardes of Northampton, innholder, in sound mind and good memory make my testament in this wise. First I bequeath my soul to Almighty God, to the Blessed Virgin Mary His mother and all the saints of the court of heaven, my body to be buried in the chapel of the Blessed Virgin Mary in the church of All Saints in the said Northampton. Item I bequeath to the high altar of the said church for tithes and oblations forgotten or not well tithed 3s 4d. Item I bequeath to each fraternity of the same church 12d. Item I bequeath to William Robardes, my brother, my gown of sanguine colour furred with squirrel fur. Item I bequeath to each son of George Dyke who is still living one silver spoon and one basin of laten. Item I give and bequeath to the said George Dyke the reversion of all my lands and properties remaining after my death and the death of Agnes, my wife, to have and to hold in entirety. The said reversion of all my lands and tenements with all their appurtenances should be given to the said George Dyke, his heirs and assigns for evermore to hold of the chief lords of the fee by services therefore due and by right accustomed. The residue of all my goods not bequeathed above I give and bequeath to the said

Agnes, my wife, and to George Dyke, to then dispose for the health of my soul and the souls of all faithful departed as seems best to them and that this testament be well and faithfully executed ordain, make and constitute the said Agnes and George my executors by these presents. With these witnesses Master Robert Mydyllham, clerk, Dom William Daffron, Thomas Malpas and others.

f87r 325 THOMAS DERWYN 13th February 1499 mercer

In Dei nomine Amen xiij die mensis Februarii anno domini millesimo ccccIxxxix Ego Thomas Derwyn
nuper de Northampton mercer compos mentis et sane memorie condo testamentum meum in hunc modum In
primis lego animam meam Deo Omnipotenti et Beate Marie Virgini ac omnibus sanctis curie celestis corpusque meum
sepiliendum in cimiterio ecclesie parochiali de Walgrave in comitatu Northampton Item lego pro meo mortuario quod
iustum est Item lego fabrice eiusdem ecclesie vjs. viijd. Item lego cuilibet domui ordinum fratrum mendicancium
ville Northampton xxd. Item volo quod Feoffati mei inmediate post decessum meum facient seu
fieri causabunt Margarate uxori mee securum et legalem statum de et in omnibus et singulis terris et tenementis
meis pratis pascius pasturis redditibus reversionibus et serviciis cum suis pertinenciis in villis et campis
Northampton et Walgrave predictis habendum et tenendum omnia et singular predicta terras tenementa prata pascue
pasturas redditus reversiones et servicia cum omnibus eorum pertinencii ut predictum est prefate Margarate ad terminum
vite sue de capitalibus domnis feodi illius per servicia inde debita et de iure consueta ita quod
inmediate post decessum predicte Margarate uxoris mee volo quod predicti Feoffati mei omnia et singula predicta terras
tenementa prata pascuas pasturas redditus reversiones et servica cum omnibus suis pertinenciis per consilium et discrecionem
executorum meorum inferius nominatorum vendent ad maximam comodum quod fieri potest et omnes pecunii inde recepti
iidem executores prefatam Margaratam uxorem meam superviventes distribuent et
disponent pro salute anime mee animarum <amicorum meorum> et animarum
omnium fidelium defunctorum Residuum vero omnium bonorum meorum superius non legatorum do et lego predicte Margarate
uxori mee Henrico Hykman de Walgrave et Johanni Barett de Faxton ad inde disponend pro salute anime
mee animarum amicorum meorum et anime omnium fidelium defunctorum prout eis melius videbitur expediri et ad
istud testamentum bene et fideliter exequendum prefatos Margaretam Henricum et Johannem ordino facio et constituo executores
meos presentes

In the name of God Amen the 13th day of February 1499 I Thomas Derwyn, formerly of Northampton, mercer, in sound mind and good memory make my testament in this wise. First I bequeath my soul to Almighty God, to the Blessed Virgin Mary and all the saints of the court of heaven, my body to be buried in the cemetery of the parish church of Walgrave in the county of Northampton. Item I bequeath for my mortuary payment whatever is right. Item I bequeath to the fabric of the same church 6s 8d. Item I bequeath to each house of mendicant brothers in the town of Northampton 20d. Item I wish that my feoffees immediately after my death should make or cause to be made to Margaret, my wife, a secure and legal title to all my lands and tenements, meadows, grazing lands and pastures, rents, reversions and services with their appurtenances in the towns and fields of Northampton and the aforementioned Walgrave to have and to hold all of the said lands etcetera as were aforementioned to the said Margaret for the term of her life of the chief lords of the fee by services therefore due and by right accustomed. Item I will that immediately after the decease of the aforesaid Margaret, my wife, my aforesaid feoffees should, by the advice and discretion of my executors named below, sell all and singular the aforesaid lands, tenements, meadows, pastures, grazing lands, rents, reversions and services with all their appurtenances for the maximum benefit that can be obtained and the same executors surviving the aforesaid Margaret, my wife, should distribute and dispose for the health of my soul, my friends' souls and the souls of all faithful departed. The residue of all my goods not bequeathed above I give and bequeath to Margaret, my wife, Henry Hykeman of Walgrave and John Baret of Faxton, to then dispose for the health of my soul, the souls of my friends and the souls of all faithful departed as seems best to them and that this testament be well and faithfully executed I ordain, make and constitute the aforesaid Margaret, Henry and John as my executors by these presents.

f87r 326 AGNES BERTILMEWE 4th March 1499 widow

In Dei nomine Amen iiij die mensis Marcii anno domini millesimo ccccIxxxix Ego Agnes Bertilmewe
de Northampton vidua compos mentis et sane memorie condo testamentum meum in hunc modum In primis
lego animam meam Deo Omnipotenti Beate Marie etcetera omnibus sanctis corpusque meum sepiliendum
in ecclesia parochiali Omnium Sanctorum ville Northampton Item lego summo altari pro decimis oblitis iijs. iiijd.
Item lego omnia tenementa fraternitati Beate Marie in ecclesia predicta excepto quod volo ut domus
pauperum Sancti Thome iuxta portam australem ville Northampton habeat sex solidos annuatim imperpetuum de predictis
tenementis meis Item lego fraternitati Sancti Johannis Baptiste vjs.viijd. Item lego campanis iijs.iiijd. Item
lego filie mee unam togam Residuum vero omnium bonorum meorum non legatorum do et lego Willelmo
Pardun' ac eciam ordino et constituo eundem Willelmum executorem meum ut ipse disponat pro

salute anime mee prout ei melius videbitur expediri Date die et anno supradictis presentibus ibidem domino Willelmo Aydroppe et domino Roberto Smyth cum aliis testibus etcetera.

In the name of God Amen the 4th day of March 1499 I Agnes Bertilmewe of Northampton, widow, in sound mind and good memory make my testament in this wise. First I bequeath my soul to Almighty God, to the Blessed Mary etcetera and all the saints, my body to be buried in the parish church of All Saints, Northampton. Item I bequeath to the high altar for tithes forgotten 3s 4d. Item I bequeath all tenements to the fraternity of the Blessed Mary in the church aforesaid except that I will that the house of the poor of St Thomas next to the south gate of Northampton should have 6s annually for ever from my said tenements. Item I bequeath to the fraternity of St John the Baptist 6s 8d. Item I bequeath to the bells 3s 4d. Item I bequeath to my daughter one gown. The residue of all my goods not bequeathed I give and bequeath to William Pardun and also I ordain and constitute the same William my executor and he to dispose for the health of my soul as seems best to him. Given the day and year abovesaid. Present at the same place Dom William Aydroppe and Dom Robert Smyth with other witnesses etcetera.

f89v 332 JOHN JAMES alias BUKBY senior 6th October 1490 tanner

In Dei nomine Amen vj die mensis Octobris anno domini mccccl xxxx Ego Johannes James alias dictus Johannes Bukby de Northampton senior Tanner compos mentis et sane memorie condo testamentum meum in hunc modum In primis lego animam meam Deo Omnipotenti etcetera
corpusque meum sepiliendum in ecclesia Sancti Gregorii ville Northampton in semitera ante principalem
crucem ibidem Item lego summo altari ecclesie predicte pro decimis oblitis etcetera iijs. iiijd. Item lego fraternitati Sancte Crucis in Muro ibidem xijd. Item lego Alicie filie mee vjs.viijd. Item lego Agneti filie mee xxs. in pecuniis muneratis et in utensilibus domesticis
ad valenciam xxvjs.viijd. Item lego Johanne filie mee ad maritagium tuum xls. in
bona moneta Anglie Item lego Elizabeth filie mee xls. in pecuniis muneratis
et in utensilibus domesticis ad valorem xxvjs.viijd. Item lego Willelmo Bukby filio
meo meam optimam togam penulatam cum lez fuches Residuum vero bonorum meorum
superius non legatorum do et lego Johanni Clerke de Northampton Baker et Alicie uxori
mee ad inde disponendum pro salute anime mee animarum omnium fidelium defunctorum
prout eis melius videbitur expediri et ad istud testamentum bene et fideliter exequendum
prefatos Johannem Clerke et Aliciam uxorem meam ordino facio et constituo executores
meos et constituo magistrum Johannem Cokkes rectorem ecclesie Sancti Gregorii predicte facio
huius testamenti mei supervisorem et volo quod predictus Johannes Clerke habeat pro labore suo
unam peciam argenti pounced cum coopertorio item volo quod predictus magister Johannes Cokkes

habeat pro labore suo in supervidendo execucionem premissorum vjs.viijd. bone monete Anglie hiis testibus Willelmo Lammer magistro scolarum gramaticum Johanne Smyth wever Ricardo Blyssworth fuller Thoma Cartewryght wever et Thoma Malpas cum multis aliis

In the name of God Amen the 6th day of October 1490 I John James, also known as John Bukby, of Northampton senior, tanner, in sound mind and good memory make my testament in this wise. First I bequeath my soul to Almighty God etcetera my body to be buried in the church of St Gregory in the town of Northampton in the half plot of ground in front of the the first cross there. Item I bequeath to the high altar in the foresaid church for tithes forgotten etcetera 3s 4d. Item I bequeath to the fraternity of the Holy Cross in the Wall there 12d. Item I bequeath to Alice, my daughter, 6s 8d. Item I bequeath to Agnes, my daughter, 20s in cash and domestic utensils to the value of 26s 8d. Item I bequeath to Joan, my daughter, on her marriage 40s of good English money. Item I bequeath to Elizabeth, my daughter, 40s in cash and domestic utensils to the value of 26s 8d. Item I bequeath to William Bukby, my son, my best gown furred with polecat. The residue of my goods not bequeathed above I give and bequeath to John Clerke of Northampton, baker, and Alice, my wife, to then dispose for the health of my soul and the souls of all faithful departed as seems best to them and that this testament be well and faithfully executed I ordain, make and constitute the aforesaid John Clerke and Alice, my wife, as executors and I ordain Master John Cokkes, rector of the church of St Gregory aforesaid, my supervisor and I wish that the aforesaid John Clerk have for his labour one piece of decorated silver with a cover also I wish that the aforesaid John Cokkes should have for his labour in supervising the execution of these premises 6s 8d in good English money. With these witnesses William Lammer, Master of the grammar school, John Smyth, weaver, Richard Blyssworth, fuller, Thomas Cartewryght, weaver, and Thomas Malpas with many others.

f90r 334 JOHN CHAUNCEY senior (1490s) (gentleman)

In the name of God Amen I John Chauncey of Northampton the elder beying in good mynd and
in the faythfull beleve of holy churche disposyt in my helth so make me redy to the mercy of God when yt shall please hym to call me owte of this mortull lyfe declare ordeyn dispose and make my wyll and testament in maner and form folowyng Firste I beqwethe my soule to Almyghty God and my body to be buryed in the chapell of ower blessyth lady hys moder and virgin Saynt Mary within the parysh churche of Saynt Gyles of Northampton
Also to the vycar of the same parysh and churche for my mortuary my best jewell or ellis xls. Item to the sayde vicar for tythes and offeringes forgoten xld.
Item to Saynt Clementis gelde vjs viijd to be payde yerly at the feste of Saynt Clement duryng the time of xxti yere nexte folowyng after my decese Item to a

preste to syng for me for one yere vii marks Item to the reparaconis of the bellys
of Saynt Giles churche ijs. Item to the reparacon of the same churche ijs
Item to the reparacon of Ower <Lady> Chapell in the same church xld. Item for my leyer in
in the same chapell vjs viijd. Item to Saynt Jamys Abbey xxvjs. viijd. Item to
Saynt Andrews to be dysposyt among the covent to pray for my sowle and all crysten
soules xld. Also I beqweth to Jane my wyfe all my lyfelode and howsold for term
of hyr lyve Also I wyll and bequeth to Annes my dogther to hyr maryage yf she
be maryed after advyce of my sayd wyfe xl marks in money Also I wyll that
every howse of freres have xxd to pray for my soule and all crystyn soules Item to
every pore man and woman within Saynt Giles paryssh dwellyng ijd. Also I wyll that the
masses wyche byeth in the boke that mayster vicar hath be sayde for my soule and
all crystyn soules on oon day with placebo and dyrige over evyn of the whyche
masses I wyll parte of them be delyveryt to Saynt Jamys Abbey Saynt Andrewes
and to every churche of the freres syche as they saye with dylyvere of the money for the same

f90v

Also I beqwethe xxs to the reparacon of the cawce in Saynt Edmund Ende by
my close Item to the brethern of Saynt Johnys of Northampton xs. Item to William
Brafeld xs. Item to Roger Belcher iijs iiijd. Item to John Lumley iijs iiijd. Item
to William Stafford xxd and to every of the maydens xxd. Also I wyll that yf
any persone make any rigthwys cleym or chealenge of any dett wrong
or extorcion that shuld be ougth or don by me in my lyfe that myn executors
make dewe satisfacdon to hem as rigth and constience requyreth and the
resydewe of all my godes and catellys on myn interment kepte by the discrecon
of myne executors I will that Jane my wyfe have the rule and disposicon of
them to do with them as shall please hyr as hyr owyn propur godys
and the resydewe of syche godes as shalbe lefte after hyr dicease to remayn
to syche issewe as shall fortun to lyve goton betwyxt hyr and me Also
I wyll that Jane my wyfe shall have and peasabully enyoye all my landys and
tenementes rentes and servyces qwyche or any othre to my use have in Northampton
and ellyswhere in the counteies of Northampton Leycester and Lincoln for terme
of hyr lyfe acordyng to my bondes and promysse wyche I made at the marrage of
hyr and me Also I wyll that Agnes Chauncy my doghtyr after the decease of
my sayde wyfe shall have and peaseably enioye my ij tenements sette godyr
in Abyndon Strete in the town of Northampton with the gardynges thereto lying
and a barn with a garthyn sett in the same strete to have and to hold to hyr
and to hyr heyres of hyr body lawfully begoten and for defawte of syche
issue to remayne to my rigth heyres forever Also I will that Antony my son
shal have and peasibly enjoye after the decease of my sayde wyfe all theyes
lands and tenements rentes and servyces undwryten wyche I have in the town
and feldes of Northampton that ys to saye the towre cald Latymers Tower
for hys mansion ij closys iij gardens and a tenement yeard sette godyr
by sayde the same towre a close with a garden in the Bryge Strete nowe in the
holde of William Mylle and bak yarde nowe in the tenure of Thomas
Bodyngton dyer a tenement with a garden nowe in the holde of John Brabson
dyer sette in the same strete a crofte with a barn in Saynt Edmundes End
in the tenure of John Smyth furzcarter a tenement with a close in the same
end in the tenure of the same John Smyth late in the holde of John Heye
a tenement with a garden late in the hold of William Stafford a close
in the hold of John Clerke xviijd of a qwryte rent goyng owte of a tenement
in the tenure of Harry Wyllymott xliijd of qwryte rent goyng owte of
a peac aruball land callyd Fayer Crofte in the feldes of Northampton late in the
hold of John Smyth carter to have and to holde to the sayde Antony and
to the heyres of hys body lawfully begoten and for defaute of siche issue

f91r

to remayn to my rygth heyres for ever Also I wyll that John Chauncy my eldyste son shal have and peasibly enjoye after the decease of my sayde wyfe all my other landes rentes tenements and servyce
not above beqwethytt qwyche I have any othyr to my use hath in Northampton or ellys where to have
to hym and to hys heyres of hys body lawfully begoten and for defaute of syche issue to remayn
to my rigth heires forever provyded all wey that yf they wylbe demeanyd and rewlyd after the mynde and counsell of my sayd wyfe this wyll to be gude and of effecte or ellys to be as voide
and as never syche graunt by me had ben made Forthermore I beqweth to the mayster & brethyrn of Saynt Johnys of the town of Northampton after the decease of my sayde wyfe all my landes and medows whyche I have in the town and feldes of Hakylton in the counte of Northampton
to have to them and to theyr sucessors for ever Also I make myn executors Jane
my wyfe and Maister Thomas Permenter clerke Maister Emson to be surveyor of this
my testament and laste wyll and wyll aswele my sayde wyfe as the sayde Maister Thomas
Permenter have to every yche of them for executing of this my last wyll xxs and
Maister Emson surveyor of this my testament have for hys labor xls theys beryng
wytnes John Clarke baker John Partys clerke William Brafeld John Peck Roger
Belcher and John Lomley

f91r 335 EDWARD ATWELL 20th May 1488 butcher

In Dei nomine Amen xx die mensis Maii anno domini mccccIxxxviij Ego Edwardus Atwell de Northampton bucher compos mentis et sane memorie condo testamentum meum in hunc modum In primis
lego animam meam Deo Omnipotenti Beate Marie Virgini sue genitrici et omnibus sanctis corpusque meum
sepiliendum in cimiterio ecclesie parochialis Omnium Sanctorum ville Northampton iuxta tumulum Matildis nuper uxoris mee
Item lego summo altari eiusdem ecclesie pro decimis meis et oblacionibus oblitis et subtractis vjs.viijd.
Item lego fraternitati Sancte Crucis in dicta ecclesia xijd. Item lego pauperibus in domo elemosinario Sancti Thome
martiris extra portam australem ville Northampton predicte xijd. Item lego ecclesie de Wotton in comitatu Northampton xxd
Item lego ecclesie de Qwynton xxd. Item lego ecclesie de Sywell vjs viijd. Item lego Domino Johanni Atwell priori domus de Suelsale filio meo meam togam coloris sangwyn ingreyn penulatem
cum le marterens Item lego Eduardo Atwell filio meo in diversis bonis et pecuniis ad valenciem
decem marcarum Item lego Thome Atwell filio meo in diversis bonis et pecuniis ad
valorem x marcarum Item lego Agneti Atwell filie mee diversis bonis et pecuniis ad
valenor decem marcarum Ulterius que do et lego Agneti uxori mee totam illud tenementum meum
principale cum domibus edificiis et omnibus aliis pertinenciis suis situatis super le corner de
Fleshmonger Strete inter tenementum nunc in tenura Margarete Elyott ex parte australi et viam regiam
ex parte boriali Item do et lego predicte Agneti uxori mee aliud tenementum in vico Sancti Egidii

nunc in tenura Walteri Wodland habendum et tenendum predicta duo tenementa cum omnibus eorum
pertinenciis prefati Agneti uxori mee heredibus et assignatis suis imperpetuum de capitalibus dominis feodi

f91v

illud per servicia inde debita et de iure consueta Item lego Emme filie mee
post decessum dicte Agnetis uxoris mee unum tenementum jacens in le Horsemarkett
iuxta tenementum principale nunc in tenura Margarete Elyott vidua cum suis pertinenciis
habendum et tenendum predictum tenementum cum suis juribus et pertinenciis prefate Emme filie
mee et heredibus suis de corpore sue legitime procreatis imperpetuum de capitalibus dominis
feodi illius per servicia inde debita et de iure consueta et si contingat predictam
Emmam obire sive heredibus de corpore suo legitime procreatis volo tunc quod dictum tenementum
remaneat et revertatur predicte Agneti uxori mee heredibus et assignatis suis ad
vendendum et ad pecunias inde receptas pro salute anime mee et omnium fidelium
defunctorum fideliter disponendum Item lego Agneti filie mee post decessum
predicte Agnetis matris sue uxoris mee aliud tenementum meum cum suis pertinenciis annexam
predicto tenemento in tenura Margareta Eliott habendum et tenendum predictum tenementia cum suis pertinenciis
prefate Agneti filie mee et heredibus suis de corpore suo legitime procreatis de capitalibus
dominis feodi illius per servicia inde debita et de iure consueta et si contingat
dictam Agnetem filiam meam obire sine heredibus de corpore suo legitime procreatis tunc volo quod
et concedo quod dictum tenementum remaneat et revertatur prefate Agneti uxori mee heredibus et
assignatis suis ad vendendum et pecunias inde recipiendum pro salute anime et omnium fidelium
defunctorum disponendum Item do et lego Anne filie mee post decessum uxoris
mee predicte duo cotagia cum suis pertinenciis situata in vico Magistorum inter tenementum
Johannis Asshwell ex parte occidentale et tenementum collegii Omnium Sanctorum ex parte orientale
habendum et tenendum predicta duo cotagia cum suis pertinenciis prefate Anne filie mee
et heredibus de corpore suo legitime procreatis imperpetuum de capitalibus dominis feodi illius
per servicia inde debita et de iure consueta et si contingat quod prefata Anna
decedat sine heredibus de corpore suo legitime procreatis tunc volo quod dicta duo cotagia
cum suis pertinenciis remaneant et reverantur predicte uxori mee heredibus et assignatis suis
ad vendendum et pecunias inde perveniendum pro salute anime mee et omnium fidelium defunctorum
Item do et lego Edmundo <Atwell> filio meo post decessum predicte Agnetis uxoris mee
unum tenementum meum cum omnibus pratis pascuis pasturis et aliis suis pertinenciis
in villa et campis de Cathorp et in campis de Lylborn in comitatu Leicester
habendum et tenendum predictum tenementum cum omnibus pratis pascuis et pasturis et pertinenciis
suis prefato Edmundo Atwell filio meo et heredibus suis de corpore suo legitime
procreatis imperpetuum de capitalibus dominis feodi illius per servicia inde debita et de
iure consuetur et si contingat predictum Edmundum obire sine heredibus de corpore sue legitime
procreatis tunc volo quod dictum tenementum cum pratis pascuis et pasturis et aliis pertinenciis suis
remaneat et revertatur prefate uxori mee heredibus et assignatis suis ad vendendum et ad disponendum

pecunias inde receptas pro salute anime mee et animarum omnium fidelium defunctorum Item do
et lego Thome Atwell filio meo post decessum Agnetis uxoris mee unam shopam
situatam in Rengo Carnifico ville Northampton inter shopam fraternitatis Corporis Christi in ecclesia
Omnium Sanctorum de Northampton ex parte orientali et shopam Thome Sosyndale ex parte

f92r

occidentali aceciam do et lego predicto Thome post decessum matris eius unum cotagium situatum
in le Flesshmonger Strete de Northampton predicte inter tenementum Sancti Leonardi ibidem ex parte occidentali et
cotagium Johannis May ex parte orientali habendum et tenendum predictam shopam et cotagium cum
suis pertinenciis prefato Thome Atwell filio meo et heredibus de corpore suo legitime procreatis imperpetuum de
capitalibus dominis feodi illius per servicia inde debita et de iure consueta et si contingat quod dictum Thomam
obierit sine heredibus de corpore suo legitime procreatis tunc volo quod dicta shopa et cotagium cum suis
pertinenciis prefate Agneti uxori mee remaneant et revertantur heredibus et assignatis suis ad vendendum et disponendum
ut supra Residuum vero omnium bonorum meorum superius non legatorum do et lego Agneti uxori mee
ad inde disponendum pro salute anime mee et animarum omnium fidelium defunctorum prout ei melius
videbitur expediri et ad istud testamentum meum bene et fideliter exequendum prefatam uxoram meam
ordino facio et constituo executricem meam et volo quod predictus dominus Johannes Atwell sit
supervisor istius testamenti mei

In the name of God Amen the 20th day of May 1488 I Edward Atwell, butcher, in sound mind and good memory make my testament in this wise. First I bequeath my soul to Almighty God, to the Blessed Virgin Mary His mother and all the saints, my body to be buried in the cemetery of the parish church of All Saints in the town of Northampton next to the grave of Matilda my late wife. Item I bequeath to the high altar of the same church for my tithes and oblations forgotten and withheld. Item I bequeath to the fraternity of the Holy Cross in the same church 12d. Item I bequeath to the poor in the almshouse of St Thomas the Martyr outside the south gate of Northampton aforesaid 12d. Item I bequeath to the church of Wootton in the county of Northampton 20d. Item I bequeath to the church of Quinton 20d. Item I bequeath to the church of Sywell 6s 8d. Item I bequeath to Dom John Atwell, Prior of the house of Suelsale, my son, my gown dyed sanguine colour furred with marten fur. Item I bequeath to Edward Atwell, my son, divers goods and money to the value of ten marks. Item I bequeath to Thomas Atwell, my son divers goods and money to the value of ten marks. Item I bequeath to Agnes Atwell, my daughter, divers good and money to the value of ten marks. Furthermore

I give and bequeath to Agnes, my wife, all my principal tenements and dwelling building and all their appurtenances situated at the corner of Fleshmonger Street between the tenement now in the tenure of Margaret Elyott on the south and the king's highway to the north. Item I give and bequeath to the aforesaid Agnes, my wife, another house in St Giles Street now in the tenure of Walter Wodland to have and to hold the aforesaid two tenements with all their appurtenances to the aforesaid Agnes, my wife, her heirs and assigns forever of the chief lords of the fee for services therefore due and by right accustomed. Item I bequeath to Emma, my daughter, after the death of the said Agnes my wife, a tenement lying in the Horsemarket next to my principal tenement, now in the tenure of Margaret Elyott, widow, with all its appurtenances to have and to hold the aforesaid tenement with its rights and appurtenances to the aforesaid Emma, my daughter, and the heirs of her body legitimately begotten forever of the chief lords by services due and by right accustomed and if it happens that the aforesaid Emma dies without heirs of her body legitimately begotten then I will that the said tenement should remain and revert to the aforesaid Agnes, my wife, and her heirs and assigns to be sold and the money received from them be disposed for the health of my soul and all faithful departed. Item I give and bequeath to Agnes, my daughter, after the death of the aforesaid Agnes, her mother and my wife, another tenement of mine with its appurtenances joined to the aforesaid tenement in the tenure of Margaret Elyott, to have and to hold the said tenement with its appurtenances to the said Agnes, my daughter, and the heirs of her body legitimately begotten of the chief lords of the fee for services therefore due and by right accustomed and if it happens the said Agnes dies without heirs of her body legitimately begotten then I will that the said tenement remain and revert to the aforesaid Agnes, my wife her heirs and assigns to be sold and the money received to be disposed for the health of my soul and all faithful departed. Item I bequeath to Anne, my daughter, after the death of my wife two cottages with their appurtenances situated in the street of the Magistrates between the tenement of John Ashwell on the west and the tenement of the college of All Saints on the east, to have and to hold the said cottages with their appurtenances to the said Anne, my daughter, and the heirs of her body legitimately begotten forever of the chief lords of the fee by services therefore due and by right accustomed and if it happens that the said Anne should die without heirs of her body legitimately begotten then I will that the said two cottages should remain and revert to my said wife, her heirs and assigns to be sold and the money received to be disposed for the health of my soul and all faithful departed. Item I bequeath to Edmund Atwell, my son, after the death of the said Agnes, my wife, my one tenement with all meadows, grazing land, pasture and other appurtenances in the town and fields of Cathorp and in the fields of Lilbourne in the county of Leicester to have and to hold the said tenement with all meadows, pastures, grazing ground and pasture land with all their appurtenances to the said Edmund Atwell, my son, and the heirs of his body legitimately begotten forever of the chief lords of the fee by services therefore due and by right accustomed and if it should happen that the said Edmund should die without heirs of his body legitimately begotten then I will that the said tenement with meadows, pastures and grazing land with all its appurtenances should remain and revert to my said wife, her heirs and assigns to be sold and the money received to be disposed for the health of my soul and the souls of all faithful departed. Item I give and bequeath to Thomas Atwell, my son, after the death of Agnes, my wife, a shop situated in the Butchers Row in the town of Northampton between the shop of the fraternity of Corpus Christi in the church of All Saints of Northampton on the east and the shop of Thomas Sosyndale on the west, and furthermore I give and bequeath to the aforesaid Thomas after the death of his mother a cottage situated in Fleshmonger Street in Northampton aforesaid between the same house of St Leonard on the west and the cottage of John May on the east to have and to hold the said shop and cottage with their appurtenances to the said Thomas Atwell, my son, and the heirs of his body legitimately begotten forever of the chief lords by services therefore due and by right accustomed and if it should happen that the said Thomas should die without heirs of his body legitimately begotten then I will that the said shop and cottage with their appurtenances should remain and revert to the said Agnes, my wife her heirs and assigns to be sold and disposed of as above. The residue of all my goods not bequeathed above I give and bequeath to Agnes, my wife, to then dispose for the health of my soul and the souls of all faithful departed as seems best to her and that this testament be well and faithfully executed I ordain, make and constitute my aforesaid wife as my executor and the aforesaid John Atwell supervisor of this my will.

f92r 336 HUGH WODSALL 20th May 1490 innholder

In Dei nomine Amen xx die Maii anno domini mccccIxxxx Ego Hugo Wodsall de Northampton
Innholder compos mentis etcetera condo testamentum meum In primis lego animam meam Deo Omnipotenti
Beate Marie Virgini sue genitrici ac omnibus sanctis corpusque meum sepiliendum in cimiterio
ecclesie Parochiali Omnium Sanctorum ibidem Item lego summo altari eiusdem pro decimis meis non bene decimatis
et oblationibus oblitis vjs. viijd. Item lego fraternitati Sancte Trinitatis in eadem ecclesia vjs.viijd. Item lego
fraternitati Sancti Georgii ibidem iijs.iiijd. Item lego lumini vocate the Bowers Lygth pendente
coram principali cruce in eadem ecclesia iijs.iiijd. Item volo quod summa <sexagenta> solidorum

in pecuniis muneratis debitis michi de fratribus Augustin' ville Northampton pro
cervisia eis diversis vicibus venditis et traditis sit remissa et perdonata imperpetuum sub hac condicione quod unus presbyter frater eiusdem domus septimanatim uno anno proximo sequente diem
decessus mei Hugonis predicti semel missam de requiem etcetera celebrabit <speciale> pro salute anime
mee et amicorum meorum et omnium fidelium defunctorum Item lego Johanni Wodsall
fratri meo omnia mea le wering clothes excepto mea optima toga de sangwyn
in greyn penulata cum le bever cum duobus deploidis vocatis dubletts of defences
quas deploides et togam volo quod executores mei vendent ad maximum valorem quo
poterint et pecunias inde pervenientes pro salute anime amicorum <meorum> et omnium fidelium defunctorum
disponent Item lego eidem Johanni fratri meo unum matricum unum par linthiamenti
vocata london shetes unum coopertorium vocatum a coverlett et unam ollam eneam continentem
duas lagenas in mensura Item lego Alicie Wodsall cognate mee unum matricum
unum par linthiamenti et unam coopertorium ac vjs.viijd. in pecuniis muneratis Item
lego Johanne Wodsall filie Roberti Wodsall fratris mei vjs.viijd. in pecuniis muneratis
Item volo quod Robertus Page puer meus elemosino sic exhibitus cum parte residui

f92v

bonorum meorum non legatorum quousque scit nomina hominium et summas pecuniarum <sci[bil]e> et ea per s[age] legare ac mar-
tinas et vesperas Beate Marie Virginis Item volo quod executores mei inferius nominati quolibet die
veneris per spacium unius anni integris inmediate decessum meum sequente septem denariatis albi pannis
inter pauperes ubi magis necesse erit distribuent et disponent ulterius quecum ego
prefatus Hugo per cartam meam feodi simplicis omnis data est octavo die mensis Januarii
anno quinto Henrici Septimi deterivi concesseravi et confirmaverivi Johanni Adams de Northampton
Innholder et Johanni Wattes de eadem corvesor totum gardinum meum cum suis pertinenciis iacens in
parochia Sancte Sepulcri ville Northampton inter tenementum cum gardino adiacentem domus sive prioratus
Sancti Andree Apostoli eiusdem ville ex parte orientali et croftum dicte domus sive prioratus
nuper in tenura Edwardi Atwell bocher parte ex occidentali ac croftum cum columbari
magistri hospitali Sancti Leonardi in Coton iuxta Northampton predictam ex parte australi necnon viam regiam
ex parte boriali habendum et tenendum totum predictum gardinum cum omnibus suis pertinenciis ut predictum est
prefatis Johanni et Johanni heredibus et assignatis suis imperpetuum volo quod predicti Johannes et Johannes feoffati
mei inmediate post decessum meum facient seu fieri causabunt Elene uxore mee secura
statum et legalem de predicto gardino cum omnibus suis pertinenciis ut prefertur prefate Elene ad terminum
vite sue ita quod inmediate post decessum eius dictum gardinum cum suis pertinenciis integre
remaneat domui elemosinario Sancti Thome Martiris extra portam australem ibidem ad sustent-
acionem pauperum pro tempore ibidem existentes pro salute anime et animarum amicorum meorum et omnium fidelium defunctorum
Residuum vero omnium bonorum meorum superius non legatorum do et lego dicte Elene uxori mee

et predicto Johanni Wattes ad inde disponendum pro salute anime mee et animarum amicorum meorum
et omnium fidelium defunctorum prout eis melius videbitur expediri et ad istud testamentum meum bene et fideliter exequendum prefatam Elenam et Johannem Wattes ordino facio et
constituo executores meos et Johannem Adams supranominatum ordino et facio istius testamenti mei supervisorem et volo quod quilibet dictorum Johannis Adams et Johannis Wattes
habeat pro labore suo vjs.viijd. per presentes hiis testibus domini Ricardo [ ] capellano confessore meo Johanne Longe tailor et Johanne Pewterer alius Waterman cum aliis etcetera

In the name of God Amen the 20th day of May 1490 I Hugh Wodsall of Northampton, innholder in sound mind etcetera make my testament. First I bequeath my soul to Almighty God, to the Blessed Virgin Mary His mother and all the saints, my body to be buried in the cemetery of the parish church of All Saints in that place. Item I bequeath to the high altar of the same church for my tithes not well tithed and oblations forgotten 6s 8d. Item I bequeath to the fraternity of Holy Trinity in the same church 6s 8d. Item I bequeath to the fraternity of St George there 3s 4d. Item I bequeath to the lamp called 'The Bowers Lygth' hanging in the centre of the main cross in the same church 3s 4d. Item I will that the sum of sixty shillings in cash owed to me by the Augustinian Friars in the town of Northampton for the ale conveyed and sold there on divers occasions, be remitted and pardoned forever under this condition that one of the priests of the same brotherhood should celebrate a single requiem mass etcetera every week for a year after my death, the aforesaid Hugh, especially for the health of my soul, the souls of my friends and the souls of all faithful departed. Item I bequeath to John Wodsall, my brother, all my wearing apparel except my best gown dyed sanguine furred with beaver with two doublets called 'dubletts of defences', which doublet and gown I wish that my executors shall sell for the maximum value they can and the money therefrom disposed for the health of the souls of my friends and all faithful departed. Item I bequeath to the same John, my brother, one mattress, one pair of sheets called 'London' sheets, one cover called a 'coverlet' and one brass jar containing two gallons measure. Item I bequeath to Alice Wodsall, my relative, one mattress, one pair of sheets and one coverlet and 6s 8d in cash. Item I bequeath to Joan Wodsall, the daughter of Robert Wodsall my brother, 6s 8d in cash. Item I will that Robert Page, my boy, be supported and trained, provided for by charity with part of the residue of my goods not bequeathed, until he knows the names of men and the sums of money and with this knowledge reads the matins and vespers of the Blessed Virgin Mary. Item I will that my executors named below on every Friday for the space of a whole year immediately after my death should distribute and allocate seven pennyworth of white bread amongst the poor where there is greatest need moreover I, the aforementioned Hugh, by my deed of fee simple on the eighth day of the month of January in the fifth year of Henry VII have determined, granted and confirmed to John Adams of Northampton, innholder, and to John Wattes of the same town, corvisor, the whole of my garden with its appurtenances lying in the parish of Holy Sepulchre in the town of Northampton, between the tenement with garden adjacent to the house or priory of St Andrew the Apostle of the same town on the east and the croft of the said house or priory, formerly in the tenure of Edward Atwell, butcher, on the west, and the croft with dovecote of the Master of the Hospital of St Leonard in Coton by the said Northampton on the south, and also the king's highway on the north, to have and to hold the whole of the aforesaid garden with all its appurtenances as mentioned above, to the aforesaid John and John and to their heirs and assigns forever. I will that the said John and John, my feoffees, should immediately after my death, make or cause to be made to Elene, my wife, a secure and legal estate of the said garden with all its appurtenances as previously mentioned to the aforementioned Elene to the term of her life on condition that immediately after her death the said garden with all its appurtenances should fully remain to the almshouse of St Thomas the Martyr outside the south gate there for the sustenance of the poor living there at that time for the health of my soul, the souls of my friends and all faithful departed. The residue of all my goods not bequeathed above I give and bequeath to the said Elene my wife, and to the aforementioned John Wattes to then dispose for the health of my soul and the souls of my friends and all faithful departed as seems best to them and that this testament be well and faithfully executed I ordain, make and constitute the aforementioned Elene and John Wattes as my executors and I ordain and make the above named John Adams supervisor of this my testament and I wish that each of the said John Adams and John Wattes should have for his labour 6s 8d by these presents. With these witnesses Dom Richard [ ] chaplain, my confessor, John Lange, tailor, and John Pewterer alias Waterman with others etcetera.

f92v 337 ROGER DAWN 2nd August 1491 haberdasher

In Dei nomine Amen secundo die Augusti anno domini mccccclxxxxj Ego Rogerus Dawn de Northampton haberdasher compos mentis et sane memorie condo testamentum meum in hunc modum In primis lego animam meam Deo Omnipotenti Beate Marie matri eius et omnibus sanctis celestis curie corpusque meum sepiliendum infra ecclesie Sancti Petri ville Northampton ad placitum uxoris mee Item lego ad honorem Dei in eadem ecclesia unum
magnum pannum sericum viridis coloris Item lego Johanni filio meo unum salte de argento sine coopertorio duo cocliaria argentea et in pecuniis xls. Item lego Edwardo filio meo xls. et ij cocliaria Item lego Ricardo filio meo xls. et duo cocliaria Item lego Johanne filie mee xls. et duo cocliaria argenti et si contingat aliquem dictorum filiorum meorum ante annos discrecionis obire tunc volo quod pars defuncti remaneat aliis filiis meis tunc viventis et si omnes moriantur ante huismodi annos tunc volo quod predicta summa <cum bonis> sic legata remaneat predicte ecclesie Sancti Petri ad orandum pro anima mea Item lego Stephano

f93r

Drewry unam togam de togis meis Item lego uxori predicti Stephani unam togarum mearum
Item lego Isabelle servienti mee <quatuor> virgatas panni lanei et in pecuniis xxs. Item
lego Anne sorori mei ij virgatas panni lanei pro una tunica videlicet a curtyll Item lego
Johanne
uxori mee totum gardinum meum cum pertinenciis ad totum terminum vite sue et inmediate
post decessum
eius volo quod totum predictum gardinum remaneat Johanni filio meo habendum et
tenendum sibi
heredibus et assignatis suis imperpetuum de capitalibus dominis feodi per servicia debita
Item lego Johanne
Dawn matri mee ij virgatas panni lanei Residuum vero omnium bonorum meorum superius
non
legatorum totaliter do et lego Johanne uxori mee ad inde ordinandum et disponendum pro
salute
anime mee et pro salute animarum omnium fidelium defunctorum prout ei melius videbitur
expediri
et facio eandem Johannam uxorem meam huius testamenti mei executricem et pro auxilio et
consilio
in omnibus concernentis dictum testamentum meum et dictam executricem facio Ricardum
Brabson shomaker
et Johannem Whyte wever supervisores et volo quod uterque eorum habebit pro labore suo
xxs. in cuius
rei testimonium sigillum meum presentibus apposui Date die et anno domini
supradictis

In the name of God Amen the 2nd day of August 1491 I Roger Dawn of Northampton, haberdasher, in sound mind and good memory make my testament in this wise. First I bequeath my soul to Almighty God, to the Blessed Mary His mother and all the saints of the court of heaven, my body to be buried within the church of St Peter in the town of Northampton at the direction of my wife. Item I bequeath to the honour of God in the same church one large silk cloth of green colour. Item I bequeath to John, my son, one large silver salt cellar without a cover, two silver spoons and in money 40s. Item I bequeath to Edward, my son, 40s and two silver spoons. Item I bequeath to Richard, my son, 40s and two silver spoons. Item I bequeath to Joan, my daughter, 40s. and two silver spoons, and if it should happen that any of my said children should die before they reach the age of discretion than I will that the deceased person's share should be handed on to my other living children and if all should die before they come of age than I wish that the said amount with goods as bequeathed should remain to the said church of St Peter for prayers for my soul. Item I bequeath to Stephen Drewry one of my gowns. Item I bequeath to the wife of the said Stephen one of my gowns. Item I bequeath to Isabella, my servant, 4 yards of woollen cloth and in money 20s. Item I bequeath to Anne, my sister, 2 yards of woollen cloth for a tunic called a 'curtyll'. Item I bequeath to Joan, my wife, all of my garden with appurtenances for the rest of her life and immediately after her death I wish that the whole of the said garden should be left to John, my son, to have and to hold by him, his heirs and assigns forever of the chief lords of the fee for services therefore due. Item I bequeath to Joan Dawn, my mother, 2 yards of woollen cloth. The residue of all my goods not totally bequeathed above I give and bequeath to Joan, my wife, to then dispose for the health of my soul and the souls of all faithful departed as seems best to her and I make that same Joan, my wife, executrix of this my will and for help and advice in all matters concerning my will and the said execution I make Richard Brabson, shoemaker, and John Whyte, weaver, supervisors and I wish that each of them should have for his labour 20s. In witness of this matter I have put my seal by these presents. Given the day and year abovesaid.

f93r 338 JOHN LEYNOWE 13th October 1491 glover

In Dei nomine Amen xiij die Octobris anno domini mcccclxxxxj Ego Johannes Leynowe de Northampton
glover compos mentis etcetera condo testamentum meum in hunc modum In primis lego animam meam Deo
Omnipotenti Beate Marie et omnibus sanctis corpusque meum sepiliendum in capella Beate Marie in ecclesia Omnium
Sanctorum eiusdem ville Item lego monasterio Sancti Andree pro decimis oblitis xld. Item lego ad reparacionem
summi altaris in dicta ecclesia xld. Item lego fraternitati Sancte Trinitatis ibidem xijd. Item lego fraternitati
Corporis Christi xijd. Item lego fraternitati Sancti Johannis Baptiste xijd. Item lego altari Sancti Jacobi xijd.
Item lego fraternitati Sancte Crucis xijd. Item lego altari Sancte Cithe xijd. Item lego altari Sancti Stephani
xijd. Item lego fraternitati Sancti Georgii xijd. Item lego fraternitati Sancte Katerine xijd. Item lego
Elizabeth filie mee xli. argenti Item lego Margate filie mee xli. bone monete
Item lego unum salarium argenti cum cooperterio Elizabeth et Margate filiabus meis equaliter inter eas
dividendum si vixerint sed si una earum decesserit altera superstite volo quod pars decedentis detur
alteri sorori viventi videlicet tam decem libre quam pars salariii et si ambo obierint volo tunc
ut uxor mea habeat dictum salarium et decem libras summe legate filiabus meis ad usum suum
et ut alie decem libre disponantur pro salute anime mee Residuum vero omnium bonorum meorum
non legatorum do et lego Margate uxori mee et ad istud testamentum meum bene et fideliter exequendum
predictam Margatam executricem meam constituo per presentes et Johannem Leynowe fratrem meum
supervisorem hiis testibus domino Willelmo Aydroppe et Simone Leynowe

In the name of God Amen the 13th day of October 1491 I John Leynowe of Northampton, glover, in sound mind etcetera make my testament in this wise. First I bequeath my soul to Almighty God, to the Blessed Mary and all the saints, my body to be buried in the chapel of the Blessed Mary in the church of All Saints of the same town. Item I bequeath to the monastery of St Andrew for tithes forgotten 40d. Item I bequeath to the repair of the high altar in the said church 40d. Item I bequeath to the fraternity of the Holy Trinity there 12d. Item I bequeath to the fraternity of Corpus Christi 12d. Item I bequeath to the fraternity of St John the Baptist 12d. Item I bequeath to the altar of St James 12d. Item I bequeath to the fraternity of the Holy Cross 12d. Item I bequeath to the altar of St Cithe 12d. Item I bequeath to the fraternity of St Stephen 12d. Item I bequeath to the fraternity of St George 12d. Item I bequeath to the fraternity of St Katherine 12d. Item I bequeath to Elizabeth, my daughter, £10 in silver. Item I bequeath to Margaret, my daughter, £10 in good money. Item I bequeath one silver salt with cover to Elizabeth and Margaret to be divided equally between them if they should live but if one of them should die with the other surviving I will that the part of the deceased should be given to the other surviving sister, that is to say the £10 and the share of the salt, and if both should die then I will that my wife should have the said salt and £10 of the sum bequeathed to my daughters for her use and the other £10 to be disposed for the health of my soul. The residue of all my goods not bequeathed I give and bequeath to Margaret, my wife, and that this testament be well and faithfully executed I constitute the said Margaret my executrix by these presents and John Leynowe, my brother, as supervisor. With these witnesses Dom William Aydroppe and Simon Leynowe.

f93v 339 THOMAS HORNE 7th December 1491

In Dei nomine Amen septimo die Decembris anno domini mcccclxxxxj Ego Thomas Horne de Northampton sane mentis condo testamentum meum in hunc modum In primis lego animam
meam Deo Omnipotenti Beate Marie et omnibus sanctis corpusque meum sepiliendum in capella Beate Marie ecclesia Omnium Sanctorum ville Northampton Item lego ad reparacionem summi
altaris eiusdem ecclesie xld. Item lego fraternitati Sancte Trinitatis xijd. Item lego fraternitati Corporis Christi xijd. Item lego fraternitati Sancti Johannis Baptiste xijd. Item lego altari Sancti
Jacobi xijd. Item lego fraternitati Sancte Crucis xijd. Item lego altaris Sancte Cithe xijd. Item lego altari Sancti Stephani xijd. Item lego fraternitati Sancti Georgii xijd. Item lego fraternitati
Sancte Katerine xijd. Item lego fabrice ecclesie de Sywell quinque oves Item lego magistro Radulpho Maryett unam togam penulatam de cremsyn Item lego fabrice ecclesie Beate Lincoln xijd. Item lego domino Willelmo Aydroppe unam togam de cremsyn lynytt
Item lego Thome Murby unam togam rosetam Item lego Rogero Clerke unam togam Residuum omnium bonorum meorum non legatorum do et lego Johanne uxori mee et ad istud
testamentum bene et fideliter exequendum predictam Johannam executricem meam facio ordino et constituo
per presentes hiis testibus domino Willelmo Aydroppe et Thoma Murby

In the name of God Amen the 7th day of December 1491 I Thomas Horne of Northampton in good memory make my testament in this wise. First I bequeath my soul to Almighty God, to the Blessed Mary and all the saints, my body to be buried in the chapel of the Blessed Mary in the church of All Saints in the town of Northampton. Item I bequeath to the repair of the high altar in the same church 40d. Item I bequeath to the fraternity of Holy Trinity 12d. Item I bequeath to the fraternity of Corpus Christi 12d. Item I bequeath to the fraternity of St John the Baptist 12d. Item I bequeath to the altar of St James 12d. Item I bequeath to the fraternity of the Holy Cross 12d. Item I bequeath to the altar of St Cithe 12d. Item I bequeath to the altar of St Stephen 12d. Item I bequeath to the fraternity of St George 12d. Item I bequeath to the fraternity of St Katherine 12d. Item I bequeath to the fabric of the church at Sywell five sheep. Item I bequeath to Master Ralph Maryett one gown trimmed with crimson. Item I bequeath to the fabric of the church of Blessed Lincoln 12d. Item I bequeath to Dom William Aydroppe one gown of crimson lined. Item I bequeath to Thomas Murby one russet gown. Item I bequeath to Roger Clerke one gown. The residue of all my goods not bequeathed I give and bequeath to Joan, my wife and that this testament be well and faithfully executed I make, ordain and constitute the aforesaid Joan my executrix by these presents. With these witnesses Dom William Aydroppe and Thomas Murby.

f94r 341 WILLIAM RUTTER 26th January 1491 draper

In Dei nomine Amen xxvj die mensis Januarii anno domini millesimo
cccclxxxxj Ego Willelmus Rutter de Northampton draper compos mentis et sane
memorie condo testamentum meum in hunc modum In primis lego animam meam
Deo Omnipotenti Beate Marie et omnibus sanctis corpusque meum sepiliendum infra
ecclesia
Omnium Sanctorum ville Northampton iuxta tumulum Alicie et Cicilie nuper uxorum
mearum Item
lego rectori eiusdem ecclesie pro decimis et oblacionibus meis oblitis sive detentis xijd.
Item lego ad sustentacionem dicte ecclesie duos lineos vocatos towellys servituros
coram sacramento in festo Pasche quamdiu duraverint Item lego capelle Sancti
Johannis in eadem ecclesia unum coopertorium de tapstry warke Item lego ad
sustentacionem
pauperum infra domum Sancti Thome Martiris extra portam australem ville predicte
unam ollam eneam et unam patenam eneam que est in custodia Elene Wodsall vidue
quatuor discos et quatuor salsarios anglice sawcers de pewter et duo cande[la]bra de
laton Item lego cuilibet ordini fratrum ville Northampton unam ollam eneam et unam
patenam
eneam que sunt in custodia predicte Elene Wodsall Item lego Magistro Roberto Mydelham
doctori confessori meo unum materas vocatum a cowcher et unum par le andyernys
ferris pro camino ac unam zonam de correo cum argento harnesato Item lego ad
sustentacionem collegii infra parochiam Omnium Sanctorum predictam et capellanorum in
eodem in

futuri existentum unum salto argenti cum coopertorio eidem <pertinent> parcellati deaurato vocatum
meum optimum salte et unam domum <vocatam a stabull> cum gardino adiacente situatum in venella vocata
the Cowe Lane ibidem ex parte australi dicte venelle habendum et tenenedum dictum stabulum
cum gardino adiacente et suis pertinenciis prefatis Collegio et Capellanis ac successoribus suis
imperpetuum de capitalibus dominis feodi illius per servicia etcetera sub hac condicione quod
dicti capellani et successores sui ibidem custodient annuatim unum obitum pro anima mea et animabus uxorum mearum infra octo dies post diem obitus mei Et si defecerint
de dicto obitu infra octo dies post diem obitus mei sic ut prefertur <annuatim> solempniter non
celebrato tunc volo quod predictus salte cum coopertorio et dictum stabulum cum gardino adiacente et pertinenciis suis totaliter remaneant ad sustentacionem camere ville Northampton
habendum et tenendum predicte camere imperpetuum de capitalibus dominis feodi etcetera Item lego aliud
stabulum cum gardino adiacente et suis pertinenciis situate in le Cowe Lane predicte capelle Beate Marie infra ecclesiam Omnium Sanctorum predictam habendum et tenendum predictum stabulum cum
gardino et suis pertinenciis prefate capelle imperpetuum de capitalibus dominis feodi Item lego Johanni Wattes corvisor omnes terminos clausi mei iacenti iuxta portam et
pontem occidentalem ville Northampton ex parte boriale eiusdem pontis habendum et tenendum predictos terminos dicti clausi mei prefati Johanni Wattys et assignatis suis prout in quibusdem indenturis inde factis plenius liquet de capitalibus dominis feodi
illius etcetera Item lego prefato Johanni Wattes et Agneti uxori sue meam optimam mappam de

f94v

dyaper et duos lineos vocatos towellys de dyaper et unam longam mensam cum le
trestyllys unam par precum de geet cum gaudiis de argento deauratis cum uno
annulo aureo eisdem precibus annexo existens in custodia antedicte Elene Woddesall
et in pecuniis vjs.viijd. Item lego Thome Wattes filio eiusdem Johannis Wattes
unum parvum ciphum vocatum a standyng maser et duo cocliaria argenti et unum librum vocatum a primarre Item lego <ad sustentacionem> ecclesie parochialis de Merston Trussell in comitatu Northampton unum
ciphum de argento cum coopertorio ad habendum animam meam et animas uxorum mearum predictarum in
speciali memoria in rotulo ibidem vocato the bede roll Item lego ecclesie parochialis Sancti Sepulcri
ville Northampton unam ciphum vocatum a nutte de argento deaurato cum coopertorio eidem
pertinente Item lego fraternitati Sancte Crucis in ecclesia Omnium Sanctorum predicto xijd. Item
lego fraternitati Sancti Georgii in eadem ecclesia xijd. Item lego altari Sancte Cithe in eadem ecclesia
xijd. Item lego fraternitati Sancte Katerine in le pardon churche yarde xijd. Item lego ad sustentacionem reparacionem terrarum et tenementorum fraternitis Sancte Trinitatis in <eadem> ecclesia vjs.viijd. et totum
[anoromium] meum Item lego Johanni Asshborn et uxori eius duas togas coloris sangwyn <penulatum> quaram una est toga mulieris et in custodia dicte Elene Wodsall et vjs.viijd. Item lego

Johanni Longe et uxori eius duas togas veridis coloris quaram una est mulieris et in
custodia predicte Elene Wodsall et vjs.viijd. Item lego Johanni Bygley et uxoris
eius duas togas de russett penulatas cum nigro unam videlicet mulioris existentem in custodia
antedicte Elene Item lego Johanni Fakon de Northampton tailor et uxori eius duas togas
videlicet unam togam de musterdevelers et alteram togam mulieris blodii coloris reman' in manibus
predicte Elene duas ollas eneas duas patenas eneas que sunt in custodia dicte
Elene duos pelves et duos ewers de laton duo candelebra de laton et duo
paria linthiaminium unam murram vocatam a standyng maser unam vaccam duo coopertoria
sex kwyshens et unam banker Item Johanni Longvyle militi unam crucem de auro
vocatam a Antony Crosse Item domine Longvyle uxori eiusdem Johannis Longvylle unam zonam
vocatam a dymysent harnasatam cum argento que est in custodia predicte Elene
Item lego duobus hominibus in Threp videlicet Bruell (Burnell) et Brere silicet pro Bruell unum
ffethir bed unum par linthiaminium unam ollam eneam unam patenam eneam et unum pelvim
cum lavacro de laten et unum candelebrum et prefato Brere unam materasse unum par
linthiaminium unam ollam eneam unam patenam eneam quo due patene sunt in custodia predicte
Elene unum pelvim cum lavacro et unum candelebrum Item lego Willelmo Russell de Daventri
unum coopertorium coloris blodii et viridis tria paria linthiaminium unam mappam duos towellys
with towrys Item lego uxori Willelmi Russell unam zonam harnessatam cum argento Item
lego Willelmo Russell filio dicti Willelmi Russell quem de sacro fonte levavi unam murram tria cocliaria
argenti Item lego Johanni Penyfathyr servienti meo pannum laneum pro una toga et
in pecuniis xiijs.iiijd. et unam par caligarum Item lego Thome Bate servienti meo
pannum pro una toga unam par caligarum et in pecuniis xiijs.iiijd. Item lego Johanni
Sutton servienti meo in omnibus soretis de le nayle infra shopam meam dimid' mille
Item eidem a C et dimidium of halpeny shone a C et dimidium of macchet shone xxiiij peny
clowtes xv machet clowtes x twopeny clowts v sharys iij burthens stele
iiij shefe osmondes a C yern Vc lath et dimidium C of all sorts of carte nayle
a materas a coveryng a payer blanketts unum par linthiamenti unum par le pothangyrs ferri

f95r

ferri pannum pro una toga unum par caligarum pannam laneum pro duobus dowplettis Residuum vero
omnium bonorum meorum non legatorum post debita mea soluta totaliter do et lego executoribus meis ad inde
ordinandum et disponendum pro salute anime mee ac pro animabus uxorum mearum predictarum parentum et amicorum
meorum et omnium fidelium defunctorum prout eis melius videbitur expediri et facio Johannem Asshborn
mercer Johannem Wattes corvesor et Johannem Long tailor huis testamenti mei executores meos et pro
implementa et performacione eiusdem testamenti mei ordino et constituo magistrum Robertum Mydelham doctorem confessor-
rem meum supervisorem hiis testibus Johanne Wellys mercer Willelmo Asshborn mercheant Willelmo Derby
Rogero Prynce et aliis

In the name of God Amen the 26th day of January 1491 I William Rutter of Northampton, draper, in sound mind and good memory make my testament in this wise. First I bequeath my soul to Almighty God, to the Blessed Mary and all the saints, my body to be buried in the church of All Saints in the town of Northampton next to the graves of Alice and Cicely, lately my wives. Item I bequeath to the rector of the same church for my tithes and oblations forgotten or withheld 12d. Item I bequeath to the maintenance of the same church two pieces of linen called towels to serve before the sacrament at the Feast of Easter as long as they last. Item I bequeath to the chapel of St John in the same church one covering of tapestry work. Item I bequeath to the maintenance of the poor in the house of St Thomas the Martyr outside the south gate of the town aforesaid one brass jar and one brass dish which are in the keeping of Ellen Wodsall, widow, four dishes and four saucers of pewter and two candlesticks of laten. Item I bequeath to each of the orders of friars of the town of Northampton one brass jug and one brass dish which are in the keeping of the aforesaid Ellen Wodsall. Item I bequeath to Master Robert Mydelham, Doctor, my confessor, one mattress called a cowcher and one pair of andirons of iron for the chimney and one belt of leather ornamented with silver. Item I bequeath to the maintenance of the college within the aforesaid parish of All Saints, and of the chaplains in the same being in the future, one salt of silver, with a cover pertaining to the same, of parcel gilt called my best salt, and a house called a stable with an adjoining garden situated in the lane called Cowe Lane on the south side of the said lane, to have and to hold the said stable with the adjoining garden and its appurtenances to the aforesaid college and chaplains and their successors forever of the chief lords of the fee for services etcetera under this condition, that the said chaplains and their successors there shall keep annually an obit for my soul and the souls of my wives within eight days after the day of my death. And if they default concerning the said obit within eight days after the day of my death as aforesaid annually solemnly is not celebrated then I will that the aforesaid salte with cover and the said stable with adjoining garden and their appurtenances, remain totally to the maintenance of the Town Hall of Northampton to have and to hold to the aforesaid Hall forever of the chief lords of the fee etcetera. Item I bequeath the other stable with adjoining garden and its appurtenances situated in Cowe Lane to the aforesaid chapel of the Blessed Mary within the aforesaid church of All Saints to have and to hold the aforesaid stable with the garden and its appurtenances to the aforesaid chapel for ever of the chief lords of the fee. Item I bequeath to John Wattes, corvisor, all the terms of my close lying next to the west gate and bridge of the town of Northampton on the south side of the same bridge, to have and to hold the aforesaid terms of my said close to the aforesaid John Wattys and his assigns just as more fully appears in certain indentures made thereon of the chief lords of the fee etcetera. Item I bequeath to the aforesaid John Wattes and Agnes, his wife, my best cloth of dyaper and two lengths called towellys of dyaper and one long table with le trestylls, one rosary of geet with beads of silver gilt with a ring joined to the same beads, in the custody of the beforesaid Elen Woddesall, and 6s 8d. in money. Item I bequeath to Thomas Wattes, son of the same John Wattes, one small cup called a standyng maser, and two silver spoons and one book called a primer. Item I bequeath to the maintenance of the parish church of Marston Trussell in the county of Northampton a silver cup with a cover to have my soul and the souls of my aforesaid wives in special memory on the roll there called a Bede Roll. Item I bequeath to the parish church of St Sepulchre, Northampton, a cup called a nutte of silver gilt with a cover belonging to the same. Item I bequeath to the fraternity of Holy Cross in the aforesaid church of All Saints 12d. Item bequeathe to the fraternity of St George in the same church 12d. Item I bequeath to the altar of St Cithe in the same church 12d. Item I bequeath to the fraternity of St Katherine in le pardon church yarde 12d. Item I bequeath to the maintenance [and] repair of the lands and tenements of the fraternity of Holy Trinity in the same church 6s 8d and my []. Item I bequeath to John Asshborn and his wife two gowns of sanguine colour furred, of which one is a woman's gown and in the keeping of the said Elen Wodsall, and 6s 8d. Item I bequeath to John Longe and his wife two gowns of green colour, one of which is a woman's and in the keeping of the aforesaid Elen Wodsall, and 6s 8d. Item I bequeath to John Bygley and his wife two gowns of russet furred with black fur, one, that is to say a woman's, is in the keeping of the beforesaid Elen. Item I bequeath to John Fakon of Northampton, tailor, and his wife two gowns, that is to say one gown of musterdevelers and the other gown a woman's of blue, remaining in the hands of the aforesaid Elen, two brass pots which are in the keeping of the said Elen, two jugs and two ewers of laten, two laten candlesticks and two pairs of blankets, one maser called a standyng maser, one cow, two coverings, six cushions and one banker. Item to John Longvyle, knight, one cross of gold called an Anthony Cross. Item to lady Longvyle, wife of the same John Longvyle, one girdle called a dymysent, ornamented with silver, which is in the keeping of the aforesaid Elen. Item I bequeath to two men in Threp, that is to say Bruell (or Burnell) and Brere, for Bruell one featherbed and one pair of blankets, one brass pot, one brass dish and one jug and ewer of laten and one candlestick, and to the aforesaid Brere one mattress, one pair of blankets, one brass pot, one brass dish, which two dishes are in the keeping of the aforesaid Elen, one jug with ewer and one candlestick. Item I bequeath to William Russell of Daventry a cover coloured blue and green, three pairs of blankets, one cloth, two towels with 'towrys'. Item I bequeath to the wife of William Russell one girdle ornamented with silver. Item I bequeath to William Russell, son of the said William Russell, whom I have raised at the holy font (godson?), one maser, three silver spoons. Item I bequeath to John Penyfathyr, my servant, one length of cloth for a gown and 12s 4d in money and one pair of boots. Item I bequeath to Thomas Bate, my servant, one length for a gown, one pair of boots and 12s 4d in money. Item I bequeath to John Sutton, my servant, all sorts of the nails inside my shop half a hundred. Item the same a 100 and a half of halfpenny shones, a 100 and a half of macchet shone, 24 penny clowts, 15 machet clowtes, 10 twopenny clowts, 5 sharys, 3 burthens stele, 4 shefe osmondes, a 100 iron, 500 lath and half a 100 of all sorts of cart nayles, one mattress, one covering, one pair of blankets, one pair of sheets, one pair of iron pothangers, one length for a gown, one pair of boots, one length of cloth for two doublets. The residue of all my goods not bequeathed above after my debts are wholly paid I give and bequeath to my executors to then ordain and dispose for the health of my soul and for the souls of my wives aforesaid, my parents and friends and all faithful departed as seems best to them and I make John Ashburn, mercer, John Wattes, corvisor, and John Longe, tailor, my executors of this testament and for implementing and performing the same testament I ordain and constitute Master Robert Mydelham, Doctor, my confessor, supervisor. With these witnesses John Wellys, mercer, William Asshborn, merchant, William Derby, Roger Prince and others.

f95r 342 WILLIAM MYLLE 11th May 1492 dyster

In the name of God Amen the xjth daye of May the yere of ower lorde God mccccIxxxx and ij I William Mylle of Northampton dyer hole of mynd make my testament in form folowyng Fyrste I beqwethe my sowle to Almyghty God etcetera my body to buryed in the chapell of Corpus Christi in the paryssh churche of All Halowes of Northampton I beqwethe to the prior and the convent of Saynt Andrews proprieteres of the same churche for my tythes forgoten or wythold xs. Item I beqwethe to the foresayd chapell of Corpus Christi for my berel ther vjs.viijd. Item I beqwethe to Ower Lady chapell in the same churche iijs.iiijd. Item I beqwethe to the fraternite of Blessytt Trinite in the church abovesayde xxd. item I gyffe to the fraternite of the Holy Rode in the same churche xijd. Also I beqweth to the fraternite of Saynt George in the sayde churche xijd. Item I beqwethe to the fraternite of Saynt John Baptiste in the same churche xijd. Item I beqwethe to the fraternite of Saynt Katteryn in the pardon churche yerd xijd.
Item I beqwethe to every howse of the frerys in Northampton to pray for my soule iijs.iiijd. Item I beqwethe toward the reparacon of Saynt Thomas howse the martyr without the southe yate of Northampton iijs.iiijd. Item I wyll that Johan my wyfe have myne howse that I nowe
dwell yn withowte the southe yate aforesayd hole as yt ys nowe with the ledys ffates vesselles
and all othir their apurtenance therto belongyng to have and to hold to hyr and hyr assignes duryng the terme of hyr lyve of the chefe lordes of the ffee etcetera and immediatly after hyr dysoese of the Johan my wyfe or ellys whan shee shall in hyr lyfe please yf shee be so dysposyt
I wyll that the sayde house with all the purtenances be solde and that money that comyth of yt to be

dysposyd in maner insewyng by the oversygth of William Flore of Northampton shereman that ys to
say I wyll that £5 of the same money be gevyn to the reparacon and mayntenance of the house
of Saynt Thomas aforesayd ther bothe I and my sayde wyfe perpetually to be prayed for Item
I wyll that Symond Ussher sonn of Emme my doghter whose soule God asoyle shall have atthe
tyme of hys comyng to lawfull age towards hys settyng upp and begynnyng of the sale of my
forsayde house yf he be than obedyent xli. in money or elys the valor therof in godes

f95v

And the resydewe of the money of the same house comyng to be dysposed in almes
dedes as by the sayde Johan my wyfe by the advyce of the sayde William Flore and
other of theyr councell beyng shalbe thogth moste nedefull and expedyent for the
helthe of my soule my kynes soules frende soules and all Crysten soules Item I gyffe
and beqwthe to Emme <Abraham> my syster all my londes and tenementes with theyer apurtenance
in Wenlyngburgh in the counte of Northampton to have and to hold to hyr and to hyr
assignes for the terme of hyr lyve of the chefe lordes of the fee etcetera and
after hyr dicese immediatly I wyll that the sayde landes and tenements with theyr
apurtenance in Wenlyngburgh afore sayde holy remayn to Richard Mylly my cosyn
to have to hym and to hys heyres of hys body lawfully begoten for ever more
of the chefe lordes of the ffee etcetera and yf yt happen the sayde Richard Milly
to decese with owte yssewe of hys body lawfully begoten than I wyll that all
my sayde landes And tenements with theyr apurtenance in Wenlyngburgh abovesayde
holy remayn to Thomas Milly brothyr to the sayde Richard Milly and to hys
heyres of hys body lawfully begoten for ever more of the chefe lordes of
the ffee etcetera and yf the sayde Thomas Milly decese with owte issewe of hys
body lawfully begoten Than I wyll that the sayde londes and tenements with theyr
apurtenance be holy sold after the dyscrecon of them then beyng an lyve
that shalbe assygned therto and the money thereof comyng to be dysposyd
for the helthe of my soule my wyfes my kynefolke soules my frendes soules
and all Crystyn soules as be them that them shall have rewle shalbe thogth
beste and moste expedyent Item I wyll that my house with the apurtenance in the
Whyte Frere Lane in Northampton abovesayde be atthe fre wyll and lyberte of the
sayde Johan by wyfe The resydewe of all my godes not beqwethed
after my dettes bepayd I holy gyffe and beqwethe to Johan my wyfe therewith
to do and dispose after hyr own ffre wyll as shee shall thynke moste nedefull
and expedyent for the helthe of my soule etcetera and I make and ordeyn the sayde
Johan of this my present testament wele and trewly to be execute in maner
and form above sayde myn executrice also I make theforsayde William Flore
overseer of the same execucion to whom I gyve for hys labor xxs. of money
by theys presentes In wittness wherof to this my present testement and laste
wyll I have sette my seale yoven the day and the yere afore rehersytt theys
wytnes mayster Robert Mydelham vicar of All Halowe chyrche abovesayd Thomas
Derby mercer Sir Antony Bowe preste with other

f97v 347 SIMON BRAYFELD 20th January 1492 dyster

In Dei nomine Amen xx die mensis Januarii anno domini mcccclxxxxij Ego Simon Brayfeld de Northampton deyster compos mentis etcetera condo testamentum meum In primis lego animam meam Deo Omnipotenti

Beate Marie Virgini etcetera corpusque meum sepiliendum in capella Beate Marie Virginis in ecclesia Omnium Sanctorum
ibidem in loco vacuo ante sedem <meam situatam> ad lavatorium altaris eiusdem capelle Item lego priori Sancti Andree Northampton
pro decimis meis <et oblacionibus> oblitis seu non sufficienter datis vjs.viijd. Item lego ad sustentacionem hospitali
Sancti Johannis Northampton xxd. Item lego ad sustentacionem fraternitatis Sancte Trinitatis in dicta ecclesia Omnium Sanctorum
vjs.viijd. Item lego ad sustentacionem fraternitatis Corporis Christi ibidem vjs.viijd. Item lego ad sustentacionem
fraternitatis Beate Marie Virginis in eadem ecclesia in pecuniis muneratis xls. sub hac condicione quod tumulus
meus et sepultura mea sunt in dicta capella sub forma predicte et quod quilibet presbyter celebraturus missam
ad horam octavam consuetam in dicta capella cotidie in missa sua tempore congruo pro anima mea et
animabus parentum <meorum> omnium amicorum et omnium fidelium defunctorum specialiter deo devote oraverit et
dixerit deprofundis cum suis suffragiis eadem oracione sub hac forma perpetuum duraturum aceciam
huiusmodi condicione et nomen meum pro speciali memoria in missali eiusdem capelle fuit intitulatum
et registrata Item lego ad sustentacionem fraternitatis Sancti Georgii in dicta ecclesia ijs. Item lego
ad sustentacionem fraternitatis Sancte Crucis in eadem ecclesia ijs. Item lego ad sustentacionem fraternitatis Sancti Johannis Baptiste
in eadem ecclesia ijs. Item lego ad sustentacionem fraternitatis Sancte Cithe ibidem ijs. Item lego cuilibet
domui fratrum in dicta villa pro relevancie omnium fratrum pro tempore ibidem residencium vjs.viijd.
Item lego Thome Brayfeld filio meo in pecuniis muneratis C marcas Item lego Johanni filio meo in pecuniis muneratis C marcas Item lego Elizabeth filie mee Lli in pecuniis muneratis Item lego Agneti filie mee in pecuniis muneratis Lli. Item lego Margarete filie mee Lli in pecuniis muneratis et volo quod omnia premissa filiis et filiabus meis superius legata fuit
in custodia Isabelle uxoris mee quousque quilibet eorum fuerit et sit de plena etate annorum discrecionis
Item do et lego predicte Isabelle uxori mee ad usum suum proprium omnia et singula bona mea et
lanas wood mader et alum que habeo in domo mea in qua iam maneo immediate post decessum
meum ulterius volo quod si contingat aliquem seu aliquam filiorum vel filiarum meorum supranominatorum obire non
maritatam antequem pervenerit ad etatem vigenti unius annorum tunc volo quod pars illius sic obinatis
equaliter dividatur inter illos <vel illas> qui vel que supervixerint Residuum vero omnium bonorum
meorum superius non legatorum do et lego predicte Isabelle uxori mee ad inde disponendum
pro salute anime mee animarum parentum meorum omnium amicorum meorum et omnium fidelium defunctorum
prout ei melius videbitur expediri Et ad istud testamentum bene et fideliter exequendum prefatam Isabellam uxorem meam Willelmum Brayfeld ac predictum Thomam Brayfeld filios

meos ordino facio et constituo executores meos et de execucione premissorum Ricardum Emson generosum ordino et facio supervisorem et volo quod Ricardus habeat pro labore suo ea intencione quod ipse defendat dictam Isabellam uxorem meam ab omnia iniuria iiij marcas
bone monete Anglie per presentes in cuius rei testimonium hunc presenti testamento meo sigillum
meum apposui hiis testibus domino Thoma Roose domino Roberto Hochekynson capellanis et aliis

In the name of God Amen the 20th day of January 1492 I Simon Brayfeld of Northampton, dyster, in sound mind etcetera make my testament. First I bequeath my soul to Almighty God, to the Blessed Virgin Mary etcetera my body to be buried in the chapel of the Blessed Virgin Mary in the church of All Saints there in the empty place in front of my seat situated at the piscina of the altar in the same chapel. Item I bequeath to the priory of St. Andrew of Northampton for tithes and oblations forgotten or not sufficiently given 6s 8d. Item I bequeath for the maintenance of the Hospital of St. John, Northampton 20d. Item I bequeath for the maintenance of the fraternity of Holy Trinity in the said church of All Saints 6s 8d. Item I bequeath for the maintenance of the fraternity of Corpus Christi there 6s 8d. Item I bequeath for the maintenance of the fraternity of the Blessed Virgin Mary in the same church in cash 40s on this condition that my grave and sepulchre are in the said chapel in the manner aforesaid and that a priest shall celebrate mass at the customary eighth hour daily in the same chapel and at the same time shall pray for my soul and the souls of my parents and the souls of my friends and all faithful departed with special devotion and shall say the De Profundis with the intercessions of the same prayer in this manner in perpetuity and also in the same way way and condition that my name should be entered and registered for special memory in the missal of the same chapel. Item I bequeath to the maintenance of the fraternity of St. George in the said church 2s. Item I bequeath to the maintenance of the fraternity of the Holy Cross in the same church 2s. Item I bequeath to the maintenance of the fraternity of St John the Baptist in the same church 2s. Item I bequeath to the maintenance of the fraternity of St. Cithe there 2s. Item I bequeath to each house of friars in the said town for the comfort of all brothers for the time of their residence 6s 8d. Item I bequeath to Thomas Brayfeld, my son, in cash 100 marks. Item I bequeath to Elizabeth, my daughter, £50 in cash. Item I bequeath to Agnes, my daughter, in cash £50. Item I bequeath to Margaret, my daughter, £50 in cash, and I will that everything above bequeathed to my sons and daughters should be in the care of my wife, Isabel, until each of them shall be of full age of the years of discretion. Item I give and bequeath to the said Isabel, my wife, to her proper use all and singular of my goods and wool, woad, madder and alum which I have in my house and which remain there immediately after my death and further I will that if it happens that any of my sons or daughters named above should die unmarried before they reach the age of twenty one years then I will that the part of the one thus dead should be equally divided among those who survive. The residue of all my goods not bequeathed above I give and bequeath to the said Isabel, my wife, to then dispose for the health of my soul, the souls of my parents, of all my friends and of all faithful departed as seems best to her and that this my testament be well and faithfully executed I ordain, make and constitute the said Isabel, my wife, William Brayfeld and the aforesaid Thomas Brayfeld, my sons, my executors and for the execution of these premises I ordain and make Richard Emson, gentleman, supervisor and I will that Richard should have for his labour, and the intention that he should protect the said Isabel, my wife, from all injury, 4 marks in good English money by these presents. In witness of this my present testament I have put my seal. With these witnesses Dom Thomas Roose, Dom Robert Hochekynson, chaplain, and others.

f98r 349 RICHARD PAKEMAN 19th April 1493 weaver

In Dei nomine Amen xix die mensis Aprilis anno domini mcccclxxxxiij Ego Ricardus Pakeman
de Northampton wever compos mentis et sane memorie condo testamentum meum ultimum continentem
voluntatem in hunc modum In primis lego animam meam Deo Omnipotenti Beate Marie matri suo
ac omnibus <celi> sanctis corpusque meum sepiliendum infra ecclesiam hospitali Sancti Baptiste ville Northampton
coram ymaginem Sancte Crucis principali ibidem Item lego magistro et confratribus eiusdem hospitali pro
sepultura mea ibidem vjs.viijd. Item lego eisdem magistro et confratribus suis pro principali
meo unum pannum laneum integrum coloris russett optimum trium pannorum eiusdem
coloris Item lego Agneti uxori mee omnia et singula terras et tenementa mea in Wenlyngburgh
Faxton in comitatu Northampton et in villa Northampton cum pratis pascuis et pasturis reditibus reversionibus
et serviciis ac cum omnibus suis pertinenciis habendum et tenendum prefate Agneti et assignatis suis durante toto
termino vite sue de capitalibus dominis feodi illorum per servicia inde debita et de iure consueta et
inmediate post decessum dicte Agnetis uxoris mee do et lego totum tenementum meum in Wenlyngburgh
predictum cum terris pratis pascuis pasturis et suis pertinenciis eidem tenemento spectantis in tenura
Thome Stoke fuller Ricardo Pakeman filio meo habendum et tenendum sibi heredibus et assignatis suis
imperpetuum de capitalibus dominis feodi illius per servicia inde debita et de iure consueta Item do

f98v

et lego inmediate post decessum Agnetis uxoris Thome Pakeman filio meo aliud tenementum

meum in Wellyngburgh predicta cum terris pratis pascuis pasturis et suis pertinenciis eidem tenemento meo spectantis modo in tenura [] Symson vidue habendum et tenendum predicto Thome filio meo heredibus et assignatis suis imperpetuum de capitalibus dominis feodi illius per servicia
inde debita et de iure consueta Item do et lego Elizabeth filie mee inter me et predictam Agnetem uxorem meam inmediate post decessum predicte Agnetis totum illud tenementum in Faxton
supradicta cum terris pratis pascuis pasturis et omnibus suis pertinenciis eidem tenemento pertinentis
habendum et tenendum predicte Elizabethe heredibus et assignatis suis imperpetuum de capitalibus dominis feodi illius
per servicia inde debita et de iure consueta Item lego prefato Ricardo Pakeman filio meo in bonis muneratis ad valenciam quadragenta solidorum Item lego Thome Pakeman filio meo predicto in bonis muneratis ad valenciam xl solidis Item lego predicte Elizabethe filie mee in bonis similiter muneratis ad valorem xl solidorum et si contingat predictum Ricardum filium meum obire
infra etatem legitimam tunc volo quod totum predictum tenementum suum in Wenlyngburgh predicta cum
omnibus suis pertinenciis premissis una cum bonis suis prescriptis indifferenter disponantur et distribuantur
inter predictos Thomam Pakeman filium meum et Elizabetham filiam meam predictam habendum
et tenendum eis heredibus et assignatis suis imperpetuum de capitalibus dominis feodi illius etcetera et si contingat prefatos Ricardum et Thomam obire infra etatem legitimam tunc volo quod predicta duo tenementa in Wenlyngburgh supradicta cum terris pratis pascuis pasturis et suis pertinenciis eisdem duobus tenementis spectantis una cum partibus bonorum suorum eis superius
legatorum totaliter remaneant predicte Elizabethe filie mee habendum et tenendum sibi heredibus et assignatis suis imperpetuum de capitalibus dominis etcetera et si contingat predictos Ricardum
Thomam et Elizabetham pueros meos obire infra etatem legitimam tunc volo quod omnia supradicta terras tenementa cum omnibus et singulis suis pertinenciis premissis una cum bonis supradictis
eisdem Ricardo Thome et Elizabethe per me legatis totaliter remaneant predicte Agneti uxori mee si tunc vixerit et volo quod predicta tenementa mea cum omnibus suis pertinenciis ut
predictum est vendantur et pecunie eorum inde perveniente distribuantur pro salute anime mee
ac animarum dictorum Ricardi Thome et Elizabethe ac pro salute animarum omnium parentum et
amicorum nostrorum et omnium fidelium defunctorum prout ei vel executoribus eorum melius
videbitur expediri. Item lego Elizabethe Westonfeld filie mee duas virgatas
panni lanei coloris russett et duas virgatas panni lanei coloris violett de
panno laneo que fuit in comuni aula ville Northampton predicte et de bonis muneratis
ad valenciam xxti solidorum Item lego Willelmo Westonfeld unam dimidiam togam coloris
violett ad orandum pro anima mea. Item lego Margarete sorori mee et viro suo quinque virgatas
panni lanei de eodem panno que fuit in comuni aula ad orandum predictam mea
Item lego Agneti Coton sorori mee unam longam togam blodii coloris ad orandum
pro anima mea Item lego Johanni Pakeman fratri meo duas virgatas panni lanei coloris
violett Item lego Thome Pakeman filio ipsius Johannis Pakeman unam virgatam
et dimidiam panni lanei coloris violett Residuum vero omnium bonorum meorum superius

non legatorum post debita mea soluta totaliter do et lego prefati Agneti uxori mee
ad inde ordinandum et disponendum pro salute anime mee ac pro animabus omnium puerorum meorum
et amicorum meorum ac omnium fidelium defunctorum prout ei melius videbitur expediri Et facio
et constituo predictam Agnetem uxorem meam huius testamenti mei executricem et facio
et ordino Ricardum Sherd magistrum hospitali Sancti Johanni supradicti et Johannem Say sherman
pro satisfacione et contentacione huius mee ultime voluntatis et testamenti supervisores et habebit
uterque eorum pro labore suo in hac parte habite sex solidos et octo denarios hiis testibus Thoma
Rose clerico Rogero Prynce literato et aliis

In the name of God Amen the 19th day of April 1493 I Richard Pakeman of Northampton, weaver, in sound mind and good memory make my last will and testament freely in this wise. First I bequeath my soul to Almighty God, to the Blessed Mary His mother and all the saints in heaven, my body to be buried in the church of St [John the] Baptist in the town of Northampton before the principal image of the Holy Cross there. Item I bequeath to the master and brothers of the same hospital for my burial there 6s 8d. Item I bequeath to the same master and his brothers for my principal one whole length of cloth of russet colour, the best of three lengths of the same colour. Item I bequeath to Agnes, my wife, all and singular my lands and tenements in Wellingborough and Faxton in the county of Northampton and in the town of Northampton with meadows, pastures, grazing land, rents, reversions and services and with all their appurtenances and services, to have and to hold by the said Agnes and her assigns during the whole term of her life of the chief lords of the fee for services therefore due and by right accustomed and immediately after the death of the said Agnes, my wife, I give and bequeath all my tenements in Wellingborough aforesaid with lands, meadows, pasture, grazing land and the appurtenances belonging to the same tenements in the tenure of Thomas Stoke, fuller, to Richard Pakeman, my son, to have and to hold to him and his heirs and assigns forever of the chief lords of the fee etcetera. Item I give and bequeath immediately after the death of Agnes, my wife, to Thomas Pakeman, my son, another of my tenements in Wellingborough aforesaid with lands, meadows, pastures, grazing land and their appurtenances belonging to my same tenement now in the tenure of [] Symson, widow, to have and to hold to the aforesaid Thomas, my son, his heirs and assigns forever of the chief lords of the fee etcetera. Item I give and bequeath to Elizabeth, my daughter, by me and the aforesaid Agnes, my wife, immediately after the death of the aforesaid Agnes, all that tenement in Faxton above said with lands, meadows, pasture, grazing land with all their appurtenances belonging to the same tenement to have and to hold to the aforesaid Elizabeth, her heirs and assigns forever of the chief lords of the fee etcetera. Item I bequeath to the said Richard Pakeman, my son, in good money to the value of forty shillings. Item I bequeath to Thomas Pakeman, my son aforesaid, in good money 40 shillings. Item I bequeath to the aforesaid Elizabeth, my daughter, likewise in good money to the value of 40 shillings and if it should happen that the said Richard, my son, should die before the legal age then I will that the whole of his aforesaid tenement in Wellingborough aforesaid with all the appurtenances bequeathed above together with the goods above written, should be disposed of impartially and distributed between the aforesaid Thomas Pakeman, my son, and Elizabeth, my daughter aforesaid, to have and to hold to their heirs and assigns of the chief lords of the fee etcetera. And if it should happen that the aforesaid Richard and Thomas should die before the legal age then I will that the aforesaid two tenements in Wellingborough aforesaid with lands, meadows, pastures, grazing land and the appurtenances belonging to the two tenements together with their share of the goods bequeathed above should wholly remain to the aforesaid Elizabeth, my daughter, to have and to hold to her, her heirs and assigns in perpetuity of the chief lords of the fee etcetera. And if it should happen that the aforesaid Richard, Thomas and Elizabeth, my children, should die below the legal age then I will that all above said lands, tenements with all and singular appurtenances above bequeathed together with the aforementioned goods bequeathed by me to the said Richard, Thomas and Elizabeth should wholly remain to the said Agnes, my wife, if she is then living and I will that my aforesaid tenements with appurtenances aforesaid should be sold and the money coming from them should be distributed for the health of my soul and the souls of all our parents, friends and all faithful departed as it may seem best to them or their executors. Item I bequeath to Elizabeth Westonfeld, my daughter, two yards of linen cloth of russet colour and two yards of linen cloth of violet colour from the linen cloth which was in the common hall of the town of Northampton aforesaid and in good money to the value of 20 shillings. Item I bequeath to William Westonfeld one short gown of violet colour to pray for my soul. Item I bequeath to Margaret, my sister, and her husband five yards of linen cloth from the same length that was in the common hall to pray for me as aforesaid. Item I bequeath to Agnes Coton, my sister, one long gown of blue colour to pray for my soul. Item I bequeath to John Pakeman, my brother, two yards of linen cloth of violet colour. Item I bequeath to Thomas Pakeman, son of the same John Pakeman, one yard and a half of cloth of violet colour. The residue of all my goods not bequeathed above after my debts are totally paid I give and bequeath to the said Agnes, my wife, to then ordain and dispose for the health of my soul and for the souls of all my children and my friends and all faithful departed as seem best to her. And I make and constitute the said Agnes, my wife, executrix of this my testament and I make and ordain Richard Sherd, Master of the Hospital of St John abovesaid, and John Say, shearman, to be supervisors for the satisfaction and contentment of this my last will and testament and they shall each have for the labour they have had in this connection six shillings and eight pence. These being witnesses Thomas Rose, clerk, Roger Prince, scrivener, and others.

f99r 351 WILLIAM WELLYNGBURGH 20th September 1493 cook

In Dei nomine Amen xx die mensis Septembris anno domini mccccclxxxxiij Ego Willelmus Wellyngburgh de Northampton cooke compos mentis et sane memorie condo presens testamentum
meum in hunc modum In primis videlicet lego animam meam Deo Omnipotenti etcetera corpusque meum sepiliendum in cimiterio ecclesie parochiali Omnium Sanctorum ville Northampton predicte iuxta sepulturam Andree
Wellyngburgh patris mei ex parte boriali eiusdem cimiterii Item lego rectoribus eiusdem ecclesie
pro decimis oblitis etcetera xijd. Item lego reparacioni ecclesie predicte xxd. Item lego fraternitati
Sancte Crucis in eadem ecclesia xijd. Item lego fraternitati Sancti Johannis Baptiste infra eadem ecclesiam
xijd. Item lego fraternitati Sancti Georgii in ecclesia predicta xijd. Item lego reparacioni domus Sancti Thome
Martiris extra portam australem eiusdem ville Northampton xijd. Item lego fraternitati Sancte Katerine in le
pardon churche yerde xijd. Item lego fraternitati Sancti Michaelis Archangeli xijd. Item lego Johanni
Hume patenmaker avunculo meo togam unam coloris violett unam tunicam vocatam a duplett
of blue worsted unam camesiam et unum par caligarum Item lego Fratribus Minoribus
ad orandum pro anima mea in pecuniis xijd. et unam pelvim <de laton> cum lavacro de laton
Item lego Henrico Potter de Newport Paynell unam togam coloris violett penulatam
cum agnellis albis Item lego Johanni Warde de Welton unam togam blodii coloris
et unam duplett de worsted Item lego Willelmo Warde filio <dicti> Johannis Warde unam togam
coloris viridis unum cocliar argentem unam pelvim et unum lavacrum de laton unum candelabrum
unam ollam eneam Item lego Petro Henke unam togam coloris tawny Item lego Roberto Dyk
de Ramiston unam togam coloris russett Item lego Margarete uxori mee totum illud gardinum
sive ortum quod <vel quem> habeo in fine Sancti Andree ville Northampton infra parochiam Sancti Sepulcri cum omnibus
suis pertinenciis habendum et tenendum totum predictum gardinum cum pertinenciis suis huiusmodi prefate Margarete
et assignatis suis durante toto termino vite eiusdem Margarete Et immediate post decessum ipsius
Margarete uxoris mee volo quod dictum gardinum sive ortum cum omnibus suis pertinenciis totaliter remaneat
abbatisse et conventui monasterii Beate Marie de Pratis iuxta Northampton predictam habendum et tenendum totum
predictum gardenum sive ortum cum omnibus pertinenciis suis prefatis abbatisse et conventui ac successoribus
et assignatis suis imperpetuum de capitalibus dominis etcetera Residuum vero omnium bonorum meorum superius non legatorum

do et lego Margarete uxori mee post debita mea soluta ad ordinandum et disponendum pro salute anime mee
etcetera prout sibi melius videbitur expediri ac predictam Margaretam ordino etcetera executricem meam et Ricardum Baxster
de Northampton jrnemonger supervisorem et habebit pro labore suo iijs.iiijd. hiis testibus magistro Roberto Midelham
vicario ecclesie Omnium Sanctorum predicte Johanne Grene carpenter et Johanne Jakeson cobelor cum aliis

In the name of God Amen the 20th day of September 1493 I William Wellyngburgh of Northampton, cook, in sound mind and good memory make my testament in this wise. First that is to say I bequeath my soul to Almighty God etcetera, my body to be buried in the cemetery of the church of All Saints in the town of Northampton aforesaid next to the grave of Andrew Wellyngburgh, my father, in the northern part of the cemetery. Item I bequeath to the rector of the said church for tithes forgotten etcetera 12d. Item I bequeath for the repair of the said church 20d. Item I bequeath to the fraternity of the Holy Cross in the same church 12d. Item I bequeath to the fraternity of St John the Baptist within the same church 12d. Item I bequeath to the fraternity of St George in the same church aforesaid 12d. Item I bequeath to the repair of the house of St Thomas the Martyr outside the south gate of the said town of Northampton 12d. Item I bequeath to the fraternity of St Katherine in le pardon church yard 12d. Item I bequeath to the fraternity of St Michael the Archangel 12d. Item I bequeath to John Hume, patten maker, my uncle, one gown of violet colour, one tunic called a doublet of blue worsted and one smock and one pair of boots. Item I bequeath to the Friars Minor to pray for my soul in money 12d and one laten jug with one ewer of laten. Item I bequeath to Henry Potter of Newport Pagnall one gown of violet colour furred with white lamb. Item I bequeath to John Warde of Welton one gown of blue colour and a doublet of worsted. Item I bequeath to William Warde, son of the said John Warde, one gown of green colour, one silver spoon, one jug and one ewer of laten, one candlestick, one brass bowl. Item I bequeath to Peter Henke one gown of tawny colour. Item I bequeath to Robert Dyk of Ramiston one gown of russet colour. Item I bequeath to Margaret, my wife all that garden and orchard which I have in the boundary of St Andrew in the town of Northampton inside the parish of Holy Sepulchre, with all their appurtenances to have and to hold all the aforesaid garden with its appurtenances in this way, the said Margaret and her assigns for the total life of the same Margaret and immediately after the death of the same Margaret, my wife, then I will that the said garden and orchard with their appurtenances wholly remain to the Abbess of the convent and monastery of the Blessed Mary of Delapre next to Northampton aforesaid, to have and to hold all the aforesaid garden with orchard with their appurtenances to the aforesaid Abbess and convent and her successors and assigns forever of the chief lords etcetera. The residue of all my goods not above bequeathed I give and bequeath to Margaret, my wife, to then ordain and dispose for the health of my soul etcetera.after the payment of my debts as seems best to her and the aforesaid Margaret I ordain etcetera. as my executrix and Richard Baxter of Northampton, ironmonger, supervisor and to have for his labour 3s 4d. With these witnesses Master Robert Midelham, vicar of the church of All Saints aforesaid, John Grene, carpenter, and John Jakeson, cobbler, with others.

f99v 352 WILLIAM LAWRENS 2nd November 1493 weaver

In Dei nomine Amen ijdo die mensis Novembris anno domini mccccIxxxxiij Ego Willelmus Lawrens de Northampton wever compos mentis et sane memorie condo testamentum meum in hunc
modum videlicet In primis lego animam meam Deo Omnipotenti Beate Marie et omnibus sanctis
celestis curie corpusque meum sepiliendum in capella Beate Marie Virginis infra hospitalum Sancti Johannis
Baptiste ville Northampton coram altari ibidem Item lego sustentacioni summi altaris parochiali ecclesie
Omnium Sanctorum eiusdem ville iijs.iiijd. Item lego fraternitati Sancte Crucis in eadem ecclesia Omnium Sanctorum xijd.
Item lego fraternitati Sancte Katerine in le pardon churche yerd xijd. Item lego fraternitati Sancti Clementis
in ecclesia Sancti Egidii ville predicte xijd. Item lego fraternitati Sancte Crucis in Muro infra parochialem
ecclesiam Sancti Gregorii eiusdem ville xijd. Item lego capelle Beate Marie in eadem ecclesia Sancti
Gregorii xijd. Item lego hospitali Sancti Johannis predicti pro sepultura mea ibidem xs. Item lego pauperibus infra firmariam eiusdem hospitalis xijd. Item lego pauperibus infra domum Sancti
(Sancti) Thome Martiris eiusdem ville xijd. Item do et lego Agneti uxori mee totum tenementum
meum in quo maneo cum omnibus suis pertinenciis situatum in vico vocato Wolmonger Strete ville
predicte habendum et tenendum sibi et assignatis suis ad totum terminum vite sue de capitalibus dominis feodi
illius per servicia inde debita et de iure consueta Et inmediate post decessum eiusdem Agnetis volo quod totum predictum tenementum meum cum omnibus suis pertinenciis totaliter remaneat
hospitali Sancti Johannis predicte habendum et tenendum eis et successoribus suis imperpetuum de capitalibus
dominis feodi illius per servicia inde debita et de iure consueta Item volo quod duo partes omnium bonorum meorum post debita mea soluta distribuantur pro salute anime mee etcetera secundum
discrecionem executorum meorum prout eis melius videbitur expediri Et do et lego prefate Agneti uxori mee terciam partem bonorum meorum superius non legatorum post debita
mea soluta ad inde ordinandum et disponendum prout ei melius placebit ac constituo prefatam Agnetem uxorem meam Johannem Smyth wever et Thomam Asplond wever

huius testamenti mei meos executores Et Thomam Roose clericum pro suo bono consilio et auxilio esse supervisorem Item lego prefato Johanni Smyth pro labore suo xs. Item lego dicto Thome Asplond pro labore suo xs. Item lego prefato Thome Roose clerico pro labore suo vj.viijd. hiis testibus Magistro Roberto Mydelham doctore Rogero Prynce scriptore Willelmo Williamson wever et aliis

In the name of God Amen the 2nd day of November 1493 I William Lawrens of Northampton, weaver, in sound mind and good memory make my testament in this wise. First I bequeath my soul to Almighty God, to the Blessed Mary and all the saints of the court of heaven, my body to be buried in the chapel of the Blessed Virgin Mary within the Hospital of St John the Baptist of the town of Northampton before the altar there. Item I bequeath to the maintenance of the high altar of the parish church of All Saints of the same town 3s 4d. Item I bequeath to the fraternity of Holy Cross in the same church of All Saint 12d. Item I bequeath to the fraternity of St Katherine in the pardon church yard 12d. Item I bequeath to the fraternity of St Clement in the church of St Giles of the aforesaid town 12d. Item I bequeath to the fraternity of the Holy Cross in the Wall within the parish church of St Gregory of the same town 12d. Item I bequeath to the chapel of the Blessed Mary in the same church of St Gregory 12d. Item I bequeath to the Hospital of St John aforesaid for my burial there 10s. Item I bequeath to the poor within the house of St Thomas the Martyr of the same town 12d. Item I bequeath to Agnes, my wife, all the tenement in which I live with all its appurtenances, situated in a street called Woolmonger Street of the aforesaid town, to have and to hold to her and her assigns for the term of her life of the chief lords of the fee for services therefore due and by right accustomed. And immediately after the death of the same Agnes I will that all my aforesaid tenement with its appurtenances shall wholly remain to the aforesaid Hospital of St John to have and to hold to them and their successors for ever of the chief lords of the fee by services therefore due and by right accustomed. Item I will that two parts of all my goods after my debts have been paid shall be distributed for the well being of my soul etcetera, according to the discretion of my executors as seems best to them. And I give and bequeath to the aforesaid Agnes, my wife, the third part of my goods not bequeathed above after my debts have been paid to be ordained and disposed as best pleases her and I constitute the aforesaid Agnes, my wife, John Smyth, weaver, and Thomas Asplond, weaver, my executors of this my testament and Thomas Roose, clerk, for his good counsel and help to be supervisor. Item I bequeath to the aforesaid John Smyth for his labour 10s. Item I bequeath to the said Thomas Asplond for his labour 10s. Item I bequeath to the aforesaid Thomas Roose, clerk, for his labour 6s 8d. With these witnesses Master Robert Mydelham, Doctor, Roger Prynce, scrivener, William Williamson, weaver, and others.

f100v 356 SIMON ROWLAND 15th November 1493 barber

In the name of God Amen the xvth day of November in the yer of ower lorde
God mccccIxxxxiij I Simon Rowland de Northampton barber hole of mynde make
my testament in maner and form hereafter folowyng ffirst I beqwethe m soule
to Almyghty God and to ower Blessyt Lady his mother Saynt Marie and to all the
company in hewyn and my body to be buryed in the chyrche yerd of the
paryssh churche of All Halowes in Northampton nygth to the great oke growyng
ther Item I beqweth to the sustentacon of the hygh awter in the same
churche iijs.iiijd. Item I beqweth to Alice my wyfe the close in Cote with purtenances
to have and to holde to hyr and hyr assignes duryng the tyme of hir
lyve of the chefe lords of the ffee by the servys therof due and acustommed
And after the decesse of the sayde Alice my wyfe I wyll that the sayde
close with all the apurtenances holy remayn to William my son to have and to hold
the same close with thapurtenances to hym and to the heyrs of hys body lawfully
begoten for evermore of the chefe lordes of the [fee] as ys before sayde and
yf yt happ the sayde Wylliam my son to decese withoute heyres of hys body
lawfully begoten that God defend then I wyll that the sayde cloose
with althe apurtenances holy remayn to the howse of Saynt Thomas
the Martyr withoute the southe yate of the town of Northampton
aforesayd to have and to holde to the sustentacon of the pore people
therin beyng and theyr successors and assignes for evermore of the cheve lords
of the ffee etcetera to thentent ther daylie to be prayed for imperpetuall
Also I wyll that the same Alice my wyfe have my copp callyt a nutt
for the terme of hyr lyfe and after hyr discess I woll that the same
nutt remayn to William my son therwith to dispose as he shall thynke
beste Also I gyff and beqweth to the same Alice my wyfe a pece
of sylver to do therwith as shee thynketh beste The residue of all my
godes above nott beqwethett after my dettes byth payed I holy gyffe
and beqwethe to the sayde Alice my wyfe therwith to do and dispose for
the helth of my soule my frendes sowles and all Crystin sowles as shee
thynkyth moste nedefull and expedyent And I make and ordeyn
of this my present testament and laste wyll the sayde Alice my wyfe
my sole executrice to performe my wyll and to be gude ayde help
and socor unto the same Alice I make John Esex oversear and he to have
for hys labor iijs.iiijd. Theys wittnes John Adam Inholder John
Apryce corvesor Roger Prynce skrevener and othyr

f101r 357 JOHN KYNG 6th April 1490 priest

In Dei nomine Amen sexto die mensis Aprilis anno domini mcccclxxxx [Ego]
dominus Johannes Kyng de Northampton presbyter compos mentis et condo testamentum
meum [in hunc]
modum In primis lego animam Deo Omnipotenti Beate Marie Virgini ac omnibus [sanctis]
corpusque meum sepiliendum in capella Beate Marie Virginis infra ecclesiam Omnium
Sanctorum
Northampton Item lego ad decorandum capud unius undecem milli' virginum in dicta
[capella]
xxs. Item lego fraternitati Sancte Trinitatis xxd. Item lego fraternitati Sancti Johannis []
Corporis Christi xijd. Item cuilibet fraternitati alii in dicta ecclesia xijd. item pauperibus
in domo Sancti Thome xxd. Item incarcaratis in gaola in victu xijd. Item monasterio Sancti
Andree iijs.iiijd. Item monasterio Sancti Jacobi Apostoli iijs.iiijd. Item quattuor ordinibus
fratribus

mendicanciis vjs.viijd. equaliter inter eos dividendum. Item Thome Langton xiijs.[iiijd]
et messuagium meum situatum in Kyslyngbery cum omnibus pertinenciis in ville et campis
Kyslyngbery predicte Item lego Emme Langton xxs. sex cocliaria argent[ia]
lectum plumalem coopertorium lecti optimum par linthiamentum pannum lineum [ ]
supra lectum meum cum cortinis circumpendentis mensam cathedram omnia stabella [ ]
pictos pendentes in camera et ciphorium meum cum omnibus pertinencii eidem Item lego [Roberto]
Kyng de Lychebarowe iijs.iiijd. et eidem Roberto unam togam de russett Item [lego]
Willelmi Kynge iijs.iiijd. Item lego Johanni Herreys filiolo meo unum superellectile [ ]
librum exequinarum unam cistam et unam togam de vyolett Item magistro Willelmo Kyng
craterem argenti et unum par precularum de awmber Item lego collegio in quo h[abito]
murram Item lego Johanni Langton vjs.viijd. Item Johanne uxori eiusdem Johannis vjs.viijd. [Item]
lego Thome Morley iijs.iiijd. Item domino Laurentio Kyng lego portoferium meum
Residuum bonorum meorum superius non legatorum do et lego magistro Johanni Cokkys domino Thome
Huett et domino Ricardo Nevell presbytris ad disponendum pro salute anime mee et <animarum> benefactorum
meorum quos ordino facio et constituo executores meos supervisorem execuc[ionis]
huius testamenti mei et ultime voluntatis constituo Johannem Langton supranominatum Date
die et anno domini supradictis magistro Roberto Preston domino Johanne Bowden et Thome
Wyrley testibus etcetera

In the name of God Amen the 6th day of April 149[0] I Dom John Kyng of Northampton, priest, in sound mind make my testament in this wise. First I bequeath my soul to Almighty God, to the Blessed Virgin Mary and all the saints, my body to be buried in the chapel of the Blessed Virgin Mary within the church of All Saints Northampton. Item I bequeath to decorate the head of one of the eleven thousand virgins in the said [chapel] 20s. Item I bequeath to the fraternity of the Holy Trinity 20d. Item I bequeath to the fraternity of St John [] of Corpus Christi 12d. Item I bequeath to each of the other fraternities in the said church 12d. Item to the poor in the house of St Thomas 20d. Item to the prisoners in the gaol for provisions 12d. Item to the monastery of St Andrew 3s 4d. Item to the monastery of St James the Apostle 3s 4d. Item to the four orders of mendicant brothers 6s 8d to be divided equally among them. Item to Thomas Langton 13s 4d and my house situated in Kislingbury with all appurtenances in the town and fields of the said Kislingbury. Item I bequeath to Emma Langton 20s, six silver spoons, one feather bed, the best bed cover, one pair of sheets, one length of linen cloth [] above my bed with the curtains hanging around it, one table, one chair and all the stools and [] painted hangings in the chamber and my cupboard with everything belonging thereto. Item I bequeath to Robert Kyng of Lichborough 3s 4d and to the same Robert one gown of russet. Item I bequeath to William Kyng 3s 4d. Item I bequeath to John Herreys, my godson, one bed cover [] one book of the offices of the dead (?) one chest and one gown of violet colour. Item to Master William Kyng one silver bowl and one rosary of amber. Item I bequeath to the college in which I live one maser. Item I bequeath to John Langton 6s 8d. Item to Joan, wife of the same John, 6s 8d. Item I bequeath to Thomas Morley 3s 4d. Item to Dom Laurence Kyng I bequeath my portable breviary. The residue of my goods not bequeathed above I give and bequeath to Master John Cokkys, Dom Thomas Huett and Dom Richard Nevell, priests, to then dispose for the health of my soul and the souls of my benefactors, whom I ordain, make and constitute my executors. I constitute the above named John Langton as supervisor of the execution of this my last will and testament. Given the day and year of Our Lord abovesaid, Master Robert Preston, Dom John Bowden and Thomas Wyrley as witnesses etcetera.

N.B. *The right hand page edge is torn and some line endings lost*

f101r 358 EM[...] WHYTE 1st August 1491 widow

In Dei nomine Amen anno domini millesimo cccc nonagesimo primo primo die mensis Augusti Ego Em[...]
Whyte relicta Thome Whyte nuper de Northampton clotheer condo testamentum meum in hunc modum
In primis lego animam meam Deo Omnipotenti etcetera corpus meum sepiliendum in cimiterio
Sancti Sepulcri iuxta virum meum Item lego summo altari pro decimis oblitis iijs. iiijd. Item lego
altari Sancte Marie in ecclesia Sancti Sepulcri predicte unum pannum linium et unum manitergium
vulgariter dictum a dyaper towell Item lego Margarete Knyghton et usum puerorum suorum
unam ollam eneam trium lagenarum et patellam quattuor lagenarum Item lego Emme Clerke unum
lectum videlicet a materas unum par linthiaminium et coopertorium et duo pulvinaria Item unam pelvim
cum lavacro Item cuilibet filio et filie de sacre fonte per me levatis iiijd. Item lego Johanni Huin
tria cocliaria argentea Residuum vero bonorum meorum non legatorum do et lego executore meo quem constituo Edwardum Huin ut disponat pro salute anime mee prout sibi melius videbitur

In the name of God Amen 1491 the first day of August I Em[...] Whyte, relict of Thomas Whyte formerly of Northampton, clothier, make my testament in this wise. First I bequeath my soul to Almighty God etcetera my body to be buried in the churchyard of Holy Sepulchre next to my husband. Item I bequeath to the high altar for tithes forgotten 3s 4d. Item I bequeath to the altar of St Mary in the church of Holy Sepulchre aforesaid one length of linen and one towel commonly called a diaper towel. Item I bequeath to Margaret Knyghton and the use of her children one three gallon brass pot and one four gallon pan. Item I bequeath to Emma Clerke one bed, that is to say one mattress, one pair of sheets and one coverlet and two pillows. Item one basin with ewer. Item to each godson and goddaughter 4d. Item I bequeath to John Huin three silver spoons. The residue of all my goods not bequeathed I give and bequeath to my executor whom I appoint Edward Huin he to dispose for the health of my soul as seems best to him.

f102r 362 ROBERT MOSE 14th August 1494

In Dei nomine Amen the xiiijth day of Auguste the yere of ower lorde God mcccclxxxxiiijth I Robert Mose of Northampton hole of mynde make this my testament and laste wyll in maner and form folowyng that ys to say fyrste I bequethe my soule to Almyghty God and to ower Blessyd Lady Saynt Marie Vyrgin and to all the company of heven my body to be buryed in the churcheyerd of the paryssh churche of All Halowes in Northampton under the chapell of Saynt George by the sepulture of my wyves ther lying Item I bequethe to the fraternite of the moste blessyt Trinite in the same churche iijs.iiijd. Item I bequethe to the fraternite of Ower Lady in the sayde churche iijs.iiijd. Item I bequethe to the fraternite of Corpus Christi in the same churche iijs.iiijd. Item I bequethe to the fraternite of the Rode in the same churche xijd. Item I bequeth to the fraternite of Saynte Kateryne in the pardon churche yerde in the parysshe beforesayde xijd. Item I bequeth to the fraternite of Saynte George in the same churche xijd. Item I bequeth to the fraternite of Saynt John Baptiste in sayde churche xijd. Item I bequeth to the reparacons of the sayde churche of All Halowes vjs.viijd. Item I bequeth to Thomas Mose my brothyr my shorte grene gown Item I bequeth to Thomas Boyse a shorte gown of blak to pray for my soule Item I bequeth to Marget Stubber my doghter a womans gown of skarlet furred with whyte menyvers Item I bequethe to Emma Smyth to pray for my soule a coferr standyng in my hall Item I bequeth to Elizabeth Grene my kynneswoman to pray for my soule a pewter plater and a pewter dyssh Item I bequeth to Alice Byrde a sheete Item I bequeth to Master Robert Mydelham doctor my confessor to pray for my soule xxd. Item I bequeth to the sustentacon of the pore pepull in Saynt Thomas house withoute the southe yate of Northampton to pray for my soule iijs.iiijd. Item I woll that William Prentece and Marget hys wife have the disposicon of the termes of my howse with owte the southe yate

f102v

of Northampton abovesayde whyche nowe I dwellin after the maner and effecte of a payer of indentors thereof made and the sayde termes to sell at their pleasors and the money therof to be disposyd emong pore poepull and in other deds of almes and charyte for the helth of my soule Johanne my wyfe soule my freends soules and all Crystin soules as they shall thynke moste nedfull and expedyent The residue of all my gods not above bequethed after my detts ben payde I holely gyff and bequeth to the forsayde William Prentece and Margaret his wyfe therwith to do and dispose also for the helth of my soule and all Cristen soules as they thynke moste beste to bedone and I make the sayde William Prentece and Margaret his wyfe of this my testament myn executors theyse beryng wytnes Master Robert Mydelham doctor and vicar of the paryshhe churche of All Halowes above sayde Nicholas Bowker fuller Roger Prynce scryvener and othyr

f102v 363 WILLIAM PRENTECE 5th December 1494 draper

In the name of God Amen the vth day of the month of December the yere of ower lord mcccclxxxxiiij I William Prentece of Northampton

draper hole of mynde beying make my testament and laste wyll in
maner here after sayng Firste I bequethe my soule to Almyghty God
and to ower Blessyt Lady Saynt Mary hys mother and to al the company in hevyn
my body to be buryed in the chapell of Saynt Kateryn in the pardon church
yerd Item I bequethe to the parsunnes of the churche of All Halowes in Northampton
for my tythes and offeryngs forgoten and negligently witholdyn vjs.viijd. Item
I bequethe to the fraternite of Ower Lady in the same church to be admytted
a brother and my wyfe a syster of the same xxs. Item I bequethe to the
fraternite of the Trinite in the same churche xxd. Item I bequeth
to the fraternite of Corpus Christi in the same churche xxd. Item I bequeth
to the fraternite of the Blessyd Rode in the sayde churche xxd. Item I
bequethe to the fraternite of Saynt George in the same churche xxd.
Item I bequeth to the fraternite of Saynt John Baptist in the same church
xxd. Item I bequeth to the fraternite of Saynt Kateryn in the pardon churche yerd
above sayde for my sepulture there vjs.viijd. Item I bequeth to the susten-
tacon of the pore peopull in Saynt Thomas howse withoute the southe
yate of the town of Northampton to pray for my soule iijs.iiijd. Item I
gyffe and bequeth to John Prentece my son in money xxli a fetherbed
a bolster a payer of blanketts a payer of shets and a coveryng to a bedd
j maser and vj sponys of sylver also I gyffe to the same John my son all
my londes and tenenments with theyr appurtenances in Bloxham in counte of Oxford
to have and to holde to hym his heyres and assignes for evermore of the lords
of the ffee etcetera Also I gyffe and bequeth to William Prentece my son <in money>
xxli a fetherbed a bolster a payer of blanketts a payer of shets a

f103r

coveryng to a bed a maser and vj sylver sponys Also I gyffe to the same William
my son al my parte of my shopp with the appurtenances upon the Carfax corner in the
town of Northampton above sayde to have and to hold to hym and to his heires and assignes
forevermore of the lords of the ffee etcetera Item I bequeth to John Brown my servant
to pray for my soule iijs.iiijd. and my shorte vyolet gown. Also I bequethe to everyeche
of my servantes in my house beying to pray for my soule xxd. Item I bequeth to Elen
my servant a materesse a bolster a payer of shets a coveryng to a bed a panne of bras
a pott of brasse a plater a dyssh of pewter a candylstyke of laton to pray for my
soule so that she continue styll <and abyde> with my wyfe to shee from hir be maryed Also
I bequeth to Willyam Jonson tanner my beste rosett gown furret with blak lams. Also
I bequeth to William Rolfe my beste dowplett The resydue of all my godes
above nott bequethyd after my dettes payed I holely gyff and bequeth to Margeret
my wyfe therwyth to do and dispose for the helthe of my soule my frends soules
and all Crystyn soules as shee thynketh moste nedefull and behovefull and I make
the same Margeret of this my testament myn executryce and for to be
to hyr gude ayder councellor and supporter I make Thomas Edward mercer
over seer and he shall have for hys labor in money xxs. and iij yerds and a quarter
of my beste wollen clothe for a gown Theys witnes Maister Robert Mydelham
doctor vicar of the paryssh churche of All Halowes above sayde Richard Goldyear
bower Roger Prynce scryvener and other

f103r 364 ALICE BULL 19th November 1494 widow

1In Dei nomine Amen xix die mensis Novembris anno domini mccccl xxxxiiij Ego Alicia
Bull de Northampton vidua compos mentis et sane memorie condo presens testamentum
meum
in hunc modum In primis commendo animam meam Deo Omnipotenti Beate Marie Virgini

ac omnibus sanctis celestis curie corpusque meum sepiliendum in cimiterio ecclesie parochialis Omnium Sanctorum
ville Northampton predicte Item do et lego rectoribus eiusdem ecclesie nomine principalis mei quod licitum fuerit
Item lego reparacionibus ecclesie parochiali de Eydon in comitatu Northampton iijs.iiijd. Item lego cuilibet
filio et filie filiorum et filiarum meorum duas oves Item lego Willelmo Bull filio meo unam vaccam
et sex oves ac unam almary ad totum terminum vite sue et si contingat dictum Willelmum obire sine herede
de corpore sue legitime procreato tunc volo quod predicta almary remaneat Thome Bull filio meo
imperpetuum Item lego eidem Thome filio meo sex cocliaria argentea meam optimumque pelvim cum
lavacro de laton et unum coopertorium lecti coloris viridis Item lego Agneti Shepard filie mee
sex oves de melioribus et unam ollam eneam continentem tres lagenas et meum optimum vas
vocatum Anglice a grete panne enei unam par linthiamium optimorum unam mappam et manutergium
de dyaper que vas olla linthamia mappa et manutergium sunt in custodia dicti Willelmi Bull filii mei
Item do et lego Johanni Bull filio meo totum illud tenementum meum situatum sive messuagium
in Eydon predicte situatum inter tenementum Ricardi Tewe ex parte australi et venellam ibidem vocatam
Langtons Lane ex parte boriali et viam regiam ibidem ex parte orientali in quo tenemento sive mesuagio
idem Johannes Bull modo inhabitat habendum et tenendum sibi et heredibus suis de corpore sue legitime procreatis
imperpetuum de capitalibus dominis feodi illius per servicia inde debita et de iure consueta Et si contingat
predictum Johannem Bull sine heredibus de corpore sue legitime procreatis obire tunc volo quod dictum tenementum
meum sive mesuagium cum omnibus suis pertinciis totaliter remaneat prefate Agneti Shepard filie
mee habendum et tenendum sibi et heredibus de corpore suo legitime procreatis imperpetuum de capitalibus dominis feodi etcetera
Et si contingat predictam Agnetem filiam meam obire sine heredibus de corpore suo legitime procreatis tunc volo
quod supradictum tenementum sive mesuagium cum omnibus et singulis pertinenciis suis ut predictum est totaliter revertitur
proximis rectis heredibus mei predicte Alicie habendum et tenendum sibi et heredibus suis et assignatis imperpetuum de capitalibus

f103v

de capitalibus dominis feodi etcetera Residuum vero omnium bonorum meorum jocalium et catallorum meorum
superius non legatorum post debita <mea> soluta totaliter do et lego predicte Thome Bull filio meo
et Hugoni Sheperd de Northampton baker ad inde ordinandum et disponendum pro salute anime mee
ac pro animabus omnium parentum et amicorum meorum ac omnium fidelium defunctorum prout eis melius
videbitur expediri ac ordino et constituo predictum Thomam Bull filium meum et Hugonem Sheperd

huius testamenti mei meos executores In cuius rei testimonium huic presenti testamento meo sigillum meum
apposui Date die et anno domini supradictis hiis testibus Magistro Roberto Midelham doctore vicario perpetuo
ecclesie parochiale Omnium Sanctorum Northampton Willelmo Klynte in eadem ecclesia capellano Johanne Esex chandeler
Rogero Prynce scriptore et multis aliis

In the name of God Amen the 19th day of November 1494 I Alice Bull of Northampton, widow, in sound mind and good memory make my present testament in this wise. First I commend my soul to Almighty God, the Blessed Virgin Mary and all saints of the court of heaven, my body to be buried in the cemetery of the parish church of All Saints in the said town of Northampton. Item I bequeath to the rectors of the said church for my principal whatever the custom is. Item I bequeath for the repairs of the parish church of Eydon in the county of Northampton 3s 4d. Item I bequeath to the sons and daughters of my sons and daughters two sheep. Item I bequeath to William Bull, my son, one cow and six sheep and one cupboard for the term of his life and if it should happen that the said William should die without legitimate heirs then I wish the said cupboard should remain to Thomas Bull, my son, forever. Item I bequeath to the same Thomas my son six silver spoons, my best bowl and ewer of laten and one bed cover of green colour. Item I bequeath to Agnes Sheparde, my daughter, six of my best sheep and one three gallon brass bowl and my best vessel called in English a great brass pan, one pair of best sheets, one cloth and towel of diaper, which vessel, bowl, sheets, cloth and towel are in the care of the said William Bull, my son. Item I give and bequeath to John Bull, my son, all my tenement and messuage situated in Eydon aforesaid between the tenement of Richard Tewe on the southern side and the lane there called Langtons Lane on the northern side and the king's highway on the east, in which tenement and messuage the same John Bull now lives, to have and to hold to him and the heirs of his body legitimately begotten forever of the chief lords of the fee by services therefore due and by right accustomed. And if it should happen that the said John Bull should die without heirs of his body legitimately begotten then I will that the said tenement with messuage and all its appurtenances should remain to the said Agnes Sheparde, my daughter, to have and to hold to her and to the heirs of her body legitimately begotten forever of the chief lords of the fee etcetera. And if it should happen that the said Agnes, my daughter, should die without heirs of her body legitimately begotten then I will that the above-named tenement and messuage with all and singular appurtenances as said before should wholly revert to the next rightful heir of me the aforesaid Alice, to have and to hold by them, their heirs and assigns forever of the chief lords of the fee etcetera. The residue of my goods, my jewels and my chattels not above bequeathed after my debts are totally paid, I bequeath to the said

Thomas Bull, my son, and to Hugh Sheperd of Northampton, baker, to then ordain and dispose for the health of my soul and for the souls of all my parents and friends and all faithful departed as seems best to them and I ordain and constitute the foresaid Thomas Bull, my son, and Hugh Sheperd my executors of this testament. In testimony of this matter, my present testament, I have affixed my seal. Given the day and year abovesaid these being witnesses Master Robert Midelham, Doctor and perpetual vicar of the church of All Saints, Northampton, William Klynte, chaplain in the same church, John Esex, chandler, Roger Prince, scrivenor and many others.

f103v 367 WILLIAM FLORE 15th February 1493 shearman

In the name of God Amen the yere of ower Lord God mccccclxxxx and three the xvth day of February I William Flore of Northampton shereman in my hole mynde and clere memory
beyng thankyt be God make (my) and ordeyn my testament and last wyll in forme
after sueyng That is to say fyrst I bequeth my soule to Almyghty God Our Lady
Saynt Marie his blessyt mother and to all the holy sayntes in hewyn My body to be
buryed within the chapell of Corpus Christi in the churche of All Halowys in Northampton
aforesayde Item I bequethe to the hee auter in the same chyrche for my tythes forgoten iijs iiijd.

f104r

Item I bequethe to the reparacon of the same chyrche iijs.iiijd. Item I bequethe to the fraternite of the Blessed
Trinite in the same chyrche xxd. Item I bequeth to the fraternite of the Holy Rode in the same church xijd. Item
I bequeth to the fraernite of Saynt John Baptist in the sayde chyrche xijd. Item I bequeth to the fraternite
of Saynt George in the same chyrche xijd. Item I bequeth to the fraternite of Saynt Kateryn the Virgin in the
newe chyrcheyerd in the same paryssh of All Halows <xijd.> Item I bequeth to the sustentacon of the pore people
of Saynt Thomas house without the south yate of Northampton abovesayd evenly among them to be dyvydyth
to pray for my soule vjs viijd. Item I bequeth to the iiij cloysters of freres in the sayde town of Northampton to pray for my soule to yche of them iijs iiijd. Item I bequethe to Richard Flowre the
son of Richard Flowre late decessett and Thomas Flowre brother to the <same> Richard Flowre <the> younger to
othyr of them vli. and yf eythyr of them decesse before othyr the survyver to have his parte that so deceses that ys to say the hole xli. and yf yt happ bothe the sayde Richard <Flowre> and Thomas his
brothyr to decesse than I wyll at the sayde xli. be kepyt styll in the handys of Margett Flowre my wyfe and to disposed for my soule and the sayde chylders soules as yt shall best please hyr
Also I wyll that the said Margett my wyfe have the hundred pounds whiche ys in specialtes of obligacon
or ellis in money that my son Richard Flowre put me in truste of as yt appereth more playnle in his testament and the same Margett to have the kepyng therof to the sayde ij chylder com to the age of xxij yeres yf they leve so longe and yf the saide Margett my wyfe decesse before

the sayde childer com to the age afore sayde than I wyll that the sayde specialtes or money be delyvyt to
Dame Elizabeth Saxby wedowe to William Robyns of More Hoghton and to Thomas Flowre my brother
and they to kepe the same specialtes or money to the behove of the foresaide Richard Flowre and
Thomas his brother in manner I afore rehersyd And yf so happen that the sayde Richard Floure and Thomas
his brothor bothe decesse before they com to the age of xxij yers then I wyll that xli. of the sayde money be disposed amonge pore people in the house of Saynt Thomas the Martyr above wrytin
to pray for my soule and for theyr soules that yt com of And also I wyll that the residue of the sayde Cli. that ys to iiijxxxli. (£90) be disposed among pore people moste nedefull by xli. a yere
till yt be fynesshytt except I wyll that the disposers and rewlers of the same then have for theyer labores and charges abowte the same xli. of the same money Also I bequethe to Thomas
Floure my brother xls. and a gowen of my wering Also I bequethe to Johanne the wyfe of the same
Thomas xxs. Item I wyll that at the day of my burying be disposed among pore people to pray
for my soule xls. Also I bequethe to John Yonge sherman to pray for my soule vjs viijd and a gown of my weryng Item I bequethe to Kateryn and Marget Skydmore my servants to pray for my
soule to eythyer of them iijs.iiijd. Item I bequethe to Margery Johann and Margarett Olney my servants
to pray for my soule to yche of theym xxd. Item I bequeth to Isbell my servant yf she wyll abyde
and dwell styll with Margett my wyfe and be rulyed by hyr to the same Isbell for time to be myreed
than to pray for my soule xxs. The residue of all my godes above nott beqwethed after my detts be payed I holy gyffe and bequethe to the foresayde Margett my wyfe therwith to do and
dispose for the helthe of my sowle my frends sowles and all Crystin sowles as shee thynketh moste
nedefull and expedyent And also I make and ordeyn of this my present testament and laste wyll
the sayde Margaret my wyfe myn executryce and to be hyr gude ayde supportacon and helper
in the same I make and ordeyn Thomas Derby mercer of this same testament overseer and supervyser and Thomas Floure my brother also to thentent at this my laste wyll be performed
and I wyll the same Thomas Derby have for his labor xxs. These beyng wytnes John Folyott tailer Thomas Mulso irmonger and othyr

f104v 368 ALICE WYNGE 4th September 1495 wife of William Wynge

In the name of God Amen the iiijth day of the moneth of September the yere of ower Lorde God mccccIxxxxv I Alice Wynge the wyfe of William Wynge wever of Northampton hole of
mynd make and ordeyn this my present testament in maner and forme

hereafter ensuyng that ys to say First I bequeth my sowle to Almighty God Our Lady and
all saints my body to be buryed under the chapell of Saynt George in parysh church of
All Halowys withoute the south dore there by the sepulture of William Mannyng sum tyme
my husband Item I bequeth to the prior of Saynt Andrewe and the covent for my tithes
and offeryngs forgeten or witholden iiis.iiijd. Item I bequeth to the fraternite
of the blessyd Trinite in the sayd churche ijs. Item to the fraternite of Corpus Christi in the
same churche ijs. to the fraternite of Our Lady there ijs. Item to the fraternite of the Rode ther
ijs. Item to the fraternite of Saynt George in the same churche ijs. Item to the fraternite
of Saynt John Baptiste in the same churche ijs. Item I bequeth to the fraternite of Saynt
Kateryn in the pardon churche yerd within All Hawlawe paryssh of Northampton ijs. Item I
bequeth
to the fraternite of Saynt Pulcre in the churche of Saynt Pulcres of Northampton ijs. Item to
the
fraternite of Saynt Clement in Saynt Gyles paryssh churche of the same town xijd. Item I
bequeth
to the fraternite of Saynt Michaell in the same town xijd. Item I bequeth to the reparacon
of Al Halawe churche aforesayde iijs.iiijd. Item I bequeth to every house of freres with-
in the town of Northampton sayng placebo and dirige with masse of requiem solemly for my
sowle ijs.
Item I bequeth to the pore people in Saynt Thomas howse withoute the southe yate of the
same town xxti ellys of lynnyn clothe the price iiijd the elle evenli to be divydyt amonges
them
to pray for my sowle Item I bequeth to Sir William Daffron preste son of Richard Daffron
late my husband vj sylver sponys a grete maser whiche was his fathyrs called Ower Lady
and a salte of sylver withoute a cover Item I bequeth to my brothyr John Withmayle of Norwych
bower to pray for my sowle xxs. Item I bequeth <to the wyfe> of my sayd brother my beste
gown of
vyolet ingreyn furred Item I bequeth to every chylde of my sayd brother vjs.viijd. Also where
as William (John) Jonson <late> of Northampton tanner owyth me a duete what yt ys I
cannot perfitely
tell I wyll that as sone and when yt ys by myn executors recoveryt that John Wyng of
Northampton corvesor have the one halfe therof what so ever yt shalbe to pray for my sowle
and the othyr parte therof to be disposed by the discrecon of myn executors in colys emong
pore people moste nedyng to pray for my sowle Item I bequeth to John Stanbryge baker xxs.
Item I bequeth to Joanna his wyfe xxs. Item I bequeth to Johanne the doghter of the same
John Stanbryge vj sylver sponys Item I bequeth to Agnes Hancok sumtyme my servant iijs.iiijd.
Item I bequeth to Margeret Wyng wyfe to sayd John Wyng <on of> my shorte russet
gownes Item
I bequeth to the sustentacon of the collage in All Halowe paryssh my beste maser Item I bequeth
to Master Robert Mydelham Doctor my gostly fathyr to pray for sowle xs. Item I bequeth to
John
Esex to pray for my sowle iijs.iiijd. Item I bequeth to Richard Greves wever to pray for
my sowle xxs. Item to Jone the wyfe of the same Richard one of my roset gownys
Also I bequeth to the syster of <the> sayd my late husband Richard Daffron to pray for my
sowle vjs.viijd.
Item I bequeth to Margeret my servant to pray for my sowle xijd. Item I bequeth thabbott
of Saynt Jamys by Northampton sayng placebo and dirige with mass of requiem for my
sowle xs.
and to the convent of the same place every xs. on the condicon that <they> pay <myn
executors> syche duete
they now owe to me Item I bequeth to Robert Paytowe a gown and to his wyfe a curtyll
Item I bequeth to every of <my> god chylder to pray for my sowle xijd. Item I wyll that yf
any of
my servants that have ben when I am departed chalenge eny duete that they wyll take

the chearge oppen theym that ther be emongst theym distributed vjs.viijd. Item I bequeth to the wyfe of Thomas Wertree wever one of my curtylls The residue of my guds above not bequeathed after my detts byth payed I holely gyff and bequeth to William Wyng my husband ther wyth to do and dispose after his owne mynd and free wyll as he shud thynke moste nedefull and expedyent for the helth of my sayde husbandes sowles and myn and all Cristen sowles and I make and ordeyn of this my testament <the> sayde William Wyng my husband and John Stanbryge above sayde myn executors and foresade Sir William Daffron to be overseer of the due performyng of this my wyll in maner afore rehersyd ffurthermore as towchyng the disposicon of sale of the howse whiche my sayde husband wyll be done for hym I remitte yt to the discrecon of the sayde Sir William and of myn executors to be performyd after the laste wyll of the <sayde> Richard Daffron These witnes Master Robert Mydelham Doctor vicar of All Halowes afore sayd John <Watts> yrnmonger John Essex chandeler and Roger Prynce wryter

f105r 370 EM HUNT 20th May 1494 widow

In the name of God Amen the xx^{ti} day of the moneth of May in the yere if our Lord God mcccclxxxxiiij I Em Hunt of Northampton wedowe beyng in my hole mynd make my testament in this wyse First I bequeth my soule to Almyghty God and to Ower Lady Saynt Mary his mother and to all the company of hewyn my body to be buryed by my husband grave in the chapell of ower lady in All Halowe churche of Northampton Item I bequeth to the fraternite <of the Blessyd Trinite> in the same chyrche vjs.viijd. Item I bequeth for my forgoten tythes vjs.viijd. Item I bequeth to the fraternite of Corpus Christi in the sayde chyrche vjs.viijd. Item I bequeth to the fraternite of Ower Blessyd Lady in the same chirche vjs.viijd. Item I bequeth to the pore pople of Saynt Thomas house xxs. Item I bequeth to Symon Markaunt my cosen that vli that Thomas Ailmers owyth me and hath in his hand Item I bequeth to my cosyn Alys Markaunt a chasyd peece kevered and parcel gyld vj sylver sponys a brasse pott a chafur' a cowcher with a bolster a payer of shetys a coverlett and ij blanketts Item I bequeth to my cosyn William Markaunt a salt seler of sylver uncoveryd for terme of his lyfe and after hys dycease I wyll that John Markaunt his eldyst son have ytt Item I bequeth to John Asshborn xxs. The residue of my godys nott bequethyd I gyff and bequeth to John Loll and to Margarett hys wyfe my doghter whyche I make myn executors for to dispose my gods in charytabull dedys and warkys as them shall seme moste expedyent. At Northampton the day and yere above rehersyd Beyng witnes Henry Humfrey John Asshborn and Thomas Flore with dyvers othyr

f105v 372 JOHN WHYTE 11th October 1495 weaver

In Dei nomine Amen xj die mensis Octobris anno domini mccccclxxxxv^{to} Ego Johannes Whyte de Northampton wever compos mentis et sane memorie condo presens testamentum meum in hunc modum In primis lego et commendo animam meam Deo Omnipotenti Beate Marie ac omnibus sanctis corpusque meum sepiliendum infra capella Sancte Katerine in ecclesia parochiali

Beate Marie ville Northampton antedicte Item lego summo altari dicte ecclesie pro decimis et oblacionibus
meis oblitis negligenter detentis xijd. Item lego ad empcionem unius libri vocati a antiphoner
pro ecclesia predicta emendem pro salute anime mee xls. solvendis equalibus porcionibus per sex annos
proximo post decessum meum sequentes videlicet quolibet anno vjs.viijd. Item lego Wilelmo filio meo
ad orandum pro anima mea iijli.vjs.viijd. Item lego alteri puero modo in ventre Cristine uxoris mee
iijli.vijs.viijd. Et si contingat aliquem dictorum puerorum meorum obire infra etatem legitimam tunc volo quod alter eorum supervivens habebit
partem alterius sic decedentis Et si contingat utrumque dictorum puerorum meorum obire ante
legitimam etatem volo tunc quod predicti vjli.xiijs.iiijd. distribuantur in donis caritativis
et elemosinis pro anima mea et animabus dictorum puerorum meorum secundum discrecionem dicte Cristine
uxoris mee prout ei melius videbitur expediri Residuum vero omnium bonorum meorum superius
non legatorum post debita mea soluta totaliter do et lego prefate Cristine uxori mee
ad inde ordinandum et disponendum pro salute anime mee ac pro animabus omnium parentum et amicorum
meorum et omnium fidelium defunctorum prout ei melius videbitur expediri Aceciam facio
ordino et constituo predictam Cristinam uxorem meam huius testamenti mei executricem et pro suo
auxilio et bono concilio circa idem testamentum meum facio Willelmum Whyte de Northampton corvesor
Johannem Bowre draper et Thomam Adam bocher supervisores hiis testibus

In the name of God Amen the 11th day of October 1495 I John Whyte of Northampton, weaver, in sound mind and good memory make my present testament in this wise. First I bequeath and commend my soul to Almighty God, to the Blessed Mary and all the saints, my body to be buried within the chapel of St Katherine in the parish church of the Blessed Mary of the town of Northampton beforesaid. Item I bequeath to the high altar of the said church for my tithes and oblations negligently withheld 12d. Item I bequeath for the purchase of a book called an antiphon to be bought for the aforesaid church for the health of my soul 40s to be paid in equal portions for six years next following after my decease that is to say 6s 8d each year. Item I bequeath to William, my son, to pray for my soul £3 6s 8d. Item I bequeath to my other child now in the womb of Christine, my wife, £3 6s 8d. And if it should happen that either of the said children die before legal age then I will that the other surviving shall have the share of the other thus deceased. And if it happens that both of my said children die before legal age then I will that the aforesaid £6 13s 4d be distributed in gifts of charity and alms for my soul and the souls of my said children according to the discretion of the said Christine, my wife, as seems best to her. The residue of all my goods not bequeathed above after my debts are wholly paid I give and bequeath to the aforesaid Christine, my wife, to then ordain and dispose for the health of my soul and for the souls of all my parents and friends and all faithful departed as seems best to her. And also I make, ordain and constitute the aforesaid Christine, my wife, my executrix of this my testament and for his help and good counsel concerning my same testament I make William Whyte of Northampton, corvisor, John Barre, draper, and Thomas Adam, butcher, supervisors with these witnesses.

f106r 374 ELIZABETH BOTELER 10th December 1495 widow

In Dei nomine Amen decimo die mensis Decembris anno domini mcccclxxxxv Ego Elizabeth Boteler de Northampton vidua compos mentis et sane memorie condo testamentum meum in hunc modum In primis lego animam meam Deo Omnipotenti Beate Marie Virgini ac omnibus sanctis curie celestis corpusque meum sepiliendum in cimiterio de ecclesie Omnium Sanctorum ville predicte iuxta tumulum Johannis Boteler nuper viri mei Item lego priori Sancti Andree pro decimis oblitis et non bene decimatis xijd. Item lego fraternitati Sancte Trinitatis in eadem ecclesia xijd. Item lego fraternitati Beate Marie Virginis ibidem xijd. Item lego fraternitati Corporis Christi in eadem ecclesia xijd. Item lego fraternitati Sancte Katerine in novo cimiterio viijd. Item lego cuilibet fratenitati in dicta ecclesia Omnium Sanctorum viijd. Item lego fraternitati Sancti Clementis in ecclesia Sancti Egidii in predicte ville Northampton xijd. Item lego Magistro Doctori xijd. Item lego fraternitati Sancti Thome Martiris extra portam australem dicte ville Northampton viijd. Item lego Matildi Boteler filie mee quinque perapsides electri et sex sawsers electri duo candelibra j pelvim unum coopertorium lecti Anglice a coverlet a payer of beds of corall gawdyd with sylver and gylt unam zonam nigri coloris harnesatam cum argento et in pecuniis xls. Item volo quod post decessum meum tenementum meum situatum in venilla vocata Cropelane ville Northampton predicte vendatur ad maximum valorem per discrecionem executorem meorum et <de> pecuniis inde receptis omnes legaciones mee supradicte per solvantur et perimpleuntur Residuum vero omnium bonorum non legatorum do et lego Johanni Esex et Thome Large ad inde disponendum pro salute anime mee animarum omnium amicorum meorum et omnium fidelium defunctorum prout eis melius videbitur expediri et ad istud testamentum bene et fideliter exequendum eosdem Johannem Esex et Thomam Large ordino et facio executores meos et lego utrumque eorum pro labore suo iijs.iiijd. per presentes hiis testibus Magistro Roberto Mydelham Doctori Thoma Malpas Roberto Holme et aliis

In the name of God Amen the tenth day of December 1495 I Elizabeth Boteler of Northampton, widow, in sound mind and good memory make my testament in this wise. First I bequeath my soul to Almighty God, to the Blessed Virgin Mary and all the saints of the court of heaven, my

body to be buried in the churchyard of the church of All Saints of the aforesaid town next to the grave of John Boteler, my late husband. Item I bequeath to the Prior of St Andrew's for tithes forgotten and not well tithed 12d. Item I bequeath to the fraternity of the Holy Trinity in the same church 12d. Item I bequeath to the fraternity of the Blessed Virgin Mary there 12d. Item I bequeath to the fraternity of Corpus Christi in the same church 12d. Item I bequeath to the fraternity of St Katherine in the new churchyard 8d. Item I bequeath to each fraternity in the same church of All Saints 8d. Item I bequeath to the fraternity of St Clement in the church of St Giles in the aforesaid town of Northampton 12d. Item I bequeath to Master Doctor 12d. Item I bequeath to the fraternity of St Thomas the Martyr outside the south gate of the said town of Northampton 8d. Item I bequeath to Matilda Boteler, my daughter, five pewter platters and six saucers, two candlesticks, 1 jug, one bed covering, in English a coverlet, a pair of beads of coral gaudid with silver and gilt, one girdle of black colour ornamented with silver and 40s in money. Item I will that after my decease my tenement in the land called Crop Lane in the town of Northampton aforesaid should be sold for its maximum value by the discretion of my executors and from the money thence received all my abovesaid legacies should be paid and fulfilled. The residue of all my goods not bequeathed I give and bequeath to John Esex and Thomas Large to then dispose for the health of my soul, the souls of all my friends and all faithful departed as may seem best to them and that this my testament be well and faithfully executed I ordain and make the said John Esex and Thomas Large my executors and I bequeath to both for his labour 3s 4d by these presents. With these witnesses Master Robert Mydelham, Doctor, Thomas Malpas, Robert Holme and others.

f106v 375 JOHN APRYCE 9th February 1495 corvisor

In Dei nomine Amen ix die mensis Februarii anno domini mcccclxxxxv Ego
Johannes Apryce de Northampton corvesor compos mentis et sane memorie existens condo
testamentum meum in hunc modum In primis lego animam meam Deo Omnipotenti creator
celi et terrre Beate Marie et omnibus celi sanctis corpusque meum sepiliendum
in cimiterio parochialis ecclesie Omnium Sanctorum ville predicte ex parte boriali eiusdem
cimiterii iuxta sepulturam Alicie nuper uxoris mee Item lego sustentacione pauperium in
domo Sancti Thome Martiris extra portam australem ville antedicte xijd Item lego fraternitati
Sancti Trinitatis in ecclesia predicta xijd Item lego fraterniti Sancte Crucis
in eadem ecclesia xijd Item lego fraternitati Sancti Johannis Baptiste in eadem ecclesia xijd Item
lego fraternitati Sancte Katerine in lez pardon chyrche xijd Item lego Fraternitati Sancti Georgii
in ecclesia Omnium Sanctorum predicta xijd Item lego Margarete Lodyngton unam mensam vocatam
a counter stantem in aula mea ad orandum pro anima mea Residuum vero omnium
bonorum meorum superius non legatorum post debita mea totaliter soluta do
et lego Alicie uxori mee ad inde ordinandum et disponendum pro salute anime mee
ac pro animabus parentum et omnium amicorum ac omnium fidelium defunctorum prout ei

melius videbitur expediri Et facio ac ordino huiis testamenti mei predictam
Aliciam uxorem meam meam executricem etcetera hiis testibus Ricardo Denton, Inholder
et Rogero Prince scriptore cum aliis

In the name of God Amen the 9th day of February 1495 I John Apryce of Northampton, butcher, in sound mind and still in good memory make my testament in this wise. First I bequeath my soul to Almighty God, Creator of heaven and earth, to the Blessed Mary and all the saints of heaven, my body to be buried in the cemetery of the parish church of All Saints of the town aforesaid on the north side of the said cemetery next to the grave of Alice, my late wife. Item I bequeath to the sustenance of the poor of the house of St Thomas the Martyr outside the south gate of the aforesaid town 12d. Item I bequeath to the fraternity of the Holy Cross in the same church 12d. Item I bequeath to the fraternity of St John the Baptist in the same church 12d. Item I bequeath to the fraternity of St Katherine in lez pardon church 12d. Item I bequeath to the fraternity of St George in the church of All SAints aforesaid 12d. Item I bequeath to Margaret Lodyngton a table called a counter standing in my hall to pray for my soul. The residue of all my goods not bequeathed above after my debts have been wholly paid I give and bequeath to Alice, my wife, to then ordain and dispose for the health of my soul and the souls of my parents and all friends and all faithful departed as seems best to her. And I make and ordain Alice, my aforesaid wife, executrix of this will etcetera. With these witnesses Richard Denton, innholder, Roger Prince, scribe, with others.

f106v 376 WILLIAM WAREN 28th March 1496 dyer

In Dei nomine Amen xxviij die mensis Marcii anno domini mcccclxxxxvj Ego
Willelmus Waren de Northampton dyer compos mentis et sane memorie condo testamentum
meum in hunc modum In primis lego animam meam Deo Patri Omnipotenti Beate Marie
Dei genitrici et omnibus sanctis eius corpusque meum sepiliendum iuxta sepulturam
Mathilde
nuper uxoris mee defuncte Item do et lego reparacionibus ecclesie Omnium Sanctorum in
villa Northampton
xxd. Item do et lego fraternitatibus Sancte Trinitatis Sancte Crucis Sancti Johannis Baptiste
Sancti
Georgii Martiris et Sancte Katerine in eadem ecclesia cuilibet videlicet earum xijd. Residuum
vero bonorum meorum superius non legatorum do et lego Edwardo Wellys quondam
servienti
meo ut ipse solvat debita mea et disponat pro salute anime mee uxoris mee
modo defuncte et parentum meorum prout ei melius videbitur expediri
Et eundam Edwardum ordino facio et constituo executorem hiuis testamenti mei
Et ut hac mea ultima voluntas fideliter compleatur constituo Willelmum Bukby
supervisorem hiis testibus Magistro Roberto Mydelham vicario dicte ecclesie Nicholao Buller
Thoma Mounforth Ricardo Mason cum aliis multis

In the name of God Amen the 28th day of March 1496 I William Waren of Northampton, dyer, in sound mind and good memory make my testament in this wise. First I bequeath my soul to God the Father Almighty, to the Blessed Mary His mother and to all the saints, my body to be buried next to the grave of Matilda, lately my wife but now deceased. Item I bequeath to the repairs of the church of All Saints in the town of Northampton 20d. Item I bequeath to the fraternities of Holy Trinity, Holy Cross, St John the Baptist, St George the Martyr and St Katherine in that same church, that is to say to each of them 12d. The residue of all my goods not bequeathed above I give and bequeath to Edward Wellys my former servant that he might settle my debts and dispose for the health of my soul as seems best to him and I ordain, make and constitute that same Edward executor of this my testament. And so that this my last will should be faithfully fulfilled I constitute William Buckby supervisor. With these witnesses Master Robert Mydelham, vicar of the said church, Nicholas Buller, Thomas Mounforth, Richard Mason with many others.

f108r 382 WILLIAM WYNGE 4th May 1496 weaver

In Dei nomine Amen iiij die mensis Maii anno domini mccccclxxxxvj Ego Willelmus Wynge de Northampton wever compos mentis et sane memorie condo presens testamentum meum in hunc modum In primis lego animam meam Deo Omnipotenti etcetera corpusque meum sepiliendum
sub capella Sancti Georgii ecclesie Omnium Sanctorum ville Northampton iuxta sepulturam Alicie nuper uxoris mee
Item lego rectoribus ecclesie predicte pro decimis et oblacionibus oblitis seu negligenter detentis
iijs. iiijd. Item lego fraternitati Sancte Trinitatis in eadem ecclesia iijs.iiijd. Item lego fraternitati Corporis Christi in eadem ecclesia iijs.iiijd. Item fraternitati Beate Marie Virginis eiusdem
ecclesie iijs.iiijd. Item lego fraternitati Sancte Crucis in eadem ecclesia ijs. Item lego fraternitati Sancti
Georgii eiusdem ecclesie ijs. Item lego fraternitati Sancti Johannis Baptiste in dicta ecclesia ijs. Item lego fraternitati Sancte Katerine Virginis in le pardon chyrche yerd ijs. Item lego cuilibet domui fratrum mendicancium ville Northampton ad solemniter celebrandum exequias et missam
die obitus mei pro anima mea iijs.iiijd. Item lego pauperibus infra domum Sancti Thome Martiris extra portam australem dicte ville Northampton inter eos indifferenter distribuendum ad
orandum pro anima mea iijs.iiijd. item lego pauperibus infra domum Sancti Johannis Baptiste
ville predicte videlicet infirmeria ibidem iijs.iiijd. indifferenter distribuendum inter eos ad orandum
pro anima mea Item lego Thome Wynge de Stamford fratri meo ad orandum pro anima mea vjs.viijd. et unam togam coloris russett penulatam cum nigris agnis. Item lego Thome Wynge filio Johannis Wynge de Eston super montem ad orandum pro anima mea vjs.viijd. unam tunicam vocatam a duplett et unum par galigarum Item lego Thome Wyghtman de Weston Favell ad orandum pro anima mea vjs.viijd. Item lego Willelmo Shitlanger de Barton comitis et duobis filiis suis xxs. equaliter inter eos dividendum Item lego sustentacioni ecclesie de Eston predicte et pauperibus in eadem villa magis indigentibus vjs.viijd. videlicet ecclesie iijs.iiijd. et pauperibus ibidem iijs.iiijd.

In the name of God Amen the 4th day of May 1496 I William Wynge of Northampton, weaver, in sound mind and good memory make my testament in this wise. First I bequeath my soul to Almighty God etcetera my body to be buried under the chapel of St George in the church of All Saints Northampton next to the tomb of Alice, my late wife. Item I bequeath to the rectors of the aforesaid church for tithes and oblations forgotten or negligently withheld 3s 4d. Item I bequeath to the fraternity of Holy Trinity in the same church 3s 4d. Item I bequeath to the fraternity of Corpus Christi in the same church 3s 4d. Item I bequeath to the fraternity of the Blessed Virgin Mary in the same church 3s 4d. Item I bequeath to the fraternity of the Holy Cross in the same church 2s. Item I bequeath to the fraternity of St George in the same church 2s. Item I bequeath to the fraternity of St John the Baptist in the said church 2s. Item I bequeath to the fraternity of St Katherine the Virgin in le pardon chyrche yerd 2s. Item I bequeath to each house of mendicant brothers in the town of Northampton to solemnly celebrate exequies and mass on the day of my obit for my soul 3s 4d. Item I bequeath to the poor people within the house of St Thomas the Martyr outside the south gate of the said Northampton to be distributed between them without distinction to pray for my soul 3s 4d. Item I bequeath to the poor people in the house of St John the Baptist in the above town that is to say in the infirmary there 3s 4d to be distributed impartially between them to pray for my soul. Item I bequeath to Thomas Wynge of Stamford, my brother, to pray for my soul 6s 8d and one gown of russet colour furred with black lamb. Item I bequeath to Thomas Wynge, the son of John Wynge of Easton on the Hill, to pray for my soul 6s 8d and one tunic called a duplett and one pair of hose. Item I bequeath to Thomas Wyghtman of Weston Favell to pray for my soul 6s 8d. Item I bequeath to William Shitlanger of Earls Barton and his two sons 20s to be divided equally between them. Item I bequeath to the maintenance of the church of Easton aforesaid and for the poor in most need in the same town 6s 8d that is to say to the church 3s 4d and to the poor there 3s 4d.

f110r 387 ROGER BUTLER 24th November 1496 baker

In Dei nomine Amen the xxiiijth day of November the yere of ower Lorde God mcccc lxxxxvj I Roger Butler of Northampton baker seke in body and thankythe God hole in mynd and perfyte remembrans make this my present testament in forme folowyng
that ys to say firste I betake my soule to Almyghty God and to his mercy etcetera my body to be buryed wythin the parysh chyrche of Saynt Gregory in Northampton abovesayd Also I bequeth to the hygh auter in the same churche xxd. Item I bequeth to the reparaciones of the same churche iijs.iiijd. Also I bequeth to every place of the iiij cloysters of freres in Northampton to pray for my soule xxd. Also I wyll ther byth disposed the day of my burying or ellys as shortly after as may be conveniently emong pore

people and other as by myn executryce and overseers shalbe thought moste expedyent for
the helth of my soule xli. Also I bequeth to Alyce Butler doughter of John
Butler my son to hyr maryage yf shee lefe so longe cs. and yf shee dye before shee
be maryed than I wyl that the sayd cs. shalbe evynly distribute & dyvydet emong
other chylderne of the sayde John my son yf he have eny levyng and yf he have no chylde
levyng than I wyll the sayde John Butler my son have the same cs. to his own use for
evermore Also I bequeth to every mayde servant in my service beyng the day of my dethe
to pray for my soule xijd. and every of them oon payer of <shetis> Also I bequeth
to the chyrche of Edyngale iijs.iiijd. Item I bequeth to the sustentacion of pore
people in the howce of Saynt Thomas withoute the southe yate of Northampton to pray
for my soule iijs.iiijd. Also I bequeth to Margery my syster a maser Also I bequethe
to the foresayde John Butler my son a hole brode wollen clothe Also I bequeth to John
Butler my brothyr my blewe gown furet with frychens Also I bequeth to Herry Atthe-
wod of Bryngton my sangwyn gown furred with lambe Also I bequeth to the foresayde
John my son my grene gown Also I gyffe and bequeth to the fraternite of Blessed Rode in
Wall in the churche of Saynt Gregory abovesayd a yerely annuite of rente of iijs.iiijd.
goyng oute of al my closys and gardyns to them belonyng in the sayde paryssh of Saynt
Gregory to have and to holde to the same fraternite for evermore on this condicon that yf the
maisteres of the same fraternite for the tyme beyng yerely kepe or cause to be kept
an obite in the churche of Saynt Gregory afore sayde for my soule and pay to the prestes
and clarkys for the observance of the same xvjd. oute of the foresayde annuite and
yf yt happen in eny yere that the sayde obite be not kepte by the sayd maistyrs of
the same fraternite for the tyme beyng after the maner before rehersed than my wyll ys
that for that yere the sayde fraternite have no peny of the sayde annuite of iijs.iiijd. And yf
the
sayd obite be not kepte by the sayde maisteres by the space of ij yeres than I wyll
that the sayde annuitye of iijs.iiijd. then I wyll the sayde <annuitye> of iijs.iiijd.
holey reverte and retorn agayn to the sayde Alyce my wyfe and to my heyres for evermore
and the sayde fraternite therof utterly excludyd by this presentes Also yt ys my wyll
that the sayde Alice my wyfe after my discesse shal have all my landys and tenements with
theyr
apurtenances in this town of Northampton and ellys where for the terme of hyr lyfe
f110v
of the chefe lordys of the ffee etcetera and inmediatly after the decesse of the
sayde Alice my wyfe I wyll that all the foresayde landes and tenements with theyr
appurtenances in Northampton aforesayde and ellis where shall holely remayne
to the abovesayde John Butler my son to have and to holde to hym and to his heirs
and assignes for evermore of the chefe lords of the ffee etcetera yerely contentyng and
paying to the fraternite afore sayde the sayde annuyte of iijs.iiijd. in manner and
forme above rehersyd The resydue of all my gods and catelles above not
bequethed no disposed I wyll that my sayde wyfe Alice levyng sole not maryed
have theym to hyr own proper use and for <to> dispose them as shee shall thynke beste and
moste expedyent for my soule and hyr soule and all Crysten soules and yf yt fortune
the sayde Alice my wyfe to marie ayen then I wyll my sayde godes and catelles
above not disposed shall evenly be dyvyded in to two parties and the sayde Alice my
wyfe have the oon partye to hyr own use for evermore and the sayd John Butler my
son have the other halfe to his own proper use for evermore to pray for my soule and
of this my present <laste> wyll and testament I make and ordeyn the sayde Alice my wyf
myn executrice and for hyr gude ayde advyce and councell in performyng of the
same I make and ordeyn my forsayde brother John Butler and Herry Atthewod overseers
wrytin the day and yere above rehersed theys bering wittness master Thomas
Parmynter clerke master John Cokkes clerke Martyn Awte gentilman John Marshall atthe
Syngne of the Harpe fullar William Mall fuller and other

f111r 389 AGNES ROBERDES 7th February 1496 widow

In the name of God Amen the vijth day of the month of February the yere of ower
Lorde God mccccIxxxxvj I Agnes Roberdes of Northampton wedowe hole of mynd thanket be God
make and ordeyne this my present testament in manner hereafter saying that ys to say fyrste I beqwethe my soule to Almyghty God and to ower Lady Saynt Mary and to all the hole company of saynts
in heven my body to be buryed in the chapell of Ower Lady in the chyrche of All Halowes of Northampton by the sepulture of John Roberds late my husband Item I beqwethe
to the fraternite of Our Lady in the same chapell for my sepulture there vjs.viijd. Item I beqwethe to the fraternite of the Blessed Trinite in the same churche xijd. Item I bequeth to the fraternite
of Corpus Christy in the sayde churche xijd. Item to the fraternite of the Rode ther xijd. Item to the fraternite
of Saynte John in the same churche xijd. Item I bequeth to the reparacon of the hygh awter in Saynte Gyles churche in Northampton xijd. Item I bequeth to the hygh awter in Saynt Gregory chyrche
in the same town xijd. Item I bequeth to every howse of the fowre orders of freres in Northampton
to pray for my sowle xijd. Item I bequeth to the sustentacon of pore people in Saynt Thomas howce of Northampton to pray for my sowle ijs. Item I bequeth to every chylde of George Dyk
my son nowe levyng a brasse pott a brasse pan a basen and a laver of laton and to everyche of the
same chylder in money vjs.viijd. Item I bequeth fferthemore to Thomas the son of the sayd George
one of the sayde chylder a fetherbed a bolster a payer of shetes a coveryng of a bedd with barres of blue in the same a cupberd a spruce cheste and a chayer. Item I bequeth to Agnes the doghter of the same George one of the sayde chylder a rede gyrdyll with sylver and gilte harnesed Item I bequeth
to Margett Dyk anothyr of the chylder beforesayd anothyr gyrdyll of rede harneysed with sylver
Item I bequeth to Isabell the wyfe of the sayde George a gurdyll of grene harneysed with sylver and
gylte and a payer of bedes of corall with gawdes of sylver and gylte Also I wyll that the forsayde George my son shall yerely duryng the space of iiij yeres nexte after my decesse make and kepe or cause to be made and kept an obite with placebo and dyrige and masse of requiem where hym beste shall please to pray for my husbands soule my soule and all Crysten sowles and at every of the sayde obites he shall distribute emong prestes and clerkes and pore people moste nedyng as by hym and his overseer shalbe thought expedient in that behalfe vjs.viijd. And also I wyll that the sayde George my son immediately after my decesse shall have all my londes and tenements with theyr appurtenances in Northampton above sayde to have and
to hold to hym and to the heyres of his body lawfully bygoten for ever and more of the chefe lordes of the ffee etcetera And yf yt happen the sayde George or his heires of his body lawfully
begoten to decesse with oute heires of theyr bodyes lawfully begoten than I wyll that all the foresayde landes and tenements with theyr appurtenances shall holy remayne to the houce
of Saynt Thomas the Martyr withoute the southe yate of the town of Northampton aforesayd to have and to hold to the master of the same houce and to theyr successors to the use and profette

of the same for evermore yeldyng to the chefe lordes of ffee etcetera there perpetually to be prayed fore
The resydue of all my godes not above bequethed after my dettes be payed I gyffe holy and bequeth to foresayde George Dyk my son therewith to do and dispose for the helth of my sayd
husbands sowle my soule our' frendes sowles and all Cristen soules as he shall seme beste and
I make and ordeyn of this my present testament the sayde George my son myn executor and John Adams otherways cald John Umfrey draper to be his gude overseer in this behalfe these
bering wyntnes Syr John Brygeman preste Dame Elizabeth Saxby wedowe and Roger Prince wryter

f111v 390 MARGARETA HANRED 1496

In Dei nomine Amen anno domini millesimo cccclxxxx sexto Ego Margareta Hanred compos mentis et sane memorie tamen egre in corpore condo testamentum meum in hunc modum In primis
lego animam Deo Omnipotenti etcetera corpusque meum sepiliendum in cimiterio ecclesie Sancti
Sepulcri ville Northampton Item lego pro decimis et oblationibus meis oblitis viijd. Item lego ad reparacionem
eiusdem ecclesie viijd. Item do et lego omnia terras et tenementa mea in Skaldwell Faxton et Wold que fuit simplicis feodi Willelmo Hanred filio meo et Johanne uxori sue
et heredibus de corporibus eorundem procreatis et pro defectu exitus inter eosdem volo quod dicta terras
et tenementa integre remaneant proximiori sanguini imperpetuum Item do et lego Ricardo filio meo
unum croftum in Pysford ut iacet in Dagland et heredibus de corpore legitime procreatis pr[] quo volo quod reddet annuatim octo denarios pro missa et dirige
semel fiendum pro tempore perpetue videlicet quattuor denarios ad preces in pulpito et quatuor
denarios pro missa et dirige Item do et lego predicto Willelmo filio meo omnia bona mea mobilia et immobilia quem ordino et constituo meum executorem ad disponendum pro anima mea prout ei melius videbitur expediri hiis testibus magistro Roberto Preston vicario ecclesie parochie Sancti Sepulcri predicte Johanne Weste irnmonger Willelmo Philyp Thome Harteshorn
Johanne Cowper et aliis

In the name of God Amen 1496 I Margaret Hanred of sound mind yet sick in body make my testament in this wise. First I bequeath my soul to Almighty God etcetera my body to be buried in the cemetery of the church of the Holy Sepulchre in the town of Northampton. Item I bequeath for tithes and oblations forgotten 8d. Item I bequeath for the repair of the said church 8d. Item I give and bequeath all my lands and tenements in Scaldwell, Faxton and Old, which were in fee simple, to William Hanred, my son, and Joan his wife and to the heirs of his body lawfully begotten and for default of issue I will that the said lands and tenements should remain entirely to my next blood relative for ever. Item I give and bequeath to Richard, my son, a croft in Pitsford which lies in Dagland and to the heirs of his body legitimately begotten on behalf of whom I will that he should give annually eight pence for a mass and dirge to be given once a year forever, that is to say four pence for preaching from the pulpit and four pence for the mass and dirge. Item I give and bequeath to the said William, my son, all my goods movable and immovable whom I ordain and constitute my executor to dispose for the health of my soul as may seem best to him. These being witnesses Master Robert Preston, vicar of the parish of Holy Sepulchre, John West, ironmonger, William Philyp, Thomas Harteshorn, John Cowper and others.

f111v 391 JOHN ESEX 3rd March 1496 chandler

In the name of God Amen the thred day of Marche the yere of ower Lord God m-cccclxxxxvj I John Esex of Northampton chaundeler hole of mynd and gud remembrans ordayn and make my testament conteynyng my laste wyll in forme and maner folowyng fyrste I bequeth my soule to Almyghty God our Blessed Lady and all sayntes and my body to be buried within the paryssh chyrche of All Halowes in Northampton aforesayd in the
chapell of Corpus Christi before the sete under the grave stone of oon Geffery Halte ther buryed
Item I bequeth to the behofe of the fraternite of Corpus Christi for my sepulture vjs.viijd. Item I bequeth to the parsonnes of the same chyrche for my duetes forgoten or witholdyn ijs. I wyll that every preste that cometh to my diryge and masse of requiem and my buryng have for his labor iiijd. <and othyr of the clerks ijd.> Item I bequeth to Master Doctor Mydellham my curate
and gostly fathyr to <pray> for my sowle ijs. Item I wyll that the day of my buryng Agnes my wyfe dele or cause to be delt among pore peopull in farthyng bred
and in mete and drynke at dyner emonge syche as she shall please then xls. Item I bequeth to every house of the iiij orders of freres in Northampton to pray for my sowle xxd. so that of every
the sayde howse there be one preste present to helpe at my dirige and masse the day of my burying Item I bequeth to the fraternite of the Blessed Rode in All Halowe chyrche above xijd. Item I bequeth to the fraternite of Saynt John Baptiste in the same chyrche xijd. Item to the fraternite of Saynte George in the same chyrche xijd. Item I bequeth to the fraterniti
of Saynt Kateryn in the pardon chyrche yerd in All Halowe paryssh xijd. item I bequeth to the
fraternite of the Blessed Rode in the Wall in Saynt Gregory chyrche of the sayde town xijd. Item I bequeth to the fraternite of Saynt Pulcre in the chyrche of Saynt Pulcre the same town viijd. Item I bequeth to the fraternite of Saynt Thomas the Martyr without the south yate of the same town of Northampton xijd. Item I bequeth to the fraternite of Saynt
Clement in the chyrche of Saynt Gyle in the same town viijd. Item to the fraternite of Saynt Michael in the sayde town iiijd. Item to the fraternite of Saynt Kateryn in the chyrche of Saynt Marie in the same town viijd. Item I bequeth to the fraternite of Saynt Ruginary in the paryssh chyrche of Saynt Peter in the same town iiijd. Item I wyll that <my> ffeoffes inmedatly after the decese of Agnes my wyfe make or cause to be made and dylyver or cause to be dylyveryt a lawfull estate and dilyvere of season of and

f112r

in the ffyssh stall as yt standyth in the fysh market in the town of Northampton abovesayd with all appertenances

as William Sywell fyssher hath yt nowe to syche persones of Saynt Peter paryssh as shalbe then rewlers there to the use and behofe of the ffysshers lyght in the same chyrche of Saynt Peter founded
after custome and maner therof afore tyme ordeyned to have and to hold to theym & to theyr successors
for ever more of the chefe lord of the fee etcetera Item I wyll that Agnes my wyfe

N.B. *The rest of page is blank.*

f114v 401 JOHN EGREMOND 5th December 1497

In Dei nomine Amen quinto die mensis Decembris anno domini mccccclxxxxvij Ego Johannes Egremond de Northampton sane mentis etcetera condo testamentum meum in hunc modum
In primis lego animam meam Deo Omnipotenti Beate Marie et omnibus sanctis corpusque meum
sepiliendum in cimiterio ecclesie Omnium Sanctorum ville Northampton Item lego unum tenementum cum
pertinenciis suis jacentem in ville de Eydon in comitatu Northampton Willelmo Halowton et Elizabeth uxori eius et post decessum illorum lego predictum tenementumWillelmo
filio dicti Willelmi Halowton Item lego fraternitati Sancte Trinitatis in ecclesia predicta xijd. Item
lego fraternitati Sancte Katerine xijd. Item fraternitati Sancti Johannis xijd. Item lego summo altari
pro decimis oblitis viijd. Item fabrice ecclesie matricis Lincoln jd. Residuum vero bonorum non legatorum lego Willelmo Halowton seniori quem constituo executorem meum ut disponendum
bona non legata ut ei melius videbitur expediri saluti anime mee hiis testibus Johanne Almey et Johanne Clerke

In the name of God Amen the fifth day of December 1497 I John Egremond of Northampton in good memory etcetera. First I bequeath my soul to Almighty God, to the Blessed Mary and all the saints, my body to be buried in the cemetery of the church of All Saints in the town of Northampton. Item I bequeath one tenement with its appurtenances lying in the town of Eydon in the county of Northampton to William Halowton and Elizabeth, his wife, and after their death I bequeath the aforesaid tenement to William, son of the said William Halowton. Item I bequeath to the fraternity of the Holy Trinity in the said church 12d. Item I bequeath to the fraternity of St John 12d. Item I bequeath to the high altar for tithes forgotten 8d. Item to the fabric of the mother church at Lincoln 1d. The residue of my goods not bequeathed I bequeath to William Halowton senior whom I constitute my executor in order to dispose my goods not bequeathed as seems best to him for the health of my soul. With these witnesses John Almey and John Clerke.

f116r 408 WILLIAM HALOWTON 1498 fuller

In the name of God Amen the yere of ower lord God mccccclxxxxviij I William Halowton of Northampton fuller in my hole mynde make my testament in this manner and forme folowyng First I beqweth my sowle to Almyghty God and to the <Blessed> mayde Mary his mothyr and to all the company of hevyn my body to be buryed in All Halowe chyrche yerd in the town of Northampton Ferthermore I beqweth to the chyrche warke of the same viijd. Item I beqweth to the reparacon of the canopy before the hee awter xxd. Item I beqweth to Herry Halowton my brother all the stuffe that longyth to my shope as wele the Walkers erthe as handylls and burlyngs yrnes with all othyr stuff Item I bequeth to William Halowton my son a houce with appurtenances in the town of Eydon after the decesse of Elizabeth my wyfe whiche was John Egremond my wyffe father Item I bequeth to William Halowton my son a peece of sylver and vj of my beste sylver sponys and the counter that standyth in the hall and my beste maser save oon that my wyfe shall have Item I bequeth to the same William my son my brasse potts my wyfe to chose the beste pott and my sonn ye Depute the nexte as long as my potts com to Item halfe a garnyssh of pewter vessel and iij of the best basynnes and iij of beste lavers save my wyfe shall chose one of the beste to hyrself Item I bequeth to William my son ij payre of the beste shetis and a payer of blanketts and a coverlett of tapestre warke with all othyr that my fathyr Egremond dyd bequeth to hym Item I bequeth to Herry Halowton wyfe my beste pott also I wyll that my brother Herry Halowton have the gydyng of William my son and all the gods that I have bequeste to hym And the resydue of my gods not bequethed I bequeth to Elizabeth my wyff shee to be myn executrix with my brother Herry Halowton they to dispose for my soule as yt shall please them wittnesses Herry Wodcok and Richard Grevys

f117r 410 NICHOLAS BOWKER 12th April 1498 fuller

In Dei nomine Amen the xijth day of Apryll the yere of our lord God mccccclxxxviij I Nicholas Bowker of Northampton fuller hole in mynde thanked be God ordeyn and make my testament and laste wyll in maner and forme hereafter sayng that ys to say fyrste I bequeth my soule to Almyghty God and to our Blessed Lady Saynt Mary the Vyrgin and to all the hole company of hewyn and my body to beryed in the chyrche yerd of All Halowes chyrche of the town of Northampton abovesayde Item I bequeth to the parsons of the same chyrche for my tythes and offeryngs forgoten negligently or wronngafly witholdyn vjs.viijd. Item I bequeth to Master Robert Mydelham Doctor and vicar of the sayde chyrche my gostely father to pray for my sowle xxd. Item I bequeth to Jone Bowker my wyfe all hyr apparell belongyng to hyr body with hyr gyrdylls beds brochys and ryngs theroppon hangyng and in money or ellys in godes to hyr necessary and behovefull xxti markes and shee noferthir to mell bot as shee and Roger Bowker my son can agree Also I bequeth to Johan Bowker my doghter yf she leve to lawfull age to be maryed to pray for my soule vjli. fferthermore I woll that Roger Bowker my son have all the termes of my house in the whiche nowe I dwell without the southe yate of the town abovesayde with the warke house within the same beyng and all the moveabyll gods that I have and detts whatsoever they be and in whosoever hands they may be found within the sayde town or elys where within the realme of England to thentent that he shall pay my deues whyche I owe to any maner of persones so ferre as any penyworth of my gods woll stretche and also I make and ordeyn of this my present testament and laste wyll the sayde Roger my son to performe this my wyll above rehersed myn executor and for his ayde councell and lawfull supportacon in this behalfe I make and ordeyn Henry Humfrey of Northampton mercer

oversear of this my wyll to be observed and he to have for his labor vjs.viijd. In wittnes
whereof to this my testament and laste wyll I have sett my seale the day and yere
above wrytin These wyttnesses the foresayd Master Robert Mydelham Doctor my gostly father
John Walker wever Thomas Mounford fuller and other moo

f117v 412 ROGER PRYNCE 1st May 1498 (scribe)

In the name of God Amen the fyrste day of May in the yere of ower lord God
mcccclxxxxviij I Roger Prynce of Northampton hole of mynde thanks
be ower Lord God make and ordeyn my testament in form hereafter ensuyng
that ys to say fyrste I bequeth my soule to Almyghty God and to Ower Blessed
Lady Saynt Marye and to all the company of sayntys in heven and my body to be
buryed in the chyrche yerd of the parysh chyrche of All Hallowes Northampton
aforesayde Item I bequeth to the parsunys of the same chyrche for my
tythes forgoten or witholde xijd. Item I bequeth to the fraternite of the Blessed
Rode in the same chyrche xijd. Item I bequeth to John Pryce my servant my
shorte musterdeveleys gown a materas j payer of shetes a rede coverlet for a
bed and yf my dettes com in I wyll he have xxs. and Gods blessyng and myn
The residue of all my godes above nott beqwethed after my dettes payed I holy giff
and bequeth to Elsabeth my wyfe therwith to do and dispose for thelthe of my soule
etcetera as <by> hyr shalbe thoght moste nedefull and expedient and I make and ordeyn the
sayde Elsabeth my wyfe myn executrice and overseer with hyr I ordeyn and make master Henry
Umfrey yf yt plese hym to take the labor and he <to> have for his labor vjs.viijd.

f119v 421 WILLIAM DONETT 13th April 1497

In the name of God Amen the xiijth day of Apryll in the yere of
our lord mcccclxxxxvij I William Donett hole of mynd make my testament
in this wyse first I bequeth my soule to Almyghty God etcetera and my body
to be buryed in the chyrche yerd of All Halowes Also I make and ordeyn
Johanne <my> wyfe to be my sole executrice and she to have all hyr gods movabyll
and un movabyll to hyr own use and profett and she for to dispose my godys and
pay my detts and when my detts bith payed she to be gude special
frend to my chylder as hyr consciens wyll bynd hyr and also I gyff to
the reparacon of All Halowe chyrche xijd. and to the fraternite of the Rode
viijd. to the hygh awter in the same chyrche xijd. Item to the chirche of
Lincoln iiijd. to the fraternite of Saynt Katerine viijd. to the fraternite of Saynt
George viijd. theys beyng record Master Robert Mydlam Doctor of Divinite my cu[rate]
John Herrys and Elizabeth Say

f121r 426 JOHN PALMER 20th November 1500 chaplain

In Dei nomine Amen xx die mensis Novembris anno domini millesimo quingentesimo Ego Johannes Palmer
capellanus cantarie Sancte Katerine in ecclesia Beate Marie ville Northampton compos mentis etecetera condo
testamentum meum in hunc modum In primis lego animam meam Deo Omnipotenti etcetera corpusque

meum sepiliendum coram ymaginem Sancte Katerine Virginis in capella eiusdem Virginis infra dictam ecclesiam
Item lego rectori eosdem ecclesia pro mortuario meo quod licitum fuerit haberi Item lego domino Stephano
canonico monasterii Sancti Jacobi iuxta Northampton unum lez ffetherbed cum lez bolster et selor Item lego Alicie
Chessyre cognate mee unam fulcrum unum coopertorium insertum cum albis lilys Item lego Johanne Walsonhed unum fulcrum cum coopertorio rubio et uno par linthiamentum Item lego Thome Palmer filio
fratris mei de Duston unam togam usualem et deploidem cum ceteris indumentis quotidianis
corpore mee pertinencis Item lego Johanne Palmer filie predicte Thome Palmer unum plater Item lego Johanni Palmer filio Ricardi Palmer meam togam optimam Item lego Thome Palmer
filio Thome Palmer unam pelvim cum lavacro Item lego Agneti Parker de Hanging Hoghton filiole meo j spete et ij cobards Item lego Willelmo Terry de Maydford oon chymor
Item lego Willelmo Barton filio Johannis Barton meum portiferium Item lego Margerie filie filie Willelmo Barton unam cistam Item lego Ricardo Tarry unum par linthiamentum Residuum vero omnium
bonorum meorum non legatorum totaliter do et lego domino Johanni Grene rectori dicte ecclesie Beate Marie
et Thome Adams bocher quos ordino executores meos ad disponandum pro salute anime mee
etcetera prout eis melius videbitur expediri preterea lego dicto Thome Adams unum goblet de argento Hiis testibus Willelmo Stonys monacho prioratus Sancti Andree ville Northampton domino
Stephano canonico monasterii Sancti Jacobi iuxta Northampton Ricardo Oxon' Roberto Poyte et aliis

In the name of God Amen the 20th day of November 1500 I John Palmer, chaplain of the little chapel of St Katherine in the church of St Mary in the town of Northampton, in sound mind etcetera make my testament in this wise. First I bequeath my soul to Almighty God etcetera, my body to be buried before the image of St Katherine the Virgin in the chapel of the said Virgin in the said church. Item I bequeath to the rector of the said church for my mortuary what is lawful to have. Item I bequeath to Dom Stephen, canon of the monastery of St James near Northampton the featherbed with the bolster and selor. Item I bequeath to Alice Chesshyre, my kinswoman, one bed, one coverlet decorated with white lilies. Item I bequeath to John Walsenhed one bed with a red coverlet and one pair of sheets. Item I bequeath to Thomas Palmer, son of my brother of Duston, one ordinary gown and doublet with the rest of the ordinary wear belonging to my body. Item I bequeath to Joan Palmer, daughter of the said Thomas Palmer, one platter. Item I bequeath to John Palmer, son of Richard Palmer, my best gown. Item I bequeath to Thomas Palmer, son of Thomas Palmer, one basin and ewer. Item I bequeath to Agnes Parker of Hanging Houghton, my goddaughter, one spit and 2 cobirons. Item I bequeath to William Terry of Maidford one chymor. Item I bequeath to William Barton, son of John Barton, my breviary. Item I bequeath to

Margery, daughter of William Barton, one chest. Item I bequeath to Richard Terry one pair of sheets. The residue of all my goods not bequeathed I wholly give and bequeath to Dom John Grene, rector of the said church of St Mary, and Thomas Adams, butcher, whom I ordain my executors to dispose for the health of my soul as seems best to them. In addition I bequeath to the said Thomas Adams one silver goblet. With these witnesses William Stonys, canon of the monastery of St James near Northampton, Richard Oxon', Robert Poyte and others.

f123v 440 THOMAS SYMSON 3rd January 1500 fuller

In the name of God Amen the iij day of January the yere of our Lord God mccccc I Thomas Symson of Saynt Edmunds Ende fuller hole of mynde make my testament in this manner Fyrst I bequethe my soule to Almyghty God etcetera my body to be buryed in the chyrche of Saynd Edmond and thyrefor I bequeth to makyng of the same chyrche iijs.iiijd. Also I bequethe to the mothyr chyrch of Lincoln ijd. Also I gyffe and bequethe to Robert Shefford
goldsmyth my bryconders with al my complete harnes and all my byllys Item I bequethe my horne to the chapell of Corpus Christi there to remayn for ever to the use of Robyn Hode to have on Wytson Monday and all othyr tymes when hee (he) nede Item I bequeth to John Lake my beste gown Item I bequeth to Robert Symson my beste dowblett and my beste
hosys Item I bequeth to Elizabeth Lake iij pewter dysshes iij sawcers j candylstyk j payer of shetes I bequeth to Robert Anderson j payer of shetes j brasse pott of iij galons j blanket and j coverlett The residue of my godes not bequethed I gyffe and bequeth to William Tomson wever to gyff and distribute for the welthe of my soule and all my benefactors whom I make myn executor theys beyng wittnes Robert Shefford goldsmyth Thomas Mulso and Thomas Kesten with moo

f123v 441 ALICE HOPWOD 27th December 1500 widow

In the name of God Amen the xxvij day of December in the yere of our Lorde God mccccc I Alice Hopwod of Northampton wedowe othyr ways cald Alice Aprees of the parissh of
Saynt Peter in the town of Northampton hole of mynd make my testament in this maner Fyrste
I bequeth my soule to Almyghty God etcetera my body to buryed in the chauncell of the paryssh
chyrch of Saynt Peter befor sayde Item I bequeth to the awter cloth of Our Lady ther xijd.
f124r
Item I bequeth for j auter clothe for the awter of Saynt John in the same chyrche xijd. Item I bequeth for a auter cloth for the awter of Saint Nicholas in the same chirche xijd. Item I bequeth for a auter cloth for the awter of Saynt Katheryn in the same chirche xijd. Item I bequeth
to the rep(ar)acon of the bellys in the same chyrche xijd. Item to the mothyr chirche of Lincoln
iiijd. Item I bequeth to Sir John Hopwod my son a cheste that ys to say the (wars) of [ ] and iij payer of shetis vj silver sponys of lightyste Item I bequeth to Gregory Hopwod my son j fethir bed with a bolster j materes ij blankettes a coverlet and iij payer of shetes

and j nothyr payer of corse shetes iiij small pottes of brasse iij brasse panays and
j water chafer j bason and j laver of luton j chasyng dyssh iiij candillstykkes ij cofers j folden
tabull iiij sylver sponys and j lytell maser with a band of sylver and gylte Item I woll that my
pari[]
pece of sylver and gilt with a fote be evenly distibuted betwen my iij sonys that ys to say
Sir John Gregory and Robert under this condicon that Robert my son gyf to Sir John for his
quantite after the rate and to Gregory for his parte after the rate in lyke condicon Item I bequeth
to Alice Inlis my servant j pott of iij galons ij blanketts j payer of shetes j coverlett and j
panne of brasse Item I bequeth to Alice Horpoll my god doghter j pott and j panne of brasse
Item I bequeth to Margett Lodyngton j corse gyrdull harnesyed with silver and my beste gowne
save oone Item I bequeth to William Weste my godson j sylver spone Item I bequeth to
Kateryn
Petyver j lytell olde corse harnysed with silver Item I bequeth to my brothyr William Horpoll
the ponde yard with appurtenances as he hath occupyed a foretyme the reversyon of my
yers paying therfor yerely to Robert Hopwod my son during the the terme xijd. The
residue of all my godes movabull and unmovabull not bequethed I gyff and bequeth to
Robert Hopwod my son and the same Robert I ordynge and make myn executor he to
dispose
for the helthe of my soule as semys beste to please God and Simon supervisor of this
present testament and he have for his labor x marks thyes bering record Sir John Hund prest
ther William Horpoll William Dawes and othyr moo

N.B. *This will has a torn right hand edge.*

f124r 442 JOHN ASSHBORN' 20th October 1500 (mercer)

In Dei nomine Amen xx die mensis Octobris anno domini mccccc Ego Johannes Asshborn' de Northampton
compos mentis etcetera condo testamentum meum in hunc modum In primis lego animam meam Deo Omnipotenti
etcetera corpusque meum sepiliendum in capella Beate Marie Virginis in ecclesia Omnium Sanctorum ville
Northampton predicta iuxta tumulum Johannis Asshborn patris mei Item lego predicte capelle residuum
omnium annorum et terminorum meorum quos habeo in uno tenemento in Veteri Draperia situato quod nuper
fuit in tenura Johannis Russden mercer inter tenementum fraternitatis Sancte Crucis in Muro ex parte borialis et
tenementum Abbatis Sancti Jacobi iuxta Northampton ex parte australi Item lego summo altari in ecclesia Omnium Sanctorum
predicta pro decimis oblitis xijd. Item lego matrici ecclesie Lincoln iiijd. Item lego Elene uxori
mee meam optimamque togam et quadraginta solidos bone monete Anglie solvendum ad Festum Pasche
proximo post datam presencium aceciam do et lego prefate Elene in quolibet anno durante vita sua
xiijs iiijd bone monete etcetera ad quattuor anni terminos videlicet Festa Nativitatis Sancti Johannis Sancti Michaelis
Archangeli Nativitatis Domini et Pasche per equales porciones Item do et lego dicte Elene dimidiam partem
omnium bonorum meorum mobilium Residuum vero bonorum meorum superius non legatorum do et
lego Willelmo Asshborn filio meo et eundem Willelmum ordino et constituo executorem meum

ut ipse disponat pro salute anime mee prout sibi melius videbitur expediri Hiis testibus Magistro Roberto Mydelham doctore Willelmo Mownford notario et aliis

In the name of God Amen the 20th October 1500 I, John Asshborn of Northampton, in sound mind etcetra make my testament in this wise. First I bequeath my soul to Almighty God etcetera my body to be buried in the chapel of the Blessed Virgin Mary in the church of All Saints of the said town of Northampton near the grave of John Asshborn my father. Item I bequeath to the said chapel the residue of all my years and terms which I have in a tenement situated in the Old Drapery which was formerly in the possession of John Russden, mercer, between the tenement of the fraternity of the Holy Cross in the Wall on the north side, and the tenement of the Abbot of St James by Northampton on the south side. Item I bequeath to the high altar in the church of All Saints aforesaid for tithes forgotten iiijd. Item I bequeath to the mother church of Lincoln 4d. Item I bequeath to Elen, my wife, my best gown and forty shillings of good English money to be paid at Easter next after the giving of these presents and also I give and bequeath to the aforesaid Elen 13s 4d of good money in each year during her life at the four terms of the year, that is the feast of the Nativity of St John, St Michael the Archangel, the Nativity of the Lord and Easter by equal portions. Item I give and bequeath to the said Elen a half part of all my movable goods. The residue of all my goods above not bequeathed I give and bequeath to William Asshborn, my son, and I ordain and appoint the same William as my executor to dispose for the health of my soul as seems best to him. These witnesses Master Robert Mydelham, Doctor, William Mounford, notary, and others.

f127v 462 WALTER ROWE 1st May 1501 fuller

In the name of God Amen the fyrste day of May in the yere of our Lord God mcccccj
I Walter Rowe of Northampton fuller hole of mynde make my testament in this wyse Fyrste
I bequeth my soule to Almyghty God etcetera my body buryed in the chirche yarde of All
Halowes of Northampton foresaid Item I bequeth to the reparacon of the same chirche xijd.
Item
I bequeth to the fraternite of the Rode in the same chirche xijd. Item to the mothyr chirche
of Lincoln ijd. Item I bequeth to Jeffrey Marshe of Dalyngton a gown the Residue of my
my gods above not bequethed I gyff and bequeth to Johan my wyfe to dispose for me in
maner

f128r

in maner and forme here folowyng that ys to say fyrste to pay my detts and to bryng my
body to the grownd and after that chearge don I wyll my gods byth dyvydyt in thre
partys of the whiche I wyll that my wyfe have ij partys and William Rowe to
have the thred parte and the sayde Johan my wyfe I make myn executrice to
dispose for my soule as shee may see beste to please god Thyes beryng witnes
Master Robert Midelham Doctor William Marshe roper John Wodford Robert Story and
othyr mo

f128r 463 JOHN PAGE 2nd April 1501 draper

In the name of God Amen the ij day of Apryll in the yere of our Lord God mcccccj I John Page of Northampton draper hole of mynd make my testament in this wyse Firste I bequeth my soule to Almyghty God etcetera my body to be buryed in the chapell of Our Lady within the
chirche of All Halowes of the town of Northampton Also I bequeth to the parson of the same chyrche for tythes for yeten xiid. Item to the reparacon of the same chyrche xxd.
Item to the iiij fraternites lawer in the same chyrche to yche fraternite xijd. Item to the pore people of Saynte Thomas howe xijd. Also I bequeth to Annes my wyfe all the yern ware and treeme ware within my shoppe here and at Daventre and my beste salte covered ij masers during
hyr lyfe and after hyr decesse oon of the masers to remayn to Elsabeth my doghter
and the othyr to gyffe and to sell Also my wyfe shall have as myche ware as comythe
to (xlljs) xlvjs.viijd. all hyr wering gere and stuffe my beste pott my best panne
a sylver pece and halfe off all my howsold stuffe paying towards my dettes xlvjs.viijd. Also shee shall have my howses nexte chyrche in Kyngesthorp duryng hyr lyfe and after hyr decess to remayn to Robert my son and to hys heirs of his body lawfully begoten
and yf he decesse withoute heyrs then to remayn to the chauntre of Kyngesthorp
foresaid Also my wyfe shall have j quateron of medowe lying over the southe syde of
the said town Also I bequeth to Robert my son and to his heires of his body lawfully begoten my garett house in Kyngesthorpe befor saide v acres of arabull land and ij quaterens of medowe and yf he decesse then to remayn to Agnes my wyfe duryng hyr lyfe and
and after hyr decesse I wyll the sayde garet house be sold and done for Stewyn Shepard soule and all Cresten soules Also I gyffe to Robert my sonn a maser a sylver salte vj sylver sponys
my beste gown ffurrett all my clothe and hosys within my shopp and v mark in money
and yf the said Robert my son decesse then I wyll that all his bequests in godes beth
departed in thre parties oon parte to have a trentall and be distribute emongs pore
people and othyr gude dedes of mercy the second parte to be gevyn after the discrecons and mynde of my supervisors and the thred parte to Agnes my wyfe Also I bequeth to the
monastery of Saynt Jamys [?s.] Item to the chapell of Marchyngton vjs viijd. Item to the chyrche
of Navisby ijs. Item to the chirche of Kyngesthorp xxd. Item to chyrche of Dalyngton
xxd. Item to the chyrche of Horpoll xxd. Item to the iiij orders of freres yche order
xxd. Item I bequeth to Elsabeth my doghter Colkens house duryng hyr lyfe and after
hyr decesse to remayn to John hyr son and his heirys and yf he dee without heirs of his body lawfully begoten then to remayn to Herry my brothyr and to his heirs Also I
gyffe to Elsabeth my doghter in howsold stuffe to the valor of xls. and yf Robert my
son decesse ix marke in money and a maser and after the decesse of my wyfe my second silver salte and vj sylver sponys Item I gyffe to John Pace my son my tawney gown newe
Item I bequeth to John the son of the same John Pace xxs. Item I bequeth to my syster
Ysod in housold stuff xxs. and in money xs. my lytell maser with a preynt lyke
a [doufe/donse] v acres of land ij quaterens of medowe and my sangwen gown and to hyr

f128v

and to hyr husband my violett gown and to yche of hyr childer xijd. Item I bequeth to Harry Page my brothyr a golde rynge with a ston my russet gown furryt with fox and xxs.
in money Item to his wyfe xijd. & to yche of his childer xijd. Item I wyll ther be a
trentall don for me and one for my mothyr and a preste for on holl yere and he to have
for his wages viij marks Item I bequeth to Robert Holme iij yerdes of violet The

residue of all my godes not bequethed I gyff to Agnes my wyfe the whiche Agnes and Herry my brothyr I make and ordeyn myn executors Also I make Master Doctor Mydelham my curate and Edward Chamerleyn my supervisors and I wyll that yche of them have for his labor vjs.viijd. Theys witnes John Obowores draper Robert Poyte wever John Bromley sharman John Pace bowear and aliis ibidem congregatis

f129r 466 JOAN JACOB 28th February 1500 widow

In Dei nomine Amen penultimo die mensis Februarii anno domini millesimo quingentesimo Ego [Johanna]
nuper uxor Thome Jacob de Cotton iuxta Northampton defuncti condo testamentum meum in hunc modum
In primis lego animam meam Deo Omnipotenti etcetera corpusque sepiliendum in cimiterio ecclesie Sancti Leonardi de Cotton predicte Item lego lumini Sancti Leonrdi ibidem xxd. Item lego
matrici ecclesie Lincoln iiijd Item lego Isabelle filie mee uxori Ricardi Bayle de Northampton corvesor meam optimam zonam Item lego Margarete Jacob filie mee <totum> illud tenementum meum predictum
situatur in Cotton predicte cum suis pertinenciis habendum et tenendum totum predictum tenementum cum
suis pertinenciis prefate Margarete ac heredibus suis sorpore sue legitime procreatis inperpetuum de capitalibus
dominis feodi illius per servicia inde debita et de iure consueta et si contingat dictam Margaretam obire sine heredibus de corpore sue legitime procreatis quod absit tunc volo quod totum predictum
tenementum cum suis pertinenciis remaneat prefate Isabelle filie mee et heredibus de corpore suo legitime procreatis imperpetuum tenendum de capitalibus dominis feodi per servicia etcetera et si contingat
dictam Isabellam obire sine heredibus de corpore suo legitime procreatis tunc volo quod dictum
tenementum revertatur rectis heredibus meis imperpetuum tenendum de capitalibus dominis feodi per servicia predicta
Item lego pauperibus magis indegentibus in panibus et pecunia muneratis iijs.iiijd. Item lego presbytris et clericis et aliis expensis funeralibus meis in die sepulture mee secundum discrecionem executorum meorum Reiduum vero omnium bonorum meorum superius non legatorum
debitis meis per executores meos solutis volo equaliter dividi inter predictas Margaretam et Isabellam
filias meas et prefatam Margaretam et Willelmum Marshall de Northampton ac Willelmum Maryet de
Cotton predicte ordino executores meos etcetera et utraque eorum habebit pro labore suo xx? et Johannem Smyth de Northampton baker facio huius testamenti mei supervisorem hiis [testibus]
testibus Willelmo Mownford notario et aliis

In the name of God Amen the 28th day of February 1500 I Joan Jacob, lately wife of Thomas Jacob of Cotton near Northampton, deceased, make my testament in this wise. First I bequeath my soul to Almighty God etcetera, my body to be buried in the cemetery of the church of St Leonard of Cotton

aforesaid. Item I bequeath to the light of St Leonard 20d. Item I bequeath to the mother church of Lincoln 4d. Item I bequeath to Isabel my daughte, wife of Richard Bayle of Northampton, corvisor, my finest girdle. Item I bequeath to Margaret Jacob, my daughter, all my tenement aforesaid situated in Cotton aforesaid with its appurtenances to have and to hold the said tenement with its appurtenances to the said Margaret, and the heirs of her body legitimately begotten, forever of the chief lords of the fee by services therefore due and by right accustomed. And if it should happen that the said Margaret should die without heirs of her body legitimately begotten then I will that all the aforesaid tenement with its appurtenances remain to the aforesaid Isabel, my daughter, and the heirs of her body legitimately begotten forever of the chief lords of the fee by services etcetera. And if it should happen that the said Isabel should die without heirs of her body legitimately begotten then I will that the said tenement should revert to my right heirs to hold forever of the chief lords of the fee by services aforesaid. Item I bequeath to the most needy poor 3s 4d in bread and money. Item I bequeath to the priests and clerks and my other funeral expenses on the day of my burial according to the discretion of my executors. The residue of all my goods not bequeathed above after my executors have paid my debts I will that they should be equally divided between the said Margaret and Isabel, my daughters. The said Margaret and William Marshall of Northampton and William Maryet of Cotton aforesaid I ordain my executors etcetera and each of them shall have for his labout 20[d] and John Smythe of Northampton, baker, I make supervisor of this will. With these witnesses William Mownford, notary, and others.

N.B. *The margin note gives this name as Joyce. Possibly a misreading of the final b as an s and Jacos could be a form of Joyce.*

f129v 468 NICHOLAS SMALLAY 17th March 1500

In Dei nomine Amen in the yere of our lord God mccccc the xvij day of March I Nicholas Smallay of Northampton beyng in gude mynd bequeth my soule to Almyghty God etcetera my body to be buryed in the chirche yard of Saynt Peter in Northampton Also I bequeth to thygh awter the j awter cloth and to Saynt Riginary j awter cloth Item j taper of dimidia of wax to brynin before our Lady Item I bequeth to my eldest son j fethyrbed j bolster j pelowe j payer of shetes j payer of blanketts a coveryng of tapestry warke and j testur Item I bequeth to my younger son j fethyrbed j bolster j pelow j payer of blanketts j payer of shetes the second coverled in the houce and j testur Item I wyll ther shalbe sold xxti shepe and v lamys and the money that they bith sold forer I wyll my wyfe have the increase theroff and then I wyll the money go to my childern that this shepe bith sold for The residue of my gods movable and un moveabull I gyffe to my wyfe and I make hyr my sole executrice she to receyfe my detts and shee to pay my detts Also I wyll yf God send his fonde of dethe to my childern I wyll my wyfe have theyer parte and yf God send visit of dethe to my wyfe (to my wyfe) I wyll my childer have that shee levyth and pay my detts

f133r 487 JOHN NEWLAND 19th July 1501 shearman

In the name of God Amen the xixth Daye of July in the yere of our Lord God mccccc
and one I John Newland of Northampton sherman hole of mynd make my testament
in this wyse First I bequeth my soule to Almyghty God etcetera my body to be buryed
in the churche yerd of All Halowys in Northampton Item I bequeth to thigh awte ther for forgoten
tythis xijd. Item I bequeth to the mothyr chirche of Lincoln ijd. Item I wyll j trentall
of massys be don for my soule by the distrecon of master doctor and he to have therfor xs.
The residue of my godes not bequethyd I gyffe and bequeth to Elsabeth my wyfe
and the same Elzabeth I make myn executrice she to dispose for the helth of
my soule as shee seyth beste to please God and Master Doctor Midelham and Adam Hochyson
sadeler overseers of this present testament Thyes witnes William Mowford
notary William Hull and othyr

f133r 488 RICHARD HOBBIS 4th January 149[ ]

In the name of God Amen the iiijth day of January in the yere of our Lord God
mccccclxxxx' I Richard Hobbis of the parysh of Saynt Gyle in Northampton hole
of mynd make my testament in this maner Fyrste I bequeth my soule to God
Almyghty etcetera my body to be buryed in the chirche of Saynt Gyle befor sayd
befor the cricifix ther Item I bequeth to thigh awter of the same chirche
for offerynges and tithis forgoten iijs iiijd. Item I bequeth to the lyght of
Saynt Clement in the same chyrche ijlb wax Item I bequeth <to light of> Saynt Mary of
Pety ther ijlb wax Item I bequeth to the reparacons of the paryssh chyrche of
Mulso in the countie of Bukks xls. Item I bequeth to the same chirche of Mulso
j blak cope of worsted to be boght by advyse of Thomas Hobbis my son and of Mawde
my wyfe the same cope to be occupied in the same chirche yerely the Sunday
before Michalmass Day specially at the diryge of Nicholas Hobbis and Johan his
wyfe my fathyr and my mother and on the morn' after theyr masse havyng in theyr
remembrans me and my three wyfes and al our childers soules and all Crysten soulys and the
same cope to be occupyed at the buryng and all housylbing of peopull in the same
parysh as long as yt wyll laste Item I bequeth to everych of my godchilder in money xijd.
Item I bequeth to the mothyr chyrche of Lincoln iiijd. Item I gyffe and bequeth to Agnes

f133v

and Johan my doghtyrs to everyeche of them in valor of stuff of howsold
or in money xxvjs.viijd. and to eyther of them iiij sylver sponys.
Item I bequeth to Mawde my wyfe all the residue of my stuff of howsold
and all hyr own stuffe on worn Item I bequeth to my sayde wyfe vj sylver
sponys nexte after vj the beste i salte with a cover parcell gylte Item I bequeth to
Thomas my son a lytyll maser notte with a cover harnest with silver and gilte and vj silver
sponys of the beste and all the risidue of my silver plate above not bequethed
I wyll yt be distribute in iij partys of the whiche I wyll my wyfe chese
firste and the othyr ij partys dyvydyd betwix my ij doghters befor namyd
Item I bequeth to my sayde wyfe all my corne excepte benys and pese
Also I gyffe frely to my sayde wyfe all maner of detts that byth owyng
to me and to hyr Item I gyff and bequeth to the same Mawde al my tenement
with apurtenance which I dwell in set in Abynde Strete of the town of
Northampton in maner and forme here folowyng that ys to say that yf
Thomas Hobbys my son wyll gyffe to my sayd wyfe within halfe yere after

my decesse x marke sterling and within yere and halfe after that payment other x marke sterling in full payment then I wyll the sayd Thomas my son have the sayde tenement with all the apurtenances after the decesse of my wyfe and the saide Thomas kepe almaner of reparacons of the sayd tenement during hir lyfe and my sayde wyfe to pay no rent therfor also longe as shee shall lefe and yf yt so be that my sayde son will nott pay the sayde xxti marke in maner and form above declared and kepe the reparacons be fore sayd for the reversion after hyr decesse than I wyll that my sayde wyfe do with ytt the same tenemente and all appurtenances as yt may please hyr beste Item I gyff and bequeth to my sayde wyfe all my purcheased landys in Bukkyngham shyre and in Bedford shyre for the terme of hir lyfe and all my othyr gods not above bequethed I gyff to my sayde wyfe. Item I bequeth of Mawde Essex my mayden to hir mariage xxs. Item I ordeyn and make Thomas Hobbys my son myn executor of this present testament as he may see to please God beste Theys beryng record William Mownford notary Thomas Aspland Thomas Berwyk and othyr moo and yf my sade son wilnott have the sayde tenement that I dwellin for the say xxti marke in maner before declared then I wyll that yf other of my doghters befor namyed shal by ytt that shee shulde <have yt> of my wyfe for xxvti marke of lawfull money payabull atthe dayes above wrytyn and my sayde wyfe to have the sayde tenement with appurtenance duryng hir lyfe withoute eny rent payng or reparacon and yf nethyr of my saide doghters in maner and forme before rehersed <will not> then I wyll that my wyfe enioye all the sayde tenement with appurtenances to rule yt at hyr pleasor for evermor as yt ys before wryten Item I bequeth to the same Mawde my wyfe my beste gown and Annes my doghter my second gown and to Johan my doghter my thrydde gown

f134r 489 THOMAS FLOWRE 27th January 1501 shearman

In the name of God Amen in the yere of our lord God mcccccj the xxvij day of January I Thomas Flowre of Northampton sherman in hole mynd etcetera make my testament in this maner and forme folowyng that ys to say fyrst I bequeth my soule to Almyghty God etcetera my body to be buryed in the chirche yerd of Saynt Gyle in the town of Northampton Item I bequeth to thygh auter of the chirche for tythis forgoten xijd. Item I bequeth to the fraternite of Saynt Clement in the same chirche xijd. Item to the reparacon of the chirche xijd. Item I bequeth to the sustentacon of the pore men in Saynt Thomas house by the southe yate of the town of Northampton iijs.iiijd. And the residue of my gods I bequeth Jone Flowre my wyfe and hyr I make myn executryce she to dispose for my soule as yt shall please hyr also I make John Holwell oversear of this my testament do bedon and he to have for his labor vjs.viijd. Witnes John Walker wever and William <Marshall> fuller

f134v 493 THOMAS KESTON 1st August 1501

In Dei nomine Amen the fyrste day of the moneth of August the yere of our lord God mccccc and one I Thomas Keston in hole mynd make my testament in this wise firste I bequeth my soule to Almyghty God etcetera my body to buryed in the chirche yarde of All Halowes in Northampton Also I bequeth to the mothyr chirche of Lincoln ijd. Item to thigh auter for forgoten tythes viijd. Item I bequeth to yeche of my thre childer xxs. and that to be in the kepyng <of my wyfe> to they byth of lawfull age And yf so

yt please God that eny of them decesse or yt com to lawfull age then
I wyll the parte of hym so decesed byth dyvyded betwen them that
lefe Also I bequeth to Mawde Weston my servant xxd. And to my othyr
mayde Ellen Smarte vs. so that she serve my wyfe the nexte yere folo'
and if she wylnott I wyll shee have but xxd. as hyr felowe hath Also
f135r
I bequeth to my brothyr John Warde my chamlett dewplet and my beste gown
The resydue of my godys not bequethed I gyff and bequeth to my wyfe whome
I make myn executrice thoru the oversight of John Warde beforesayd they
to order and dispose them as they thynke beste for the helthe of my soule theys
beyng Master Doctor my gostely fathyr William Whitfeld John Langton and othyr mo

f135r 494 JOHN HASILBYCHE 14th March 1500 blacksmith

In the name of God Amen the xiiijth day of Marche in the yere of our lord God
mccccc I John Hasilbyche of Northampton smith in hole mynd make my testament
in this maner fyrste I bequeth my soule to Almyghty God my body to be buryed
in the chirche yarde of All Halowys in Northampton agayn the weddyng dore
Item I bequeth to the mothyr chyrche of Lincoln iiijd. Item I bequeth to thigh
awter in the chyrche of All Halowys for forgoten tythis xijd. Item I bequeth to
Alice my wyfe the reversion of my yers of the house on the corner agayn
Saynt Pulcri chircheyard in the town of Northampton beforsayde whiche I holde of
the heirs of John Lubnam Item I gyff and bequeth to the same Alice my wyfe
all my tenement with medowys pasturs and lesowes with their apurtenance within the
town and feld of Brykesworth to have and to hold all the sayde tenement with
medowys pasturs and lesuys with ther apurtenance to the sayde Alice and hir assignes
for the terme of hyr lyfe and after hyr decesse I wyll that all the sayd tenement
with medowis pasturs and lesuys with theyr apurtenance shal remayn to John Hasilbych
my son and to the heyrs of his body lawfully begoten for ever more and yf yt
happen the sayd John Hasylbyche to decesse with oute heirs of his body lawfully
begoten then I wyll the forsayd tenement with medowys pasturs and lesueys
with their appurtenances shal remayn to the chyrche of Brykesword afore sayd
for ever more to pray for me and my godedoers and for them that yt com off
The residue of all my gods above not bequethed I gyff and bequeth to the sayde
Alice my wyfe to pay my detts and the same Alice I make and ordeyng myn
executrice to dispose for the helthe of my soule as shee beste may see
to please God theys beryng witnes Robert Rygby Symond Cley William
Sewale and othyr moo

f135v 499 ROBERT TESTWOD 16th July 1501 capper

In the name of God Amen the xvj day of July in the yere of our lord
God mccccc and one I Robert Testwod of Northampton capper hole of mynd
etcetera make my testament in this maner ffirste I bequeth my soule to
God my body to be buryed in the chirche yerd of All Halowys of Northampton
f136r
afore sayd Item I bequeth to thigh awter of the same chirche for tythis and
offryngs not duly don xijd. Item I bequeth to v prestes to bryng my body to
the chirche and to say placebo and dirige for my soule etcetera and masse on the morowe
xxd. Item I bequeth to the prior and supprior of the frere Austyns in Northampton to
pray for me soule in lyke wyse every of hem iiijd. Item I bequeth to Sir John

Overton to pray for my soule and all Cristen soulys vs. Item I bequeth to Robert Testwod my son my beste fethyr bed with the coveryng of the same of tapestre warke with bolster pelowys tester curtens blanketts and shets to the same belongyng after the decesse of Emme my wyfe and yf yt happen the sayde Robert decesse be for my sayde wyfe then I wyll that all my foresayd legacy made to Robert shal remayn after decesse of my wyfe to Johan Testwod my doghter Item I bequeth to the same Johan my doghter j materasse v payer of shets j tabul cloth vj plateres vj disshis vj saucers and j cheargeer of pewter j basyn j ewer vj candilstikks of laton j brass pott j brasse pan j postnet j chafer with iii fete of brasse j chafyng dysh of laton j towell of dyaper and ij towells of playn cloth Item I bequeth to William Rugby late my servant j materes j bolster j coverlett of grene warke The residue of my gods not above bequethed I gyff and bequeth to Emme my wyfe and hyr I make myn executrice to dispose for the helth of my soule as shee beste may se to please God and Richard Goldyears to be supervisor of this present wyll theys men beryng witnes Master Doctor Midelham Sir Richard Jankyn Sir John Overton and othir moo

f142r 526 ADAM HOCHYNSON 24th January 1501 saddler

In the name of God Amen the xxiiijth day of January in the yere of our lord God mccccc and one I Adam Hochynson of Northampton sadeler hole of mynde etcetera make my testament in this wyse ffyrste I bequeth my soule to Almyghty God my body to be buryed in the chyrche of All Halowys in the

f142v

mydell place before the rode and to pay for my berying as the maner ys vjs. viijd. Item I bequeth to the fraternite of the Rode in the same chirche xxd. Item I bequeth to the fraternite of Saynt John Baptiste in the same chirche xxd. Item I bequeth to the fraternite of Saynt Kateryn to the same chirch petenyng xxd. Item I bequeth to the fraternite of Saynt George in the same chirche xxd. Item to the hospitall of Saynt Thomas the Martyr withoute the southe yate of Northampton xxd. Item I bequeth to pore peopull to be distribute the day of my burying v dosen brede Item I bequeth to the mothir chirche of Lincoln vjd. The residue of all my gods not bequethed I gyffe and bequeth to Johan my wife and hyr I make and ordeyng myn executrice to dispose for the helthe of my soule as shee beste may see to please God and William Mownford notary survyar of this present testament wytnes of this Master Robert Midelham Doctor of Divinite Sir Richard Hikks parson of Wheleton and othyr

f145r 539 RICHARD CHEAD 3rd July 1502 corvisor

In the name of Almyghty God Amen the thred day of the moneth of July the yere of our lord God mccccc and ij I Richard Chead de Northampton corvisor in hole mynd etcetera make my testament in this wyse ffurste I bequeth my soul to Allmyghty God etcetera my body to be buryed by my doghter Margett in the chirche yerd of All Halowys of Northampton afore sayde Item I bequeth to the reparacon of the same chyrche iijs.iiijd. Item I bequeth to the fraternite of Saynt Kateryn in the newe chirche yarde in the sayde paryssh of All Halowys iijs.iiijd. Item I bequeth to the reparacon of the almushowse of Saynt Thomas the Martyr withoute the southe yate of Northampton iijs.iiijd. Item I bequeth to a preste to syng masse and pray for my soule by the space of halfe yere ls. Item I bequeth to Domini John Leicester monke of Daventre to pray for me vjs.viijd. Item I bequeth to the mothyr chyrche of Lincoln ijd. Item I bequeth to my own mothyr a gown clothe of russett Item I bequeth to my brothyr Thomas Chead my tawny gown furred Item I woll that my wyfe distribute emonge pore folke the day of my burying vjs.viijd. The residue of all my gods not above bequethed I gyffe and bequeth to Annes my wyfe and hyr I make myn executrice to dispose for thelth of my soule as she beste may se to please God and Richard Goldyear my wyfees fathyr to be oversear of this my my testament Thyese bering wittnes Master Robert Midelham vicar of All Halowys afore sayde William Mownford notary and William Palmer with othyr

f147r 547 THOMAS HENDYMAN 6th May 1502 weaver

In Dei nomine Amen sexto die mensis Octobris anno domini millesimo quingentisimo secundo Ego Thomas
Hendyman de Northampton wever compos mentis etcetera condo testamentum <meum> in hunc modum
In primis lego animam meam Deo Omnipotenti etcetera corpusque meum sepiliendum in cimiterio
ecclesie parochiali Sancti Petri ville Northampton Item lego summo altari ibidem xijd. Item do et lego
quinque presbytris exequiis meis et misse interessentibus xxd. Item lego matrici ecclesie Lincoln ijd.
Item do et lego Margarete Hendyman unam <ci>stam Item volo quod ortus meus iuxta castello
vulgariter the Castelgrene vendatur ad ultimum precium sui valoris et distribuetur
pauperibus secundum discreceonem executricis mee Item do et lego residuum omnium bonorum meorum
non legatorum disposicioni Margarete Hendyman uxoris mee quam ordino et constituo executricem
meam Willelmum Horpoll et Johannem Wall supervisores huius testamenti qui recepient pro suis
laboribus iijs.iiijd. ut ipsa disponat ea pro salute anime mee Hiis testibus Domino Willelmo Kyrkeby et Johanne Wall cum circumstantibus

Note - The almost identical will appears on f147v will no. 549

In the name of God Amen the 6th day of October 1502 I Thomas Hendyman of Northampton, weaver, in sound mind etcetera make my testament in this wise. First I bequeath my soul to Almighty God etcetera, my body to be buried in the cemetery of the parish church of St Peter in the town of Northampton. Item I bequeath to the high altar there 12d. Item I give and bequeath to five priests being present at my funeral and mass 20d. Item I bequeath to the mother church of Lincoln 2d. Item I give and bequeath to Margaret Hendyman a chest. Item I will that my garden by the castle commonly called the Castle Grene should be sold for the highest price and distributed among the poor according to the discretion of my executrix. Item I give and bequeath the residue of all my goods to the disposition of Margaret Hendyman, my wife, whom I make and ordain my executrix, William Horpoll and John Wall supervisors of this testament who shall receive for their labour 3s 4d, that she should dispose for the health of my soul. With these witnesses Dom William Kyrkeby, John Wall and others around.

f148v 553 WILLIAM ADAMS 26 August 1502

Festum Nativtalis Domini anno domini
millesimo quingentesimo secundo

In Dei nomine Amen the xxjth day of Auguste the yere of our lord God m-
ccccc and ij I William Adams othir wyse cald William Reve in hole mynd
make my testament in this wyse fyrste I bequeth my soule to Almyghty
etcetera my body to be buryed in the chyrcheyerd of Saynt Gyles in Northampton
also I bequeth to thygh awter of the same chyrche for forgoten tythes
xijd. Item to the mothyr chyrche of Lincoln iiijd. Item to iiij awters
in the same chyrche of Saynt Gyles to yche of them iiijd. Item to the bells
viijd. Item to hygh awter of Saynt Gyles j torche Item to the awter of Saynt
Clement j torche Item to Saynt Thomas house vjd. Item to thygh awter of Ekton
vjd. Item to the bellys of the same chyrche vjd. Item to the fraternite of Our Lady
of Overston vjd. Item to the bellys ther vjd. Item to the freres of the horse
market xxd. Item to the Austyn ffrerys xxd. Item to the Whyte ffrers
xxd. Item I gyff and bequeth to Alice my wyfe all that my messuage that
and tenement with all the appurtenances sett on the Crope Lane within the paryssh of
Saynt Giles within the town of Northampton to have to hyr for terme of hyr lyfe
and to pay oute of the same yerely to the maisteres of the fraternite of Saynt
Clement in the chirche of Saynt Gyles aforesayde xijd. by yere and
yf yt be so that Alice my wyfe be with childe atthe tyme of my deth then
I wyll atthe sayde mesuage and tenement with all thappurtenances remayn to the same
child after the deth of my sayd wyfe to have to my sayde childe And to the
heirs of the body of the sayde childe therof comyng and yf my sayde wyfe
be <not> with childe at the tyme of my deth then I wyll and bequeth the sayde
mesuage and tenement with al thappurtenances after the decesse of my wyfe that yt
remayne to John Walker and John Warwyk maisteres of the fraternite of
Saynt Clement in the sayde chirche chirche of Saynt Gyles and to theyr
successors maisteres of the saide fraternite for ever and that the maisteres of
same fraternite for the tyme beyng shall yerly kepe on obytt for me
my wyfe and my childer in the foresayde paryssh chyrche of Saynt Gyles for ever
atthe feste of Saynt Nicholas yerely to be kepte and to expend yerely
atthe same obbytt ijs. and yf the sayde maisteres do not kepe the same
obbyt yerely I wyll that Thomas Reve my brothyr shall enter into the
sayde house to the behofe of hym and his childer The residue of my gods
not bequethed I gyff and bequeth to Alice my wyfe and I make my sole
executrice William Lyceras and Robert Marshall to be overseers witnes of this my
laste will Thomas Higham baker John Walker Richard Haywarte and many othyr

f152v 567 RICHARD BARKER (alias DYER) 7th March 1502 dyer

In Dei nomine Amen decimo <septimo> die mensis Marcii anno millesimo quingentisimo
secundo Ego Ricard Barker

alias Dyer de Northampton dyer compos mentis condo testamentum meum in hunc modum. In primis commendo animam meam Deo celi et terre Creatori corpusque meum sepiliendum in cimiterio ecclesie parochiali Sancti Gregorii in Northampton predicte Item lego Alicie filie mee
togam meam de russet penulatam et unum signum argenti videlicet a broche olim matris sue post decessum Margerie nunc consortis mee Item lego fabrice ecclesie Sancti Gregorii predicti xxd. Item lego Johanni Goldeston qui duxit aliam filiam meam duas togas deploidem tunicam et pelvim Residuum bonorum meorum do et lego Margerie uxori mee ad solvendum debita mea et eandem constituo meam executricem per presentes et Johannem
Cokkys clericum ac Robertum Ushere supervisores Date die et anno supradictis hiis testibus Johanne Cockys et Roberto Usshere et Thoma Pytman cum aliis

In the name of God Amen the seventeenth day of March 1502 I Richard Barker alias Dyer of Northampton, dyer, in sound mind make my testament in this wise. First I commend my soul to God, Creator of heaven and earth, my body to be buried in the cemetery of the parish church of St Gregory in Northampton aforesaid. Item I bequeath to Alice, my daughter, my gown of russet furred and a silver device known as a brooch, once belonging to her mother, after the decease of Margery, now my wife. Item I bequeath to the fabric of the church of St Gregory aforesaid 20d. Item I leave to John Goldeston, who married my other daughter, two gowns, a doublet, a tunic and a basin. The residue of my goods I give and bequeath to Margery, my wife, to pay my debts and the same I constitute my executrix by these presents. And John Cokkys, clerk, and Robert Ushere supervisors. Given the day and year abovesaid. With these witnesses John Cokkys and Robert Ushere and Thomas Pytman and others.

f152v 568 ALICE CUTLERD 7th October 1502 widow

In Dei nomine Amen the vij day of October the yere of our lord God mcccccij I Alice Cutlerd of Northampton wedowe in gude mynd make my testament in this wyse ffyrste I bequeth my soule to Almyghty God etcetera my body to be buryed in the chapel of Corpus Christi in the churche of All Halowes of Northampton Item I bequeth for my burying ther as the maner is vjs.viijd. Item I bequeth to thygh auter in the same churche for tythis for koten vjs.viijd. Item I bequeth to the fraternite of Corpus Christi to be sister ther xxs. and a torche Item I bequeth to the fraternite of Rode in the same chyrche xxd. Item I bequeth to the fraternite of Saynt John Baptiste xxd. Item to fraternite of Saynte George in the same churche xxd. Item to the fraternite of Saynt Kateryn in the newe chyrche yerd in the same paryssh xxd. Item I bequeth to every of the iiij orders of freres in the town of Northampton iijs.iiijd. Item I bequeth to the mothyr chyrche of Lincoln iiijd. Item I bequeth to the reparacions of aye wayes (highways) ijs. Item I wyll that myn executors bye for my dirige and masse an wax to bryn above my herse ijs.viijd. Item I bequeth to prests and clerkys that shalbe at my dirige and masse xs. Item I bequeth for ryngyng at my diryge and masse and burying xvjd. Item I wyll that myn executors pay for wyndyng shete xxd. Item I wyll that the vj torchis that shall bren at my diryge masse and burying byth distribute in maner folowyng that ys to say to chyrche of Myche Billyng a torche to Qwynton chyrche a torche Item to the fraternite of the Rode in All Halowe Chirch before sayde a torche Item

to Saynt Kateryn in the newe chirche yerd a torche Item to Saynt Thomas hows
a torche Item to the honour of moste blessed sacrament in the sayde chyrche of All Halowes
a torche Item I bequeth to Sir Rowland Messenger to syng for me the space of
oon yere vij markes sterling Item I woll that iiijli sterlyng bith distribute emongys
pore folke in Northampton that ys to say in every quarter of the iiij quarters of the town
xxs. Item I bequeth to William Cutlerd my son my beste pece with the cover of silver
gylt with oute and my beste coveryng of a bed Item I bequeth to John Napton sadeler
and to Elsibeth his wyfe my doghter my beste maser and vj sylver sponys knoppytt
with lyons valued at xls. and my second best coveryng of a bed Item I bequeth to
my foresayd doghter Elsabeth Napton my gown of puke that come from London
ij payer of my beste beds and a holde blak ffurre of shankis and my gowns pervelyt with
whyte and a chased pece of sylver parcell gylte with a bace fote and ij gylte gyrdyllys

f153r

Item I bequeth to iiij doghters of the sayd John Napton everyche of them a fethyrbed
a bolstyr a brasse pott a laton basyng and vis.viijd. in redy money Item I bequeth to
Thomas Purvey oon olde gown lately Thomas Clerks Item I bequeth to Emmott
Clerke my servant a materasse j payer of shetis and a vyolet gown lynytt and velwhett
in coler and vjs.viijd. in money Item I bequeth to John Freman of Billyng one olde
russett gown Item I bequeth to my cosyng a younge woman of Horpoll a corse gyrdyll
harnesett with sylver Item I wyll that there remayn in the house I dwell in
for standards to contynue ther a great bruyng lede a panne in fornes and iij
worte leds The resydue of my gods above nott bequethed I gyff and bequeth
to William Cutlerd my son and to John Napton of Northampton and them I make
myn executors to dispose for the elth of my soule as they may se beste to
please God and Robert Shefford of Northampton goldsmyth to be supervisor
of this my present testament Item I bequeth to Elsabeth Napton my doghter
ij women capps of sylke Item I bequeth to Alyce Napton my god doghter my
my salte of sylver and gylte Item I bequeth to Elsabeth Napton the younger ij sylver
sponys Item I bequeth to Annes Napton ij sylver sponys Item to Johane Napton
ij sylver sponys Item where as Thomas Radborn owthe me for blankett
xxvjs. I wyll that the one halfe of that money be waryd in wodd and gevyn
to pore folke agaynst Cristemasse that shalbe in the yere of our Lorde God
mvc and iiij and the othyr halfe of the sayde money I wyll in lyke wyse
be waryd in wodd and gevyng to pore folks agaynst Cristemasse that shalbe
in the yere of our lord God mvc and v Theys men beryng witnes Robert
Shefford goldsmyth John Napton and William Mownford notary with othyr

f154v 575 SIR RICHARD SHERD 16th May 1503 priest

Registered also at number 597

In the name of God Amen the yere of our lord God mccccc and iij xvjth day of
May I Sir Richard Sherd preste late Master of the hospital of Saynt John Baptiste
in Northampton beyng of gude remembrance make my testament and laste wyll in thys
wyse ffirste I bequeth my soule to almyghty God etcetera and my body to be buryed in the
chancell of the foresayd hospitall Also I bequeth to the mothyr chirche of
Lincoln xijd. Also for my mortuary due to the Bishop of Lincoln for my benefice
of Bourton xiijs.iiijd. Also to Maister Thomas Knyght commissary xxs. Also to
Maister Richard Grene notary and scrybe to the same commissary xs. Also to Adam
Free sommoner ijs. Also I bequeth to the sustentacion of the chirche of Blisworth
a mese with ij cotages and j yeard of arabulle land with the purtenance for ever more
more so that the chirche men and wardens yereli gyff to the curate ther xijd

to say placebo and diryge and masse of requiem in the day of my obite for my soule my fathyr and mothyr sowles and for all Crysten soules and to the ryngers of the bellys atthat tyme iiijd. Also I bequeth to mayster Thomas Parmenter maister of the hospitall of Saynt Jonys to fede prestes and clerks beyng at my berying xxs. Also to the sayd maister a foldyn tabull iiij cheyars standyng ij long setyls ij awmbres ij cofers of Stirbryge j fether bed with a bolster a materasse with a bolster ij payer blanketts ij payer of shets iij coverletts a pane of counterfete aresse with all manner of hanyngs within the parlor and the chambers Also a lytyll pece gylte with a cover standyng Item ij laton basens ij euers of laton oon Saynt George iij of my beste candyllstykks vj whysshons of one sorte and vj of anothyr sorte also all thyngys longing to the chymnethes also a great brasse pott a presse a closse cheyre a towell of dyaper a Saynt Johanys hede a payer of tabullys with the men also to the same maister to pray for my soule xiijs.iiijd. Also I bequeth to every preste brothyr or not brothyr servyng within Saynt Jonys at the tyme of my berying to pray for my soule vjs.viijd. Also to Maister Thomas Knyght commissary a chawferen Also I bequeth to Alice Lawrens a salte of sylver with the cover also to the same Alyce ij sylver sponys Also I bequeth John Lawrens and Alice his wyfe xli. in money lawfull of Yngland Also I bequeth to Sir William Emerton vycar of Wendore my beste gown to Sir John Calcote my second gowne to Sir Richard Morden my thred gown to Sir William Chadok a gown to John Chadok a gown a candylstyke a cofer standyng under the shelfe to William Cowper a gowne and a candylstyke The resydue of all my gods not bequethed I bequeth to the disposicion of Maister Thomas Permenter Maister Thomas Knyght Maister William Wake swyer and Richard Grene notary whome I make and ordeyng myn executors that they dispose them to Gods pleasor and the welthe of my sowle Theys beyng witnes Sir William Chaddok Sir Richard Morden John Chaddok and John Lawrens with othyr moo

f157r 591 JOHN LANGTON 1503 (singer)

In the name of God Amen in the yere of our lord God mccccc and iij I John Langton beyng in hole mynde make my testament in this maner fyrste I bequeth my sowle to God Almyghty etcetera my body to be buryed in Cristen sepulcre* Also I bequeth to our Lady chapell for my brethyrhed to be payed by ij yere of the rente of the Whyte House in Kyngesthorpe Item I bequeth to the reparacion of the bokys in All Halowes chyrche iijs.iiijd. Item I bequeth to iiij fraternites that ys to say to the fraternite of the Rode Saynt John Saynt George and Saynt Kateryn to everyche of them xijd. Item I bequeth to my son Thomas Langton j pece of sylver j maser with the handyll and halfe a dosen sylver sponys my beste coverlet j payer of blanketts ij peyer of shets with a materasse iij brasse potts a byg pott that was at Morys house a medyll pot and a lasse potte a greate cofer that standyth in the hall a basyn with a laver ij candilstykks iiij platers iiij pewter dysshys and iiij sawcers Item I bequeth to Eme my doghter a maser

f157v

and iij brasse potts a byg pott a mydyll pott and a lasse pott a peyr of blanketts with a payer of shets and a longe spete Item I bequeth to my wyfe the Whyte House at Kyngesthorp as longe as shee levyth to pay my detts and after hyr decesse and after hyr decesse and my detts payed I wyll that retern to Eme my doghter for ever Item I bequeth to my wyfe my shoppe with the purtenans and al' othyr of my gods not bequethed I gyff fully to my wyfe and hyr I make myn sole executrice and to over sear this my laste wylle performed I ordeyng Edward Chamberleyn wever and John Aras clerke wittnes of this my testament George Aras husbandman of Lytill Billing and John Gibbard of Kyslyngbery with othyr mo

* *The church is All Saints*

f158r 592 ANNES ESEX 8th January 1503 widow

In the name of God Amen the viijth of the moneth of January in the yere of our Lord God mccccc and iij I Annes Esex of Northampton wedowe hole of mynd make my testament conteynyng my last wyll in form folowyng revokyng and anullyng all syche wyllys or testaments as byfore this day warre made yf eny siche happen to be fownd and I wyll that the present testament procede and take effecte and be execute by myn executors under namyd ordeyned and made ffyrste I bequeth my soule to Almyghty God etcetera my body to be buryed in the chapell of Corpus Christi in All Halowes chirche of Northampton aforesayd Item I bequeth to thygh awter ther for tythis and oblacions forgoten etcetera iijs.iiijd. Item I bequeth to hygh awter in Corpus Christi chapell a awter clothe of lynyn Also I bequeth to the awter of the Holy Rode in the same chirche a awter cloth of lynyn Item I bequeth to the awter in the chapell of Saynt Kateryn in the newe chyrche yerd a awter clothe of lynyn Item I bequeth to the awter of Saynt Mychaell in the paryssh chyrche of Saynt Michaell a awter clothe in the sayd town of Northampton a awter cloth of lynyng Item I bequeth to mothyr chyrche of Lincoln xijd. Item I wyll that a preste be found to syng and to pray for me and my husband John Esex and for all our gude frends soules in the chyrche of Saynt Michaell in Northampton by the space of on hole yere and the same preste to have for his salary viij markes of gode and lawfull money of Yngland Item I wyll that in the day of my buryng xl dosen brede be distribute emong pore folke where moste nede ys after discrecon of my executors Item I bequeth to the wyfe of John Olye in howsold stuffe to the valor of vjs.viijd. Item I bequeth to Elizabeth Reve my servant in howsold stuff to the valor of vjs.viijd. Item I bequeth to Margett Myllys my lytill mayden in stuff of howsold to the valor of iijs.iiijd. Item I wyll that John Adyngton be found of my gods after discrecon of myn executors by the space of on hole yere Item I bequeth to mayntenans of the fyssher lyght in Saynt Petri chirche in Northampton to the performans of my husband laste wyll a ffysshstall now in the tenur of William Sywell fyssher
The residue of all my gods above not bequethed I gyf to Richard Williamson preste and to John Malory gentilman and the same Richard and John I make myn executors to dispose for the elth of my soule as they may beste se to pleise God and Mayster Robert Mydelham Doctor and vicar of Alhalow chirche in Northampton to be supervisor of this present
testament and he to have for his labor vjs.viijd. Theys bering witnes John Spenser John Wele Thomas Williamson and John Olye with othir moo

f158v 595 WILLIAM HORPOLL 18th December 1503

In Dei nomine Amen I William Horpoll hole of mynd make my testament in this maner in the yere of our Lord God mccccc and iij the xviij day of December Firste I bequeth my soule to God Almyghty etcetera and my body to beryed in the chirche yerd of Saynt Peter in Northampton Also I bequeth all my moveabill gods and immoveabull to Margarett my wyfe Also I wyll that the howse and the pasture beyng in Multon the whiche longyth unto me be at the disposicion of my wyfe Also I wyll that all the tenements and pastures that belongyth unto me within the town of Northampton and oute of the foresaid town be at the disposicon of my wyfe And I make the oversear of this my laste will Master Thomas Haselwod Witnes herof William Dawes dyar and Robert Warde tanner

f159r 597 SIR RICHARD SHERDE 19th May 1503
ex Master of St Johns

Registered also at number 575

In the name of God Amen the yere of our lord God mcccccth iij the xix day of
the moneth of May I Syr Richard Sherde sometyme Master of the hospital of Saynt John
of the towne of Northampton beyng in my hole mynd makys my testament in this
maner of wyse ffirst I bequeth my sowle to Almyghty God to Our Lady Seynt Mary and
to all the holy company of heven And my body to be buryed in the chawnsell of the
forseid hospitall Also I bequeth for my mortuarye due to the Bysshepe of Lyncolne xiijs.
iiijd. Also I bequeth to the moder chirch of Lyncolne xijd. Also I bequeth to Master Thomas
Knyght comissary xxs. Also to Master Richard Grene xs. Also to Adame Fre sommoner ijs.
Also to Master of Seynt Johns for meyte and drynke to prestes and clerks in day of
my burynge xxs. Also I bequeth to the chirch of Blisworth I meyse
with ij cotagers and i yerd of ayrable land with the purtenances for ever so that the chirch
wardens yerly gyf to the curatt xijd. to say placebo and dirige and masse of
Requiem in my mynnyng day and iiijd. to the ryngers of the bells for the weyle of
my sowle my ffather and moder sowlls and all Cristen sowlls Also I gif and be-
queth to the Master of Seynt Johns all thes thyngs ffolowyng that is to say
a foldyng tabyll iiij cheyres ij long settlys ij amberys ij cofers of Stere-
bryge a feder bedd with a bolster a materys with a bolster ij payr of blanketts
ij payr of shetts iij coverletts a pane of cowntterffett arres and al maner
of hangyns within my parlors and chawmebers a lityll gilt peyse stondyng with the
covers ij laten basyns ij euers of laten oon of Saynt Jorge iij of the best
candylstykks xij qwysshyns and althyng longyng to the chymeneth Also a gret
brase pott a presse a closse cheyere a towell of diaper a Seynt Johns hedd and a
payre of tabylls with the menne Also to the same Master to pray for my sowle xiijs.iiijd.
Also I bequeth to Dame Elizabeth* nonne of Dalapra vjs.viijd. Also I bequeth to
every brother servyng in Sent Johns at the tyme of my deth and to every prest conduckt
servyng ther the same tyme vjs.viijd. Also to the master comissary a chawforne Also I
bequeth to Alys Lawrens a salt of sylver with the cover Also to John Lawrens and to
the seid Alys xli. in money and iij sylver spownnes Also to Sir Wylyam Everdon my best
gown to Sir John Calcote my second to Sir Richard Morden my thirde gown to Sir Wylyam
Chadok a noder gown to John Chadok a noder gown a cofer and a candylstyke
Also to Wylyam Cowper a gown and a candylstyke The residue of all my goods nott be-
quethed I gif and bequeth to Master Thomas Parmenter Master of Seint Johns Master
Thomas
Knyght commissary Master Wylyam Wake squyer and Richard Grene notary to dispoyse
them
for the weyle of my sowll whom I make my executors
thes beyng recorde Sir Wylyam Chadoke Sir Richard Morden John Chadok and John
Lawrens etcetera

** this is Dame Elizabeth Saxby*

f164r 609 WILLIAM MARCHALL 22nd May 1504 mercer

In Dei nomine Amen vicesimo secundo die mensis Maii anno
domini millesimo quingentesimo quarto Ego Willelmus Marchall de Northampton
mercer compos mentis et sane memorie condo testamentum meum

in hunc modum In primis lego animam meam Deo Omnipotenti Beate Marie omnibus que sanctis eius corpusque meum sepiliendum in cimitorio ecclesie parochialis Omnium Sanctorum ville Northampton prope tumulum parentum meorum Item lego summo altari ecclesie parochialis Omnium Sanctorum pro decimis meis oblitis xijd. Item lego ffraternitati Sancti Georgii Martiris in ecclesia predicta viijd. Item lego ffraternitati Sancte Katerine Virginis in novo cimitorio viijd. Item lego Hospitaliti Sancti Leonardi in Coton iuxta Norhampton in comitatu Norhampton ad reparacionem ecclesie dicte Sancti Leonardi iijs.iiijd. Item do et lego Thome Marchall

f164v

filio meo in pecuniis xs. et tria cocliaria argenti Item do et lego Willelmo Marchall filio meo in pecuniis xs. tria cocliaria argenti Item unum par lynthiaminium duas ollas eneas et unam patellam Item tres perapsides tres discos et tres sausers electri unum candelabrum et meam optimam togam Item lego Johanni Marchall filio meo decem solidos in pecuniis tria cocliaria argenti unum par linthiaminium duas ollas eneas unam patellam tres perapsides tres discos et tres sausers electri unum candelabrum Item do et lego Johanne filie mee in pecuniis xs. unum par linthiaminium duas ollas eneas duas patellas tres perapsides tres discos tres sausers electri duas candelabras meam togam coloris violet et unum sipurs foser Item do et lego Roberto Marchall filio meo in pecuniis xs. unum par linthiaminium duas ollas eneas duas patellas tres perapsides tres discos tres sausers electri duas candelabras et unam togam Item do et lego Willelmo Marchall filio meum tenementum situatum in vico Boriali ville Northampton et heredibus suis de corpore suo legittime procreatis imperpetuum Et si contingat predictum Willelmum obire sine heredibus de corpore suo legitime procreatis quod absit tunc volo quod Thomas Marchall filius meus habebit predictum tenementum cum pertinenciis sibi et heredibus suis
de corpore suo legittime procreatis imperpetuum Et si contingat dictum Thomam obire sine heredibus de corpore suo legittime procreatis quod absit tunc volo quod Johannes Marchall filius meus habebit dictum tenementum cum pertinenciis sibi et heredibus suis de corpore suo legittime procreatis imperpetuum et si contingat predictum Johannem Marchall obire sine heredibus de corpore suo legittime procreatis quod absit tunc volo quod Robertus Marchall filius meus habebit dictum tenementum cum pertinenciis sibi et heredibus suis de corpore suo legittime procreatis imperpetuum Et si contingat prefatum Robertum obire sine heredibus de corpore suo legittime procreatis quod absit tunc volo quod Johanna filia mea habebit dictum tenementum cum pertinenciis sibi et heredibus suis de corpore suo procreatis legittime imperpet-
uum Et si contingat prefatam Johannam obire sine heredibus de corpore suo legittime procreatis quod absit tunc volo quod predictum tenementum cum pertinenciis venditur pro pecuniis ut distribuantur pauperibus et indegentibus pro salute anime mee et parentum meorum Item do et lego Willelmo filio meo unum par de breganders et unum salet Item Johanne filie mee unam mirram argenti et deaurati et unum cover cum uno le knoppe argenti et deaurati Item lego Thome Marchall filio meo unum chafyndishe de laten Item lego Roberto filio meo unum chafyndishe Item volo quod Willelmus Marchall habebit tenementum meum cum gardino situatum in the Olde Drapery ville Northampton ut patet per indenturas Item volo quod dabitur in die sepultura mee pauperibus in panibus vs. et presbiteris et clericis

f165r

vs. et in aliis expensis iijs.iiijd. Item lego Roberto filio meo meam clavem argenti Item do et lego Johanne filie mee unum le spi[tt]e unum par de cobberdes et unum chafyndishe de laten Residuo vero omnium bonorum meorum superius non legatorum volo quod distribuantur post mortem mei et Johanne uxoris mee quatuor prenominatis filiis meis et Johanne filie mee prenominate per equales porciones per supervisionem executorum meorum inferius prenominandorum huius autem testamenti mei executores facio ordino et constituo Christoferum Massenger et Willelmum Grene mercer ut ipsi omnia predicta legaciones et donaciones fideliter exequantur et compleant cum effectu prout sibi pro salute anime mee melius videbitur expediri Et ut quilibet eorum habeat pro labore suo vjs.viijd. Hiis testibus Roberto Medilham vicario ecclesie Omnium Sanctorum curato meo Willelmo Newall de Northampton et Johanne Bagley de eadem cum aliis Date die et anno domini supradictis anno vero Regni Regis Illustrissimij Henrici Septimi post conquestum decimo nono

In the name of God Amen the twenty second day of May 1504 I William Marchall of Northampton, mercer, in sound mind and good memory make my testament in this wise. First I bequeath my soul to Almighty God, to the Blessed Mary and all their saints, my body to be buried in the cemetery of the parish church of All Saints in the town of Northampton near the grave of my parents. Item I bequeath to the high altar of the parish church of All Saints for my tithes forgotten 12d. Item I bequeath to the fraternity of St George the Martyr in the church aforesaid 8d. Item I bequeath to the fraternity of St Katherine the Virgin in the new cemetery 8d. Item I bequeath to the Hospital of St Leonard in Coton next to Northampton in the county for the repair of the church of St Leonard 3s 4d. Item I give and bequeath to Thomas Marchall, my son, in money 10s and three silver spoons. Item I give and bequeath to William Marchall, my son, in money 10s and three silver spoons. Item one pair of sheets, two brass pots and one pan. Item three dishes, three plates and three saucers of pewter, one candelabra and my best gown. Item I bequeath to John Marchall, my son, ten shillings in money, three silver spoons, a pair of sheets, two brass pots, one pan, three dishes, three plates and three saucers of pewter and one candelabra. Item I give and bequeath to Joan, my daughter, in money 10s, one pair of sheets, two brass pots, two pans, three dishes, three plates and three saucers of pewter, two candelabra, my gown of violet colour and one ? ? Item I give and bequeath to Robert Marchall, my son, in money 10s, one pair of sheets, two brass pots, two pans, three dishes, three plates, three saucers of pewter, two candelabra and one gown. Item I give and bequeath to William Marchall, my son, my tenement situated in North Street in the town of Northampton and the heirs of his body legitimately begotten forever. And if it should happen that the aforesaid William dies without legitimate heirs of his body legitimately begotten then I will that Thomas Marchall, my son, have the said tenement with its appurtenances. And if it should happen that the said Thomas dies without heirs of his body legitimately begotten then I will that John Marchall, my son, have the said tenement with its appurtenances and the heirs of his body legitimately begotten. And if it should happen that the aforesaid John dies without heirs of his body legitimately begotten then I will that Robert Marchall, my son, have the said tenement with its appurtenances and the heirs of his body legitimately begotten. And if it should happen that Robert dies without heirs of his body legitimately begotten I will that Joan, my daughter, have the said tenement have the said tenement with its appurtenances and the heirs of her body legitimately begotten. And if it should happen that the aforesaid Joan should die without heirs of her body legitimately begotten then I will that the aforesaid tenement with appurtenances be sold and the money distributed among the poor and needy for the health of my soul and my parents. Item I give and bequeath to William, my son, one pair of briganders and one salet. Item to Joan, my daughter, one silver and gilt maser and a cover with a silver and gilt knoppe. Item I bequeath to Thomas Marchall, my son, one chafing dish of laten. Item I bequeath to Robert, my son, one chafing dish. Item I wish that William Marchall have my tenement with garden situated in the Old Drapery in the town of Northampton as appears by his indentures. Item I will that on the day of my burial 5s in bread be given to the poor, and the priests and clerks 5s and in other expenses 3s 4d. Item I bequeath to Robert, my son, my silver clavem. Item I give and bequeath to Joan, my daughter, one 'le spi[tt]e', one pair of cobberdes and one chafing dish of laten. The residue of all my goods not bequeathed above I will that they be distributed after my death and Joan my wife, to my four aforenamed sons and Joan, my aforenamed daughter, in equal portions by the supervision of my below named executors. To this end I make, ordain and constitute Christopher Massenger and William Grene, mercer, my executors in order that all the aforesaid legacies and donations are faithfully executed and completed with effect for the health of my soul as seems best. And that each have for his labour 6s 8d. With these witnesses Robert Medilham, vicar of the church of All Saints, my curate, William Newall of Northampton and John Bagley of the same with others. Given the day and year abovesaid, in fact the nineteenth year of the most illustrious Henry the seventh after the Conquest.

f165r 610 WILLIAM JONSON 16th June 1504 carpenter

In the name of God Almyghty Amen The yere of our Lord God mccccc and iiij The xvith day of the moneth of Junii I William Jonson carpenter of the towne of Northampton beying in hole memory and mynde do makith my will and testament in forme folowyng Fyrst I bequeth my soule to God Almyghty to Our Lady Saint Mary and to all the holy company of heven and my body to be buryed in the chirchyard of Saint Gyles within the towne of Northampton Alsoo I bequeth to the hygh altere of the saide chirche for tithes forgoten xijd. Alsoo to the fraternite of Saint Clement xijd. Alsoo to the moder chirch of Lincoln xijd. Alsoo to the iiij orderes of freres to eche of them

xijd. Also to Sir Thomas Serjant paryshe preste at that tyme beyng
f165v
to pray for my xxd. Alsoo I bequeth to Master Lole to be good master to my wiff vjs.viijd. Alsoo to Mestrice Lole to be good maistres to my wiff vj.viijd. Alsoo I gyfe and bequeth to John Cokys and to Emme hys wiff to eche of them vjs.viijd. Alsoo I bequeth to the said John Cokys to his wiff and to their children all my rayment belong-gyng to my body Alsoo I gife and bequeth to Elizabeth my wife my howse beying in Knyght Strete duryng here lyff and immediatly after decease of my wiff I give the saide howse to John Cokys to Emme hys wiff and to the children of their bodyes lawfully begoten in the yeres of my endentures Alsoo I bequeth to the howse of Saint Thomas without sowth yate of Northampton to be prayed fore xijd. Also to the Maister of Saint Johns ijs. Alsoo to the Rode loft within the chirche of Saint Gyles xijd. Alsoo to Our Lady altere within the chirch of Alhalowen xijd. Alsoo to the Prior of Cano[n]s Asshby xijd. Alsoo to Thomas Worley iijs.iiijd. Alsoo to John Waucar iijs.iiijd. The residue of alle my goodes not bequethed my detts ffully payed I gyve and bequeth to Elizabeth my wiff and the saide Elizabeth I make and ordeyn my sole executryce to dispose for the helth of my soule as it its best seyn unto here and Maister Lole and his wiff to be over sears of this my laste wyll witnesses Sir Thomas Serjant Thomas Worley and John Waucar with other moo

f172r 625 JOHN FAWCET 20th October 1509 bowyer

In the name of God Amen the yere of our lord mcccccix the xxth dae of the monthe of Octobre I John Fawcet hole of mynde of Northampton boyer make my will in this maner Firste I bequeth my soull to Almyghty God to his modre Seynt Mary and to all the holy company of hevyn my body to be buryed in the church yarde of Alhalows in Northampton Also I bequeth to the high auter for my forgoten tythes iiijd. Item to the modre church of Lincoln ijd. Item I bequeth to my modre Alice Fawcet xxvjs.viijd. ij paire of shets a keverlett and my russett gowne furred with white lambe and also iijs. that Robert Malory oweth unto me to bye a matteres to her bedde Item I bequeth to William Fawcett my sone xls. Item to John Fawcett my sone xls. and if any of theis ij children depart out of this world I wille that the hole iiijli remayn to the child beyng a live And if both my children departe I wille my wife have xls. and the other xls. to be disposed for the welth of my soulle and if my wif mary aftir my decesse I wille that my bequest be delyvered to thands of my supervisers till my children be of lawfull age also I bequeth to Margarett my sustre xiijs.iiijd. The residue of my goods not bequethed I gif and bequeth to Margaret my wif and her I ordeyn and make my sole executrice and also I will that Richard Goldikar and Thomas Akeley be supervisours of this my wille they to dispose my goods to the honor of Almyghty God and helpe of my soull and I will that my supervisors have eche of theym xd. for theire busynes and labor Records of this will Sir Thomas Goodchild preste Jamys [L]ench with other moo

f175v 630 EDMUND TATHAM 12th November 1509 corvisor

In Dei nomine Amen the yere of our lord God anno mccccc and ix the xijth daie of Novembre I Edmunde Tatham corvisor of this parish of Alhalows in Northampton hole of mynde make my testament in this maner Firste I bequeth my soull to Almyghty God to Our Lady Seynt Mary and to all angells and seynts of hevyn and my body to be buryed in the church of Alhalows aforsaid Also I bequeth to the modre church of Lincoln viijd. Also I bequeth to the reparations of the forsaid church of Alhalows xld. Also I bequeth to the pore folks in Seynt Thomas house xijd. Also to every house of ffreres in Northampton xxd. Also I bequeth to Alice my doughter in money xli. and iiij sillver sponys Also to my doughter Agnes xli. and iiij silver sponys Also to my doughter Elisabeth xli. and iiij sylver sponys yf eche of theym wilbe councellyd and rulyd after the councell of Agnes my wife their modre and if it fortune any of my said doughters to deceasse within thage of xviij yeres than I will that the childs parte deceassed be devided bitwixt the susters over levyng her and if it fortune ij of the said iij to deceasse within the forsaid yers then I woll that there ij partes remayne to the suster over levyng

f176r

and if it fortune all my iij doughters to deceasse within the tyme of xviij yeres of their age than I will that Agnes my wife have the half parte that is to say xvli. and the other xvli. to be disposed to a preste to synge for me and my wif the space of iij yers at Seynt Stephens alter in the church of Alhalows aforesaid Also I bequeth to Kateryn my moder xxs. Also to Johan my sustre vjs.viijd. Also to Alice my sustre vjs.viijd. Also to William Tatham my brodre my russett gown The residue of all my goods not bequethed I gyve to Agnes my wife whom I make sole executrice of this my last will and I make John Marsely vicar of Thorpe oversear of this forsaid testament and he to have for his labor vjs.viijd. Witnessing Robert Middylham my curat Richard Goldikar and William Chadoke prests

f179v 635 JOHN DAWKYNS 3rd July 1505 baker

In Dei nomine Amen anno domini millesimo 5c quinto tercio die mensis Julii Ego Johannes Dawkyns ville Northampton pistor condo testamentum meum cum sum sane memorie et eciam corporis in hunc modum In primis do et lego animam meam Deo corpusque meum sepiliendum in cimiterio Omnium Sanctorum Item Capellane Sancti Georgii eiusdem capelle xijd. Item crucifixo xijd. Item capelle Sancte Katerine xijd. Item capelle Sancti Johannis xijd. Item ecclesie parochiali de Milton vjs.viijd. Item cuilibet ordini fratrum in Northampton xijd. Item Abathie de Betlesden

unam ollam eneam Item dompno Johanni filio monacho
de Betelsden cs. et unam pelvim cum lavacro Item lego
Thome Hyams pannam pro toga Residuum vero omnium bonorum meorum
superius non legatorum do et lego Johanne uxori mee et eandem
Johannam ordino facio et constituo executricem meam cum Thome
Highams antedicto ut ipsa cum Thoma disponant pro anima mea
prout eis <melius> videbitur expediri Et Johannem filium meum monachum
predictum constituo presentis testamenti mei supervisorem Date die et anno
antedictis Hiis testibus Doctore Myddelham ecclesie Omnium Sanctorum
vicario Willelmo Marshe et Ricardo Deyntyth

In the name of God Amen the third day of July 1505 I John Dawkyns of Northampton, baker, make my testament, being in good memory and also body, in this wise. First I give and bequeath my soul to God, my body to be buried in the cemetery of All Saints. Item to the chaplain of St George of the same chapel 12d. Item to the Cross 12d. Item to the chapel of St Katherine 12d. Item to the chapel of St John 12d. Item to the parish church of Milton 6s 8d. Item to each of the orders of friars in Northampton 12d. Item to the Abbot of Betlesden one brass pot. Item to Dom John, monk of Betlesden 100s and one basin and ewer. Item I leave to Thomas Hyans cloth for a gown. The residue of all my goods not bequeathed above I give and bequeath to Joan, my wife, and the same Joan I ordain, make and constitue my executrix with Thomas Highams abovesaid that she with Thomas dispose for my soul as seems best to them. And John, my son, monk aforesaid, I constitute supervisor of my present testament. Given the day and year before said. With these witnesses Doctor Myddelham, vicar of the church of All Saints, William Marshe and Richard Deyntyth.

f183v 643 JOHN COBBE 26th September 1505

In Dei nomine Amen Vicesimo die mensis Octobris
anno domini millesimo quincentesimo quinto in ecclesia hospitalis
Sancti Johannis Northampton coram nobis Thoma
Knyght probatum fuit etcetera onusque etcetera
commissa fuit etcetera dat etcetera
Northampton
In the name of God amen the xxvjth day of September
f184r
in the yere of our Lord God a thousand vc and v I John Cobbe of
Northampton hole of mynde and of good memore beyng thanked
be our Lord Jesu make my testament in thys wyse First I
bequeth my soule to Almyghty God to Our Lady Saynt Mary
and to al the holy company of hevyn My body to be buried
in the church of Saynt Mighell in the towne of Northampton
before the image of Our Blessyd Lady there Item I bequeth to
the reparacion of the same church for my buryeng []
vis.viijd. sterling Item I bequeth to the reparacion of the church
of Sprotton xxd. Item I bequeth to the moder church of

Lincoln vjd. Item I bequeth to the church of Bosworth xxd. Item I bequeth to William Cobbe my sone my best maser and ij sylver sponys and my fetherbed in the solar and the curteyns Item I bequeth to Margaret my daughter a pott and a panne that was her moders a candlestik a chaforn an almery ij keverletts my best cofer a cheyre and a table Item I bequeth to every house of the iiij orders of freres withyn the town of Northampton xiijd. Item I bequeth to the house of the frere Carmalites in the said Northampton to say a masse and dirige for me yerely at my yeres mynde for the space of vii yeres xiid. Item I bequeth to Alice my wife the iijrd parte of al my goodes The residue of al my goodes above not bequethed I give and bequeth to William Cobbe my sonne And the same William and William Wykyn of Shutlanger I orden and make myne executors to dispose for the helth of my soule as they may best see to please Almyghty God and I bequeth to the same William Wykyn for hys labor to see thys testament truly executed viijs viijd. Theys men berying witnesse William Mownford notary and William Handred poticary and other moo

In the name of God Amen the fifth day of October 1505 in the church of the Hospital of St John, Northampton, before Thomas Knyght was proven etcetera effected etcetera granted etcetera given etcetera

f188r 649 JOAN GETYN 6th May 1503 widow

In the name of God Amen the vj day of the moneth of May the yere of our Lord mccccc and iij I Johane Getyn of Northampton wedow hole of mynd and in good memorye beyng thanyd be our Lord Jehu make my testament in this wise Firste I bequeth my soule to All myghtty God to Our Lady Saint Mary and to all the holy company of hevyn my body to be buried in the chirche of Alhalows in the chapell of Corpus Christi Item I bequeth to the hie auter of the same chirche for tithes and oblacions forgotyn and not dewly don xijd. Item I bequeth to the fraternite of the Trinitie in the same chirche xijd. Item I bequeth to the fraternite of Corpus Christi in the same chirche xijd. Item I bequeth ti the fraternyte of Our Blessed Lady in the same chirche xijd. Item I bequeth to the fraternite of the Rode in the same chirche xijd. Item I bequeth to the fraternite of Saynt John Baptist in the same chirche xijd. Item I bequeth to the fraternite of Saint George in the same chirche xijd Item I bequeth to the fraternite [called Saint Kat]eryne in the newe chirchyard xijd. Item I bequeth to the [reparacion] of Saynt Stevyns chapell xijd. Item I bequeth to the reparacion of Saint Sithes auter xijd. Item I bequeth to the reparacion of the auter of Saint James in the same chirche xij. Item I bequeth to Agnes my dowghter a cowcher one of the best and a bolster to the same a peyre of shets a peyre of blanketts a coverlett of grene with rede lyons and white a latyn bason a laver to the same iij pewter platers iij pewter dischis and iij pewter sawcers ij laten candulstykks a white seler with the valence a pleyne tabull cloth and ij towells of playn clothe and

a cofer my best skarlet kyrtyll and my best blewe gown furrid a great
bras pott of iij galons and iij kuschyns with bestis Item I bequeth to Richard
Mylly a bras pott and a peyre of shets Item I bequeth to Alice my
mayde a bras pott of ij galons Item I bequeth to everyche hows
of the iiij orders of ffreris within the towne of Northampton xijd Item
I woll that my husbandes wille of William Milly be ffulfilled to Saynt
Thomas howse withoute the south yate of Northampton of cs. as in

f188v

the same testament therof made more pleynly apperith Item I gyfe bequeth
to the fratenite of Corpus Christi in the chirche of Alhalows in Northampton a
forsaide my hows in the White Frer Lane lately in the tenure of
Savage the cardemaker to kepe an obit fo my husband William
Milly and me onys in the yere yerly for evermore Item I will that
myn executors dispose for me in funerall expenses the day of my burying
ls. of lawfull money of England and likwyse at my monthly
mynd in expencis and almysdede ls. sterlinge The Residewe of all my
goods a bove not bequethed after my detts paid I woll that Robert
Ussher and John Pervyn be myn executors to dispose for
my husbonds soulis and myn as they best may se to please God and
the said Robert Ussher and John Pervyn everyche of them to have
for ther labur xxs. sterling and Master Richard Crispe late Maire
of Northampton to be supervisor [of this my] present testament and he to have
for his labor other xxs. sterling [ ] These men beryng witnesse
Master Doctor Robert Middelham vicar of Alhalow in Northampton
John Harris bayly ther Thomas Brafeld senior William
Mownford notary and other moo

Appendix 1

ALPHABETICAL LIST OF ALL THE WILLS IN THE VOLUME.
The index in the volume, which was complied in the later sixteenth century, has a number of spelling variants which show how usage had already begun to change e.g. replacing y with an i, but for this list we have used the spelling in the original registrations. There is still room for doubt, however, in a number of names, with e and o being particularly difficult to distinguish. For example is it Honyborn, Honybern or Henybern? Suspension marks, e.g. Leycestr' have not been transcribed.

Where the testator has not been described as 'of', the place of burial has been given instead. Modern versions of place-names have been used, e.g. Greens Norton rather than Norton Davy: in some cases where there are a number of places with similar names it has not been possible to be more specific without more extended research. Places known to be in Rutland have been identified as such.

'Aka' – 'also known as' has been used rather than 'alias'.
(Northampton wills are listed in bold type).

Abraham	Richard	Finedon	474
Adams	Guy	Brington	611
Adams	**William**	**Northampton**	**231**
Adams (aka Reve)	**William**	**Northampton**	**553**
Aleyn	John	Blakesley	329
Allin	Margaret	Doddington	282
Alward	Edward	Lutton	67
Alyson	John	Cogenhoe, parson of	519
Andrewe	John	Kettering	540
Appyltoft	Richard	Peterborough	600
Apryce	**John**	**Northampton**	**375**
Arderon	**Thomas**	**Northampton**	**4**
Armeston	Richard	Fineshade	206
Arnold	William	Corby	582
Ashebye	Margery	Hannington	79
Ashebye	Thomas	Hannington	41
Asplond	**John**	**Northampton**	**59**
Asser	Thomas	Stoke Albany	205
Asshborn	**John**	**Northampton**	**442**
Asshwell	Robert	Wilbarston	550
Astell	William	Heyford	560
Atkyns	Thomas	Blatherwycke, rector of	270
Atthewell	William	Abington	172

Atthrope	John	Middleton	289
Atwell	**Edward jun.**	**Northampton**	**86**
Atwell	**Edward**	**Northampton**	**335**
Atwell	**William**	**Northampton**	**87**
Atylburgh (aka Leycestr)	**John**	**Northampton**	**74**
Aungell	Thomas	Little Houghton	616
Austyn	**William**	**Northampton**	**321**
Awnten	Thomas	Culworth	501
Ayle	Edward	Hardingstone	267
Ayleward	John	Collingtree	569
Aynsworth	Thomas	Ecton	434
Bacon	John	Kingsthorpe	29
Baker	John	Whissendine, Rutland	265
Baker	Robert	Peterborough	399
Baker	Robert	Peterborough	418
Ball	**Joan**	**Northampton**	**11**
Barker	John	Kingsthorpe	301
Barker (aka Dyer)	**Richard**	**Northampton**	**567**
Barnard	**John**	**Northampton**	**88**
Barnard	Margaret	Abington	383
Baron	Thomas	Irchester, vicar of	477
Barrette	Thomas	Sulgrave	215
Basse	John	Oakham, Rutland	509
Basse	William	Milton Malsor	548
Bassett	Richard	Pilton, rector of	543
Bassett	Thomas	Rushton St Peter	541
Bastard	John	Broughton	121
Bawston	William	Bulwick	221
Bay	William	Peterborough	228
Bayle	John	Towcester	272
Bayle	**William**	**Northampton**	**102**
Belcher	Roger	Nortoft, Guilsborough	639
Bele	Nicholas	Benefield	176
Benett	Katherine	Scaldwell	380
Bentley	Alice	Cold Ashby	361
Bentley	Henry	Cold Ashby	360
Berington	Joan	North Luffenham Rutland	573
Bertilemewe	**Agnes**	**Northampton**	**326**
Berwyk	Edmund	Whiston	386
Berwyk	Joan	Whiston	479

Bylling	John	Woodford [...]	37
Byry	William	Helmdon	242
Calcott	Alexander	Barby	593
Campyon	John	Wedon Beck	515
Campyon	Simon	Weedon	248
Canfield	John	Peterborough, clerk	17a
Carter	John	Guilsborough	113
Carter	John	Creaton, rector of	536
Carter	**Margery**	**Northampton**	**22**
Carter	**Thomas**	**Northampton**	**20**
Carter	William	Farthinghoe	8
Catlyn	Thomas	Great Addington	141
Caumvyle	William	Alderton	328
Cave	Alice	Kettering	157
Cave	Alice	Heyford	250
Cave	Joan	Stanford-on-Avon	152
Chamberlayn	William	Watford	9
Chambre	**Agnes**	**Northampton**	**56**
Chambre	William	Aldwinkle All Saints	355
Chambur	Elizabeth	Aldwinkle All Saints	343
Chambur	John	Watford	266
Chamerleyn	John	Higham Ferrers	63
Chandeler	William	Chesham, Woburn	559
Chapelen	Thomas	Gayton	230
Chapman	John	Brixworth	129
Chauncy	**John**	**Northampton**	**334**
Chead	**Richard**	**Northampton**	**539**
Chelever	William	Walgrave	81
Chese	John	Broughton, parson of	478
Chessam	William	Bainton	645
Christopher	Chaplain of St Michael's Chapel,	Upton	85
Clarke	**Thomas**	**Northampton**	**30**
Claydon	Richard	Bulwick	642
Clerke	**Agnes**	**Northampton**	**58**
Clerke	John	Blisworth	150
Clerke	John	Weedon Bec	400
Clerke	Richard	Wellingborough	454
Clipston	John	Kingsthorpe	160
Clypesham	Thomas	Little Houghton	247
Clypsham	Katherine	Weekley	196
Clypston	John	Kingsthorpe	262

Dove	John	Harpole	531
Dovse	John	Upton	311
Drake	William	Kettering	651
Drayton	William	Brington	613
Drinkewell	Joan	Irchester	427
Dunkeley	Henry	Guilsborough	145
Dunmowe	Richard	Harringworth	116
Durant	John	Broughton	158
Durant	Thomas	Kings Cliffe	587
Durward	John	Sibbertoft	187
Dyer (aka Barker)	**Richard**	**Northampton**	**567**
Dyk	**George**	**Northampton**	**298**
Dyng	Richard	Ashwell, Rutland	290
Eddon	John	Middleton	576
Edgosse	William	Bulwick	64
Edwards	John	Aston	223
Egremond	**John**	**Northampton**	**401**
Else	George	Kingsthorpe	320
Elyngton	William	Greetham, Rutland vicar of	293
Emerton	William	Stanion	287
Ernold	John	Upton	565
Esex	**Annes**	**Northampton**	**592**
Esex	**John**	**Northampton**	**391**
Ewod	Gervase	Oakham, Rutland	178
Eyre	Robert	Hardwick	619
Fawcet	**John**	**Northampton**	**625**
Faxton	Thomas	Kettering	346
Fenton	William	Kingsthorpe	195
Ferman	John	Braunston	60
Ferman	Thomas	Moulton	271
Ferndon	Henry	Byfield	211
Ferrour	**William**	**Northampton**	**78**
Flore	**William**	**Northampton**	**367**
Flowre	Thomas	Oakham, Rutland	70
Flowre	**Thomas**	**Northampton**	**489**
Foster	William	Tinwell, Rutland	457
Fowler	John	Hambledon, Rutland	579
Frake	Roger	Kingsthorpe	167
Freman	John	Little Bowden	453
Freman	Thomas	Hardingstone	495

Freman	William	Brixworth	209
Freman	William	Geddington	461
Furtho	William	Furtho	623
Fyssh	**Thomas**	**Northampton**	**224**
Fyssher	Thomas	Great Doddington	143
Garard	John	Crick	631
Garre	William	Norton	6
Geffron	**Isabel**	**Northampton**	**257**
Geffron	John	Overstone	108
Gente	Isabel	Brixworth	214
George	**William**	**Northampton**	**103**
German (aka Tailor)	Henry	Geddington	100
German	Henry	Draughton	350
German	Robert	Geddington	512
Geytyn	**Joan**	**Northampton**	**649**
Gilberte	Alexander	Barby	483
Glapthorn	John	Oundle	66
Goldwyre	**William**	**Northampton**	**68**
Golofor	John	Faxton	629
Gregory	John	Peterborough	135
Grene	John	Helmdon	286
Grene	John	Wootton	71
Grene	Margaret	Lowick	32
Grenewod	William	Lowick	437
Grenway	William	Ecton	260
Gressy	Robert	Preston	417
Gretham	Thomas	Oakham, Rutland	323
Grevyle	Robert	[ ]	69
Grey	William	Hambleton, Rut.	473
Greyby	John	Whitfield	24
Gryffyn	Richard	Wappenham	264
Gryggs	Thomas	Pytchley	277
Gryndyll	Agnes	Braybrooke	491
Gryndyll	John	Braybrooke	369
Gryndyll	Thomas	Titchmarsh	14
Gudezere	William	Corby Woodland	295
Gulliver	John	Faxton	629
Gun	Symkyn	Weston Favell	236
Guyn	John	Stanwick	644
Gybbis	William	Little Harrowden	604
Gybson	**Robert**	**Northampton**	**39**
Gyldeale	John	Overstone	439
Gylys	William	Higham Ferrers	415

Ha [ ]	Thomas	Kingsthorpe	319
Halam	John	Great Doddington	151
Haldenby	Robert	Ravensthorpe	5
Haldenby	William	Holdenby	146
Hall	John	Belton, Rutland	180
Halowton	**William**	**Northampton**	**408**
Hamwell	John	Tansor	622
Hancok	**John**	**Northampton**	**36**
Hancok	**Margaret**	**Northampton**	**53**
Hanred	**Margaret**	**Northampton**	**390**
Hardewyn	John	Upton	498
Harowdon	**Thomas**	**Northampton**	**93**
Harowedon	**Margaret**	**Northampton**	**101**
Harowedon	**Richard**	**Northampton**	**49**
Harre	Thomas	Desborough	258
Haryngton	James	Brixworth	394
Harys	Margery	Polebrook	217
Harysson	**William**	**Northampton**	**26**
Hasilbyche	**John**	**Northampton**	**494**
Hasylwode	Thomas	Braybrooke, rector of	61
Hathorne	John	Canons Ashby	333
Hawke	John	Kingsthorpe	620
Hawley	Robert	Amston	578
Hayte	Richard	Bozeat	446
Hayward	Thomas	Hardingstone, priest	423
Hendyman	**Thomas**	**Northampton**	**547**
Hendyman	**Thomas**	**Northampton**	**549**
Heron	William	Ravensthorpe	216
Herysson	John	Seaton	138
Hions	Joan	East Haddon	605
Hobbis	**Richard**	**Northampton**	**488**
Hobson	Richard	Wootton	316
Hochyn	Robert	Helpston	617
Hochynson	**Adam**	**Northampton**	**526**
Holand (aka Randyll)	William	Oundle	580
Holyzeth	John	Wilbarston	241
Honybern	Henry	[ ]	203
Honyborn	Thomas	Higham Ferrers	524
Hopkyns	Simon	Towcester	235
Hopwod	**Alice**	**Northampton**	**441**
Hopwod	**Hugh**	**Northampton**	**44**
Horley	John	Milton Malsor	288
Horne	**Thomas**	**Northampton**	**339**
Horpoll	**Richard**	**Northampton**	**106**

Horpoll	**William**	**Northampton**	**595**
Hotofte	John	Easton Maudit	513
Hoton	Nicholas	Moulton	602
House	John	Oundle	507
Howman	Richard	Silverstone	514
Hudson	John	Lowick	156
Hull	Isabel	Doddington	612
Hunt	**Emma**	**Northampton**	**370**
Hunte	John	Bradden	243
Hunte	James	Hardwick	299
Hyckman	John	Pitsford	529
Hyde	John	Guilsborough	147
Hygham	**John**	**Northampton**	**18**
Hykman	Henry	Walgrave	414
Hykman	Thomas	Old, clerk	322
Hylles	Richard	Watford	603
Idlefylde	John	Raunds	65
Irland	Robert	Thrapston	202
Isham	Dame Margaret	Pytchley	53
Jabott	William	Syresham, rector of	546
Jacob/Joyce	**Joan**	**Northampton**	**466**
Jakys	John	Old	275
James (aka Bukby)	**John**	**Northampton**	**332**
January	Nicholas	Harlestone	283
Jeffcokke	Simon	Brixworth	213
Jeffrey	Matilda	Irchester	452
Jeffrey	Thomas	Irchester	451
Jelley	John	Brampton	570
Jogges	Thomas	Thenford	212
Jonson	Henry	Bugbrooke	191
Jonson	**William**	**Northampton**	**610**
Jurden	Thomas	Oakham	179
Kayso	Alice	Piddington	200
Kebyter	Thomas	Tansor	584
Kente	John	Burley, Rutland	227
Keston	**Thomas**	**Northampton**	**493**
Keysoo	William	Hackleton, Piddington	104
Knottinge	Ralph	Rockingham	72
Knottyng	**Richard**	**Northampton**	**28**
Kyllom	William	Oakham, Rutland	48

Kylworth	Richard	Edgcote	344
Kyng	Charles	Rockingham	492
Kyng	John	Hanging Houghton	226
Kyng	**John**	**Northampton**	**357**
Kyng	Laurence	Desborough, vicar of	371
Kyng	Robert	Byfield	193
Kyng	Simon	Hanging Houghton	197
Kynton	Thomas	Croughton	273
Lambert	William	Silverstone	403
Langton	**John**	**Northampton**	**591**
Launden	John	Horton	627
Law	John	Towcester	161
Lawrens	**William**	**Northampton**	**352**
Lawson	Margaret	Higham Ferrers	606
Ledys	John	Barnwell All Saints, rector of	554
Leeke	Agnes	Daventry	245
Lenton	Thomas	Aldwincle All Saints	588
Leycestr (aka Atylburgh)	**John**	**Northampton**	**74**
Leynho	**John**	**Northampton**	**75**
Leynowe	**John**	**Northampton**	**338**
Lodyngton	Andrew	Old	163
Lokkyng	Richard	Finedon	155
Longe	**John**	**Northampton**	**139**
Lovington	Thomas	Teigh, Rutland	238
Lowthe	Phillip	Kings Cliffe	353
Lucas	Robert	Coton, Ravensthorpe	601
Lumbard	William	Grafton	144
Lyne	John	Higham Ferrers	204
Lynes	Henry	Guilsborough	268
Lythyll	William	Finedon	345
Magode	John	Overthorpe Middleton Cheney	291
Makelesse	Thomas	Daventry	481
Marchall	**William**	**Northampton**	**609**
Margates	Nicholas	Towcester	626
Margettes	Agnes	Ryhall, Rutland	98
Martyn	John	Lowick	47
Maryett	William	Quinton	249
Maryot	Thomas	Cotton, Hardingstone	485

Olyver	Thomas	Oundle	397
Osbern	Richard	Whitfield	628
Page	John	Edith Weston, Rutland	3
Page	**John**	**Northampton**	**463**
Page	Simon	Irchester	556
Pakeman	**Richard**	**Northampton**	**349**
Palady	John	Barton	428
Palmer	**John**	**Northampton**	**426**
Palmer	Thomas	East Haddon	561
Palmer	William, esq.	East Carlton	95
Parker	John	Oakham, Rutland	459
Parmynter	**Isabel**	**Northampton**	**31**
Patryk	Richard	Spratton	253
Payne	John	Sibbertoft	269
Peche	**Isabel**	**Northampton**	**45**
Pecke	John	Kingsthorpe	624
Pecke	John	Kingsthorpe	633
Pedder	**John**	**Northampton**	**10**
Pedyvor	William	Hambleton, Rutland	378
Pelle	Richard	Pattishall	255
Penne	Richard	Kislingbury	318
Peny	**Alice**	**Northampton**	**112**
Pepe	**Thomas**	**Northampton**	**84**
Peper	Edmund	Seaton, Rutland	475
Pereson	Thomas	Brampton	551
Perkyns	Thomas	Naseby	120
Perte	John	Oakham, Rutland	621
Perwyn	**William**	**Northampton**	**297**
Petyfer	Robert	Everdon	396
Plomer	Thomas	Watford	528
Porter	William	Moulton, vicar of	42
Pounce	**Thomas**	**Northampton**	**99**
Power	Harry	Oundle	636
Prentece	**William**	**Northampton**	**363**
Preston	William	Piddington	105
Prynce	**Roger**	**Northampton**	**412**
Pullay	William	Lilford	490
Pulton	Dame Agnes	Rothwell	563
Pykyn	Henry	Ashley	581
Radborn	Richard	Wadenhoe	174
Radburne	Thomas	Barnwell All Saints	173
Ragdale	Henry	Ryhall, Rutland	472

Skyrnyng (aka Reve)	Richard	Higham Ferrers	284
Smalbon	Thomas	Evenley	280
Smale	William	Irthlingborough, priest	496
Smallay	**Nicholas**	**Northampton**	**468**
Smyth	Henry	Watford	574
Smyth	Joan	Middleton	132
Smyth	John	Stoke Bruerne	142
Smyth	John	Wootton	430
Smyth	John	Potterspury	585
Smyth	Richard	Clipston	133
Smyth	Richard	Piddington	166
Smyth	Richard	Haselbeech	198
Smyth	Richard	Bugbrooke	618
Smyth	William	Muscott, near Brockhall	38
Smyth	William	Woodford	188
Smyth	William	Stanion	392
Smyth	William	Wellingborough	470
Smyth	William	Brockhall	520
Smyth	William	Wellingborough	670
Snokstubbes	Thomas	Market Overton, Rut.	413
Somerfield	John	Newnham	594
Sounde	Richard	Geddington	239
Spenser	Thomas	Badby	348
Sprott	John	Walgrave	500
Stafford	Constance	(see Wiltshire, Countess of)	
Stanbryge	**John**	**Northampton**	**57**
Staunton	William	Harringworth	117
Stephen	**Thomas**	**Northampton**	**15**
Stevens	Richard	Sulgrave	192
Stewyns	John	Rushden	555
Stok	William	Boughton	433
Stretford	Richard	Weston by Welland, vicar of	525
Styffe	Robert	Grendon	444
Styffe	William	Grendon	207
Sutton	Lettice	Towcester	149
Swyfte	Robert	Everdon	124
Swillington	John	Brackley	422
Symmys	Robert	Braunston	533
Symson	**Thomas**	**Northampton**	**440**

Warner?	Peter	Stoke Albany	511
Warren	Henry	Everdon	123
Wattes	Richard	Lowick	436
Wattys	John	East Haddon	566
Wawe	John	Everdon	168
Webbe	Simon	Broughton	615
Welche	Nicholas	Winwick	535
Wellyngburgh	**William**	**Northampton**	**351**
Wellys	Henry	Kingsthorpe	261
Wellys	**John**	**Northampton**	**107**
Wellys	Simon	Kelmarsh	153
Werall	William	Hartwell	497
Wermyngton	Robert	Tansor	469
West	**Ralph**	**Northampton**	**27**
Weste	Margery	Braybrooke	234
Weste	Thomas	Hanging Houghton	263
Weste	William	Braybrooke	233
Westfeld	William	Farthinghoe	251
Westley	Robert	Irthlingborough	632
Westron	William	Farndon	447
Whitlinge	Alice	Ketttering	405
Whitwell	John	Egleton, Rutland	542
Whitwell	William	Harrowden	438
Whyrlatt	John	Potterspury	169
Whyte	**Emma**	**Northampton**	**358**
Whyte	**John**	**Northampton**	**372**
Whyte	Richard	Drayton	429
Whyte	**Thomas**	**Northampton**	**111**
Whytehed	Robert	Braybrooke	294
Whythe	John	Easton Neston	309
Whytynge	Robert	Kettering	354
Wilcocks	John	Seaton, Rutland	476
Wilkokkes	**John**	**Northampton**	**115**
Wilkynson	Robert	Naseby	641
Williams	Henry	Stanford on Avon	471
Wiltshire	Countess of	[Lowick]	33
Wodyll	Elizabeth	Chacombe	25
Wodsall	**Hugh**	**Northampton**	**336**
Wolaston	Henry	Aldwinkle	175
Worley	John	Sulgrave	244
Worley	William	Heyford	199
Wower	John	Guilsbrough	534
Wright	John	Hanging Houghton	278
Wright	John	Abington	465

Appendix 2

LIST OF OCCUPATIONS IN NORTHAMPTON
(The first figure is for the whole Northampton sample and the figure in brackets for testators themselves)

apothecary	1
baker	13 (6)
barber	5 (3)
bailiff	1
blacksmith	1 (3)
bowyer	3 (1)
brasier	1
butcher	8 (4)
capper	1 (1)
cardmaker	1
carpenter	2 (1)
chandler	1 (1)
clothier	1 (1)
cobbler	1
commissary	1
cook	2 (2)
corvisor/ shoemaker	12 (4)
dyster	11 (5)
esquire	12 (4)
fisher	4 (2)
fletcher	1
fuller	14 (7)
furze carter	1
gentleman	8 (3)
glover	1 (2)
goldsmith	1
grammar scholar	1
grazier	1 (1)
haberdasher	1 (1)
inn holder	6 (4)
ironmonger	5 (1)
knight	6
mercer/draper	29 (14)
merchant	2
notary	3
pattenmaker	1
roper	2 (1)
saddler	2 (1)
scribe/writer	3 (1)
servant	26
shearman	5 (2)
shopkeeper	1
singer	1 (1)
summoner	1
tailor	2 (1)
tanner	7 (4)
vinter	3
weaver	18 (7)
wiredrawer	1 (1)
yeoman	2
canon	1
monk	2
priest	41 (4)
chaplain	14
Total	297 (91)

Glossary

almery/armariolum/aumbre	a cupboard
alum	an astringent mineral salt used in dyeing and tanning
andirons	a pair of horizontal bars, with upright posts in front, placed in the hearth to support burning wood
anniversary	anniversary of a person's death on which a memorial mass would be said
antiphon	a religious book of musical or verbal resonses
appurtenances	belongings, minor properties, rights and privileges, part of a larger system, usually relating to land and property
aresse	superior kind of tapestry from Arras in Flanders
bayley	a bailiff
banker	cloth to cover a bench or seat
barker	one who works with bark in the tanning and dyeing industry
bede roll	a list of persons to be prayed for
bereloy	a carying basket
blackloge	black lamb fur
blakelyr	black cloth from the Brabant
borcloth/bordcloth	altar or table cloth
brazier	a worker in brass
brentis	black or dark colour
breviary	book containing the Divine Office for each day
bruge	a bridge
bryconders	briganders - pliable armour made from small plates sewn onto quilted linen or leather
brynded cow	brindle or brownish with streaks of other colour
buckram	fine linen or cotton (not stiff)
burthen stele	possibly a weight bearing bar
byllys	a halberd or combined spear and battle axe
carpet	cloth used to cover a table or other furniture but not on the floor

cawse	a causeway
celer/celour/seler	a canopy over a bed
chafing dish	a small enclosed brasier containing hot coals or charcoal for heating food and drink
chalice	a communion cup
charger	a large platter, plate or dish, usually of pewter
chymer	a loose or light gown
close	a small area of enclosed land near a house or building
clowt	a kind of nail
cobard/ cobiron/gobbarde	irons for supporting the spit in front of the fire
cocher	a mattress
coffer	a strong box, usually of wood, for storing clothes, valuables and money
conduit	channel for carrying water
Corpus Christi livery	a gown with a hood worn by members of the Corpus Christi guild
corse girdle	a belt worn around the waist and often used for carrying light articles. Usually made from silk and often ornamented with embroidery or metal work
corvisor	a shoemaker
cotyer	a cottager or smallholder
curtyll	a short gown or petticoat
demesne	manorial 'Home Farm' - land retained by the lord for his own use
diaper/dyaper	woven linen cloth with a diamond pattern used for table linen and towels
dyester	a dyer or a preparer of dyes and colourings most often for cloth
dirige	part of the funeral service, a psalm, often with the **placebo** in response
dyker	a bundle of ten hides or skins
ell	a measue of length in cloth of 45ins.
engrayned	cloth that is dyed before it is woven, or dyed in fast colours
esquire	next below knight
ewer	a jug with a wide spout used for carrying water for washing

exequies funeral rites, ceremonies or processions

fan of wyker a shallow basket used in winnowing

fattes vats used to hold liquid, often used in brewing and dyeing processes

fee an interest in land or property which could be inherited. **fee simple** freehold tenure which allowed an owner to dispose of his propeerty freely. **lords of the fee** lords of the manor to whom tenants owed a variety of dues

feoffee a holder of land with conditions attached

feoffment/feftament a deed of conveyance recording the granting of land

firkin a small cask holding 9 gallons of beer or 8 gallons of ale

flecher a fletcher - one who makes or deals in arrows

flesshook flesh hook - a hook with a long handle for removing meat from the cooking pot

flokkys coarse tufts of wool or cotton waste used for stuffing mattresses and pillows

fodyn folding

freize coarse woollen cloth with a nap on one side

fuller one who treads or beats cloth to thicken it

furred edged or trimmed

frychen polecat

garye/gerys a member of a working team of oxen or horses

gaudis the larger beads of a rosary indicating that the Lord's Prayer should be said

gete jet

girdle see **corse**

gobbardes see **cobard**

garnish a complete set of 12 each of pewter platters, saucers, cups and small plates

godryd oxe not known

halling wall hanging of fabric

hardyn	sheets of coarse material
harnessed	threaded and ornamented with precious materials, usually relating to girdles
hemp	fibre used to make ropes or coarse fabric
hogerells/ogerellys	sheep from 6 months old to shearing
homage	a pledge of loyalty by a tenant to his lord or an assembled body of tenants
hovell	a hut or shed for storage of grain, peas, tools etc.
kerchief	a square piece of cloth worn to cover the head or neck
kwyshens, qwyshens	cushions
laten	Latten - an alloy of copper, zinc, lead and tin, yellow and resembling brass
laver	a basin in which to wash hands after meals. Usually paired with an **Ewer**
madder	a red vegetable dye obtained from the roots of the plant
mark	a common unit of currency in medieval Europe worth 13s 4d
marten	the fur of the pine marten
maser	a bowl or drinking cup usually made from a hard wood such as maple; often very large and with a metal rim. They usually were without feet unless referred to as a **standing maser** and they often had a decorated cover
mercer	a dealer in fabrics, silks and velvets
miniver	pure white or ermine fur
Missal	a book containing the complete service for mass throughout the year
monthmynd	the thirtieth day after death on which a memorial service would be held
mortar	morter, a vessel of hard material such as marble, brass, iron or stone in which ingredients were pounded with a **pestle**
mortuary/principal;	a customary due claimed by the incumbent of the parish church from the estate of a deceased person. Sometimes an animal

musterdevelere	mixed grey woollen cloth from the town of Montvilliers in Normandy.
narke	an ark, coffer or chest
nayle	nail
nutte	a cup or maser made from a coconut shell
oblations	offerings to church funds for the relief of the poor and other pious purposes
obit	a memorial mass performed in commemoration of or on behalf of the soul of a deceased person, usually on the anniversary of his death
oggyes	hogs
osmondes	highly ductile iron used for arrow heads; **shefe osmondes** - sheaf of 24 arrows
Ossy	from the old French Aussey, a sweet wine of Alsace.
pardon	an indulgence offered to penitents for remission of time in purgatory
parcel gylt	partly gilded e.g. having the inner surface gilded
Pater noster	the Lord's Prayer
patten maker	one who makes overshoes of wood or metal which raise the wearer above the mud
pestle	see **mortar**
placebo	see **dirige**
platter	flat dish or plate
portowse	a service book
posnet	a small metal pot with three feet and a long handle
pothanger	a chain or rod to which a pot or kettle is hung over a fireplace by means of a pot hook
pottell	pottle, a measure of 16 pints or a pot of this size, often funnel shaped
Primer/Primour	a prayer book or devotional manual for use by the laity
principal	see mortuary
puke	imported woollen cloth, usually nearly black.
quartern	a measurement of capacity. 1 quartern = 8 bushels = 64 gallons

redall and ryeng sefe	riddle and sieve
reversion	a temporary conveyance of property in which a future interest is safeguarded
rone russet	reddish brown colour of cloth originally from Rouen
russet	a colour or coarse cloth
rood	the great crucifix placed on the roodbeam under the chancel arch in church.
salet	a light head-piece of armour
salt	a salt cellar
sanguine	blood red colour
sefe	see redall and ryeng sefe
seler	see **celer**
shankys	fur from the lower legs of animals
sharys	shares or iron blades for ploughs
shedde carte	a cart with iron rimmed wheels
shearman	one who shears woollen cloth after fulling
shones/machet shones	possibly nails
Sir	courtesy title given to priests educated at Oxford or Cambridge, or chantry priests?
skemer	a skimmer for taking the ashes out of the fire or for use in cooking
skillet	a metal cooking vessel with three or four feet and a long handle, to stand over a fire.
soresse	unknown
spete/spit	a tapering pointed instrument of iron on which meat was roasted over a fire
standing maser	see **maser**
stansil	probably a fence around a grave or tombstone
sterryd horse	unknown
stryke	a dry measure of 1 bushel, often of barley
tawney	yellowish brown colour
tenement	a holding - a house or other building or land
tenter yard	an area where cloth was pegged out on frames to dry, stretch and bleach
tester	the ceiling of a bed often of carved wood of various kinds of fabric

thyll a cart with shafts for a horse

thyll gerys the wheelers in a working team of oxen or horses

tithe a levy or tax of a tenth part of the produce of land and stock paid annually to the church

torches candles or tapers of wax, tallow or resin to be carried in the hand or placed in holders to give light. Can be very large and often used in ceremonies

towrys cheap coarse fabric?

tre wood

trental set of thirty masses or the money to pay for them

Trimonelis a prayer, often requested immediately after death, for the health of the soul

vintner a dealer in wine

virgas a measure of 1 yard, ususally of cloth

vyrly plough a plough with a share reinforced with iron

wiredrawer one who reduces metal rope to fine fibres by pulling through successively smaller holes in a hard steel block

woad a blue dye

worsted superior woollen cloth originally made at Worsted in Norfolk

yat a gate

yelyng house unknown

yeoman a freeholder farming his own land worth 40s who served on juries.

yern ware iron ware

yog yoke, contrivance by which two oxen were coupled together for drawing a plough

Index of Persons

References to Part 1 (introductory chapters) are by *page number*, indicated by p. in brackets. References to Part 2 (the wills) are by *will number*; bold type indicates the name of an actual testator.

Index of Places

References to Part 1 (Introductory chapters) are by *page numbers*, and indicated by p. in brackets. References to Part 2 (the wills themselves) are by *will number*.

Index of Subjects

This index is not in strict alphabetical order. In some cases subheadings have been used to demonstrate the range of 'items' in a particular category. References to Part 1 (Introductory chapters) are by *page numbers*, and indicated by p. in brackets. References to Part 2 (the wills themselves) are by *will number* .